lone

D0342922

# Colombia

### Krzysztof Dydyński

*carrera 3 10-80*
*ron ringsrud*

*www.emeralddynna.com*

*310 478 8579*

## LONELY PLANET PUBLICATIONS
### Melbourne • Oakland • London • Paris

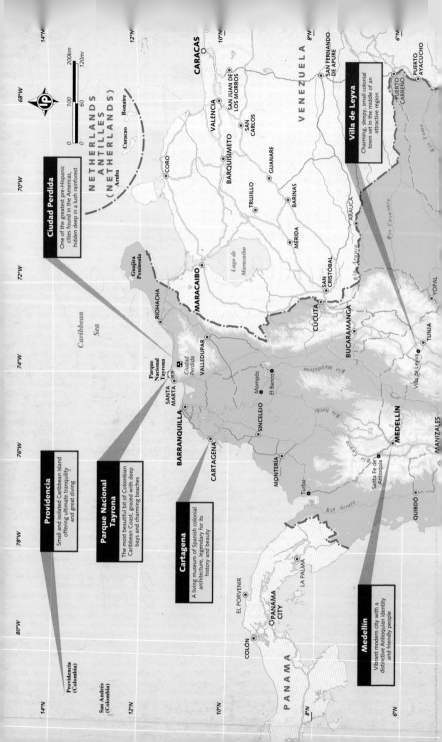

**Ciudad Perdida**

One of the greatest pre-Hispanic cities found in the Americas, hidden deep in a lush rainforest

**Villa de Leyva**

Charming, sleepy, small colonial town set in the middle of an attractive region

**Providencia**

Small and isolated Caribbean island offering ultimate tranquility and great diving

**Parque Nacional Tayrona**

The most beautiful bit of Colombian Caribbean Coast, graced with deep bays and charming beaches

**Cartagena**

A living museum of Spanish colonial architecture, legendary for its history and beauty

**Medellin**

Vibrant modern city with a distinctive Antioquian identity and friendly people

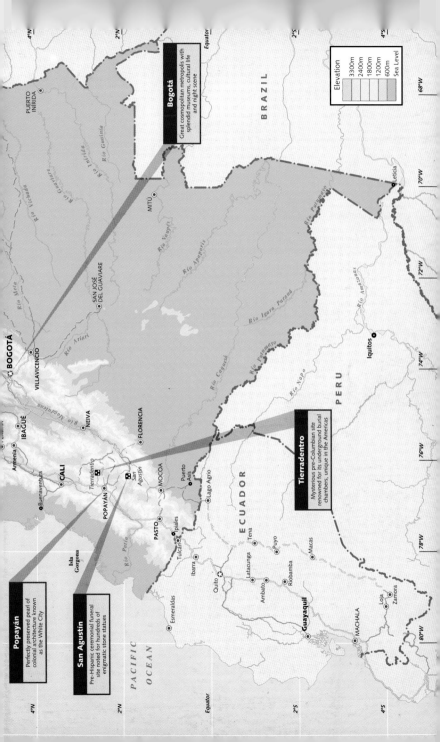

**Bogotá**
Great cosmopolitan metropolis with splendid museums, cultural life and night scene

**Tierradentro**
Mysterious pre-Columbian burial site renowned for its underground burial chambers; unique in the Americas

**Popayán**
Perfectly preserved pearl of colonial architecture known as the White City

**San Agustín**
Pre-Hispanic ceremonial funeral site noted for hundreds of enigmatic stone statues

Elevation
3300m
2400m
1800m
1200m
600m
Sea Level

PUERTO INÍRIDA

MITÚ

SAN JOSÉ DEL GUAVIARE

VILLAVICENCIO

BOGOTÁ

IBAGUÉ

Armenia

CALI

Buenaventura

NEIVA

FLORENCIA

Tierradentro

San Agustín

POPAYÁN

MOCOA

Puerto Asís

PASTO

Ipiales

Lago Agrio

Tulcán

Isla Gorgona

Ibarra

Tena

Quito

Latacunga

Puyo

Ambato

Riobamba

Macas

Esmeraldas

Guayaquil

MACHALA

Loja

Zamora

Leticia

Iquitos

B R A Z I L

P E R U

E C U A D O R

P A C I F I C   O C E A N

Río Guaviare

Río Vichada

Río Inírida

Río Guainía

Río Vaupés

Río Apaporis

Río Igara Paraná

Río Caquetá

Río Putumayo

Río Igara Paraná

Río Amazonas

Río Napo

Río Putumayo

Río Meta

Río Ariari

Río Magdalena

Río Patía

4°N

2°N

Equator

2°S

4°S

4°N

2°N

Equator

2°S

4°S

68°W

70°W

72°W

74°W

76°W

78°W

80°W

**Colombia**
**3rd edition** – June 2003
**First published** – December 1988

**Published by**
**Lonely Planet Publications Pty Ltd** ABN. 36 005 607 983
90 Maribyrnong St, Footscray, Victoria 3011, Australia

**Lonely Planet Offices**
**Australia** Locked Bag 1, Footscray, Victoria 3011
**USA** 150 Linden St, Oakland, CA 94607
**UK** 10a Spring Place, London NW5 3BH
**France** 1 rue du Dahomey, 75011 Paris

**Photographs**
Many of the images in this guide are available for licensing from
Lonely Planet Images.
w www.lonelyplanetimages.com

**Front cover photograph**
Chiva, traditional Colombian bus, Colombia (Krzysztof Dydyński)

ISBN 0 86442 674 7

text & maps © Lonely Planet Publications Pty Ltd 2003
photos © photographers as indicated 2003

Printed through Colorcraft Ltd, Hong Kong
Printed in China

Although the author
and Lonely Planet try
to make the informa-
tion as accurate as
possible, we accept
no responsibility for
any loss, injury or
inconvenience sus-
tained by anyone
using this book.

# Contents – Text

1

# Contents – Maps

## COLOMBIA CHAPTERS INDEX

CARIBBEAN COAST
page 131

VENEZUELA

NORTH OF BOGOTÁ
page 106

NORTHWEST
COLOMBIA
page 178

SOUTHWEST COLOMBIA
page 212

BOGOTÁ
page 77

COLOMBIA

ECUADOR

BRAZIL

San Andrés &
Providencia
page 166

PERU

AMAZON BASIN
page 238

OTHER MAPS
Colombia at front of book
Locator page 9
Administrative Divisions page 20
Main Domestic Flights page 71

# The Author

## KRZYSZTOF DYDYŃSKI

Krzysztof was born and raised in Warsaw, Poland. Though he graduated in electronic engineering and became an assistant professor in the subject, he soon realised that there's more to life than microchips. After exploring Europe, he took off to Asia, then to Latin America where he lived for four years. He established a base in Colombia from where he travelled pretty much everywhere, from Mexico to Argentina. In search of a new incarnation, he made Australia his next home and worked at Lonely Planet's Melbourne office as a cartographer and designer before opting for freelance travel writing. Apart from this guide he is the author of our *Venezuela*, *Poland* and *Kraków* guidebooks, and has contributed to other Lonely Planet books.

## FROM THE AUTHOR

Many friends, colleagues and travellers have kindly contributed to this book and deserve the highest praise. I would like to thank all those people for their advice, information, hospitality and much else. Warmest thanks to Tim Abercrombie, Ignacio Aris, Yaneth Arrieta, Marion Bouillon la Rana, Germán Escobar, Axel Antoine-Feill, Leonardo Franco, Alessandro Ghiselli, Jean-Philippe Gibelin, Lucho and Oscar Guerrero, Hans Kolland, Angela Melendro, Juan Carlos Méndez, José Peláez, Ziga Ramsak, Sebastián Rojas, Ugo Salvagno, Hanneke Stolk and Miguel Velásquez.

# This Book

The previous two editions of *Colombia*, like this edition, were written by Krzysztof Dydyński. Thanks also to Danny Palmerlee who conducted a prebriefing research trip and helped develop this edition.

## FROM THE PUBLISHER

The coordinating editor was Craig MacKenzie. The coordinating cartographer was Laurie Mikkelsen. Craig was assisted by Lara Morcombe, Melissa Faulkner and Linda Suttie. Laurie was assisted by Anneka Imkamp, Csanád Csutoros and Karen Fry. The layout designer was Sally Morgan. The cover was designed by Maria Vallianos and final artwork done by James Hardy. The Language chapter was produced by Quentin Frayne. The project manager was Celia Wood, the commissioning editor was Wendy Smith and the series publishing manager was Robert Reid. David Burnett provided Word XP support and Mark Germanchis provided In-Design support.

**THANKS**

Many thanks to the travellers who used the last edition and wrote to us with helpful hints, advice and interesting anecdotes. Your names appear in the back of this book.

# Foreword

## ABOUT LONELY PLANET GUIDEBOOKS

The story begins with a classic travel adventure: Tony and Maureen Wheeler's 1972 journey across Europe and Asia to Australia. There was no useful information about the overland trail then, so Tony and Maureen published the first Lonely Planet guidebook to meet a growing need.

From a kitchen table, Lonely Planet has grown to become the largest independent travel publisher in the world, with offices in Melbourne (Australia), Oakland (USA), London (UK) and Paris (France).

Today Lonely Planet guidebooks cover the globe. There is an ever-growing list of books and information in a variety of media. Some things haven't changed. The main aim is still to make it possible for adventurous travellers to get out there – to explore and better understand the world.

At Lonely Planet we believe travellers can make a positive contribution to the countries they visit – if they respect their host communities and spend their money wisely. Since 1986 a percentage of the income from each book has been donated to aid projects and human rights campaigns, and, more recently, to wildlife conservation.

## UPDATES & READER FEEDBACK

Things change – prices go up, schedules change, good places go bad and bad places go bankrupt. Nothing stays the same. So, if you find things better or worse, recently opened or long-since closed, please tell us and help make the next edition even more accurate and useful.

Lonely Planet thoroughly updates each guidebook as often as possible – usually every two years, although for some destinations the gap can be longer. Between editions, up-to-date information is available in our free, monthly email bulletin *Comet* (Ⓦ www.lonelyplanet.com/newsletters). You can also check out the *Thorn Tree* bulletin board and *Postcards* section of our website which carry unverified, but fascinating, reports from travellers.

**Tell us about it!** We genuinely value your feedback. A well-travelled team at Lonely Planet reads and acknowledges every email and letter we receive and ensures that every morsel of information finds its way to the relevant authors, editors and cartographers.

Everyone who writes to us will find their name listed in the next edition of the appropriate guidebook. The very best contributions will be rewarded with a free guidebook.

We may edit, reproduce and incorporate your comments in Lonely Planet products such as guidebooks, websites and digital products, so let us know if you don't want your comments reproduced or your name acknowledged.

**How to contact Lonely Planet:**
**Online:** Ⓔ talk2us@lonelyplanet.com.au, Ⓦ www.lonelyplanet.com
**Australia:** Locked Bag 1, Footscray, Victoria 3011
**UK:** 10a Spring Place, London NW5 3BH
**USA:** 150 Linden St, Oakland, CA 94607

# Introduction

For most travellers, Colombia is unknown territory – a land of myths, of cocaine barons, guerrillas, emeralds and the mysterious El Dorado. It is the land of Gabriel García Márquez and his famous novel, *One Hundred Years of Solitude* – a tale as magical as the country itself. And it is the land that bears the name of Columbus, who never got as far as Colombia, but where people have rearranged the name to spell 'Locombia', or 'the mad country', and not without reason.

Colombia has been largely the forgotten part of the popular Latin American 'gringo trail' that wends from Mexico down through Ecuador, Peru and Bolivia. It is looked upon as a country to get through quickly rather than as a place to visit. As a result, there are only a handful of popular tourist sites while the rest of Colombia hardly ever sees a foreign traveller. This makes Colombia a wonderful country for independent travel.

Colombia's geography is among the most varied in South America, as are its flora and fauna. Its people form a palette of ethnic blends uncommon elsewhere on the continent and include a few dozen Indian groups, some of which still maintain traditional lifestyles. It's a country of amazing natural and cultural diversity and contrast, where climate, topography, wildlife, crafts, music and architecture

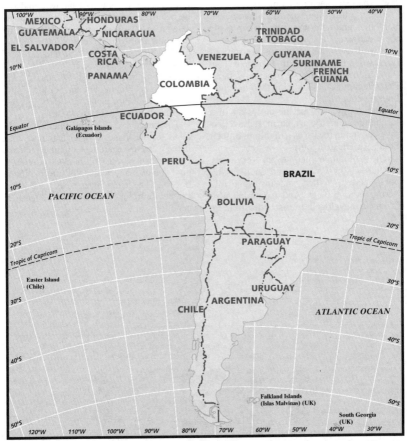

change within hours of overland travel – it's as if Colombia were several countries rolled into one.

Through its stormy and turbulent history, Colombia has been soaked with blood in innumerable civil wars and has endured the continent's most massive and persistent guerrilla insurgency. The country is also the world's major producer of cocaine. With such a background, it's no wonder that violence may occur here more frequently than in neighbouring countries.

Yet, travellers to Colombia are often immediately amazed by how normal and orderly everyday life is despite all the problems the country is going through. And most visitors leave Colombia with fantastic experiences and enthusiastic comments – very few experience security problems.

Yes, it's true, there are kidnappings, car bombings and hold-ups, but you can avoid these dangers.

If you take the necessary precautions (and we've been careful to document them throughout this book) you actually don't risk much more in Colombia than in neighbouring countries.

Your reward will be the discovery of a fascinating country, which most travellers rave about and regard as a highlight of their South American sojourn.

The Colombian people are very, very special – you'll rarely find such joyful, open-hearted, skilled and inspiring folk during your travels. And Colombia also boasts a developed tourist infrastructure and is one of the cheapest countries on the South American continent.

If you take the necessary precautions, Colombia is well worth the challenge. It is one of the world's most exotic, sensual, wild, complex and fascinating countries.

This book is geared for safe travel in Colombia. It focuses on reasonably safe regions and provides comprehensive information on how to get around as safely as possible. Since safety has been a priority, this book is different from most Lonely Planet guidebooks.

This book doesn't seek to comprehensively cover the whole of Colombia. On the contrary, some of the most potentially unsafe areas have been deliberately omitted. These are essentially remote regions, way off the beaten track, which had been rarely visited in the past anyway and can be positively unsafe to travel in. Relatively safe areas have been covered in great detail meaning that you have a thinner, lighter book which covers the best and safest of what Colombia has to offer.

Apart from a thorough Dangers & Annoyances section in the Facts for the Visitor chapter, there are plenty of safety tips and comments throughout this book.

The boxed text 'Colombia Online' in the Facts for the Visitor chapter features a long list of websites regarding Colombia (actually far longer than most LP books), in order to give you as many sources of information as possible. The list includes news sites, which can be useful for checking out current safety conditions in various regions.

# Facts about Colombia

## HISTORY
### Pre-Columbian Times

Colombia is the only overland gateway to South America and must have been part of the route pioneered by the continent's first human inhabitants who migrated from North and Central America. Some tribes headed farther south, later developing well-known cultures such as the Nazca, Tiahuanaco and Inca, while other groups established their settlements in what is now Colombia and eventually reached a remarkably high level of development. However, these groups are little known internationally, partly because few left spectacular, enduring monuments.

There are only three important archaeological sites in Colombia. They are San Agustín, Tierradentro and Ciudad Perdida. Other communities left behind artefacts – mainly gold and pottery – some of which are now in museums across the country. Yet their art reveals a high degree of skill, and their goldwork is the continent's best, both for the techniques used and for artistic design.

In contrast to the Aztecs or Incas, who dominated vast regions, a dozen independent Colombian groups occupied relatively small areas scattered throughout the Andean region and along the Pacific and Atlantic (Caribbean) Coasts. Despite trading and cultural contacts, these cultures developed largely independently. Among the most outstanding were the Calima, Muisca, Nariño, Quimbaya, San Agustín, Sinú, Tayrona, Tierradentro, Tolima and Tumaco. Most of the groups are believed to have reached the height of their cultural and social development by the time of the Spaniards' arrival.

San Agustín is one of the most extraordinary ceremonial burial sites in South America, famous for hundreds of monolithic stone statues and tombs that are scattered over a mountainous area of present-day southwest Colombia. Another culture with elaborate funeral rites flourished in nearby Tierradentro, which is noted for impressive underground burial chambers (unique in South America), laboriously carved out of the soft rock and decorated with paintings.

The Muiscas developed a flourishing culture in what are now the Boyacá and Cundinamarca departments in central Colombia. They took advantage of fertile soil and rich salt and emerald mines, and created extensive trading links with other communities. They were Colombia's largest indigenous group at the time of the Spanish Conquest, with a population estimated by some chroniclers to have been as high as 500,000. Often confusedly called the Chibchas because they were the major group of the Chibcha linguistic family, the Muiscas are widely known for the myth of El Dorado, created by the Spaniards.

The Tayrona, in the Sierra Nevada de Santa Marta on the Caribbean Coast, had long been considered one of the most advanced early Indian civilisations, yet it was only after an accidental discovery of Ciudad Perdida (the Lost City), in 1975, that their greatness as architects and urban planners was confirmed. Ciudad Perdida, thought to be their major centre, is one of the largest ancient cities ever found in the Americas. Resplendent with several hundred stone terraces linked by a network of stairs, it is spectacularly situated in the heart of a tropical rainforest.

The Tumaco culture on the Pacific Coast is one of the oldest in Colombia, dating from about the 10th century BC. It is noted for the erotic art associated with its fertility cult. The Tumaco were influenced by the coastal cultures of Ecuador, Costa Rica, Guatemala and Mexico.

### Spanish Conquest

Colombia is named after Christopher Columbus, even though he never set foot on Colombian soil. It was Alonso de Ojeda, one of his companions on his second voyage, who landed at the Cabo de la Vela on the Guajira Peninsula in 1499. He briefly explored the Sierra Nevada de Santa Marta and was astonished by the wealth of the local Indians. Their gold and their stories about fabulous treasures inland gave birth to the myth of El Dorado, a mysterious kingdom abundant in gold. In its most extreme interpretation, it was believed to be a land of gold mountains littered with emeralds.

From the moment the Spaniards arrived, their obsession with El Dorado became the principal force driving them into the interior. They did not find El Dorado, but their search resulted in rapid colonisation.

The legend of El Dorado became linked to the Muiscas and their famous Laguna de Guatavita. There, the expectations of the Spaniards were to some degree confirmed by the rituals of the Indians, who threw gold offerings into the sacred waters, though very little has been found despite numerous efforts (see Laguna de Guatavita in the later Bogotá chapter).

Attracted by the presumed riches of the Indians, the shores of present-day Colombia became the target of numerous expeditions by the Spaniards. Several short-lived settlements were founded along the coast, but it was not until 1525 that Rodrigo de Bastidas laid the first stones of Santa Marta, the earliest surviving town. In 1533, Pedro de Heredia founded Cartagena, which soon became the principal centre of trade.

In 1536, a general advance toward the interior began independently from three different directions, under Jiménez de Quesada, Sebastián de Benalcázar (known in Colombia as Belalcázar) and Nikolaus Federmann. Although all three were drawn by the Indian treasures, none intended to reach Muisca territory, where they finally met.

Quesada set off from Santa Marta, pushed up the Valle del Magdalena, then climbed the Cordillera Oriental, arriving in Muisca territory early in 1537. At the time, the Muiscas were divided into two clans – the southern one ruled by the Zipa from Bacatá (present-day Bogotá), and the northern empire under the Zaque in Hunza (present-day Tunja). The two caciques quarrelled over territory and the rivalry considerably helped Quesada conquer the Muiscas without undue difficulty. In August 1538, he founded Santa Fe de Bogotá on the site of Bacatá.

Belalcázar deserted from Francisco Pizarro's army, which was conquering the Inca empire, and mounted an expedition from Ecuador. He subdued the southern part of Colombia, founding Popayán and Cali along the way, and reached Bogotá in 1539. Federmann started from the Venezuelan coast and, after successfully crossing Los Llanos and the Andes, arrived in Bogotá shortly after Belalcázar. Thus, in a short period of time, a large part of the colony was conquered and a number of towns were founded.

The three groups fought tooth and nail for supremacy, and it was not until 1550 that King Charles V (Carlos V) of Spain, in an effort to establish law and order, created the Real Audiencia del Nuevo Reino de Granada, a tribunal based in Bogotá. It was principally a court of justice, but its duties went beyond normal legal and penal affairs. Administratively, the new colony was subject to the Viceroyalty of Peru (Virreynato del Perú), ruled from Lima.

## The Colonial Period

In 1564, the Crown established a new system, the Presidencia del Nuevo Reino de Granada, which had dual military and civil power and greater autonomy. Authority was in the hands of the governor, appointed by the King of Spain. The Nuevo Reino at that time comprised present-day Panama and all of Colombia, except what is today Nariño, Cauca and Valle del Cauca, which were under the jurisdiction of the Presidencia de Quito.

The population of the colony, initially consisting of indigenous communities and the Spanish invaders, diversified with the arrival of blacks, brought from Africa to serve as the workforce. Cartagena was granted the privilege of being the exclusive slave-trading port in which blacks were sold as slaves and distributed throughout the colony. Most of them were set to work in mines and plantations, mainly on the Caribbean and Pacific Coasts. During the 16th and 17th centuries the Spaniards shipped in so many Africans that they eventually surpassed the indigenous population in number.

The demographic picture became more complex when the three racial groups began to mix, producing various fusions, including mestizos (people of European-Indian blood), mulatos (of European-African ancestry) and *zambos* (African-Indian). However, throughout the whole of the colonial period, power was almost exclusively in the hands of the Spaniards.

With the growth of the Spanish empire in the New World, a new territorial division was created in 1717, and Bogotá became the capital of its own viceroyalty, the Virreinato de la Nueva Granada. It comprised the territories of what are today Colombia, Panama, Ecuador and Venezuela.

## Independence Wars

As Spanish domination of the continent increased, so too did the discontent of the inhabitants. Slavery, and the monopoly of commerce, taxes and duties – among other factors – slowly gave rise to protests. The first open rebellion against colonial rule was the Revolución Comunera in Socorro in 1781, which broke out in protest against tax rises levied by the Crown, before taking on more pro-independence overtones.

Disillusionment was also experienced by the higher Creole class. The *criollos* (Colombian-born whites) were generally excluded from senior administrative posts. Of the 170 viceroys who governed the New World, only four were Creoles. In 1794, Antonio Nariño translated Thomas Paine's *Rights of Man* into Spanish. The pamphlet was a touchpaper of revolt in a country where slavery was widespread.

All this, together with a series of external events (the North American and French revolutions and, more importantly, the invasion of Spain by Napoleon Bonaparte), paved the way to independence. When Napoleon put his own brother on the Spanish throne in 1808, the colonies refused to recognise the new monarch. One by one, Colombian towns declared their independence.

The Corte Suprema de la Nueva Granada (Supreme Court) was established in Bogotá. It was the first central state body whose members were to be elected from the provinces. Some provinces, however, refused to send their representatives, becoming instead fierce advocates of regional autonomy. Thus, in spite of a united front against Spain, internal rivalries between centralists and federalists ensued. This continued to be the central political division of post-independence Colombia and gave rise to numerous conflicts and civil wars.

In 1812, Simón Bolívar, who was to become the supreme hero of the independence struggle, appeared on the scene. He left Caracas, his place of birth, and launched a brilliant campaign to seize Venezuela from Cartagena in 1813. He won six battles against Spanish troops, but was unable to hold Caracas and withdrew to Cartagena.

When Napoleon was defeated at Waterloo, Spain recovered its throne and then set about reconquering its colonies. Troops were sent under Pablo Morillo and Cartagena was retaken in 1815 after a four-month siege. The 'pacifying' Spanish troops then reconquered the interior and colonial rule was re-established by 1817.

Bolívar retreated to Jamaica after the defeat of Cartagena, and took up arms again. He went back to Venezuela, and after assembling an army of horsemen from Los Llanos, strengthened by a British legion, he marched over the Andes into Colombia, claiming victory after victory. The last and most decisive battle took place at Boyacá on 7 August 1819. Three days later he arrived triumphantly in Bogotá. Colombia's independence was won.

## After Independence

With Colombia free, a revolutionary congress was held in Angostura (modern-day Ciudad Bolívar, in Venezuela) in 1819. Still euphoric with victory, the delegates proclaimed the Gran Colombia, a new state uniting Venezuela, Colombia and Ecuador (although Ecuador and large parts of Venezuela were still under Spanish rule).

The Angostura congress was followed by another one, held in Villa del Rosario, near Cúcuta, in 1821. It was there that the two opposing tendencies, centralist and federalist, came to the fore. Bolívar, who supported a centralised republic, succeeded in imposing his will. The Gran Colombia came into being and Bolívar was elected president. Francisco de Paula Santander, who favoured a federal republic of sovereign states, became vice-president.

From its inception, however, the vast state began to disintegrate. Bolívar was far away fighting for the independence of Ecuador and Peru, leaving effective power in Santander's hands. It soon became apparent that a central regime was incapable of governing such a vast and diverse territory. The Gran Colombia had split into three separate countries by 1830 and Bolívar's dream of a sacred union of the nations he had freed came to an end even before he died.

Thus began a new inglorious page of Colombia's history. The political currents born in the struggle for independence, centralist and federalist, were formalised in 1849 when two political parties were established: the Conservatives (with centralist tendencies) and the Liberals (with federalist leanings). Fierce rivalry between these two forces resulted in a sequence of insurrections and civil wars and throughout the 19th century, Colombia experienced no fewer than eight civil wars. Between 1863

## Simón Bolívar – the Extraordinary El Libertador

'There have been three great fools in history: Jesus, Don Quixote and I.' This is how Simón Bolívar summed up his life shortly before he died. The man who brought independence from Spanish rule to the entire northwest of South America – today's Venezuela, Colombia, Panama, Ecuador, Peru and Bolivia – died abandoned, rejected and poor.

Bolívar was born in Caracas on 24 July 1783, the second child of a wealthy Creole family which had come to Venezuela from Spain in 1589. He was just three years old when his father died and nine when his mother died. The boy was brought up by his uncle and was given a tutor, Simón Rodríguez, an open-minded mentor who had a strong formative influence on his pupil.

In 1799, the young Bolívar was sent to Spain and France to continue his education. After having mastered French, he turned his attention to that country's literature. Voltaire and Rousseau became his favourite authors. Their works introduced him to new, progressive ideas of liberalism and, as it turned out, would determine the course of his career.

In 1802, Bolívar married his Spanish bride, María Teresa Rodríguez del Toro, and soon after the young couple sailed to Caracas. However, their married life lasted only eight months as María Teresa died of yellow fever. Bolívar never remarried, even though he had many lovers. The most devoted of these was Manuela Sáenz, whom he met in Quito in 1822 and who stayed with him almost until his final days.

The death of María Teresa marked a drastic shift in Bolívar's destiny. He returned to France where he met with the leaders of the French Revolution, and then travelled to the USA to take a close look at the new order after the American Revolutionary War. By the time he returned to Caracas in 1807, he was full of revolutionary theories and experiences taken from these two famous events and it didn't take him long to join clandestine pro-independence circles.

Bolívar's military career began under Francisco de Miranda, the first Venezuelan leader of the independence movement. After Miranda was captured by the Spaniards in 1812, Bolívar assumed command. Over the following decade, battle followed battle with astonishing frequency until 1824. Of the battles personally directed by Bolívar, the forces of independence won 35, including three key ones: the Battle of Boyacá (7 August 1819), which secured the independence of Colombia; the Battle of Carabobo (24 June 1821), which brought freedom to Venezuela; and the Battle of Pichincha (24 May 1822), which led to the liberation of Ecuador.

Bolívar's long-awaited dream materialised: Gran Colombia, the unified state comprising Colombia (which then included Panama), Venezuela and Ecuador, became reality. However, the task of setting the newborn country on its feet proved to be even more difficult than that of winning battles. 'I fear peace more than war,' Bolívar wrote in one of his letters, aware of the difficulties ahead.

The main problem was the question of Gran Colombia's political organisation. Bolívar, then president, favoured a strong central rule, but the central regime was incapable of governing such an

and 1885 alone there were more than 50 antigovernment insurrections.

In 1899, a Liberal revolt turned into a full-blown civil war, the so-called War of a Thousand Days. That carnage resulted in a Conservative victory and left 100,000 dead. In 1903, the USA took advantage of the country's internal strife and fomented a secessionist movement in Panama, then a Colombian province. By creating an independent republic, the USA was able to build a canal across the Central American isthmus under its control. It wasn't until 1921 that Colombia eventually recognised the sovereignty of Panama and settled its dispute with the USA.

## La Violencia

After a period of relative peace, the struggle between Liberals and Conservatives broke out again in 1948 with La Violencia, the most destructive of Colombia's many civil wars. With a death toll of some 300,000, La Violencia was one of the bloodiest conflicts in the western hemisphere, comparable only to the Mexican Revolution and the American Revolutionary War. Urban riots broke out on 9 April 1948 in Bogotá, following the assassination of Jorge Eliécer Gaitán, a charismatic populist Liberal leader. Liberals soon took up arms throughout the country.

To comprehend the brutality of this period, one must understand that generation after

## Simón Bolívar – the Extraordinary El Libertador

immense country with its great racial and regional differences. Gran Colombia began to collapse from the moment of its birth.

As separatist tendencies escalated dangerously, Bolívar ousted his vice-president Francisco de Paula Santander by decree and, in August 1828, assumed dictatorship. This step brought more harm than good. His popularity waned and after miraculously escaping an assassination attempt he resigned from the presidency in early 1830 disillusioned and in poor health. The formal disintegration of Gran Colombia was just months away.

Following Venezuela's separation from Gran Colombia, the Venezuelan congress approved a new constitution and – irony of ironies – banned Bolívar from his homeland. A month later, Antonio José de Sucre (remembered for inflicting final defeat on Spain in the Battle of Ayacucho on 9 December 1824), Bolívar's closest friend, was assassinated in southern Colombia. These two pieces of news reached Bolívar just as he was about to board a ship bound for France. Depressed and ill, he accepted the invitation of a Spaniard, Joaquín de Mier, to stay at his home, Quinta de San Pedro Alejandrino, in Santa Marta. A bitter remark written in Bolívar's diary at that time reads: 'America is ungovernable. Those who serve the revolution plough the sea.'

Bolívar died on 17 December 1830 of pulmonary tuberculosis. A priest, a doctor and a few officers were by his bed, but none of his close friends. Joaquín de Mier donated one of his shirts to dress the dead body, as there had been none among Bolívar's humble belongings. So died perhaps the most important figure in South America's history.

It took the Venezuelan nation 12 years to acknowledge its debt to the man to whom it owed its freedom. In 1842, Bolívar's remains were brought from Santa Marta to Venezuela and placed in Caracas' cathedral. In 1876, they were solemnly transferred to the National Pantheon in Caracas, where they now rest.

El Libertador – as he was called at the beginning of the liberation campaign and is still commonly known – was without doubt a man of extraordinary gifts. An idealist with a poetic mind and visionary ideas, his goal was not only to topple Spanish rule but also to create a unified America. This, of course, was an impossible ideal, yet the military conquest of some five million sq km remains a phenomenal accomplishment.

This inspired amateur, without any formal training in war strategy, won battles in a manner that still confounds experts. The campaign over the Andean Cordillera in the rainy season was described 100 years later as 'the most magnificent episode in the history of war'.

Today, Bolívar's reputation is inflated to almost superhuman dimensions. His cult is particularly strong in Venezuela, but he is also widely venerated in all the other nations he has freed. His statue graces nearly every central city plaza, and at least one street in every town bears his name.

generation of Colombians were raised as either Liberals or Conservatives and imbued with a deep mistrust of the opposition. In the 1940s and 1950s, these 'hereditary hatreds' were the cause of countless atrocities, rapes and murders, particularly in rural areas.

By the early 1950s, some groups of Liberal guerrillas had begun to demonstrate a dangerous degree of independence, in some cases making alliances with small bands of communist guerrillas that also operated during this period. As it became evident that the partisan conflict was taking on revolutionary overtones, the leaders of both the Liberal and Conservative parties decided to support a military coup as the best means to retain

power and pacify the countryside. The 1953 coup of General Gustavo Rojas Pinilla was the only military intervention the country experienced in the 20th century.

The dictatorship of General Rojas was not to last. In 1957, the leaders of the two parties signed a pact to share power for the next 16 years. The agreement, later approved by plebiscite (in which women were allowed to vote for the first time), became known as the Frente Nacional (National Front). During the life of the accord, the two parties alternated in the presidency every four years.

In effect, despite the enormous loss of lives, the same people returned to power. Moreover, they no longer needed to contest power. Party leaders repressed political activity thus sowing the seeds for the emergence of guerrilla groups.

## Guerrillas & Paramilitaries

Guerrillas have been quite an important part of Colombian political life, and a headache for the government. With roots that extend back to La Violencia, they are the oldest and largest insurgent forces in Latin America. They continue to engage in armed struggle and are more active than ever.

Colombia has given birth to perhaps a dozen different guerrilla groups, each with its own ideology and its own political and military strategies. The movements that have had the biggest impact on local politics (and left the largest number of deaths) include the FARC (Fuerzas Armadas Revolucionarias de Colombia), the ELN (Ejército de Liberación Nacional) and the M-19 (Movimiento 19 de Abril).

Until 1982, guerrillas were treated as a problem of public order and persecuted by military forces. President Belisario Betancur (1982–86) was the first to open direct negotiations with guerrillas in a bid to reincorporate them into the nation's political life. Yet the talks ended in failure. The rupture was poignantly symbolised by the takeover of Bogotá's Palacio de Justicia by M-19 guerrillas in November 1985. The military surrounded the building and, in 28 hours of fierce fighting, it went up in flames. When the fighting was over, more than 100 people lay dead, including an estimated 35 guerrillas and 11 Supreme Court justices.

In 1990, after long and complex negotiations with M-19, the Liberal government of President Virgilio Barco (1986–90) signed an agreement under which the guerilla group handed over its arms, ceased insurgent activity and transformed itself into a political party. However, the two largest and militarily strongest guerrilla groups – the 18,000-strong FARC and the 5000-strong ELN – remain under arms.

The FARC was founded in 1964 as a military wing of the Communist Party of Colombia and was pro-Soviet. The ELN, founded in 1965 by urban intellectuals inspired by Fidel Castro's communist revolution, was originally pro-Cuban, but later became a hardline Christian Marxist group headed by former Spanish priests. Having lost support from Moscow and Havana, the two guerrilla groups now rely on extortion, robbery and kidnapping to finance their struggle. They are also heavily involved in drug production and trading and have largely lost their ideological and political goals as well as popular support. In 2002, the USA and the EU included them on their list of terrorist organisations.

Colombia's peculiar geography facilitated much of the country's endemic political violence. Over 50% of the country comprises vast lowlands to the east of the Andes – the Llanos to the north and the Amazon to the south – which are sparsely populated and relatively inaccessible. Guerrilla groups prospered in these regions, often controlling significant areas.

The FARC and ELN remain in control of large chunks of Los Llanos and the Amazon, but they have also expanded over many other regions in recent years. They are now present in most departments across the country, and are stronger than ever before. It's estimated that they currently control about 40% of the country's area.

Since the state has been unable to control the areas lost to guerrillas, private armies (so-called *paramilitares* or *autodefensas*) have mushroomed, with the Colombian military turning a blind eye and even supporting them. These right-wing squads operate against rebels in many regions, including Urabá, Cesar, Córdoba, Antioquia, Magdalena Medio, Santander, Cundinamarca and Caquetá, and have committed some horrendous massacres of civilians allegedly supporting the guerrillas.

In 1997, they formed a loose alliance known as the AUC (Autodefensas Unidas de Colombia), and grew dramatically in recent years, from an estimated 8000 fighters nationwide in 2000 to perhaps 12,000 in 2002. They have also been included on the above-mentioned list of terrorist organisations.

## Drug Cartels

The government's other major headache is caused by drug lords. Colombia is the world's largest producer of cocaine, controlling 80% of the global market.

Regional mafias or cartels started in a small way in the early 1970s, but, within a short time, developed the trade into a powerful industry, with their own plantations, laboratories, transport services and protection rackets.

The boom years began in the early 1980s. The Medellín Cartel, led by Pablo Escobar, became the principal mafia, and its bosses lived in freedom and luxury. They even founded their own political party and two newspapers, and in 1982 Escobar was elected to Congress. By 1983, Escobar's personal wealth was estimated to be US$2 billion, making him one of the richest criminals in the world. He financed the construction of a suburb for 200 poor families in Medellín, and for this and several other benevolent actions, he was called the Robin Hood Paisa.

In 1983, the government launched a thorough campaign against the drug trade. In response, the cartel bosses disappeared from public life and proposed an unusual 'peace treaty' to President Betancur. For immunity from both prosecution and extradition, they offered to invest their capital in national development programmes. More tantalising still, they proposed to pay off Colombia's entire foreign debt, some US$13 billion at that time. After much consideration, the government turned down the proposals then war broke out. The cartel responded violently and managed to liquidate many of its adversaries. The war became even bloodier in August 1989, when the drug lords gunned down Luis Carlos Galán, the leading Liberal contender for the 1990 presidential election.

The government retaliated with the confiscation of nearly 1000 mafia-owned properties, and announced new laws on extradition – a nightmare for drug barons.

All hell broke loose. Drug traffickers responded with a hair-raising campaign of terror, burning the farms of regional politicians and detonating bombs in banks, newspaper offices, political party headquarters and private homes in Bogotá, Cali, Medellín and Barranquilla. In November 1989, a midair bombing killed all 101 passengers and six crew members aboard an Avianca flight from Bogotá to Cali.

The election of Liberal César Gaviria (1990–94) brought a brief period of hope. Following lengthy negotiations, which included a constitutional amendment to ban the extradition of Colombians, Escobar and the remaining cartel bosses surrendered and the narcoterrorism subsided. However, Escobar escaped from his palace-like prison (called La Catedral) following the government's bumbling attempts to move him to a more secure site. An elite 1500-man special unit sought Escobar for 499 days, until they tracked him down in Medellín and killed him in December 1993.

Despite this, the drug trade continued unabated. While the military concentrated on hunting one man and persecuting one cartel, the other cartels were quick to take advantage. The Cali Cartel, led by the Rodríguez

## Watergate Colombia-style

The 1994 elections put Liberal Ernesto Samper into the presidency. Just before he took office, his major opponent, Andrés Pastrana, released tapes (dubbed 'narcocassettes') of wire-tapped telephone conversations in which Cali Cartel bosses discussed making 'donations' to Samper's presidential campaign. The issue was glossed over, but resurfaced in 1995 when Santiago Medina, Samper's campaign treasurer, testified that the party had received some US$6 million from the cartel. A further blow came when Fernando Botero, Samper's campaign manager, claimed during a television interview that Samper knowingly took the cartel's money (dubbed 'narcodinero').

Both Medina and Botero – as well as some members of parliament, former ministers and a former attorney general – were linked to an amazing web of corruption, referred to as the Proceso 8000 (dubbed 'narcoproceso'), and some ended up in jail. Meanwhile, the president maintained he was unaware that drug money had gone into his campaign fund. An investigation was carried out by Congress and, predictably, Samper was not indicted. This is Colombian democracy (dubbed 'narco-democracia').

While the drug-money issue was at the top of the political agenda for most of Samper's term in office, the government (dubbed 'narcogobierno') largely lost its grasp over domestic affairs, and guerrilla and paramilitary activities intensified dramatically. By the end of Samper's term, the country faced its worst economic outlook and public order situation in decades.

Orejuela brothers, swiftly moved into the shattered Medellín Cartel's markets and became Colombia's largest trafficker. It also diversified into opium poppies and heroin. However, most of the cartel's top bosses were captured in 1995 and put behind bars, and the cartel was largely dismantled.

However, drug trafficking hasn't diminished as the government hoped it would; instead it has just moved elsewhere. Other regional cartels and, principally, the guerrillas and paramilitaries have quickly filled the gap left behind by the two original mafias, and the drug trade continues to flourish. Until the USA rethinks its drug strategy there appears little hope that the Colombian bad guys will simply walk away from a US$6-billion-a-year business.

## Into the 21st Century

The 1998 elections brought 12 years of Liberal domination to an end by placing independent conservative Andrés Pastrana into the top office. Just after the elections Pastrana met secretly with the FARC's top commander Manuel Marulanda, known as Tirofijo (Sure Shot), in order to end the bloody guerrilla war.

Before entering into talks, the FARC insisted on the withdrawal of government troops from the guerrilla-controlled areas of Caquetá and Putumayo departments. In a politically risky move to start the peace process, in November 1998 Pastrana ceded to the FARC a 42,000 sq km demilitarised zone the size of Switzerland (or twice the size of Massachusetts), which effectively became the rebels' country.

Talks began in January 1999 and inched on and off with practically no results. The guerrillas refused a cease-fire as a precondition of the peace dialogue, so the war went on as it had for decades. The FARC also wanted the government to dismantle the right-wing paramilitary groups, but the government denied any links with them.

It soon became evident that the FARC just temporised to gain control over the region and to strengthen its grip on power. By February 2002, the government eventually lost its patience and reclaimed the demilitarised zone. However, this wasn't a straightforward process as the FARC was already well established in the region and had no intentions of leaving its jungle stronghold. In fact the guerilla group set about capturing new spots in other regions. In April 2002, shortly before presidential elections, the FARC began a campaign of terror including car bombs aimed at the civilian population.

The May 2002 election was carried out in a climate of violence, a fragile economic situation and with both traditional political parties in crisis. Six presidential candidates campaigned for the top post, but one of them, Ingrid Betancourt, was kidnapped by the FARC. Álvaro Uribe, who ran as an independent hardliner, claimed a landslide first-round victory, capturing 53% of the vote.

## Who Is Álvaro Uribe?

The 43rd Colombian president elected by popular vote, Álvaro Uribe is an independent hardline politician with a brilliant education and a remarkable political career. Born in Medellín in 1952, he graduated in law and political sciences from the Universidad de Antioquia, and later continued his education at Harvard and Oxford. He gained experience in politics as the governor of Antioquia and the mayor of Medellín before challenging for the presidency.

In 1983, Álvaro's father was assassinated by the FARC guerrillas in a kidnap attempt at the family ranch in Antioquia. A fierce adversary of the guerrillas, Álvaro Uribe survived 15 assassination attempts even before he became president, including three serious attacks during his presidential campaign.

Married to Lina Moreno, with whom he has two sons, Uribe doesn't drink and has a reputation as a workaholic. He has been a yoga practitioner for over 20 years and still tries to find an hour a day for meditation in between his presidential tasks.

It all seems to suggest that Uribe's politics will differ significantly from that of his predecessors. The first bombshell broke soon after he took office and appointed his cabinet. Six of a total of 13 ministers are women, including two in the key posts of defence and foreign affairs. This is not common anywhere in the world, let alone in traditionally machismo-ridden Latin America.

Uribe ran on a strong anti-guerrilla ticket, promising a more intensive military campaign against the two enduring rebel groups as the best way to end Colombia's lengthy and bloody civil war. Predictably, his policy curried favour with the electorate, which was by then fed up with what seemed a never-ending conflict involving bombings, kidnappings and extortion.

Uribe's presidential term is likely to be a difficult period for the nation and crucial for Colombia's future. Both the government and the guerrillas are determined to win their battle, but what will come from their strong initial declarations remains to be seen. The first few months of the new government did not bring any radical changes although the war intensified, claiming more victims on both sides. Despite that (or perhaps because of it), Uribe enjoyed a remarkable 75% popular support towards the end of 2002, more than any other president in recent history.

## GOVERNMENT & POLITICS

Colombia is a parliamentary republic. The president is elected by direct vote for a four-year term and cannot be re-elected. If no candidate obtains an absolute majority (half of all votes) in the first round, a second and deciding round between the two leading contenders is held three weeks later. The president is the head of state, of the government and of the armed forces, as well as the supreme administrative authority. The president is empowered to nominate ministers.

The Congress consists of two houses, the 102-seat Senate and the 161-seat Chamber of Representatives. The members are also elected in a direct vote for a four-year term.

The Supreme Court, the highest judicial body, can review legislation and judge the president and the members of the Congress. The death penalty was abolished in 1910.

There are various political parties, of which the Conservatives and the Liberals have been the major traditional forces since their foundation in 1849. Colombian presidents were always members of one of these parties until the 1998 elections when Andrés Pastrana, an independent, was successful. The 2002 election was won by another independent, Álvaro Uribe, confirming that the traditional parties were in crisis.

A new constitution came into effect in July 1991, extensively reforming the institutional structure of Colombian politics, replacing the bipartisan power-sharing arrangement of the National Front. In its place, the constitution affirmed a more pluralist conception of politics, which incorporated former guerrilla groups, Indian communities, blacks, non-Catholics and others who had previously felt excluded from the political process. The new constitution is pioneering in its concepts of human rights, ethnic pluralism and ecological preservation.

Administratively, the country is divided into 32 departments ruled by governors, and Bogotá's special district (Distrito Capital) ruled by the city's mayor. The governors and the mayor are elected by popular vote.

The Colombian flag has three horizontal belts: the upper half is yellow and the lower one is half-blue and half-red.

## GEOGRAPHY

Colombia covers 1,141,748 sq km, roughly equivalent to the combined area of France, Spain and Portugal. It is the fourth-largest country in South America, after Brazil, Argentina and Peru. Colombia occupies the northwestern part of the continent and is the only South American country with coasts on both the Pacific (1448km long) and the Caribbean (1760km). Colombia is bordered by Panama, Venezuela, Brazil, Peru and Ecuador.

Colombia's physical geography is amazingly diverse. The western part, almost half of the total territory, is mountainous, with three Andean chains – the Cordillera Occidental, Cordillera Central and Cordillera Oriental – running roughly parallel north–south across most of the country and featuring some peaks above 5000m.

Two valleys, the Valle del Cauca and Valle del Magdalena, are sandwiched between the three cordilleras. Their rivers flow northwards, more or less parallel, until the Cauca River (1350km long) joins the Magdalena (1538km), which then flows into the Caribbean near Barranquilla.

Apart from the three Andean chains, Colombia features an independent and relatively small formation, the Sierra Nevada de Santa Marta, which rises from the Caribbean coastline to permanent snows. It is the world's highest coastal mountain range, and its twin peaks of Simón Bolívar and Cristóbal Colón (both 5775m) are the country's highest.

# ADMINISTRATIVE DIVISIONS

More than half of the territory east of the Andes is vast lowland, which is generally divided into two regions: Los Llanos to the north and the Amazon to the south. Los Llanos, roughly 250,000 sq km in area, is a huge open savannah lying in the basin of the Río Orinoco. The Amazon, stretching over some 400,000 sq km, occupies all of Colombia's southeast and lies in the Amazon basin. Most of this land is covered by a thick rainforest crisscrossed by rivers.

Colombia has a number of islands. The major ones are the archipelago of San Andrés and Providencia (in the Caribbean Sea, 750km northwest of mainland Colombia), the Islas del Rosario and San Bernardo (near the Caribbean Coast) and Gorgona and Malpelo (in the Pacific Ocean).

## The Bewitching Green Gem

Emeralds have been known since at least 3500 BC. The earliest mines were in Egypt, but later on emeralds were found at many other locations. Today, emeralds are mined by a number of countries on most continents, including Australia, Brazil, Colombia, India, Madagascar, Pakistan, Russia, Tanzania, Zambia and Zimbabwe. Colombia produces about 50% of all the world's emeralds, followed by Zambia (20%) and Brazil (15%). Judging by quality, however, an estimated 80% of the finest emeralds come from Colombia.

Technically speaking, emeralds are a green-coloured transparent variety of a mineral known as beryl, which is found in coarse granites and igneous rocks all over the world. Emeralds in their original state don't usually look particularly attractive. It's only after a skilful stonecutting process that they reveal their full splendour, making them some of the most valued precious stones in the world. Emerald cutting is a delicate and difficult task, since the stones are fragile and usually have some impurities.

Emeralds are aristocrats of the gem family and have always been highly prized by royalty, from the ancient Egyptians to the tsarist Russians. They are among the priciest stones, often more expensive than diamonds. They are difficult to judge; their value hugely depends on their colour, purity, transparency, brilliance and luminosity, and obviously the size of the stone and its cutting style.

The two most famous emeralds are the *Devonshire* and the *Patricia*, both mined in Colombia. The *Devonshire* is a 1384-carat uncut stone of amazing green colour – it's now in the British Museum of Natural History. The 632-carat *Patricia* is in New York's Museum of Natural History. The stone has been labelled 'too perfect to cut'.

There are two sites in Colombia where emeralds are mined, Muzo and Chivor, both in the Boyacá department. The stones from Muzo are noted for their brilliant grass-green colour, whereas those from Chivor show bluish-green tones. Both are considered among the finest you can get.

The Muzo area, in western Boyacá, lies at around 600m above sea level and features several mines, including Tequendama, Cosquez, Santa Bárbara and Peñas Blancas. The *Patricia* stone was found in Peñas Blancas in the early 20th century. Chivor, in eastern Boyacá, is on the eastern slopes of the Cordillera Oriental at an altitude of roughly 2300m. The principal mines here include Buena Vista, Mundo Nuevo, El Toro and Las Vegas.

Muisca Indians, who lived in Boyacá since perhaps the 3rd century BC, knew about emeralds and mined them long before the Spaniards arrived. They used the stones as ritual offerings for their gods, as well as funerary objects left in tombs to accompany the dead into their hereafter. Emeralds were also commonly used for barter in trading with other indigenous groups in the region and beyond. Since Muiscas had no gold mines of their own, they often traded emeralds for gold.

Once the Spaniards arrived they quickly learned about emeralds and pinpointed the Muisca mines. They enslaved the Indians to mine the gems for them, then shipped the stones back to Spain. Later, during the independence wars, emeralds helped to finance Bolívar's liberation campaign.

Mining continued after Colombia gained independence, though the government never managed to gain full control over the mines. Fierce battles were repeatedly fought between rival bands of miners, claiming lives and ravaging the mines. Between 1984 and 1990 alone, in one of the bloodiest 'emerald wars' in recent history, 3500 people were killed in Muzo. Yet, 'green fever' continues to burn among fortune hunters and adventurers from the four corners of the country. And the mines are believed to still contain plenty of bewitching green stones...

## CLIMATE

Colombia's proximity to the equator means its temperature varies little throughout the year. However, the temperature does change with altitude, which creates various climatic zones from hot lowlands to freezing Andean peaks, so you can experience completely different climates within just a couple of hours of travel.

As a general rule, the temperature falls about 6°C with every 1000m increase in altitude. If the average temperature at sea level is 30°C, it will be around 24°C at 1000m, 18°C at 2000m and 12°C at 3000m.

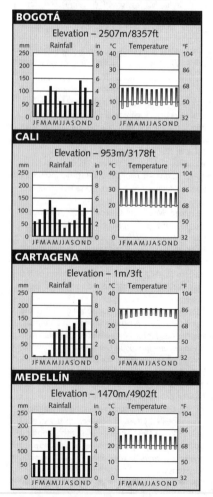

The altitude also affects the difference between daytime and night-time temperatures. The higher the altitude, the greater the difference. Consequently, in the highlands there can be warm days but freezing nights, while in the lowlands days and nights are almost equally hot.

Colombia has two seasons: dry or *verano* (literally 'summer') and wet or *invierno* (winter). The pattern of seasons varies in different parts of the country, and has been greatly affected over recent years by El Niño and La Niña.

As a rough guideline only, in the Andean region there are two dry and two rainy seasons per year. The main dry season falls between December and March, with a shorter and less dry period between July and August. This general pattern has wide variations throughout the Andean zone.

The weather in Los Llanos has a more definite pattern: there is one dry season, between December and March, while the rest of the year is wet. The Amazon doesn't have a uniform climate but, in general, is quite wet year-round.

## FLORA & FAUNA

Colombia claims to have more plant and animal species per unit area than any other country in the world. Its variety of flora and fauna is second only to Brazil's, even though Colombia is seven times smaller than its neighbour. This abundance reflects Colombia's numerous climatic zones and microclimates, which have created many different habitats and biological islands in which wildlife has evolved independently.

Colombia is home to the jaguar, ocelot, peccary, tapir, deer, armadillo, spectacled bear and numerous species of monkey, to mention just a few of the 300-odd species of mammals. There are more than 1920 recorded species of birds (about 20% of the world's total), ranging from the huge Andean condor to the tiny hummingbird. More than 140 bird species are endemic to Colombia. There is also abundant marine life in the country's extensive river systems and along its two coastlines.

Colombia's flora is equally impressive and includes some 3000 species of orchid alone (see the boxed text 'Orchids, Orchids Everywhere' in the later Northwest Colombia chapter). The national herbariums have classified more than 130,000 plants, including many endemic species. This richness still does not convey the whole picture as large areas of the country, such as the inaccessible parts of the Amazon, have never been investigated by botanists.

## National Parks

Colombia has 34 national parks and 12 other state-run nature reserves. Their combined area constitutes 8.1% of the country's territory. This figure may sound impressive but, unfortunately, there have never been sufficient funds or personnel to properly guard the parks. Simply decreeing an area as a national park has not eliminated colonisation, logging, ranching and poaching, let alone guerrilla activities.

Only a dozen parks provide accommodation and food; several more offer only camping. The remaining parks have no tourist amenities at all and some, especially those in remote regions, are virtually inaccessible. Many parks can be unsafe for tourists because of the guerrilla presence.

National parks are managed by the Unidad Administrativa Especial del Sistema de Parques Nacionales, a department of the Ministry of the Environment. Their central office is in Bogotá, and there are regional offices in most large cities and other localities close to the parks. If you plan on visiting the parks, you should first visit the park office to pay the entrance fee (US$2 to $US$4 per person). Accommodation, when available, costs US$6 to US$12 per bed. The most popular parks include Tayrona, Los Corales del Rosario, Los Nevados, Isla Gorgona and Amacayacu, and Santuario de Iguaque. They all are detailed in this book.

The Bogotá park office (called Oficina de Ecoturismo) handles visits to all the parks, and some, including Isla Gorgona, have to be booked here. Most other parks can be booked in subsidiary offices which service the parks in their regions.

## Private Nature Reserves

Growing ecological awareness has led to the creation of privately owned and run nature reserves. They are administered by individual proprietors, rural communities, foundations and other nongovernmental organisations. They are usually small, but often contain an interesting sample of habitat. They are scat-

tered countrywide, although most are in the Andean region. Some reserves offer accommodation, food and guides.

The reserves are affiliated with the Red de Reservas Naturales de la Sociedad Civil, an association based in Cali (see that entry in the Valle del Cauca section of the later Southwest Colombia chapter for contact details). As of 2002, there were 120 reserves affiliated with this association, but more than half were closed due to security problems.

## ECONOMY

Colombia managed to avoid the debt crises and bouts of hyperinflation which plagued most of its neighbours in the 1980s, and until the mid-1990s had one of the continent's steadiest economies. Despite social and political problems, the country's GDP growth rate hovered around 5% annually for three decades until 1995.

Sadly, this remarkable economic performance was badly affected during the Samper presidency. The GDP growth rate fell to 2.1% in 1996, then to just 0.6% in 1998, and slumped to a dangerous -4.2% in 1999, which was the first year of negative economic growth since 1932. It since has recovered and stood at 1.5% in 2002 and is expected to maintain similar growth in 2003.

Despite these problems, Colombia has managed to build a diversified economy and produces an array of domestically manufactured products to meet local demand. The country exports coffee, oil, coal, nickel, flowers, bananas, sugar, cotton, textiles, pharmaceuticals and a host of other manufactured goods. Colombia has a relatively large middle class, and an economy robust enough to support sustained economic growth.

Colombia's traditional export is coffee, and until the late 1970s the crop was responsible for about half of the country's legal foreign exchange earnings. Coffee was introduced to Colombia in the 18th century and the first commercial plantations began operating at the beginning of the 19th century. Today, the country is the world's second-largest coffee producer, after Brazil. Coffee is cultivated in most departments, but the majority comes from Caldas, Risaralda and Quindío, the so-called Zona Cafetera.

Other main agricultural products include sugar (with production concentrated in the Cali region), cotton and bananas. Thanks to the diverse climate there's a variety of other crops such as rice, maize, potatoes, tobacco, barley, beans and cocoa, making Colombia agriculturally the most self-sufficient of all the Latin American countries. It is also an important producer and exporter of flowers, particularly carnations.

Mineral resources are plentiful, but remain underexploited. Colombia possesses the largest deposits of coal in Latin America, and coal mining has become one of the most dynamic sectors of the economy. Coal is mined in La Guajira where a gigantic Cerrejón project was built in the 1980s.

With the discovery of rich oilfields in Casanare in the early 1990s, Colombia has joined the ranks of the world's oil-exporting nations. However, after 10 years of intensive exploitation, the fields are now half-empty and production has waned. Oil exports in 2002 still accounted for about 20% of fiscal revenues (down from 35% in 2000), but experts warn that if no new oilfields are found soon, Colombia will need to start importing oil by around 2006.

The country also has deposits of gold, silver, platinum, nickel, copper and iron among other minerals. It produces half of the world's emeralds, and Colombian stones are considered to be the best (see the boxed text 'The Bewitching Green Gem' earlier in this chapter).

Industry has grown over recent decades, primarily in the fields of petrochemicals,

## The Shadowy Side of Colombia's Economy

The unknown element in any portrait of the Colombian economy is the impact of the underground economy and of Colombia's illegal exports which, by all estimates, account for a significant portion of GNP.

Undoubtedly, the biggest illegal export is cocaine, which earns an estimated US$6 billion annually, half of which is thought to be reinvested in Colombia. In 2001, Colombia exported about 480 tonnes of cocaine (1.3 tonnes per day), over 10 times more than 10 years earlier.

Colombia is the world's third-leading producer of marijuana. In the 1980s, the US DEA (Drug Enforcement Agency) sprayed most of Colombia's marijuana fields with herbicide, practically eliminating all production. At this time, production was concentrated mostly in the Sierra Nevada de Santa Marta and La Guajira areas. Today, the crop is back and is grown in many regions of the country, and has become a significant revenue earner.

A newer, illicit export is that of heroin. The industry began in the early 1990s and has quickly made inroads into northern markets, taking advantage of transport networks established for the cocaine trade. Colombian heroin is evidently of high quality and easily competes with the best available from traditional Asian suppliers.

However, illegal exports are not confined to drugs. Colombia has been commercially producing emeralds for over a century, but the state has been unable to control the trade. Colombia produces half of the world's emeralds and the Colombian stones are generally regarded as the finest. An estimated US$500 million worth of emeralds comes from Colombia, roughly 60% of which is exported illegally.

It is hardly surprising that Colombia has become an illegal exporter of animals, mostly birds, given the amazing variety of exotic wildlife here. The birds are caught in Colombian forests and reappear in US or European pet shops or are sent directly to clients.

Colombia is also thought to be one of the leading producers of counterfeit US dollars. According to rough estimates, about a quarter of all fake US dollars circulating worldwide are printed in Colombia, mainly in Cali. Like other illegal products, they are of excellent quality, and are virtually indistinguishable from the genuine article.

The shadow economy doesn't always involve exports. There is a lot of illicit trading done within the country when large amounts of money move outside state control. One of the most lucrative deals over recent years has been the theft of petrol from the pipelines, a crime committed mostly by guerrillas and paramilitaries. They simply puncture the pipeline, extract the petrol, then sell it or use it for their own purposes, eg, for cocaine production (which requires a lot of fuel). Large parts of pipeline pass through territories controlled by guerrillas and paramilitaries, so access for these groups is pretty straightforward. The pipelines are now so densely perforated that locals refer to them as flutes.

metallurgy, car assembly (Renault, Chevrolet, Mazda), textiles, domestic electrical appliances and food and agriculture.

Inflation in 2002 was 6.5%, unemployment peaked at 19% and minimum monthly wages were around US$125. Foreign debt in that year reached US$39 billion.

## POPULATION & PEOPLE

No census has been conducted since 1993, so population figures are estimates calculated on the basis of the previous data and projections. According to these calculations, Colombia's population reached 44 million in late 2002, making it the second-most populous country in South America, after Brazil. Population growth is about 1.7%. Average life expectancy is about 71 years. Literacy stands at 91%, though it's much lower (about 60% on average) among blacks and Indian groups.

Population density varies a great deal across the country. The western half of Colombia, which consists of the Andean region and the two coasts, is home to more than 90% of the total population. The three Andean Cordilleras are pretty densely populated, and here also are Colombia's three biggest cities. This is largely the result of the Spanish Conquest; whereas in other parts of South America the Spaniards mainly colonised only coastal areas, in Colombia they quickly ventured into the interior in search of El Dorado.

Colombia's rough topography limited contact between regions, forcing them to be self-sufficient and develop independently and the result is still noticeable today. In contrast to most other countries in South America, which tend to be dominated by one or at most two metropolises, Colombia has four distinct regional centres, each based on a city with more than a million inhabitants. Bogotá, the capital, has seven million people and is the nucleus of central Colombia; Medellín, the second-largest urban centre, has two million inhabitants, and dominates the northwest; Cali, the centre of the southwest, is almost as big as Medellín; and Barranquilla, the smallest of the four, is the centre of the Caribbean Coast.

Colombia has significant racial integration. About 75% of the population is of mixed blood, composed of 50% to 55% mestizos (of European-Indian blood) and 15% to 20% mulatos (of European-African blood). There are also about 3% zambos (of African-Indian blood).

The rest of the population, roughly a quarter of the nation, are pure whites, blacks or Indians. Whites, who are mainly descendants of the Spaniards, constitute about 20% of the population. Antioquia and the coffee region (Caldas, Risaralda and Quindío) are 'white' departments due to the traditional reluctance of European settlers to mix with either blacks or Indians.

Blacks represent about 4% of the total population and are most numerous on the Caribbean Coast (which was formerly the centre of the slave trade), the Pacific Coast and in the Cali region. The department of Chocó is home to the largest proportion of the black population.

Indians number between 400,000 and 600,000, representing just a bit more than 1% of the total population. This seemingly insignificant number comprises about 80 different Indian groups speaking about 65 languages and nearly 300 dialects belonging to several linguistic families. They live in communities scattered throughout the country, usually occupying quite small areas. Some groups live in relative isolation, while others maintain close contact with the outside world. In spite of these contacts, several groups have managed to preserve their culture and traditions.

## ARTS

Colombia is an ethnic mosaic and its culture, folklore, arts and crafts reflect this. The different roots and traditions of the Indians, Spaniards and Africans have combined with external influences to produce interesting fusions.

### Pre-Columbian Art

The pre-Hispanic cultures of what is now Colombia left behind a number of artefacts, mostly stone sculpture, pottery and goldwork, which show a high degree of development.

The greatest masters of stone sculpture were the people from San Agustín, who left behind several hundred monumental stone statues. Some statues feature anthropomorphic figures, presumably depicting ancestors and gods, while others have zoomorphic forms, representing the animals of the complex religious cult of the group.

## Colombia's Who's Who

Colombia is not exactly a nation known worldwide for its famous citizens. Go on, try and name some contemporary Colombians who have become internationally renowned. How many could you name? Let's give you some help:

**Ingrid Betancourt** (born 1961) – Bogotá-born, Paris-raised prominent politician and senator, best known for her fearless attacks on corruption, drug trafficking and the destruction of the natural environment. Her account of her political life, *La Rage au Coeur*, written in French and published in 2000, was a big success in France where the media has not hesitated in calling her a heroine and even the new Jeanne d'Arc. She ran for the 2002 presidency as a candidate for her own party, Oxígeno, but in February, just three months before the elections, she was kidnapped by FARC guerrillas and has been captive ever since, despite numerous release pleas from people and organisations all over the world.

**Fernando Botero** (born 1932) – The most internationally recognised Colombian painter and sculptor. Born in Medellín, he had his first individual painting exhibition in Bogotá at the age of 19 and gradually developed his easily recognisable style characterised by the unusual fatness of his figures. In 1972, he settled in Paris and began experimenting with sculpture, which resulted in a collection of *gordas* and *gordos*, as Colombians call these creations. Today, his paintings dot the walls of world-class museums and his monumental public sculptures adorn squares and parks in cities around the globe, including Paris, Madrid, Lisbon, Florence and New York.

**Gabriel García Márquez** (born 1928) – One of Latin America's greatest writers, born in the small Caribbean town of Aracataca, which came to be a prototype of the legendary Macondo. He became a journalist and reporter for local newspapers, and a foreign correspondent in Europe and New York, but it was as a novelist that he achieved fame. His hypnotic, magical *One Hundred Years of Solitude*, published in 1967, became an international bestseller and one of the greatest novels ever written. It was followed by several other extraordinary novels including *Love in the Time of Cholera*. He was awarded the Nobel Prize for literature in 1982.

**Juan Pablo Montoya** (born 1975) – Williams Formula One team driver born and raised in Bogotá, now living in Monaco. He first drove a go-kart at the age of five and after 20 years of kart racing and a drive in the Indianapolis 500, he debuted in the Australian Grand Prix in March 2001. He secured his maiden victory at Italy's Monza circuit in September 2001 and finished sixth in the drivers' championship in his first Formula One season. He received the 2001 Ibero-American Community Trophy, awarded annually for the most eminent Latin American sportsperson. He finished third in the drivers' championship in the 2002 Formula One season.

The statues reveal a remarkable level of technical skill.

Pottery developed as people became sedentary farmers, although the objects they made were not always utilitarian. Funeral jars, anthropomorphic and, less frequently, zoomorphic figures have also been found, along with ritual dishes and vases. Decorative motifs, in colour or in relief, were sometimes applied. Pre-Columbian pottery can be seen today in many Colombian museums.

Colombia's pre-Hispanic goldwork is commonly considered the best on the continent. Several cultures using similar techniques developed individual styles and forms. Gold was used in jewellery (nose rings, breastplates, headwear and bracelets) and ritual artefacts (mainly stylised human and animal figures).

The best-known piece of pre-Columbian goldwork is the famous Balsa Muisca (Muisca Raft), which depicts a ceremonial raft holding the cacique, his dignitaries and oarsmen. The Muiscas are also known for their *tunjos* – flat, gold figurines depicting human figures, often warriors.

Other cultures noted for their remarkable goldwork include the Quimbaya, Tolima

## Colombia's Who's Who

**Álvaro Mutis** (born 1923) – Bogotá-born novelist and poet, considered one of Latin America's most innovative writers, yet overshadowed by his great friend, Gabriel García Márquez. Mutis began his literary career in the 1950s and is said to have written every day ever since. A series of his novels features the mythical Maqroll el Gaviero, a mysterious vagabond travelling around the globe through high seas and seedy ports. Mutis was awarded the 2001 Miguel de Cervantes prize for literature, the top literary award in the Spanish-speaking world.

**Laura Restrepo** (born 1950) – Bogotá-based peace activist, journalist and novelist. Graduated in arts and political sciences, Restrepo lectured at Colombian universities and worked as a journalist and an editor before turning to literature. Her novel *Angel of Galilea*, published in 1997, brought her national and international prizes, including France's Prix France-Culture. She has written other remarkable novels including *Leopard in the Sun* and the recently translated *The Dark Bride*. Her novels combine reporting with fiction, reflecting her journalistic background.

**Shakira** (born 1977) – A girl from Barranquilla who has become a huge pop-music phenomenon. Shakira Mebarak (who has used only her first name during her career) wrote her first song at the age of eight and recorded her debut album *Magia* (Magic) when she was just 14. However, it wasn't until 1996 that her third album *Pies Descalzos* (Bare Feet) sold over four million copies and brought her fame. Four years later, her album *MTV Unplugged* won her the 2000 Grammy for the best Latin pop album. In 2002, her first English-language album *Laundry Service* stormed pop charts in the USA and cemented her status as a global superstar.

**Totó La Momposina** (born 1932) – Afro-Caribbean music vocalist and researcher nicknamed the 'Queen of the Folklore'. Born into a four-generation-long musical family in the steamy Caribbean plains, since her childhood she studied, collected and interpreted local folk songs and dances, such as *cumbia, porro* and *mapalé*. She graduated from the conservatory of Bogotá's Universidad Nacional and later studied the history of dance at the Sorbonne in Paris. She has performed with various ensembles since 1968, and toured extensively across Europe. Her songs reflect the musical culture of Colombia's Caribbean Coast noted for the fusion of Spanish and indigenous traditions with vibrant African rhythms.

**Carlos Vives** (born 1961) – One of the major Latin pop vocalists who successfully transformed *vallenato*, a popular traditional musical genre rooted in Colombia's Caribbean Coast, into a lively and captivating pop beat which includes elements of rock, jazz and reggae. Born in Santa Marta, Vives began as a rock musician in the bars of Bogotá and Puerto Rico, but it wasn't until the mid-1990s that his creative take of the vallenato captivated audiences all over Latin America and, later, in Spain and the USA. In 2002, his album *Déjame Entrar* (Let me in) won him a Grammy.

and Tayrona. The Quimbayas were masters at making *poporos*, finely proportioned lime containers embellished with realistic bas-relief human images. The Tolimas are particularly remembered for their flat pectorals, depicting simplified human figures. The Tayrona artwork is renowned both for its detail and the simplicity of its lines. Unlike most other cultures, Tayronas rarely used pure gold in their jewellery, opting instead for a mixture of gold and copper.

The largest collection of pre-Columbian goldwork is displayed in the Museo del Oro (Gold Museum) in Bogotá.

## Folk Arts & Crafts

Colombia's folk art and craft tradition goes back to the pre-Hispanic period. After the Spanish Conquest, the Indians incorporated Spanish inventions and techniques into their work, but maintained their ancient motifs and patterns. The great variety of available plants and materials contributed considerably to the diversity of crafts developed, which include basketry, weaving and pottery.

Baskets come in all sizes, shapes, colours and vegetable fibres. Fique, the agave fibre, widespread in Colombia, is popular but plenty of other materials such as bamboo, palm leaf, reed, and even horse hair, are employed.

Weaving was well developed during pre-Columbian times, but sheep, and thus wool, were introduced by the Spaniards. Although the techniques have changed, rudimentary hand looms are still used by artisans in many regions.

Pottery manufacture has adapted to present-day needs, and mainly utilitarian and decorative items are produced. Though some pottery is still made using traditional methods, the pottery wheel, introduced by the Spanish, is the norm. The shape and decoration of modern pottery reveals many similarities with the pottery made a millennium ago.

Folk art differs widely between the regions, and is best represented in the areas where Indian groups still live such as on the Pacific Coast, in the Amazon and La Guajira. The Boyacá department is the biggest producer of handicrafts. Although there are no pure indigenous descendants living there, the mestizo population has maintained and developed the ancient craft of the Muiscas and enriched it with new forms.

## Architecture

No pre-Columbian dwellings have survived because they were generally built from perishable materials. Stone was used only by the most developed groups, and on a limited scale, mostly for foundations and cult centres. The most outstanding example of pre-Columbian urban planning is the Ciudad Perdida of the Tayronas in the Sierra Nevada de Santa Marta. Although the dwellings haven't survived, the stone structures, including a complex network of terraces, paths and stairways, remain in remarkably good shape.

After the arrival of the Spaniards, bricks and tiles became the main construction materials. The colonial towns followed rigid standards prescribed by the Spanish Crown. They were constructed on a grid plan and centred around the Plaza Mayor (Main Square), with a church facing the square. This pattern was applied throughout the colonial period and is the dominant feature of most Colombian cities, towns and villages.

Spain's strong Catholic tradition left behind loads of churches and convents in the colony – the central areas of Bogotá, Cartagena, Tunja and Popayán are good examples. The churches built in the early days of the Conquest were generally small and modest, but in the later period they tended to reach monumental dimensions. Unlike in Mexico or Peru, colonial churches in Colombia have rather austere exteriors, but their interiors are usually richly decorated.

In the 19th century, despite independence, the architecture continued to be predominantly Spanish in style. Very little French, English or Italian influence was felt and new houses hardly differed from the colonial constructions of a century earlier. There were some regional variations, notably in Antioquia, which developed a decorative, intricate style of ornamental carving for doors and windows.

Modern architectural trends made their way to Colombia after WWII. This process accelerated during the 1960s when skyscrapers began to appear in urban centres, most notably in Bogotá and Medellín.

## Fine Arts

The colonial period was dominated by Spanish religious art and although paintings and sculptures of this era were mostly created by local artists, they reflected Spanish trends of the time. Much of their work consisted of paintings of saints, carved wooden statues, gilded retables and elaborate altarpieces, some of which can still be seen in old churches and museums.

Two interesting variations – both originating from Spain – left a strong mark on Colombia's colonial art. One is the Islamic-influenced Mudéjar art *(arte mudéjar)* which developed in Spain between the 12th and 16th centuries and is at its best in the internal decoration of the churches in Tunja and Bogotá. The other is the style known as the Quito School *(escuela quiteña)* which flourished in Quito after the Conquest and influenced religious woodcarving in southern Colombia.

Gregorio Vásquez de Arce y Ceballos (1638–1711) was clearly the most remarkable painter of the colonial era. He lived and worked in Bogotá and left behind a collection of more than 500 works, now distributed among churches and museums across the country.

With the arrival of independence, fine arts departed from strictly religious themes, but it was not until the revolution in European painting at the turn of the 19th century that Colombian artists began to experiment and create original art.

Many painters and sculptors who started their careers in the 1930s and 1940s developed interesting individual styles. Among the most distinguished are Pedro Nel Gómez, known for his murals, watercolours, oils and sculptures; Luis Alberto Acuña, a painter and sculptor who used motifs from pre-Columbian art; Guillermo Wiedemann, a German painter who spent most of his creative period in Colombia and drew inspiration from local themes, though he later turned to abstract art; Alejandro Obregón, a Cartagena painter tending to abstract forms; Edgar Negret, an abstract sculptor; Eduardo Ramírez Villamizar, who expressed himself mostly in geometric forms; and Rodrigo Arenas Betancur, Colombia's most famous monument-maker.

These masters were followed by a slightly younger generation, born mainly in the 1930s, such as Armando Villegas, a Peruvian living in Colombia, whose influences ranged from pre-Columbian motifs to surrealism; Leonel Góngora, noted for his erotic drawings; and the most internationally renowned Colombian artist, Fernando Botero.

The recent period has been characterised by a proliferation of schools, trends and techniques. The artists to watch out for include Bernardo Salcedo (conceptual sculpture and photography), Miguel Ángel Rojas (painting and installations), Lorenzo Jaramillo (expressionist painting), María de la Paz Jaramillo (painting), Doris Salcedo (sculpture and installations), María Fernanda Cardozo (installations) and Catalina Mejía (abstract painting).

Today, Colombia is considered one of Latin America's leading fine arts representatives. Plenty of exhibitions featuring contemporary art are put on by museums and private commercial art galleries.

Bogotá, with university art faculties and loads of art galleries, has the most active cultural life, making it the main centre for contemporary art.

## Literature

Almost all literature during the colonial period was written by Spaniards who imposed not only the Spanish language, but a Spanish cultural perspective. A more independent approach emerged only at the end of the 18th century, with the birth of revolutionary trends which led to the publication of political literature expressing the ideals and ambitions of the nation.

Following independence, Colombian literature became intoxicated with the imagery of freedom and the Romanticism then dominant in Europe. Rafael Pombo (1833–1912) is generally acclaimed as the father of Colombian romantic poetry. Jorge Isaacs (1837–95), another notable author of the period, is particularly remembered for his romantic novel *María*, which is still popular.

José Asunción Silva (1865–96) is one of Colombia's most remarkable poets, considered the precursor of modernism in Latin America. He planted the seeds that were later developed by Nicaraguan poet Rubén Darío. Another literary talent, Porfirio Barba Jacob (1883–1942), known as 'the poet of death', introduced the ideas of irrationalism and the language of the avant-garde.

After WWII, Latin America experienced an unprecedented literary boom that thrust many great authors into the international sphere. One of these was Gabriel García Márquez (born 1928), who has become the major ambassador of Colombian literature for nearly four decades.

García Márquez began writing as a journalist in the 1950s, but gained fame through his novels, particularly *One Hundred Years of Solitude*, published in 1967. It mixed myths, dreams and reality, and amazed readers with a new form of expression which critics dubbed *realismo mágico* (magic realism). In 1982, García Márquez won the Nobel Prize for literature. Since then, he has created a wealth of fascinating work, and it's a surprisingly diverse bag. *The General in his Labyrinth*, published in 1989, is a historical novel which recounts the tragic final months of Simón Bolívar's life. *Strange Pilgrims*, published in 1992, is a collection of 12 stories written by the author over the previous 18 years. *Of Love and Other Demons*, from 1994, is the story of a young girl, raised by her parents' black slaves, who becomes a victim of Cartagena's Inquisition after being bitten by a rabid dog. In one of his more recent works, *News of a Kidnapping*, published in 1996, García Márquez returns to journalism, where his career began. The book relates a series of kidnappings ordered by Medellín Cartel boss, Pablo Escobar. The combination of the author's literary talents and Colombia's action-movie-like modern history makes the book a fascinating but terrifying read.

García Márquez's most recent book, the first volume of his memoirs, *Vivir Para Contarlo*, was released in October 2002 and created sales records throughout Colombia and the Spanish-speaking world. In the first 10 days of release it sold 160,000 copies in Colombia and 300,000 in Spain. By the time you read this, there will probably be an English translation of the book.

Gabo, as he is affectionately known, is the key figure of Colombian literature. His phenomenal success has, to a great extent, overshadowed both the accomplishments of his contemporaries and an emerging group of younger authors. Several talented contemporaries who deserve recognition include poet, novelist and painter Héctor Rojas Herazo (born 1921) and Álvaro Mutis (born 1923), a close friend of Gabo. Of the younger generation, seek out the works of Rafael Humberto Moreno Durán (born 1946) and Laura Restrepo (born 1950), both of whom are among the most outstanding Colombian writers of recent years.

## Music

Music formed an integral part of religious ceremonies, festivities and battles during pre-Columbian times. The indigenous people used only wind and percussion instruments (there were no string instruments on the continent before the Spanish Conquest), but little is known of their musical forms and only a handful of instruments have survived.

The musical world became much more complex and diversified with the arrival of the Spaniards and the blacks, both of whom brought their own musical traditions and instruments. The imported musical rhythms gradually fused with one another and with traditional indigenous music, to produce new forms and rhythms. And different forms evolved in different regions, giving Colombia a heterogeneous musical identity.

Colombia's geographical location has made it a melting pot for two flourishing, although wholly distinct, musical cultures: the African-origin music of the Caribbean basin, and the Andean Indian music of the highlands of Bolivia and Peru. Both have influenced local rhythms, although the Caribbean contribution is far more noticeable.

In very broad terms, Colombia can be divided into four musical zones: the two coasts, the Andean region and Los Llanos. All the rhythms listed below have corresponding dance forms.

The Caribbean Coast vibrates with hot African-related rhythms, such as the *cumbia*, *mapalé* and *porro*, which share many similarities with other Caribbean musical forms. Possibly the best known interpreter of these beats is the internationally acclaimed Totó La Momposina, nicknamed the 'Queen of the Folklore' (see the boxed text 'Colombia's Who's Who' earlier in this chapter).

The traditional music of the Pacific Coast, such as the *currulao*, is more purely African, with strong use of drums, but tinged with Spanish influences.

Colombian Andean music has been strongly influenced by Spanish rhythms and instruments, and differs noticeably from the indigenous music of the Peruvian and Bolivian highlands. Among typical old genres

### Cumbia – Popular Rhythm from the Caribbean Plains

Of all old Afro-Caribbean rhythms of the Colombian Atlantic Coast, such as porro, *merecumbe*, mapalé and *gaita*, cumbia is the most popular. Its roots are African, and its name is thought to derive from '*kumb*', which is a West African word meaning 'noise and celebration'. Cumbia was born on the hot Caribbean coastal plains when the traditional songs of the black slaves, based on a strong hand drum, merged with simple melodies played on flutes and ocarinas by local indigenous communities. The Spanish contributed by adding some verses, and the fusion eventually evolved into a vibrant rhythm, which includes singing and dancing.

Cumbia has a rural background and is still most popular in the countryside where it's played by home-bred bands in small villages across the region. It's here that it's at its most authentic and spontaneous. Over recent decades, cumbia has gradually made it into the city auditoria and recording studios, and today it's arguably the most popular Colombia-born musical folk genre after the vallenato.

are the *bambuco, pasillo* and *torbellino*, all of which are instrumental and feature predominantly string instruments.

The music of Los Llanos, known as *música llanera* or *joropo*, is sung and accompanied by a harp, *cuatro* (a sort of four-stringed guitar), and maracas. It has much in common with the music of the Venezuelan Llanos.

Apart from these traditional forms, there are some newer musical styles, the most popular of which is the *vallenato*. Born a century ago on the Caribbean Coast, vallenato is based on the European accordion and, unlike other beats, succeeded in conquering large parts of the country. This was partly due to Carlos Vives, one of the best-known, modern Latin artists, who transformed vallenato into a vibrant pop beat (see the boxed text 'Vallenato – Musical Beat that Conquered a Country' in the later Caribbean Coast chapter).

Another hugely popular rhythm is the Cuban-rooted salsa, which spread throughout the Caribbean and hit Colombia by the late 1960s. Cali and Barranquilla have since become Colombia's bastions of salsa music, but it's heard all across the country. Today, Colombia has more than 50 salsa bands and plenty of excellent *salseros*. Among the best are Joe Arroyo from the Caribbean Coast and Grupo Niche from Cali.

Colombia's most famous musical export is Shakira, today a global pop superstar, whose songs regularly hit pop charts worldwide (see the boxed text 'Colombia's Who's Who' earlier in this chapter). Not as famous, but rising quickly over recent years, is Colombian rock vocalist Juanes, who won a Grammy in 2002 for his song *'A Dios Le Pido'*. Colombia's most famous rock group is Los Aterciopelados. Formed in 1990 in Bogotá, it has toured far beyond Colombia and won a Grammy in 2001 for the best Latin rock album (entitled *'Gozo Poderoso'*).

## Theatre

Although theatre first developed in the middle of the 19th century, it mainly followed foreign trends and remained insignificant. A genuine national theatre emerged in the mid-20th century in Bogotá and Cali. Since then, some 100 theatre groups have been founded, most of them small, amateur troupes.

Theatre activity is almost exclusively confined to the largest urban centres. Only Bogotá, Medellín and Cali have several groups working permanently in their own theatres. Teatro de la Candelaria in Bogotá (founded in 1966) and the TEC in Cali (1955) are pioneers of the national theatre and are still interesting and innovative. Several theatre schools are now contributing to the development of a national theatre, and foreign and local performers gather at the two international theatre festivals, in Bogotá and Manizales.

## Cinema

Colombian cinema is still immature and inexperienced, way behind that of, say, Mexico or Argentina. Films of better technical quality and artistic content began to appear during the 1980s. Local production is small and few domestically produced films reach the screens because distributors prefer foreign movies, which are more likely to realise a profit.

In contrast to the dearth of cinematic productions, the production of films for TV has been burgeoning. Colombians, like most Latin Americans, are fans of *telenovelas* (soap operas) and producers and directors are doing everything they can to meet that demand.

## SOCIETY & CONDUCT

Although Colombia is a palette of ethnic blends, and traditional culture is still alive in the countryside, in many ways the urban population follows Western lifestyles. Cities offer plenty of Western-style facilities, local shops are crammed with Western products and you will have little problem locating McDonald's, Kodak Express and Citibank outlets. Locals dress much the same as in London or Sydney, use the same laptops and mobile phones, and go to the cinema to see the same Hollywood fare.

Although some manifestations of Western culture are evident, you'll find many local habits, manners and attitudes quite different from those at home. Some may be strange or even irritating if you haven't been to this country before.

On the whole, Colombians are courteous, polite and hospitable. They are open, willing to talk and are not shy about striking up a conversation with a stranger. This may vary from a big city to the countryside and from region to region, but wherever you are, you are unlikely to be alone or feel isolated, especially if you can speak a little Spanish.

You will probably meet many friendly people promising you the earth, but keep in mind that such effusiveness often has a short life span. Their statements may well gloss over reality, their promises can be just wishful thinking, and appointments are often not kept. Few locals will return your phone call after you've left a message, and the passionate friend of one day might hardly recognise you the next. This attitude (common in most of the continent) is largely rooted in the Latin American concept of life *aquí y ahora* (here and now), with little importance given to the future or past. Don't worry, there will be plenty of new faces and new promises coming your way.

Everyday life is remarkably open and public. One reason might be the restricted space of the humble Colombian homes in which a vast majority of the population live. The climate, too, invites the outdoor life. Consequently, much family life takes place outside the home: in front of the house, in the street, in a bar or at the market. Many Colombians seem indiscreet about their behaviour in public places. Someone in a bar may discuss personal problems at a volume that allows all the patrons to follow the conversation. A female employee in a bank or travel agency may talk by phone for quite a while about private matters (including love affairs), and doesn't seem embarrassed or ashamed that you're waiting right in front of her to be served. The driver may urinate on the tyre of his bus after he has stopped for a break on the road and disembarked along with most passengers. People waiting to use public phones will be squashed up against the person calling. And couples hug and kiss passionately in parks and in the street.

Noise is a constant companion in Colombia and locals seem to be undisturbed by volume levels many decibels above what Europeans or North Americans are used to. Music blares in restaurants, is pumped into buses, and climaxes at night in discos, taverns and private parties. Powerful portable cassette players are an important part of equipment for beachgoers and holidaymakers. Televisions are at full volume, especially during telenovelas and sports transmissions. Some vehicles are as noisy as army tanks, and horns are used constantly, even in traffic jams. Street vendors screech at potential customers, and people converse at a volume that to outsiders might suggest a heated argument.

Like noise, litter is an integral part of Colombian life, so you'd better get used to it. Colombians are accustomed to throwing things away wherever they happen to be – in the streets, on the floor in restaurants, hotel rooms, buses, cinemas, in the countryside and also on the beach. Litter bins are virtually nonexistent, except for some in central streets in major cities. In budget hotels and restaurants you will rarely find an ashtray and asking for one may embarrass the management. It's normal to throw cigarette butts on the floor, and nobody pays the slightest attention. In buses, all disposables, including empty glass bottles, are thrown out the windows.

Colombians (like most other Latin Americans) seem to have their own notion of time. Time-related terminology does exist but its interpretation is not necessarily what visitors might expect. For example, *mañana* (literally 'tomorrow') can mean anytime in the indefinite future. Similarly, the word *ahora* (literally 'now', or 'in a moment'), often used in its more charming, diminutive forms such as *ahorita* or *ahoritica*, also has a flexible meaning.

If, for example, you're waiting for a bus and ask bystanders when the bus should arrive, their *ahorita viene* ('it's coming') may mean anytime from a minute to a few hours. By the same token, when the driver of the bus waiting at the terminal assures you that *ya nos vamos* ('we are leaving right now'), take it easy – it may still take an hour before the bus departs.

Colombians invited to lunch or a party might arrive a few hours late and, by their understanding of time, regard it as normal. The same applies to meetings in the street, cafés, bars etc. Arriving half an hour later than arranged may still give you time to read a newspaper before your friends arrive (if they arrive at all). Many offices and institutions have a similarly flexible grasp of their official working hours. Don't expect to arrange anything in an office if you arrive less than half an hour before its statutory lunch break or the end of work in the afternoon.

Some Colombians, particularly the rural dwellers, also have a different notion of space. If they say that something you're looking for is *allí mismito* ('just round here') or *cerquitica* ('very close'), it may still be an hour's walk to get there.

If you ask for information or directions, don't always expect a correct answer, especially in the countryside. The *campesinos* (country folk), even if they have no idea, may often tell you anything just to appear helpful and knowledgeable. Ask several people the same question and if one answer seems to pop up more frequently than others it may be the correct one. Avoid questions which can be answered by just 'yes' or 'no'; instead of 'Is this the way to…?' ask 'Which is the way to…?'.

## Photographing People

Be sensitive about photographing people; if in doubt, don't take photos at all. Indigenous people may be reluctant to be photographed so ask for permission and don't insist or take a picture if permission is denied. It's not a good idea to photograph soldiers, police, or any suspicious individuals or groups of characters – use common sense.

## RELIGION

The great majority of Colombians are Roman Catholic. Other creeds exist but their numbers are small. However, over the past decade there has been a proliferation of various Prot-

estant congregations, which have succeeded in converting some three million Catholics.

Many Indian groups have adopted the Catholic faith, sometimes incorporating some of their traditional beliefs. Only a few remote indigenous communities still practise their ancient native religions. The blacks also converted to Christianity, almost entirely losing their ancestral religions.

Roman Catholicism was brought from Spain by the missionaries and introduced rapidly across the colony. Catholic clergy played an important role in power during colonial times. The Inquisition was introduced in 1610, and the first court was established in Cartagena.

After independence, Colombia remained a deeply Catholic nation, a fact that is enshrined in the country's constitution. Although other creeds were officially permitted, their followers were minimal – San Andrés and Providencia islands, which were colonised by the English, were one of the few settled areas to avoid the influence of Catholicism; they remain partly Protestant to this day.

The 1991 constitution marked possibly the most important religious revolution in Colombia's history. References to the 'Sacred Heart of Jesus' were replaced by a universal 'God', eliminating the concept of a Catholic nation as it had been defined in the previous constitution.

# Facts for the Visitor

## HIGHLIGHTS

Colombia has plenty of attractions, both cultural and natural, some of which rank among the best on the continent.

## Colonial Cities & Towns

The old port of Cartagena, on the Caribbean Coast, is arguably South America's most amazing colonial city, and a must for every visitor. Popayán, in southern Colombia, is another pearl of colonial architecture, known as the 'White City'. Among smaller colonial towns, the finest and best preserved are Mompós, Barichara and Villa de Leyva, all charming but totally different from each other.

## Museums & Churches

Bogotá's Museo del Oro is generally regarded as the world's best gold museum, worth much more than just one visit. The Donación Botero, also in Bogotá, is one of the richest art collections in South America. Bogotá also has some of Colombia's best colonial churches, including Iglesia de Santa Clara. There are plenty of other great colonial churches elsewhere, but probably nothing as spectacular as Iglesia de Santo Domingo and Iglesia de Santa Clara la Real, both in Tunja.

## Archaeological Sites

Colombia has three world-class archaeological sites: Ciudad Perdida, San Agustín and Tierradentro. Ciudad Perdida, in the mountainous jungles near the Caribbean Coast, is one of the largest pre-Hispanic cities ever found and is accessible only by foot on a six-day trip – a perfect South American adventure as fascinating as the famous Inca Trail, but without as many tourists on your heels. San Agustín, in southern Colombia, is a mysterious ceremonial funeral site noted for

hundreds of monumental stone statues scattered over a mountainous area. Tierradentro, near San Agustín, is another funeral site, renowned for dozens of underground burial chambers, unique in the Americas.

## Festivals

Carnaval de Barranquilla has been described by some travellers as the maddest and most colourful carnival after Rio's world-famous event. Alternatively, try the almost-as-crazy Carnaval de Cartagena, with its legendary beauty pageant in which Miss Colombia is crowned. For something more divine, the night-time processions during Semana Santa (Holy Week) in Popayán are among the most elaborate religious ceremonies you will experience. Finally, Festival Iberoamericano de Teatro de Bogotá is one of the best theatre festivals in Latin America, attracting entertainers from all over the globe.

## Nightlife

Colombian nightlife is exciting and fun, and there are plenty of night spots to suit all guises. You'll find the best and most varied nightlife on offer in Bogotá, Cali and Medellín.

## National Parks

Thanks to Colombia's diverse geography there's a great variety of parks, and some of the best, fortunately, are safe to visit. Parque Nacional Tayrona protects possibly the most amazing bit of Colombian coast, with its deep bays, coconut groves and beautiful small beaches. Parque Nacional Los Nevados reveals splendid high-mountain volcanic scenery while Parque Nacional Amacayacu provides an insight into the lush Amazon rainforest and its wildlife.

## Outdoor Activities

Diving in Colombia is good, operated by professionals and among the cheapest you can get anywhere in the world. The best places to try include San Andrés, Providencia and Taganga. Rafting is a great new attraction and is cheap as well. San Gil is the major rafting centre. Medellín is one of South America's best places to try paragliding – it's also one of the cheapest on the continent.

---

### Unesco's Famous Five

The Unesco World Heritage list includes five sites in Colombia: the historic cities of Cartagena and Mompós; the archaeological sites of San Agustín and Tierradentro; and the national park of Los Katíos (currently closed).

---

## SUGGESTED ITINERARIES

Your itinerary will largely depend upon your particular interests, your budget, the amount of time you have, the season, the method of transport and the state of safety in particular regions at the time of travel. Some travellers will rush through half of the country in a week, while others will prefer to spend the same time on the one beach. Some travellers will be crazy about colonial architecture while others will be mad about scuba diving.

But for many visitors Colombia will be just a short or long stopover on their South American trip. Depending on where they are coming from and where they are heading, they may be inclined to keep close to their route without longer detours. Some travellers arrive from Central America via San Andrés or San Blas and head south to Ecuador (or vice versa), in which case the usual route includes Cartagena, Bogotá, Cali and Popayán. There is also a number of visitors coming through Colombia from Venezuela via Cúcuta; some of these take a detour to Colombia's Caribbean Coast (Cartagena and Parque Nacional Tayrona), while others head straight south via Bogotá and Popayán.

To sum up, it's difficult to recommend any hard and fast itineraries. The following suggestions have been made assuming you arrive at Bogotá and plan on visiting just Colombia, but please consider them as rough guidelines only. Various options are given to suit your personal preferences.

### One Week

Spend two to three days in Bogotá and its environs, and go for the rest of the week to Cartagena, visiting the city and its surroundings. It only makes sense if you fly because bus travel takes 20 hours each way. If you're not up to this, explore Bogotá as above and spend the remaining time in Villa de Leyva and its surroundings.

### Two Weeks

To the above add one of the three following options: do the southern loop including Popayán, San Agustín and possibly Tierradentro; go for a week to Zona Cafetera with a possible detour to Medellín; or stay a week longer on the coast, visiting Santa Marta and some of the sites in the area (Parque Nacional Tayrona, Taganga and Ciudad Perdida).

### One Month

You'll be able to do most of the options listed above, or stay longer in some regions, eg, three weeks on the coast including Ciudad Perdida; also consider a week in Leticia exploring the jungle, and/or a week on Providencia diving, sunbathing and completely forgetting about the outside world.

## PLANNING
### When to Go

The most pleasant time to visit is in the dry season, between December and March or in July and August. This is particularly true if you plan on hiking or some other outdoor activities. The dry season also gives visitors a better chance to savour local cultural events because many festivals and fiestas take place during these periods.

Apart from the weather, you may also consider Colombian holiday periods. There are basically three high seasons when Colombians rush to travel: from late December to mid-January, during Semana Santa, and from mid-June to mid-July. During these three periods transport gets more crowded, hotels tend to fill up faster and prices may rise in holiday destinations. If you travel at this time, you will have to plan your trip a little ahead and do more legwork to find a place to stay, but you'll also enjoy more contact with travelling Colombians, who will be in a relaxed, holiday spirit.

### Maps

You'll probably find it difficult to buy anything other than general maps of Colombia outside the country itself. Check with good travel bookshops and map shops to see what is available. In the USA, **Maplink** (☎ 805-965 4402; 25 E Mason St, Dept G, Santa Barbara, CA 93101) has an excellent supply of maps. A similarly extensive selection of maps is available in the UK from **Stanfords** (☎ 020-7836 1321; 12-14 Long Acre, London WC2E 9LP).

Within Colombia, folded road maps of the country are produced by various publishers and are distributed through bookshops. They are of varied quality so check exactly what you're buying.

The widest selection of maps of Colombia is produced and sold by the **Instituto Geográfico Agustín Codazzi** (IGAC; Carrera 30 No 48-51, Bogotá), the government mapping body which has its head office in the Colombian capital and branch offices in departmental capitals.

## Orientation

Colombian cities, towns and villages have traditionally been laid out on a grid plan. The streets running north–south are called *Carreras*, often abbreviated on maps to Cra, Cr or K, whereas those running east–west are called *Calles*, labelled on maps as Cll, Cl or C. This simple pattern may be complicated by diagonal streets, called either *Diagonales* (more east–west and thus like Calles), or *Transversales* (more like Carreras).

All streets are numbered and the numerical system of addresses is used. Each address consists of a series of numbers, eg, Calle 23 No 5-43 (which means that it's the building on Calle 23, 43m from the corner of Carrera 5 towards Carrera 6), or Carrera 17 No 31-05 (the house on Carrera 17, 5m from the corner of Calle 31 towards Calle 32). Refer to the Orientation map for examples.

The system is very practical and you will soon become familiar with it. It is usually easy to find an address. It's actually one of the most precise address systems in the world. If you have an address you can determine the location of the place with pinpoint accuracy.

In the larger cities the main streets are called *Avenidas* or *Autopistas*. They both have their own names and numbers, but are commonly known just by their names.

Cartagena's old town is the only Colombian city where centuries-old street names have withstood the modern numbering system. Streets in some other cities (eg, Medellín) have both names and numbers, but elsewhere only numbers are used.

The Colombian system of designating floors is the same as that used in the USA; there is no 'ground floor' – it is the *primer piso* (1st floor). Thus, the European 1st floor will be the *segundo piso* (2nd floor) in Colombia.

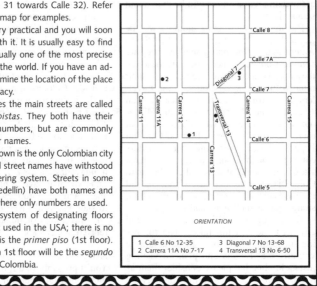

ORIENTATION

| | |
|---|---|
| 1 Calle 6 No 12-35 | 3 Diagonal 7 No 13-68 |
| 2 Carrera 11A No 7-17 | 4 Transversal 13 No 6-50 |

The IGAC produces general and specialist maps of the country, departmental maps, city maps, and 1:100,000 scale *planchas* (sheets), broken down into more detailed 1:25,000 scale maps. Unfortunately, most maps are long out of date. If the office runs out of colour maps (which is usually the case) it will make a black-and-white copy of the original. Maps cost somewhere between US$2 and US$5 per sheet, depending on the type and size.

### What to Bring

Pack light as almost everything you might need can easily be bought in Colombia.

The Colombian climate varies with altitude, so you need to be prepared for both hot and cold weather. A warm shirt with long sleeves is essential, but also pack a T-shirt for the lowlands, and a jacket and sweater for the highlands. Take a light, waterproof jacket because the weather changes constantly, and even the dry season can be fickle in some regions. A sleeping bag is necessary only if you intend to go trekking; even the cheapest hotels provide sheets and blankets.

A small day pack is recommended for city walks, short side trips and for carrying your essential items and valuables with you on buses and planes. A swimming suit is essential if you're heading for beaches. Bring a mask and snorkel (to save on rental fees). Bookworms might want to bring along some paperbacks as the choice offered by local bookshops may not be extensive.

Some other essentials which might be worth packing include a travel alarm clock (for those early morning buses), a small torch (for Tierradentro tombs and dodgy electricity supplies), sunglasses and a hat, a

Spanish/English dictionary and flip-flops or thongs (to protect feet against fungal infections in shabby hotel bathrooms).

The rest is up to you. Whatever you pack, however, don't bring any khaki-coloured clothing or any army surplus uniforms. You will look like a soldier, paramilitary or a guerrilla and shooting is the only form of communication among these three.

## RESPONSIBLE TOURISM

A responsible tourist is, perhaps, one who treats the visited place as if it were home. Would you wander into your hometown church during a service and start taking flash photos? Would you bluntly point your camera at your friends while they go about their daily business? Would you leave rubbish scattered in your favourite park?

Respect rituals and ceremonies, traditions and beliefs. Be aware that some customs can challenge your own belief system and avoid trying to impose on the locals your own view of the world. Encourage ecotourist projects that aim to preserve or restore local environments. Support native communities by buying their crafts, but avoid those made from corals, turtles or fossils.

Littering in Colombia is widespread, but you don't have to follow suit. Make a little extra effort and carry your own rubbish until you find an appropriate disposal bin. Be particularly careful when visiting areas with delicate ecological balances such as coral reefs, the *páramos* (open highlands) or rainforests. Carry your own rubbish out of all national parks. Remember that the plastic bags, cans, silver foil, tampons or condoms you leave behind can endanger wildlife.

## TOURIST OFFICES

The provision of tourist information is administered by municipal tourist information offices in departmental capitals and other tourist destinations. Some are better than others, but on the whole they lack city maps and brochures. The staff members may be friendly but rarely speak English. The practical information they provide sometimes leaves a bit to be desired and the quality of information largely depends on the person attending to you.

In some cities, tourist offices are supported by the Policía de Turismo, police officers specially trained to attend tourists.

Abroad, Colombian consulates and embassies may provide limited tourist information. Overseas offices of Colombian airlines occasionally have brochures.

## VISAS & DOCUMENTS
### Passport

A valid passport is an essential document and it must be stamped with a visa if you need one. If your passport is due to expire within a year, get a new one before you leave on a South American circuit. Many countries won't issue a visa or admit you at the border if your passport has less than six months or even one year validity remaining. Even if expiry isn't a problem, make sure that your passport has a few blank pages left for visas and entry and exit stamps.

Once in Colombia, you must carry your passport with you at all times. Identity document checks are not uncommon on country roads and city streets. Your passport is the first document the police will ask for. Some police officers may be satisfied with a certified photocopy of your passport, but most won't accept it as a valid document.

### Visas

Nationals of some countries, including most of Western Europe, the Americas, Japan, Australia and New Zealand, don't need a visa to enter Colombia. It's a good idea to check this before your planned trip, because visa regulations change frequently. Over recent years, Colombia has reintroduced visas for nationals of various countries, partly as a retaliatory response to the decision of other countries demanding visas for Colombians.

All visitors get an entry stamp or print in their passport from DAS (the security police responsible for immigration) upon arrival at any international airport or land border crossing. The stamp says how many days you can stay in the country. The maximum allowed is 90 days, but DAS officials often stamp 60 or just 30 days.

**Visa Extensions** You are entitled to a 30-day extension (US$25), which can be obtained from DAS in any departmental capital. Apply shortly before the expiration of your allowed stay because the extension runs from the day it is stamped in your passport. Most travellers apply for an extension in Bogotá (see that chapter later for further details).

## Where's my Entry Stamp?

When you arrive at Colombia and pass through immigration, check twice whether DAS officials have put an entry stamp in your passport. If you don't have this stamp, you are illegally in Colombia. You may be stopped on departing the country and not allowed to board your flight before the situation is formally solved. You then have to pay a fine of about US$60 and get a *salvoconducto* from the DAS office which will allow you to leave the country legally. Without the stamp, you can also have problems when changing money in banks.

Upon departure, immigration officials should put an exit stamp in your passport. Again, check if they've done so. Travellers have reported that some immigration posts didn't stamp passports. However, the central DAS office in Bogotá firmly states that you do need this stamp; without one you may have problems entering Colombia next time around.

## Onward Tickets

Officially, every tourist entering Colombia should have an onward ticket. You may be asked by immigration officials to present it, though that rarely happens these days.

## Travel Insurance

Ideally, all travellers should have a travel insurance policy, which will provide some security in the case of a medical emergency, or the loss or theft of money or belongings. It may seem an expensive luxury, but if you can't afford a travel health insurance policy, you probably can't afford medical emergency charges abroad if something goes wrong.

If you do need to make a claim on your travel insurance, you must produce a police report detailing loss or theft (see Dangers & Annoyances later in this chapter). You also need proof of the value of any items lost or stolen. Receipts are the best bet, so if you buy a new camera for your trip, for example, hang onto the receipt.

## Driver's Licence

If you plan on driving in Colombia, make sure you bring your driver's licence. The driver's licence from your country will normally do, but if you want to be 100%

sure, bring along an International Driving Permit as well.

## Vaccination Certificates

The International Health Card is not required for entry into Colombia unless you're arriving from an area infected with yellow fever, but even in this case you'll rarely be asked for the card. Yet, it's a good idea to get inoculated against some diseases before you set off for the trip – see the Health section later in this chapter for details.

## Other Documents

A student card is of very limited use in Colombia. It will help you save a few pesos on museum admission fees, but that's about it. A hostelling card is not much use either as there's just one youth hostel in the country. However, it's worth having photo identification other than your passport. It can be either of the above or just any of your old identity cards (ICs), permits, membership cards or whatever. Because of Colombia's fragile safety situation, many office buildings (including some tourist offices) are these days staffed by security guards, and all visitors need to leave their ICs at reception. It's a bit inconvenient to pull your passport out of a hidden inside pocket, and it's probably not absolutely safe to leave it with someone. In fact, you can leave virtually any IC-looking document and nobody will raise an eyebrow.

## Copies

Make photocopies of important documents such as your passport (data pages plus visas), credit cards, airline tickets, travel insurance policy and travellers cheques receipt slips. Take notes of the serial numbers of your cameras, lenses, camcorder, laptop computer and any other pieces of high-tech stuff you'll be taking on the trip. Make a list of phone numbers of emergency assistance services (credit cards, insurance, your bank etc). Keep all that material separate from your passport, money and other valuables. It's a good idea to keep one copy with you, one copy inside your luggage and (if applicable) deposit another with a travelling companion. Also leave a copy of all these things with someone at home. Slip US$50 or US$100 into a safe place on your person to use as an emergency stash.

## EMBASSIES & CONSULATES
### Colombian Embassies & Consulates

Colombia has embassies and consulates in all neighbouring countries, and also in:

**Australia**
(☎ 02-6257 2027) 101 Northbourne Ave, Turner, ACT 2601
(☎ 02-9955 0311) 100 Walker St, North Sydney, NSW 2060

**Canada**
(☎ 514-849 4852) 1010 Sherbrooke St West, Suite 420, Montreal, Quebec H3A 2R7
(☎ 416-977 0475) 1 Dundas St West, Suite 2108, Toronto, Ontario M5G 1Z3

**France**
(☎ 01 53 93 91 91) 12 rue de Berri, Paris 75008

**Germany**
(☎ 030-263 96 10) Kurfürsternstrasse 84, 10787 Berlin

**UK**
(☎ 020-7495 4233) Suite 14, 140 Park Lane, London W1Y 3AA

**USA**
(☎ 202-387 8338) 2118 Leroy Place NW, Washington, DC 20008
(☎ 305-441 1235) 280 Aragon Ave, Coral Gables, Miami, FL 33134
(☎ 212-949 9898) 10 East 46th St, New York, NY 10017

### Embassies & Consulates in Colombia

Most countries which maintain diplomatic relations with Colombia have their embassies and consulates in Bogotá. Some countries also have consulates in other Colombian cities.

**Argentina**
(☎ 1-570 5047) Av 40A No 13-09, Piso 16, Bogotá

**Australia**
*Honorary Consulate:* (☎ 1-636 5247) Carrera 18 No 90-38, Bogotá

**Bolivia**
(☎ 1-629 8252) Carrera 9 No 114-96, Bogotá
(☎ 2-553 6386) Carrera 40 No 5C-102, Cali

**Brazil**
(☎ 1-218 0800) Calle 93 No 14-20, Piso 8, Bogotá
(☎ 2-893 0615) Carrera 2 Oeste No 12-44, Cali
(☎ 8-592 7530) Carrera 9 No 13-84, Leticia
(☎ 4-265 7565) Calle 29D No 55-91, Medellín

**Canada**
(☎ 1-657 9800) Carrera 7 No 115-33, Piso 14, Bogotá

### Your Own Embassy

It's important to realise what your own embassy – the embassy of the country of which you are a citizen – can and can't do to help you if you get into trouble. Generally speaking, it won't be much help in emergencies if the trouble you're in is remotely your own fault. Remember that you are bound by the laws of the country you are in. Your embassy will not be sympathetic if you end up in jail after committing a crime locally, even if such actions are legal in your own country.

In genuine emergencies you might get some assistance, but only if other channels have been exhausted. For example, if you need to get home urgently, a free ticket home is exceedingly unlikely – the embassy would expect you to have insurance. If you have all your money and documents stolen, it might assist with getting a new passport, but a loan for onward travel is out of the question.

Some embassies used to keep letters for travellers or have a small reading room with home newspapers, but these days the mail holding service has usually been stopped and even newspapers tend to be out of date.

**Chile**
(☎ 1-214 7990) Calle 100 No 11B-44, Bogotá

**Costa Rica**
(☎ 1-256 1105) Carrera 8 No 95-48, Bogotá
(☎ 8-512 4938) Novedades Regina, Av Colombia, San Andrés

**Ecuador**
(☎ 1-635 0322) Calle 89 No 13-07, Bogotá
(☎ 2-661 2264) Av 5AN No 20N-13, L-103, Cali
(☎ 2-773 2292) Carrera 7 No 14-10, Ipiales
(☎ 4-512 1303) Calle 50 No 52-22, Oficina 603, Medellín

**France**
(☎ 1-638 1400) Carrera 11 No 93-12, Bogotá

**Germany**
(☎ 1-423 2600) Carrera 69 No 43B-44, Piso 7, Bogotá

**Honduras**
(☎ 1-213 0073) Transversal 13 No 114A-51, Bogotá
(☎ 8-512 3235) in Hotel Tiuna, Av Colombia, San Andrés

**Israel**
(☎ 1-288 4637) Calle 35 No 7-25, Piso 14, Bogotá

**Italy**
(☎ 1-218 6680) Calle 93B No 9-92, Bogotá

**Japan**
(☎ 1-317 5001) Carrera 7 No 71-21, Torre B, Piso 11, Bogotá
**Mexico**
(☎ 1-629 5189) Carrera 9 No 113-90, Torre A, Local 106, Bogotá
**Netherlands**
(☎ 1-611 5080) Carrera 13 No 93-40, Piso 5, Bogotá
**Panama**
(☎ 1-257 4452) Calle 92 No 7-70, Bogotá
(☎ 5-360 1872) Carrera 54 No 64-245, Barranquilla
(☎ 2-880 9590) Calle 11 No 4-42, Oficina 316, Cali
(☎ 5-664 1433) Plaza de San Pedro Claver No 30-14, Cartagena
(☎ 4-268 1358) Carrera 43A No 7-50, Oficina 1607, Medellín
**Peru**
(☎ 1-257 0505) Calle 80A No 6-50, Bogotá
(☎ 1-257 3147) Calle 90 No 14-26, Bogotá
(☎ 2-668 6966) Av 7N No 24N-57, Cali
(☎ 8-592 7204) Calle 13 No 10-70, Leticia
**Spain**
(☎ 1-622 0090) Calle 92 No 12-68, Bogotá
**Switzerland**
(☎ 1-255 3945) Carrera 9A No 74-08, Oficina 1101, Bogotá
**UK**
(☎ 1-317 6690) Carrera 9 No 76-49, Piso 9, Bogotá
**USA**
(☎ 1-315 0811) Calle 22D Bis No 47-51, Bogotá
**Venezuela**
(☎ 1-640 1213) Carrera 13 No 87-51, Bogotá
(☎ 1-636 4011) Av 13 No 103-16, Bogotá
(☎ 5-358 0048) Carrera 52 No 69-96, Barranquilla
(☎ 5-665 0382) Carrera 3 No 8-129, Cartagena
(☎ 7-579 1956) Av Camilo Daza, Cúcuta
(☎ 4-351 1614) Calle 32B No 69-59, Medellín

## CUSTOMS

Customs procedures are usually a formality, both entering and leaving the country. However, thorough luggage checks can occur, more often at airports than at overland borders, and they can be very exhaustive, with a body search included. They aren't looking for your extra Walkman, but for drugs. Trying to smuggle dope across the border is the best way to spend some years seeing what the inside of a Colombian jail looks like.

Customs regulations don't differ much from those in other South American countries. You can bring in personal belongings and presents you intend to give to Colombian residents. The quantity, kind and value of these items shouldn't arouse suspicion that they may have been imported for commercial purposes. You can bring with you cameras (still, video and movie), camping equipment, sports accessories, a laptop computer and the like without any problems.

On departure, you may be asked for receipts for any emeralds, antiques and articles of gold and platinum purchased in Colombia.

## MONEY

Given the country's hazards, it's better to carry travellers cheques (American Express are by far the easiest to change) rather than cash, though some US dollar bills may be useful. With the recent proliferation of ATMs, however, the best way to carry money in Colombia is by credit card.

Note that large amounts of counterfeit US dollars 'made in Cali' circulate on the market. According to rough estimates, about a quarter of all fake US dollars circulating worldwide are printed in Colombia. They are virtually indistinguishable from the genuine article.

### Currency

Colombia's official currency is the peso, but you'll find almost all the prices in this book provided in US dollars. There are 50, 100, 200, 500 and 1000 peso coins, and paper notes of 1000, 2000, 5000, 10,000, 20,000 and 50,000 pesos. Forged peso notes do exist, so watch exactly what you get. In contrast to perfect dollar fakes, peso forgeries are usually of poor quality and easy to recognise. There are also some fake 1000-peso coins in circulation. Many businesses don't accept 1000-peso coins and neither should you.

### Exchange Rates

Approximate exchange rates are:

| country | unit | | peso |
|---|---|---|---|
| Australia | A$1 | = | 1216 |
| Canada | C$1 | = | 1242 |
| euro | €1 | = | 1878 |
| Japan | ¥1 | = | 15 |
| New Zealand | NZ$1 | = | 965 |
| UK | UK£1 | = | 2881 |
| USA | US$1 | = | 1840 |

Banks change travellers cheques at rates 2% to 5% lower than the official rate, and usually pay about a further 1% to 3% less for cash. Exchange rates vary from bank to bank, so shop around. Some banks charge a commission for changing cheques.

## Exchanging Money

Some banks change cash and travellers cheques, but others don't. Some branches of a bank will change your money while other branches of the same bank will refuse. Banks that are most likely to exchange your cash and/or travellers cheques include: Lloyds TSB Bank, Banco Unión Colombiano, Bancolombia, Bancafé and Banco Santander.

Banks (except for those in Bogotá) are open 8am to 11.30am and 2pm to 4pm Monday to Thursday, and 8am to 11.30am and 2pm to 4.30pm on Friday. However, they usually offer currency exchange services within limited hours, which may mean only one or two hours daily; your best chances are in the morning. Banks close at noon on the last working day of the month, and it may be difficult to change money on that day so plan ahead.

Your passport is required for any banking transaction. Banks are often crowded and there's much paperwork involved in changing money, so the process may prove time-consuming – set aside up to an hour.

You can also change cash (and sometimes travellers cheques) at *casas de cambio* (authorised money exchange offices), found in virtually all major cities and border towns. They are open until 5pm or 6pm on weekdays, and usually until noon on Saturday. They deal mainly with US dollars, offering rates comparable to, or slightly lower than, banks. The whole operation takes seconds.

Titán Intercontinental is one of the largest casas de cambio, with branch offices in most large cities. It changes both cash and travellers cheques, gives reasonable rates and charges no commission on cashing cheques. Many other casas have mushroomed over recent years and also change both cash and travellers cheques.

You can change cash dollars on the street, but it's not recommended. The only street money markets worth considering are those at the borders, where there may be simply no alternative. There are moneychangers at every land border crossing.

**Credit Cards & ATMs** Although the use of credit cards in Colombia is still not as common as it is in Western countries, they have become wildly popular over the past decade. They can be used for cash advances from banks and ATMs, and for purchases of goods and services in a variety of establishments.

The most useful card for cash advances is Visa, as it's accepted by most banks, including all those listed in the previous section. Another possibility is MasterCard, which is honoured by Bancolombia and Banco de Occidente. Other cards are of limited use.

You can get advance payments on cards from the cashier in the bank (it takes less time than changing travellers cheques) or from the bank's ATM (almost all major banks have adjacent ATMs, and they usually work fine with cards issued outside Colombia).

Make sure you know the number to call if you lose your credit card, and be quick to cancel it if it's lost or stolen.

**International Transfers** If you need money sent to you quickly, it's probably best to use Western Union, which has over 80,000 agencies worldwide. Your sender pays the money at their nearest Western Union branch, along with a fee, and gives the details on who is to receive it and where. You can have the money within 15 minutes. When you pick it up, take along photo identification.

Western Union is represented in Colombia by Giros & Finanzas, which has offices in virtually all cities around the country and also in some smaller localities. There are about 20 offices in Bogotá alone. Call from anywhere in the country on ☎ 9800 111 999 toll-free for information. In the USA, call ☎ 1800 325 6000 toll-free. Or simply check the website at Ⓦ www.westernunion.com.

## Costs

Colombia is a reasonably cheap country to travel in, provided you are travelling overland. Backpackers should be prepared to

### How Much Does It Cost?

Here are price guidelines for some goods and services in Colombia:

| Item | US$ |
| --- | --- |
| 1L of milk | 0.60 |
| Loaf of bread | 0.50 |
| 0.33L bottle of local beer in a shop | 0.30 to 0.40 |
| 0.75L bottle of aguardiente (spirit) in a shop | 3 to 5 |
| 1L bottle of mineral water in a shop | 0.60 |
| Budget set lunch or dinner | 1.50 to 2.50 |
| Dinner in a fine restaurant | 10 to 15 |
| Double room in a budget hotel | 6 to 15 |
| Double room in a mid-range hotel | 20 to 30 |
| 100km intercity bus fare | 3 to 4 |
| Bogotá–Cartagena air fare | 75 to 125 |
| City bus ride | 0.25 to 0.40 |
| 5km daytime taxi ride in the city | 2 |
| Cinema ticket | 2 to 3 |
| Museum admission fee | 1 to 2 |
| Local newspaper | 0.40 to 0.60 |
| Three-minute local phone call | 0.10 |
| Three-minute long-distance domestic phone call | 0.80 |
| Three-minute phone call to the USA | 4 |
| Postcard to Europe | 1 |
| An hour logging on in an Internet café | 0.80 to 2 |
| Colombian-made CD | 10 to 15 |
| 24-exposure Kodak print film | 3 to 4 |
| Packet of 20 Colombian-made Marlboro cigarettes | 1.50 |

shell out US$15 to US$25 per day on the average. If you want a more comfy trip, with mid-range hotels, some better restaurants and a flight from time to time, you'll average somewhere between US$25 and US$45 daily.

## Tipping & Bargaining

Tipping is essentially limited to upscale restaurants (leave about 10% of the bill) and posh hotels. As in most neighbouring countries, bargaining is limited to informal trade and services, such as markets, street stalls, taxis, and sometimes long-distance buses.

## POST & COMMUNICATIONS
### Post

The Colombian postal service is operated by two companies, Avianca and Adpostal. Both cover international post, but Avianca only deals with airmail, so if you want to ship a parcel overseas, you'll need Adpostal. Both companies seem to be efficient and reliable, but Avianca is much more expensive: a 10g letter sent with Avianca to Europe costs US$3 (and only US$1 with Adpostal).

The poste restante system is operated by Avianca. You can receive poste restante letters in any city where Avianca has a post office, but not all provincial offices do a good job. The most reliable office is in Bogotá (Your Name, c/o Lista de Correos Avianca, Edificio Avianca, Carrera 7 No 16-36, Bogotá).

### Telephone & Fax

The telephone system is largely automated for both domestic and international calls. Until not long ago, Telecom was the only national telecommunication company, with its offices even in the most remote villages. In 1998 two new companies, Orbitel and ETB, entered the market and a price war broke out.

Public telephones exist in cities and large towns but, except for the centres of the largest cities, they are few and far between, and many are out of order. Those which do work often have lines of people waiting to place calls. Street phones are usually the most besieged, so look for public phones in more secluded locations such as hotel lobbies, shopping malls etc. As a rule, Telecom offices have some operable phones. Local calls are charged by timed rate (not flat rate).

## International Collect Calls

Reverse-charge or collect calls *(llamadas de pago revertido)* are possible to most major countries. Here are the international direct-dialling numbers of some countries.

| | |
|---|---|
| Australia | ☎ 9809 61 00 57 |
| Canada | ☎ 9809 19 00 57 |
| France | ☎ 9809 33 00 57 |
| Germany | ☎ 9809 49 00 57 |
| UK | ☎ 9809 44 00 57 |
| USA (AT&T) | ☎ 9809 11 00 10 |
| (MCI) | ☎ 9809 16 00 01 |
| (Sprint) | ☎ 9809 13 00 10 |

Public telephones use coins, although newly installed telephones accept *tarjeta telefónica* (phone cards). Phone cards can be used for international, intercity and local calls, so it's worth buying one if you think you might be using public telephones frequently. The cards can be bought at Telecom offices.

You can call direct to just about anywhere in Colombia. All phone numbers are seven digits long countrywide. Area codes are single digits, and you'll find them included immediately under the headings of the relevant destinations throughout this book.

However, before using them you need to dial the index of the provider you want to use – ☎ 05 for Orbitel, ☎ 07 for ETB and ☎ 09 for Telecom. As yet, Orbitel and ETB provide connections only between some of the major cities, so in most cases you'll be using Telecom.

All three companies provide an international service and may temporarily offer significant discounts – watch out for their advertisements in the electronic and print media. Calling abroad from Colombia, you dial ☎ 005, ☎ 007 or ☎ 009, respectively, then the country code etc.

Colombia's country code is ☎ 57. If you are dialling a Colombian number from abroad, drop the prefix (05, 07 or 09) and dial only the area code and the local number.

Larger Telecom offices offer fax services. You can also send faxes from Internet cafés.

### Email & Internet Access

Virtually all large cities and many smaller urban centres have Internet cafés. Bogotá probably has more than 100. Internet cafés are usually open, without a lunch break, until 7pm to 10pm weekdays, and many are also open all day Saturday. Some also open on Sunday. Most cafés provide a range of related services such as printing, scanning and faxing, and some offer cheap international calls. Internet connections are fastest in the major urban centres, while they can be pretty slow in some remote places such as San Andrés or Leticia. The access normally costs US$0.80 to US$2 per hour.

We have included quite a number of Internet cafés in the relevant sections in this book, but note that this is one of Colombia's fastest developing facilities, so there are likely to be many more (and perhaps better, faster, cheaper) places by the time you come.

## Colombian Computer Jargon

If you surf the Web at a Colombian Internet café you may have to do it in Spanish. The following list contains useful local Webspeak:

| | | | | | |
|---|---|---|---|---|---|
| Back | *Atrás* | Format | *Formato* | Refresh | *Actualizar* |
| Bookmarks | *Favoritos* | Forward | *Adelante* | Save | *Guardar* |
| Close | *Cerrar* | Help | *Ayuda* | Search | *Búsqueda* |
| Copy | *Copiar* | Insert | *Insertar* | Send | *Enviar* |
| Cut | *Cortar* | New | *Nuevo* | Start | *Inicio* |
| Delete | *Suprimir* | Open | *Abrir* | Stop | *Detener* |
| Edit | *Edición* | Page | *Página* | Tools | *Herramientas* |
| Enter | *Ingresar* | Password | *Contraseña* | Website | *Portal* |
| Exit | *Terminar* | Paste | *Pegar* | View | *Ver* |
| File | *Archivo* | Print | *Imprimir* | Window | *Ventana* |

## DIGITAL RESOURCES

A good place to start your Net explorations is the **Lonely Planet website** (w *www .lonelyplanet.com*). Here you'll find succinct summaries on travelling to most places on earth, postcards from other travellers and the Thorn Tree bulletin board, where you can ask questions before you go or dispense advice when you get back. You can also find travel news and updates for many of our most popular guidebooks, and the subwwway section links you to the most useful travel resources elsewhere on the Web.

There are quite a few websites concerning Colombia and the number is growing.

## BOOKS

You will get far more out of your visit if you read about the country before you go. There are plenty of books in English which cover various aspects of Colombia, some of which are recommended below. If you read Spanish, you'll find invaluable sources of information in Colombia itself. The country publishes many books and other publications, few of which have been translated into foreign languages.

### Lonely Planet

If you're planning a wider journey than just Colombia, consider taking LP's *South America on a Shoestring*, which covers the whole continent. LP's *Read This First: Central & South America* may be useful predeparture reading.

You may also want to consult LP's *Healthy Travel Central & South America*. Also note that LP has individual guidebooks to most Latin American countries, including Colombia's neighbours: Venezuela, Ecuador, Peru, Brazil and Panama. Finally, LP's *Latin American Spanish phrasebook* can prove a worthwhile addition to your backpack.

## Colombia Online

Following are some useful sources of general, specific and tourist information on Colombia available online. Many of them feature links to further sites, giving virtually unlimited possibilities.

w **www.colombiaemb.org**
Website of Colombian embassy in Washington, which includes plenty of news on Colombia from various US and Colombian newspapers and TV and radio broadcasters (in English and Spanish), plus links to Colombian travel resources

w **www.colombiaupdate.com**
Comprehensive source of news on Colombia (in English), with plenty of links to the country's history, culture etc

w **www.colombiareport.org**
Another excellent news site (in English) providing plenty of information on current politics, economy, human rights issues etc

w **www.realworldrescue.com/latin.htm**
Detailed source of information (in English) about acts of violence in Latin American countries; unfortunately, most cases refer to Colombia

w **www.paislibre.org.co**
Website of the Fundación País Libre, an organisation providing support to the victims of kidnapping and their families; the site features up-to-date, detailed information (in Spanish) on kidnapping-related issues

w **www.poorbuthappy.com/colombia**
English-language site providing a lot of tourist and practical information

w **www.latinnews.com**
Website of Latin American Newsletters – economic and political information (in Spanish and English) on Latin America, including Colombia (only part is available free; you need to subscribe for the rest)

w **www.lab.org.uk**
Website of the Latin American Bureau with good country profiles, including Colombia

w **www.lanic.utexas.edu/la/colombia**
Website of the Latin American Network Information Center – one of the best sites for information on Colombia, including plenty of useful links to the government, politics, art and culture, society,

## History & Politics

A good overview of the period of Spanish colonisation is provided by John Hemming's *The Search for El Dorado*. The book is a fascinating insight into the conquest of Colombia and Venezuela.

Equally captivating is *The Explorers of South America* by Edward J Goodman, which brings to life some of the more incredible explorations of the continent, from Columbus to Humboldt, some of which refer to Colombia.

Colin Harding's *In Focus: Colombia – A Guide to the People, Politics and Culture*, is a good, brief introduction to the country's history, economy and society. *Colombia: Portrait of Unity and Diversity* by Harvey F Kline is a well-balanced overview of Colombian history.

Titles covering Colombia's modern history include: *The Politics of Colombia* by Robert H Dix; *Colombia: Inside the Labyrinth* by Jenny Pearce; *The Politics of Coalition Rule in Colombia* by Jonathan Hartlyn; and *The Making of Modern Colombia: A Nation in Spite of Itself* by David Bushnell.

## Geography & Wildlife

The famous German geographer and botanist Alexander von Humboldt explored and studied regions of Colombia (as well as Venezuela, Ecuador and Peru). He describes it all in amazing detail in his three-volume *Personal Narrative of Travels to the Equinoctial Regions of America, 1799-1801*.

Travellers with a serious interest in South American wildlife have quite a choice when it comes to background reading and practical guides. *A Neotropical Companion: An Introduction to the Animals, Plants, and Ecosystems of the New World Tropics* by John C Kricher is an excellent source of information and fascinating reading. *World of Wildlife – Animals of South America* by

### Colombia Online

media (some articles in English, other in Spanish); not focusing on tourism but has some travel information
**W** www.presidencia.gov.co
  Spanish-language official government site featuring information related to state issues such as governmental institutions, the constitution, and a full list of Colombian embassies and consulates around the world and the foreign diplomatic missions in Bogotá
**W** www.businesscol.com
  Extensive Spanish-language site of Colombia's economy, trade, business etc
**W** www.latinworld.com/sur/colombia
  General site including politics, culture, economy and a bit of tourism
**W** www.gosouthamerica.about.com/cs/colombia
  A mixed bag of general and tourist information in English
**W** www.locombia.org
  Comprehensive site featuring Colombian news, comments, opinions (in English)
**W** www.samexplo.org
  Website of the South American Explorers Club, a helpful source of information for visitors to South America comprising a short coverage of Colombia
**W** www.onlinenewspapers.com/colombia.htm
  Links to 19 Colombian online newspapers
**W** www.quehubo.com
  Website directory comprising 93 categories and over 4500 links to Colombian pages (mostly in Spanish), including hotels, tourist attractions, sporting events etc
**W** www.terra.com
  Comprehensive information and links to newspapers and magazines, forums, entertainment, cultural events, nightlife etc (in Spanish)
**W** www.southamericadaily.com
  Site from The World News Network, specialising on news related to South America, including Colombia
**W** www.minrelext.gov.co
  Official site of the Ministry of Foreign Affairs, including lists of Colombian diplomatic missions abroad and of foreign embassies and consulates in Colombia (Spanish only)

FR de la Fuente is a good, basic, reference work. *Neotropical Rainforest Mammals – A Field Guide* by Louise H Emmons is a practical guide containing descriptions and illustrations of several hundred species, many of which can be found in Colombia.

If birds are what interest you most, you might start with *A Guide to the Birds of South America* published by the Academy of Natural Science, Philadelphia. There's also the helpful *Where to Watch Birds in South America* by Nigel Wheatley.

For the trip itself, get a copy of *A Guide to the Birds of Colombia* by Stephen L Hilty & William L Brown, which is a good, illustrated field-guide. *South American Birds – A Photographic Aid to Identification* by John S Dunning might be another good companion on your trip. A number of the bird species featured in the book are found in Colombia.

A recommended rainforest guide is *Rainforests – A Guide to Research and Tourist Facilities at Selected Tropical Forest Sites in Central and South America* by James L Castner. This book has useful background information and has descriptions of 40 rainforests in half a dozen countries.

## NEWSPAPERS & MAGAZINES

All major cities have daily newspapers. Bogotá's leading newspaper, *El Tiempo*, has reasonable coverage of national and international news, culture, sports and economics. It has the widest national distribution. The leading newspapers in other large cities include *El Mundo* and *El Colombiano* in Medellín, and *El País* and *El Occidente* in Cali.

*Semana* is the biggest national weekly magazine. It features local and international affairs and has an extensive cultural section. Another major weekly, *Cambio*, is an important opinion-forming magazine.

## RADIO & TV

Hundreds of FM and AM radio stations operate in Colombia, mainly broadcasting music programmes. Even middle-size towns have their own local radio stations.

Colombian TV dates from 1954 and since 1981 all programmes have been broadcast in colour. There are three nationwide television channels, all broadcast by the state-run monopoly Inravisión. They are Cadena Uno, Canal A and Señal Colombia. During the late 1980s, three regional channels –

Telepacífico, Teleantioquia and Telecaribe – began broadcasting, and more recently were joined by Telecafé.

Satellite TV boomed in Bogotá in the 1990s and, to a lesser extent, in other major cities. The *parabólica* (satellite dish) became the ultimate status-symbol, and a new feature of the city skyline. More recently, cable TV became another success story and has captured some satellite-TV clients.

## VIDEO SYSTEMS

If you want to record or buy videotapes to play back home, you won't get a picture if the image registration system is different. Colombia uses the NTSC system, the same as in North America and Japan, but incompatible with the French SECAM system, and PAL which is used in most of Europe and Australia.

## PHOTOGRAPHY & VIDEO

Given the country's spectacular and varied geography, wildlife, architecture and its ethnic mosaic, there's plenty to capture on film or video.

### Film & Equipment

Bring all necessary equipment from home. Cameras and accessories can be bought in Colombia, but the choice is limited, unpredictable and prices hardly welcoming. It's difficult to get cameras repaired in Colombia, so make sure your gear is reliable.

Film is easier to come by and there's quite a choice in Bogotá and some other big cities. Elsewhere, particularly in remote areas, it may be difficult to get the film type and speed you require. Film is reasonably cheap in Colombia, with prices comparable to those in the USA.

Kodak, Fuji and, to a lesser extent, Agfa are the most popular brands in Colombia. Negative film is found almost everywhere. Slide film, especially high-speed and professional types, is harder to find. Prints can be processed in any number of laboratories, often within an hour or two, and the quality is usually acceptable, but E6 slide processing is rare and the quality is not always good.

### Restrictions

Except for usual restrictions on photographing military installations and other strategic facilities, you theoretically can take pictures almost anywhere and of just about anything. However, it may be a bit different in practice. Due to the delicate internal situation, combined with the rise of terrorism worldwide, you may be watched with suspicion while taking photos of skyscrapers, bridges, even discotheques. Private and public security guards (and there are plenty of them these days) may not allow you to take pictures of some buildings, shops, shopping malls etc. Be discreet with your camera and use common sense (see Photographing People under Society & Conduct in the earlier Facts about Colombia chapter).

## TIME

All of Colombia lies within the same time zone, five hours behind Greenwich Mean Time. There is no daylight saving time.

## ELECTRICITY

Electricity is 110V, 60 cycles AC throughout the country. US-type, flat, two-pin plugs are used, so take conversion plugs if you need them.

## WEIGHTS & MEASURES

The metric system is commonly used, except for petrol which is measured in US gallons. Food is often sold in *libras* (pounds) which is roughly equivalent to 500g. There is a conversion chart at the back of this book.

## LAUNDRY

There are dry-cleaners in large cities and it usually takes a couple of days to get your clothes cleaned. Top-class hotels offer laundry facilities for guests, but prices for this service are rather high. In budget hotels, you can usually make arrangements with the hotel staff, or their relatives, to have clothes washed (usually by hand) at fair rates.

Self-service laundrettes don't exist, but there are laundrettes which offer service washes. Just ask the locals for the *lavandería automática*. They normally offer the full service including washing, drying and ironing, if requested. It usually takes a few hours to wash and dry, and costs US$2.50 to US$5 for a 5kg load, detergent included.

## TOILETS

There are virtually no self-contained public toilets in Colombia. If you are unexpectedly caught in need, use a toilet in a restaurant.

Choose better-looking establishments because basic eateries either have no toilets or, if they do, you're better off not witnessing them. If you feel uncomfortable about sneaking in just to use the toilet, order a soft drink, a coffee or whatever. Museums and large shopping malls usually have toilets, as do bus and airport terminals. Toilets are usually the sit-down style, but they often lack boards, so they effectively become the squat variety.

You will rarely find toilet paper in toilets, so make sure you carry some at all times. Some toilets charge fees (normally not exceeding US$0.25), but in return you can receive some toilet paper. If it seems to be too little for your needs, do not hesitate to ask for more.

Except for toilets in some upmarket establishments, the plumbing might not be of a standard you are accustomed to. The pipes are narrow and water pressure is weak, so toilets can't cope with toilet paper. A wastebasket is normally provided.

The most common word for toilet is *baño*. Men's toilets will usually bear a label saying *señores*, *hombres* or *caballeros*, while the women's toilets will be marked *señoras*, *mujeres* or *damas*.

## HEALTH

Colombia is not the most disease-ridden part of the world, but certain precautions should be taken. The medical standards and the variety of diseases make health more of a problem than in the West.

Fortunately, the local pharmacy network is quite developed and extensive: there are *droguerías* (pharmacies) even in small towns, and those in the cities are usually well stocked.

This section includes some preventative measures, descriptions of symptoms and suggestions about what to do if there is a problem. It isn't meant to replace professional diagnosis or prescription. If a serious medical problem arises during the trip, seek qualified help wherever possible because self-diagnosis and treatment can be risky. Your embassy or consulate can usually recommend a good place to go for medical help. So can five-star hotels, although they often recommend doctors with five-star prices – this is when your medical insurance really is useful.

## Predeparture Preparations

**Health Insurance** Purchasing a travel insurance policy to cover medical problems is highly recommended. Regardless of how fit and healthy you are, you might be involved in an accident. There is a wide variety of policies and your travel agent will have recommendations.

**Medical Information Services** Useful health information is available from several public information services. In the USA the Center for Disease Control & Prevention (CDC) has an international **travellers' hot line** (☎ 877-394 8747). In Canada there's **Health Canada** (☎ 613-957 8739). In the UK you can obtain a printed health brief for any country by calling **MASTA** (*Medical Advisory Services for Travellers Abroad;* ☎ 0906-8-224 100). In Australia call the Australian Government Health Service or consult the **Travellers Medical & Vaccination Centre** (*TMVC;* ☎ 1300 658 844), which has 19 clinics in Australia and New Zealand.

You'll find a number of excellent travel health sites on the Internet and from the Lonely Planet home page there are links at www.lonelyplanet.com/weblinks/wlheal.htm to the World Health Organisation and the US Center for Disease Control & Prevention.

**Travel Health Guides** If you plan to travel in remote areas, you might consider taking a health guide. Here are some suggestions:

*Healthy Travel Central & South America* by Isabelle Young includes guidelines on treating travel illnesses in the region.

*Staying Healthy in Asia, Africa & Latin America* by Dirk Schroeder is one of the best all-round guides to carry as it's compact, detailed and well organised.

*Travelers' Health* by Richard Dawood is comprehensive, easy to read, authoritative and highly recommended, although it's rather large to lug around.

**Immunisations** No immunisations are necessary for Colombia, unless you are coming from an area infected with cholera or yellow fever. However, the further off the beaten track you go, the more necessary it is to take precautions. All vaccinations should be recorded on an International Health Certificate, which is available from your doctor or government health department.

Plan your vaccinations ahead of time; some of them require an initial shot followed by a booster, and some vaccinations should not be administered at the same time. Most travellers from Western countries will have been immunised against various diseases during childhood, but your doctor may still recommend booster shots. The list of possible vaccinations includes:

**Diphtheria & Tetanus** Diphtheria can be a fatal throat infection and tetanus can be a fatal wound infection. Vaccination for these two diseases are usually combined and are recommended for everyone. Most people in developed countries have been vaccinated against these diseases at school age. Boosters are necessary every 10 years and are recommended as a matter of course.

**Hepatitis A** This is the most common travel-acquired illness after diarrhoea, and can put you out of action for weeks. A vaccine such as Havrix 1440, Avaxim or VAQTA provides long-term immunity (possibly more than 10 years) after an initial injection and a booster at six to 12 months.

**Hepatitis B** Vaccination involves three injections, the quickest course being over three weeks with a booster at 12 months. A combined hepatitis A and hepatitis B vaccine called Twinrix is also available; three injections over a six-month period are required.

**Malaria** So far, there is no effective vaccine against malaria, only antimalarial drugs. They don't prevent you from being infected, but they kill malaria parasites during a stage of their development and reduce the risk of serious illness or death. Expert advice on medication should be sought, as there are many factors to consider, including the area to be visited, the risk of exposure to malaria-carrying mosquitoes, the side effects of medication and your medical history.

**Polio** Westerners will usually have had an oral polio vaccine while at school, but you should undertake a booster dose if more than 10 years have elapsed since your last vaccination.

**Typhoid** This is an important vaccination to have in areas where hygiene is a problem, and is recommended to anybody travelling for longer periods in rural tropical areas. It's available either as an injection or as oral capsules.

**Yellow Fever** This vaccination is a legal requirement for entry into many countries when a visitor comes from an infected area. Protection lasts 10 years and is recommended for travel in most lowland tropical areas of South America, where the disease is endemic.

**Medical Kit** Give some thought to a medical kit for your trip, particularly if you're going far off the beaten track.

It's not necessary to take every remedy for every illness you might contract during your trip. Colombian pharmacies stock all kinds of drugs, and medication can be cheaper than in Western countries. There are few restricted drugs; almost everything is sold over the counter. Many drugs are manufactured locally under foreign licence. Be sure to check expiry dates.

Ideally, antibiotics should be administered only under medical supervision and should never be taken indiscriminately. Overuse of antibiotics can weaken your body's ability to deal with infections naturally, and can reduce the drug's efficacy in future. Take only the recommended dose at the prescribed intervals and continue using the antibiotic for the prescribed period, even if the illness seems to have been cured.

Remember that antibiotics are quite specific to the infections they treat, so if there are any serious unexpected reactions, discontinue use immediately. If you are not sure whether you have the correct antibiotic, don't use it at all.

**Other Preparations** Make sure you're healthy before you start travelling. Have your teeth checked and make sure they are OK. If you wear glasses or contact lenses, bring a spare pair and your optical prescription. Losing your glasses can be a real problem, although in many Colombian cities you can get new spectacles made up quickly, cheaply and competently.

At least one pair of good-quality sunglasses is essential because there is strong glare, and dust and sand can get into the corners of your eyes. A hat, sunscreen lotion and lip protection are also important.

If you require a particular medication take an adequate supply with you, as it may not be available locally. Take the original prescription specifying the generic rather than the brand name; it will make getting replacements easier. It's also wise to have the prescription with you to prove you're using the medication legally.

## Environmental Hazards

**Altitude Sickness** Popularly referred to as *soroche*, altitude sickness, and its more serious form known as acute mountain sickness (AMS), occur at high altitudes and in extreme cases can be fatal. They are caused by ascending to high altitudes so quickly that the body does not have time to adapt to the lower oxygen concentration in the atmosphere. Minor symptoms can occur at altitudes as low as 2500m, and they become increasingly severe the higher you go. Most people are affected to some extent at altitudes between 3500m and 4500m.

The best way to minimise the risk of altitude sickness is to ascend slowly, to increase liquid intake and to eat meals containing energy-rich carbohydrates. Even with acclimatisation, however, you may still have trouble if you visit high-altitude areas. Headaches, nausea, dizziness, a dry cough,

## Basic Health Rules

Paying attention to what you eat and drink is the most important health rule. Stomach upsets are the most common travel health problem, but most of these upsets will be relatively minor. Don't be paranoid about trying local food – it's part of the travel experience and you wouldn't want to miss it.

### Water & Drinks

The tap water in Bogotá and several other large cities is considered safe to drink, but it's better to avoid it, and that's pretty easy; bottled water and soft drinks are readily available in shops, supermarkets, restaurants, bakeries etc. Outside the big cities, tap water should never be drunk, but even in the most remote villages bottled drinks are almost always available.

### Food

Salads and fruit should, theoretically at least, be washed with purified water, or peeled whenever possible. Thoroughly cooked food is safe, but not if it has been left to cool or if it has been reheated. Take great care with shellfish or fish, and avoid undercooked meat. If a place looks clean and well run and if the vendor also looks clean and healthy, then the food is probably all right. In general, places that are packed with locals will be fine, while empty restaurants are questionable.

breathlessness and loss of appetite are the most frequent symptoms. If the symptoms become more pronounced or there is no improvement after a few hours, descend to a lower altitude.

**Heat Exhaustion** Serious dehydration or salt deficiency can lead to heat exhaustion. Salt deficiency, which can be brought on by diarrhoea or vomiting, is characterised by fatigue, lethargy, headaches, giddiness and muscle cramps. Salt tablets may help. The best way to avoid heat exhaustion is by drinking lots of liquids and eating salty foods.

**Motion Sickness** If you are prone to motion sickness, try to choose a place that minimises disturbance – near the wing on an aircraft, midship on a boat or between the front and the middle of a bus. Eating lightly before and during a trip will reduce the chances of motion sickness. Fresh air almost always helps, while reading or cigarette smoking make matters worse.

**Prickly Heat** This is an itchy rash caused by excessive perspiration trapped under the skin. It usually strikes people who have just arrived in a hot climate and whose pores have not yet opened sufficiently to cope with increased sweating. Frequent baths and applications of talcum powder will help relieve the itchiness.

## Infectious Diseases

**Diarrhoea** Simple things like a change of water, food or climate can all cause a mild bout of diarrhoea, but a few rushed toilet trips with no other symptoms is not indicative of a major problem.

Dehydration is the main danger with any diarrhoea, particularly in children or the elderly as dehydration can occur quite quickly. Fluid replacement is the most important thing to remember. You need to drink at least the same volume of fluid that you are losing in bowel movements and vomiting. Urine is the best guide to the adequacy of replacement – if you have small amounts of concentrated urine, you need to drink more. Stick to a bland diet as you recover.

Lomotil or Imodium can be used to bring relief from the symptoms, although they do not actually cure the problem. Only use these drugs if you do not have access to

toilets, eg, if you must travel. Do not use these drugs if you have a high fever or are severely dehydrated.

In some situations antibiotics are required: diarrhoea with blood or mucous (dysentery), any fever, watery diarrhoea with fever and lethargy, persistent diarrhoea not improving after 48 hours and severe diarrhoea. In these situations gut-paralysing drugs like Imodium or Lomotil should be avoided.

A stool test is necessary to diagnose which kind of dysentery you have, so you should seek medical help urgently. Where this is not possible the recommended drugs for dysentery are norfloxacin 400mg twice daily for three days or ciprofloxacin 500mg twice daily for five days.

Amoebic dysentery is more gradual in the onset of symptoms, with cramping abdominal pain and vomiting less likely; fever may not be present. It will persist until treated and can recur and cause other health problems.

Giardiasis is another type of diarrhoea. The parasite causing this intestinal disorder is present in contaminated water. The symptoms are stomach cramps, nausea, a bloated stomach, watery, foul-smelling diarrhoea and frequent gas. Giardiasis can appear several weeks after you have been exposed to the parasite.

**Cholera** This disease is transmitted orally by the ingestion of contaminated food or water. The symptoms, which appear one to three days after infection, consist of a sudden onset of acute diarrhoea with rice-water stools, vomiting, muscular cramps, and extreme weakness. You need medical attention but your first concern should be rehydration. Drink as much water as you can – if it refuses to stay down, keep drinking anyway. If there is likely to be a considerable delay in getting medical treatment, begin a course of Tetracycline, but it should not be administered to children or pregnant women.

**Fungal Infections** Fungal infections occur more commonly in hot weather and are most likely to be found between the toes or fingers or around the groin. The infections are spread by infected animals or humans; you may contract them by walking barefoot in damp areas, for example. Moisture encourages these infections.

To prevent fungal infections wear loose, comfortable clothes, avoid artificial fibres, wash frequently and dry thoroughly. Use thongs (flip-flops) while taking a shower in bathrooms of cheap hotels. If you become infected, wash the infected area daily with a disinfectant or medicated soap, and rinse and dry well. Apply an antifungal cream or powder.

**Hepatitis** This is a disease that's common throughout the world. The symptoms are fever, chills, headache, fatigue, feelings of weakness and aches and pains, followed by loss of appetite, nausea, vomiting, abdominal pain, dark urine, light-coloured faeces and jaundiced (yellow) skin. The whites of the eyes may turn yellow. There are several strains of hepatitis, denominated with the consecutive letters of the alphabet.

The most common is hepatitis A, which is transmitted by contaminated food and drinking water. If you contract it, you should seek medical advice, but there is not much you can do apart from resting, drinking lots of fluids, eating lightly and avoiding fatty foods. People who have had hepatitis should avoid alcohol for some time after the illness, as the liver needs time to recover.

Hepatitis B is spread through contact with infected blood, blood products or body fluids (eg, through sexual contact, unsterilized needles and blood transfusions, or contact with blood via small breaks in the skin). Other risk situations include having a shave, tattoo, or having your body pierced with contaminated equipment. The symptoms of hepatitis B may be more severe than type A and the disease can lead to long-term problems, such as chronic liver damage or liver cancer.

There are vaccines against hepatitis A and B, but there are currently no vaccines against other types.

**HIV & AIDS** Infection with the human immunodeficiency virus (HIV) may lead to acquired immune deficiency syndrome (AIDS), which is a fatal disease. Any exposure to blood, blood products or body fluids may put the individual at risk. The disease is often transmitted through sexual contact, and in South America it's primarily through contact between heterosexuals.

HIV and AIDS can also be contracted through infected blood transfusions, and you should be aware that not all the hospitals screen blood supplies. The virus may also be picked up through injection with an unsterilised needle. Acupuncture, tattooing and body piercing are other potential dangers. There is currently no cure for AIDS.

**Intestinal Worms** These parasites are common in most humid, tropical areas. They can be present on unwashed vegetables or in undercooked meat, or you can pick them up through your skin by walking barefoot. Infestations may not show up for some time and, although they are generally not serious, they can cause further health problems if left untreated. A stool test on your return home is not a bad idea if you think you may have contracted them. Once the test pinpoints the problem, medication is usually available over the counter and treatment is easy and short.

**Rabies** This is present in most of South America. It is caused by a bite or scratch by an infected animal. Bats and dogs are the most notorious carriers. Any bite, scratch or lick from a mammal should be cleaned immediately and thoroughly. Scrub the site with soap and running water and then clean it with an alcohol solution. If there is any possibility that the animal is infected, medical help should be sought. Avoid any animal that appears to be foaming at the mouth or acting strangely. If bitten, try to capture the offending animal for testing. If that's impossible, you must assume the animal is rabid. Rabies is fatal if untreated, so don't take the risk. Medical attention should not be delayed.

Treatment consists of a series of injections (usually seven) around the navel over consecutive days. A rabies vaccination is now available and should be considered if you intend to spend a lot of time around animals.

**Sexually Transmitted Diseases** Sexual contact with an infected partner can result in you contracting a number of diseases. While abstinence is the only 100% effective prevention, the use of condoms lessens the risk of infection considerably.

The most common sexually transmitted diseases are gonorrhoea and syphilis, which in men first appear as sores, blisters or rashes around the genitals and a discharge or pain when urinating. Symptoms may be less marked or not present at all in women.

Syphilis symptoms eventually disappear, but the disease continues and may cause severe problems in later years. Gonorrhoea and syphilis are treatable with antibiotics.

**Tetanus** This potentially fatal disease is difficult to treat, but is easily prevented by immunisation. Tetanus occurs when a wound becomes infected by a germ which lives in soil in the faeces of horses and other animals. It enters the body via breaks in the skin, so the best prevention is to clean all wounds promptly and thoroughly and use an antiseptic. Use antibiotics if the wound becomes hot or throbs or pus is seen. The first symptom may be discomfort in swallowing, or stiffening of the jaw and neck; this can be followed by painful convulsions of the jaw and whole body.

**Typhoid** This is a gut infection which travels via contaminated water and food. Vaccination against typhoid is not 100% effective and, since it is one of the most dangerous infections, medical attention is necessary if you are infected. Early symptoms are similar to those of many other travellers illnesses – you may feel as though you have a bad cold or the flu combined with a headache, a sore throat and a fever. The fever rises a little each day until it exceeds 40°C (104°F), while the pulse rate slows – unlike a normal fever where the pulse increases. These symptoms may be accompanied by vomiting, diarrhoea or constipation.

In the second week, the high fever and slow pulse continue and a few pink spots may appear on the body. Trembling, delirium, weakness, weight loss and dehydration set in. If there are no further complications, the fever and other symptoms will slowly fade during the third week. However, medical attention is essential, since typhoid is extremely infectious and possible complications include pneumonia or peritonitis (burst appendix). The recommended antibiotic is Chloramphenicol.

## Insect-Borne Diseases

**Malaria** This serious and potentially fatal disease is spread by mosquito bites and in Colombia the high-risk areas are essentially in the eastern half of the country (Los Llanos and Amazonia), and along the Pacific and Caribbean Coasts.

Since antimalarial tablets are not 100% effective, the primary prevention should always be to avoid mosquito bites. Wear long trousers and long-sleeved shirts, use mosquito repellents, avoid highly scented perfumes or aftershaves and use a mosquito net.

Symptoms range from fever, chills and sweating, headache, diarrhoea and abdominal pains to a vague feeling of ill-health. Seek medical help immediately if malaria is suspected. Without treatment malaria can rapidly become more serious and can be fatal.

The symptoms of malaria only appear several weeks after contraction, which may lead to confusion in diagnosis. By that time you may be home and local doctors will not be looking for an exotic disease. Make sure you give your doctor details of your trip. Malaria can be diagnosed by a simple blood test.

**Dengue Fever** This serious disease is a rapidly growing problem in tropical South America. The *Aedes aegypti* mosquito, which transmits the dengue virus, is most active during the day and is found mainly in urban areas, in and around human dwellings.

Signs and symptoms of dengue fever include a sudden onset of high fever, headache, joint and muscle pains, nausea and vomiting, and sometimes a rash of small red spots appears three to four days after the onset of fever.

In the early phase, dengue may be mistaken for other diseases, including malaria and influenza. Later it can progress to the potentially fatal dengue haemorrhagic fever (DHF), a severe illness characterised by heavy bleeding. Full recovery even from simple dengue fever may be prolonged, with tiredness lasting for several weeks.

If you think you may be infected, seek medical attention quickly. A blood test can exclude malaria and indicate the possibility of dengue fever, for which there is no specific treatment. Aspirin should be avoided, as it increases the risk of haemorrhaging.

There is no vaccine against dengue fever. The best prevention is to avoid mosquito bites at all times, as for malaria.

**Yellow Fever** This is found in most of South America, except for the Andean highlands and the southern part of the continent. This viral disease, which is transmitted by mosquitoes, first manifests itself as fever, headaches, abdominal pain and vomiting. There may appear to be a brief recovery before it progresses into its more severe stages, including possible liver failure. There is no treatment apart from keeping the fever as low as possible and avoiding dehydration. The yellow fever vaccination gives protection for 10 years, and is highly recommended for every person travelling on the continent.

**Typhus** This is spread by ticks, mites and lice. It begins as a severe cold followed by a fever, chills, headaches, muscle pains and a body rash. There is often a large and painful sore at the site of the bite, and nearby lymph nodes become swollen and painful.

## Cuts, Bites & Stings

**Cuts & Scratches** In warm, moist, tropical lowlands, skin punctures can easily become infected and may have difficulty healing. The best treatment for cuts is to cleanse the affected area frequently with soap and water and to apply an antiseptic cream. Whenever possible, avoid using bandages, which keep wounds moist and encourage the growth of bacteria. If the wound becomes tender and inflamed, use a mild, broad-spectrum antibiotic.

**Bites & Stings** Cover your skin, especially from dusk to dawn when many insects, such as malaria-transmitting mosquitoes, feed. Wear long-sleeved shirts and long trousers, instead of T-shirts and shorts, and wear shoes instead of sandals or thongs. Use insect repellent on exposed skin and, if necessary, spray it over your clothes. Sleep under a mosquito net if you are outdoors or if your hotel room does not have a sufficiently strong fan.

Use creams and lotions which alleviate itching and deal with infection. They are sold in local pharmacies. Body lice and scabies mites are common, but shampoos and creams are available to eliminate them.

Leeches may be present in damp rainforests. They attach themselves to your skin and suck your blood. Trekkers may get them on their legs or in their boots. Salt or a lighted cigarette end will make them fall off. Do not pull them off because the bite is more likely to become infected and the head

of the leech can remain in your body. An insect repellent may keep them away.

Vaseline, alcohol or oil will persuade a tick to let go. You should always check your body if you have been walking through a tick-infested area because ticks can spread typhus. They like the warmest parts of the body and often go to the genital area or the armpits, so be sure to inspect all of these areas.

**Snakebite** There's only a small chance of being bitten by a snake in Colombia, but you should take precautions. To minimise the chances of being bitten, wear boots, socks and long trousers when walking through undergrowth. A good pair of canvas gaiters will further protect your legs.

Snakebites do not cause instantaneous death and antivenins are available. If someone is bitten, it's vital that you identify the snake immediately, or at the very least, are able to describe it. Keep the victim calm and still, wrap the bitten limb tightly, as you would a sprain, then attach a splint to immobilise it. Seek medical help immediately and, if possible, bring the dead snake along for identification.

## Women's Health

Antibiotic use, synthetic underwear, sweating and contraceptive pills can lead to fungal vaginal infections when travelling in hot climates. Maintaining good personal hygiene, and loose-fitting clothes and cotton underwear will help to prevent these infections.

Fungal infections are characterised by a rash, itch and discharge, and can be treated with a vinegar or lemon-juice douche, or with yoghurt. Nystatin, Miconazole or Clotrimazole pessaries or vaginal cream are the usual treatment.

Sexually transmitted diseases are a major cause of vaginal problems. Symptoms include a smelly discharge, painful intercourse and sometimes a burning sensation when urinating. Sexual partners must also be treated. Medical attention should be sought. Remember that, in addition to these diseases, HIV or hepatitis B may also be acquired from sexual contact.

Women who are pregnant need to take special care on the road. Most miscarriages occur during the first three months of pregnancy, so this is the most risky time to travel.

The last three months should also be spent within reasonable reach of good medical care because serious problems can develop at this stage. Pregnant women should avoid all unnecessary medication, but vaccinations and malarial prophylactics should still be taken when possible.

## Back Home

Be aware of illnesses after you return home; take note of odd or persistent symptoms of any kind, get a check-up and remember to give your physician a complete travel history. Most doctors in temperate climates will not be looking for unusual tropical diseases. If you have been travelling in malarial areas, have yourself tested for the disease.

## WOMEN TRAVELLERS

Like most of Latin America, Colombia is very much a man's country. Machismo and sexism are palpable throughout society. The dominant Catholic church with its conservative attitude towards women doesn't help matters. In this context, it's not difficult to imagine how a gringa travelling by herself is regarded.

Women travellers will attract more curiosity, attention and advances from local men than they would from men in the West. Many Colombian men will stare at women, use endearing terms, make comments on their physical appearance and, in some cases, try to make physical contact. It is just the Latin-American way of life, and local males would not understand if someone told them that their behaviour constituted sexual harassment. On the contrary, they would argue that they are just paying the woman a flattering compliment.

Men in large cities, especially when they are in male-only groups, and particularly when they are drunk, will generally display more bravado and be more insistent than those in small villages. To balance things a little, some male travellers have reported that they themselves felt hassled by Colombian women, who are seen as being rather sexually aggressive.

The best way to deal with unwanted attention is simply to ignore it. Maintain your self-confidence and assertiveness and don't let macho behaviour disrupt your holiday. Dressing modestly may lessen the chances of you being the object of macho interest, or at least make you less conspicuous to the local peacocks. Wearing a wedding band and carrying a photo of a make-believe spouse may minimise harassment.

Travelling with a man solves much of the problem because local men will see your male companion as a protector and a deterrent. Travelling with another woman will make things easier; the harassment is likely to continue, but you will at least have the emotional support of your companion.

Harassment aside, women travelling alone face more risks than men. Women are often targets for bag-snatchers and assault, and rape is a potential danger. However, female travellers need not walk around Colombia in a constant state of fear. Just be conscious of your surroundings and aware of situations that could be dangerous. Shabby barrios, solitary streets and beaches, and all places considered male territory, such as bars, sports matches, mines and construction sites should be considered risky.

There isn't much in the way of women's support services in Colombia, let alone resources specifically for women travellers. Books which might be worth looking at before the trip include *Handbook for Women Travellers* by Maggie & Jemma Moss and *Women Travel – Adventures, Advice & Experience* by Natania Jansz & Miranda Davies.

## GAY & LESBIAN TRAVELLERS

The gay and lesbian movement is still very underdeveloped. Bogotá has the largest gay and lesbian community and the most open gay life, and therefore is the best place to make contacts and get to know what's going on. Also check the local gay website ⓦ www.ventanagay.com, which lists bars, discos, events, activities, publications and other related matters.

Gay bars, discos and other venues are limited to the larger cities, but because of social pressures they come and go frequently. Again, Bogotá offers the largest choice. See that chapter for some gay hang-outs.

## DISABLED TRAVELLERS

Colombia offers very little to people with disabilities. Wheelchair ramps are available only at a few upmarket hotels and restaurants, and public transport will be a challenge for any person with mobility problems. Hardly any office, museum or bank provides special facilities for disabled travellers, and wheelchair-accessible toilets are virtually nonexistent.

Disabled travellers in the USA might like to contact the **Society for the Advancement of Travel for the Handicapped** (☎ 212-447 SATH, fax 725 8253; 347 Fifth Ave, Suite 610, New York, NY 10016). In the UK, a useful contact is the **Royal Association for Disability & Rehabilitation** (☎ 020-7242 3882; 25 Mortimer St, London W1N 8AB).

## SENIOR TRAVELLERS

By and large, senior travellers may expect more respect and help from locals than young visitors, though this attitude doesn't necessarily prevail with some attendants in shops, bank tellers and employees of public institutions. The difference in attitudes towards the youth and elderly is likely to be more pronounced among rural communities.

As far as discounts go, senior travellers get reductions on air fares with some airlines, but that's about it. So far, there are no discounts for senior citizens on bus fares, accommodation rates, cinema and theatre tickets etc.

## TRAVEL WITH CHILDREN

As with most Latin Americans, Colombians adore children. Due to a high rate of population growth, children are a significant proportion of the population, and they are omnipresent. Few foreigners travel with children in Colombia, but if you do plan on taking along your offspring, he or she will easily find plenty of local companions.

Basic supplies are usually no problem in the cities. There are quite a few shops devoted to kids' clothes, shoes and toys, and you can buy disposable nappies and baby food in supermarkets and pharmacies.

## DANGERS & ANNOYANCES

Colombia definitely isn't the safest of countries, and you should be careful at all times. Keep your passport and money next to your skin and your camera inside your bag, and don't wear jewellery or expensive watches. Always carry your passport with you, as document checks on the streets are not uncommon. Some police officers may accept a photocopy of the passport, but legally only the genuine document is valid.

### Safe Travel in Colombia

Here are 10 basic rules of safe travel in Colombia:

• Use common sense and don't get paranoid. Travellers do come to Colombia and few have any problems.

• Upon arrival in Colombia, check available air passes and budget air fares, to limit land travel as much as possible.

• Travel by bus during the daytime.

• Consider air travel if the overland route is notorious for a lack of safety.

• Seek local advice about the safety of the region you are travelling in and the one you're heading for.

• Unless the rural area you plan to visit is regarded as safe, make cities the focus of your travel rather than the countryside.

• Don't use a rented car (but if you insist on travelling this way we provide some guidelines under Car & Motorcycle in the Getting Around chapter later in this book).

• Avoid off-the-beaten-track travel.

• Should you feel compelled, however, to go off the beaten track, leave details about your planned whereabouts prior to departure.

• Don't accept any food, drink or cigarettes from strangers.

### Theft & Robbery

Theft is the most common travellers' danger. Generally speaking, the problem is more serious in the largest cities. The more rural the area, the quieter and safer it is. The most common methods of theft are snatching your day-pack, camera or watch, pickpocketing, or taking advantage of a moment's inattention to pick up your gear and run away.

Distraction is often part of the thieves' strategy. Thieves often work in pairs or groups; one or more will distract you, while an accomplice does the deed. There are hundreds, if not thousands, of possible ways to distract you, and new scams are dreamt up every day. Some thieves are even more innovative and will set up an opportune situation to separate you from your belongings. They may begin by making friends with you, or pretend to be the police and demand to check your belongings.

If you can, leave your money and valuables somewhere safe before walking the

## Ten Precautions Against Theft & Robbery

• Keep your money and documents as secure as possible, preferably in a moneybelt next to your skin.

• Distribute your valuables about your person and luggage to avoid the risk of losing everything in one fell swoop.

• Don't venture into poor suburbs, desolate streets or suspicious-looking surroundings, especially after dark.

• Wear casual and inexpensive clothes, preferably in plain, sober tones rather than in bright colours.

• Keep your camera out of sight as much as possible and only take it out to take a photo.

• Behave confidently on the street; don't look lost or stand with a blank expression in the middle of the street.

• Before arriving in a new place, make sure you have a map or at least a rough idea about orientation.

• Use taxis if this seems the appropriate way to avoid walking through risky areas.

• Look around to see whether you're being observed or followed, especially while leaving a bank, casa de cambio or an ATM.

• Arrange comprehensive travel insurance just in case something goes wrong.

streets. In practice it's good to carry a decoy bundle of small notes, the equivalent of US$5 to US$10, ready to hand over in case of an assault; if you really don't have a peso, robbers can become frustrated and, as a consequence, unpredictable.

Armed hold-ups in the cities can occur even in some more upmarket suburbs. If you are accosted by robbers, it is best to give them what they are after, but try to play it cool and don't rush to hand them all your valuables at once – they may well be satisfied with just your decoy wad. Don't try to escape or struggle – your chances are slim. Don't count on any help from passers-by.

Be careful when drawing cash from an ATM as some robberies have been reported. Criminals may watch you drawing money, then assault you either at an ATM or a convenient place nearby. It may be safer to get an advance from the cashier inside the bank, even if this takes a while.

### Police

Colombian police have a mixed reputation. Cases of police corruption, abuse of power and use of undue authority have been known, so it's probably best to stay a safe distance from them if you don't need them. This, of course, doesn't mean that they will stay away from you.

On a more positive note, there's an increasing number of the so-called tourist police. They are uniformed and easily recognisable by the Policía de Turismo labels printed on their arm bands. These forces have been formed and trained to attend to tourist needs and, accordingly, operate mainly in popular tourist destinations. They are usually friendlier and more helpful than ordinary police.

If your passport, valuables or other belongings are stolen, go to the police station and make a *denuncia* (report). The officer on duty will write a statement according to what you tell them. It should include the description of the events and the list of stolen articles. Pay attention to the wording you use, make sure you include every stolen item and document, and carefully check the statement before signing it to ensure it contains exactly what you've said. Your copy of the statement serves as a temporary identity document and you will need to present it to your insurer in order to make a claim. Don't expect your things to be found, as the police are unlikely to even try to do anything about it.

If you happen to get involved with the police, keep calm and be polite, but not overly friendly. Don't get angry or hostile – it only works against you. Keep a sharp eye out when they check your gear because things sometimes 'disappear'.

Be wary of criminals masquerading as plain-clothes police. They may stop you on the street, identify themselves with a fake ID, then ask to inspect your passport and money. Under no circumstances should you agree to a search. Call a uniformed police officer, if there happens to be one around, or decent-looking passers-by to witness the incident, and insist on phoning a bona fide police station. By that time, the 'officers' will probably walk discreetly away.

### Drugs

Cocaine is essentially an export product but it is also available locally. More widespread is marijuana, and it is even more easily available. However, be careful about drugs – never carry them. The police and army can be very thorough in searching travellers, and have been known to accept bribes.

Sometimes you may be offered dope on the street, in a bar or a disco, but never accept these offers. The vendors may well be setting you up for the police, or their accomplices will follow you and stop you later, show you false police documents and threaten you with jail unless you pay them off.

There have been reports of drugs being planted on travellers, so keep your eyes open. Always refuse if a stranger at an airport asks you to take their luggage on board as part of your luggage allowance. Needless to say, smuggling dope across borders is a crazy idea. Have you ever seen the inside of a Colombian prison?

### Burundanga

This is another security risk. Burundanga is a drug obtained from a species of tree widespread in Colombia and is used by thieves to render a victim unconscious. It can be put into sweets, cigarettes, chewing gum, spirits, beer – virtually any kind of food or drink – and it doesn't have any noticeable taste or odour.

The main effect after a 'normal' dose is the loss of will, even though you remain conscious. The thief can then ask you to hand over your valuables and you will obey without resistance. Cases of rape under the effect of burundanga are known. Other effects are loss of memory and sleepiness, which can last from a few hours to several days. An overdose can be fatal.

Burundanga is not only used to trick foreign tourists – many Colombians have been on the receiving end as well, losing their cars, contents of their homes, and sometimes their life. Think twice before accepting a cigarette from a stranger or a drink from a new 'friend'.

### Guerrillas & Paramilitaries

There's intense guerrilla and paramilitary activity in many regions, consequently the area of reasonably safe travel is limited. As a general rule, avoid any off-the-beaten-track travel. It's best to stick to main routes

### Some Sombre Statistics

Dry as they are, statistics are reputedly the most precise way of reflecting facts. In Colombia's case, some of the figures may look pretty scary. Perhaps they don't fit well on the pages of a tourist guidebook, but we think you should know both sides of the coin, just to have a more balanced and objective image of the country.

The nearly 40-year-long armed conflict has claimed 250,000 Colombian lives and inflicted enormous material losses. In 2002 alone, the civil war cost the state's coffers an estimated US\$4.7 billion (5.8% of the country's GDP) which included losses to industry, a drop in foreign investment, and damage to the oil industry's infrastructure.

In 2001, about 3700 civilians lost their lives as a result of the armed conflict between various internal forces, including guerrillas, paramilitaries, drug lords and the army. About 190,000 peasants were internally displaced that year. In other words, every hour there were 42 displaced persons in Colombia. Some 1.1 million rural Colombians were internally displaced by the country's violence during the four-year presidency of Andrés Pastrana (August 1998 to August 2002).

It's estimated that there are about one million illegal guns in Bogotá, or one gun per seven persons (men, women and children included). Only 4% of all arms in Bogotá are registered and the picture is similar in other large cities. About 80% of violent deaths in Colombia are caused by guns.

There were 27,840 murders in Colombia in 2001, or three murders per hour. About 160 trade unionists and 10 journalists were murdered that year, and 260 people are considered missing.

Colombia bears an infamous world record number for kidnapping – more than 3000 reported cases a year. During Pastrana's presidency, 12,948 persons (including 1162 children) were taken hostage, principally for ransom. However, this is not the complete picture as many kidnappings (an estimated 5000) go unreported and are dealt with privately. Since 1996, more than 270 foreigners of 49 nationalities have been kidnapped. The vast majority of kidnappings is attributed to guerrilla groups, principally the FARC.

and travel during daytime only. Yet, even main routes can be risky. Among these, the Popayán–Pasto road has possibly the worst reputation, but there also have been many assaults on buses and cars on the Bogotá–Medellín–Cartagena and the Bogotá–Santa Marta roads, to name just a few.

Many regions may be unsafe for travel. The entire area east of the Andes (except Leticia and its environs) should be avoided as it's the guerrilla heartland. Parts of Cundinamarca, eastern Antioquia, Chocó, Córdoba, Magdalena, Bolívar, La Guajira, Cesar, southern Tolima, Valle del Cauca, Huila, Cauca and Nariño are considered high-risk areas due to the presence of guerrillas and paramilitaries.

Kidnapping for ransom has been part of guerrilla activity for quite a while and is on the increase. The main targets are well-off locals and foreign executives and the ransoms go up to US$1 million or more. In Colombia in 2001, about 3100 people, including some foreigners, were kidnapped (a world record).

Guerrillas don't specifically target tourists, but cases have been reported. Statistically, backpackers travelling by bus face a low risk, at least less than VIPs moving around in 4WD Toyotas.

More frequent than kidnapping is ambushing cars and buses then robbing the passengers. These normally occur at night at roadblocks and the perpetrators are mostly common criminals and guerrillas.

There's no need to be paranoid, but you should be aware of the potential risk, and avoid the regions that are notorious for guerrilla activity. Air travel may be worth considering to skip over some unsafe regions, even though it may eat a bit into your pocket.

Monitor current guerrilla movements. It's not that easy because things change rapidly and unexpectedly, but the regional press and TV news can be useful. Possibly better and more specific is the advice of locals who best know what's going on in their region. Also, inquire at regional tourist offices, travel agents and bus terminals. Ask other travellers along the way and check online resources.

## BUSINESS HOURS

The office working day is, theoretically at least, eight hours long, usually from 8am to noon and 2pm to 6pm weekdays, but in practice offices tend to open later and close earlier. Many offices in Bogotá have adopted the so-called *jornada continua*, a working day without a lunch break, which finishes two hours earlier. However, it's nearly impossible to arrange anything between noon and 2pm, as most of the staff are off for their lunch anyway. Most tourist offices are closed on Saturday and Sunday, and travel agencies usually only work on Saturday until noon.

As a rough guide only, the usual shopping hours are from 9am to 6pm or 7pm Monday to Saturday with some shops closing for lunch. Large stores and supermarkets usually stay open until 8pm or 9pm or even longer, and some also open on Sunday. Shopping hours vary considerably from shop to shop and from city to countryside. In remote places, opening hours are shorter and are often taken less seriously.

Most of the better restaurants in larger cities, particularly in Bogotá, tend to stay open until 10pm or longer, whereas restaurants in smaller towns often close by 9pm or earlier. Many restaurants don't open at all on Sunday.

The opening hours of museums and other tourist sights vary greatly. Most museums are closed on Monday, but are open on Sunday. The opening hours of churches are even more difficult to pin down. Some are open all day, others for only certain hours, while the rest remain locked except during mass, which in some villages may be only on Sunday morning.

## PUBLIC HOLIDAYS

The following days are observed as public holidays in Colombia.

**Año Nuevo** (New Year's Day) 1 January
**Los Reyes Magos** (Epiphany) 6 January*
**San José** (St Joseph) 19 March*
**Jueves Santo** (Maundy Thursday) & **Viernes Santo** (Good Friday) March/April (Easter)
**Día del Trabajo** (Labour Day) 1 May
**La Ascensión del Señor** (Ascension) May*
**Corpus Cristi** (Corpus Christi) May/June*
**Sagrado Corazón de Jesús** (Sacred Heart) June*
**San Pedro y San Pablo** (St Peter and St Paul) 29 June*
**Día de la Independencia** (Independence Day) 20 July
**Batalla de Boyacá** (Battle of Boyacá) 7 August
**La Asunción de Nuestra Señora** (Assumption) 15 August*

**Día de la Raza** (Discovery of America) 12 October*
**Todos los Santos** (All Saints' Day) 1 November*
**Independencia de Cartagena** (Independence of Cartagena) 11 November*
**Inmaculada Concepción** (Immaculate Conception) 8 December
**Navidad** (Christmas Day) 25 December

When the dates marked with an asterisk do not fall on a Monday, the holiday is moved to the following Monday to make a three-day long weekend, referred to as the *puente*.

## SPECIAL EVENTS

The Colombian calendar is full of festivals, carnivals, fairs and beauty pageants. Colombians love fiestas and they organise them whenever they can or whenever they feel like it. There are some 200 festivals and events annually, ranging from small one-day local affairs to international festivals lasting several days. This means that almost every day there is a fiesta going on somewhere in Colombia.

Given the strong Catholic character of Colombia, many feasts and celebrations follow the Church calendar. Accordingly, Christmas, Easter and Corpus Christi are often solemnly celebrated, particularly in more traditional rural communities. The religious calendar is dotted with saints' days, and every village and town has its own patron saint – you can take it for granted that the locals will be holding a celebratory feast on that day. In many cases, solemn religious ceremonies are accompanied by popular fiestas that may include beauty pageants and bullfights. Some events are celebrated throughout the country, but most are local, confined to a particular region or town.

The following list is a brief selection of the biggest events, where they are held and in which month. More information on these and other fiestas can be found in the appropriate sections.

**Carnaval de Blancos y Negros** Pasto; January
**Feria de Manizales** Manizales; January
**Carnaval de Barranquilla** Barranquilla; February or March
**Festival Internacional de Cine** Cartagena; March or April
**Semana Santa (Holy Week)** climaxes on Good Friday; the most prominent celebrations are in Popayán and Mompós; March or April
**Festival Iberoamericano de Teatro** Bogotá; biennially in March or April

**Feria de las Flores** Medellín; August
**Festival Latinoamericano de Teatro** Manizales; September
**Reinado Nacional de Belleza** Cartagena; November
**Feria de Cali** Cali; December

## ACTIVITIES

The national parks in Colombia offer walks ranging from easy, well-signposted trails to jungle paths where you may need a machete. Many parks are notorious for a guerrilla presence and may be unsafe for visitors, but those included in this book are generally OK for hiking. If you arrive in Bogotá, contact hiking associations, which organise weekend walks in Bogotá's environs (see Organised Tours in the later Bogotá chapter).

Colombia's coral reefs provide good conditions for snorkelling and scuba diving. The main dive centres are San Andrés, Providencia, Santa Marta, Taganga and Cartagena, each of which has several diving schools offering courses and other diving services. Colombia is considered one of the world's cheapest countries for diving.

Colombia has also developed greatly as a centre of paragliding. The main hub is Medellín, but there are also gliding schools in Bogotá, Cali and elsewhere. Paragliding in Colombia is reasonably cheap.

White-water rafting is pretty new in Colombia, but is developing fast with its major base in San Gil. Like most other outdoor activities in Colombia, rafting is cheap.

Cycling is one of Colombia's favourite spectator sports, yet only in recent years have bicycle-rental agencies begun to appear. You can go cycling in San Andrés, Providencia, and Villa de Leyva among other places.

Horse riding can be practised in many places including Villa de Leyva, San Agustín, Valle de Cocora, San Gil and Providencia.

Other possible activities include mountaineering, rock climbing, windsurfing, canoeing, fishing, caving and even bathing in a mud volcano (see Around Cartagena in the later Caribbean Coast chapter).

## LANGUAGE COURSES

Spanish language courses are run by universities and language schools in some large cities, of which Bogotá has the widest choice. Most travellers, however, opt for informal arrangements with the local tutors.

Popular travellers hotels (in Bogotá, Medellín, Cali and Cartagena) are the best places to ask about independent teachers.

## ACCOMMODATION

There is a constellation of places to stay in Colombia, from large cities to the smallest villages. There are actually so many places that the problem is not finding a hotel, but choosing which one to stay in. The vast majority are straightforward Colombian hotels where you are unlikely to meet foreigners, but some budget traveller haunts have appeared over the past decade. You'll find them in most large cities (Bogotá, Medellín, Cali and Cartagena) and popular tourist destinations.

Accommodation listed in this book is ordered according to price, beginning with the cheapest. Budget travellers should read these sections from the beginning; more affluent visitors would be wise to leapfrog to the closing paragraphs.

Where sections are broken down into price categories, budget accommodation includes anything costing less than about US$15 per double room, the mid-range bracket covers hotels rated from approximately US$15 to US$30 per double, and anything over US$30 a double is top-end.

### Camping

Camping is not popular in Colombia, and there are only a handful of genuine camp sites in the country. Unofficial camping is theoretically possible almost anywhere outside the urban centres, but given the country's dangers you should be very careful. If you intend to camp, get permission to pitch your tent next to a peasant's house or in the grounds of a holiday centre so that you have some protection.

### Youth Hostels

Colombia is a member of the International Youth Hostel Federation, but there's only one youth hostel in the country, in Bogotá.

### Hotels

Accommodation appears under a variety of names including *hotel*, *residencias*, *hospedaje*, *pensión*, *hostería*, *hospedería* and *posada*. Residencias and hospedaje are the most common names for budget places. A hotel generally suggests a place of a higher standard, or at least a higher price, though the distinction is often academic.

**Budget** This type of accommodation is usually clustered around the market, bus terminal and in the back streets of the city centre. On the whole, residencias and hospedajes are unremarkable places without much style or atmosphere, but there are some pleasant exceptions.

Many cheapies have a private bathroom (in this book simply called 'bath'), which includes a toilet and shower. The bathroom is sometimes separated from the room by only a partition (eg, a section of wall which doesn't even reach the ceiling), and there is hardly ever a door between the two areas. Note that cheap hotel plumbing can't cope with toilet paper, so throw it in the wastebasket which is normally provided.

In hot places (ie, the lowland areas), a ceiling fan or table fan is often provided. On the other hand, at altitudes above 2500m where nights can be chilly, hotels may offer hot water in baths. By and large, residencias (even the cheapest) provide a sheet and some sort of cover (another sheet or blankets, depending on the temperature). Most will also give you a towel, a small piece of soap and a roll of toilet paper.

The cheapies cost US$3 to US$8 a single, US$5 to US$15 a double. Payment is almost exclusively upfront and by cash. Hardly any budget hotel will accept a credit card.

Many budget hotels have *matrimonios*, rooms with a wide double bed intended for couples. A matrimonio is usually cheaper than a double and can be only slightly more expensive than a single (or even the same price). Travelling as a couple considerably reduces the cost of accommodation.

Always have a look at the room before booking in and paying. When inspecting the room, make sure the toilet flushes and the water runs in the shower. Check that the fan works and that the lock on the door is sufficiently secure. In hotels in the highlands pay attention to how many blankets you are given and check the hot water if the hotel claims to have it. If you're not satisfied with the room you're shown, ask to see another.

Colombians enjoy TV, so many budget hotels provide TV sets in rooms. Since the insulation between the rooms is often flimsy, TV noise can be a nightmare. If there are no

TV sets in rooms, you can be sure that there's one around the reception area, and it's usually kept at top volume until late at night. Try to take a room as far from the TV set as possible.

By and large, hotels are reasonably safe places, but precautions and common sense are always advisable. Most budget places lock their doors at night, and some even keep them locked during the day, opening them only for guests. The biggest danger of being ripped-off is most likely to come from other guests (and occasionally from staff). The thieves' task is made easier by partial hardboard partitions between rooms and flimsy catches and easily picked padlocks on doors. Hotels provide padlocks, but it may be better to use your own combination lock (or padlock) instead. As a rule, bigger hotels are less safe than smaller ones because the atmosphere is more impersonal and a thief won't stand out in a crowd.

Some of the budget hotels offer a deposit facility which practically means that the management will guard your gear in their own room as there are no other safe places. This reduces the risk, but doesn't eliminate it completely. In most cheapies, the staff don't give any receipts for receiving your valuables, and if you insist on one they may simply refuse to guard them. Decide for yourself if it's safe.

**Mid-Range & Top-End**  Mid-range hotels are usually in the city centre, and you can expect to find one or two right on Plaza Bolívar or in its immediate vicinity. They provide more facilities than the cheapies, but often lack character. They will almost always have private baths and fan, sometimes even air-conditioning (but it can be noisy). Many of these hotels are reasonably priced for what they offer, but some can be outrageously overpriced. It's a good idea to inspect the room in these hotels before you commit yourself. Some of the mid-range hotels can be great value offering a spacious, comfortable double room in the heart of the city for US$25 to US$30.

Top-end hotels usually offer more facilities and better standards than the mid-range establishments, including silent, central air-conditioning and a reception desk open round the clock with proper facilities to safeguard guests' valuables. There are usu-ally some top-class hotels in the centre, but most prefer quieter and greener locations in upmarket residential districts, sometimes far from the centre. Prices vary greatly and don't always reflect quality. Most top-end hotels will accept payment by credit card. Some of these hotels are world-class and cheaper than in the West. The best choice of top-end hotels is in Bogotá and Cartagena.

**Love Hotels**  These places are designed for couples with an urgent need for privacy and togetherness. They have rooms with a double bed and a private bath, which are rented by the hour. Many budget (and some mid-range) hotels double as love hotels, and it's often impossible to recognise them and to avoid staying in one from time to time. This shouldn't be a major problem, though, as love hotels are probably safer than some other places (the guests have more on their minds than stealing your belongings). The staff normally don't admit prostitutes and keep the sex section separate from other hotel rooms so the sound of excited couples won't stop you sleeping at night. There are also upmarket love hotels, but these are well outside central areas, usually tucked away on the city outskirts.

## FOOD

Colombia has countless places to eat, ranging from street stalls to excellent, well-appointed restaurants. Even the smallest village will have a place to eat – a restaurant, the market or, at the very least, a private house which serves meals.

Colombian cuisine is varied and regional. The most typical snacks and dishes, collectively referred to as *comida criolla*, include *ajiaco, bandeja paisa, cabro, chocolate santafereño, cuchuco, cuy, hormiga culona, lechona, mondongo, mute, puchero, sancocho, sobrebarriga* and *tamales*. See the Language chapter at the back of this book for details.

Variety does not normally apply to the basic *comida corriente* (set meal), which is the principal diet of the majority of Colombians eating out. It is a two-course meal consisting of *sopa* (soup) and *bandeja* or *seco* (main course), and usually includes a *sobremesa* (a bottled fizzy drink or juice). The main course contains a small piece of meat, chicken or fish (look closely, it can be very small!) served with rice, pasta, red beans, lentils or vegetables, sometimes with fried plantains and a small salad. The drink may or may not be included in the meal price.

At lunch time (noon to 2pm), the meal is called *almuerzo*; at dinner time (after 6pm), it becomes *comida*, but it is in fact identical to lunch. Despite some local additions, it's much the same throughout the country.

The almuerzos and comidas are the staple, sometimes the only, offering in countless budget restaurants. Some serve them continuously from noon until they close at night, but most only serve them during lunch time and, less often, at dinner time. The almuerzo/comida corriente is the cheapest way to fill up, costing between US$1.50 and US$3 – roughly half the price of an average à la carte dish. The set meals also appear on the menus of higher-class establishments, where they are usually more diversified and tastier, and you can expect a genuine dessert rather than a drink only. They may be great value at US$3 to US$5.

Budget restaurants supplement the comida with a short list of popular dishes, which almost always includes *carne asada* (roasted or grilled beef) and *arroz con pollo* (rice with chicken).

If you're on a tight budget, be prepared to stick to the comida corriente in budget restaurants. The way to diversify and enrich your diet is to eat at street stalls and markets. Food stalls are a common part of the urban landscape and every town has a market with stalls serving food, which is usually fresh, tasty and cooked in front of you.

Roasted or barbecued chicken restaurants (there are plenty of them) are an alternative to the comida. Half a chicken with potatoes will cost around US$3 to US$4.

Western food is readily available, either in fast-food outlets (including chains such as McDonald's and Pizza Hut) or in upmarket restaurants. Over the last decade there has been a trend toward vegetarian food, and most major cities have budget vegetarian restaurants.

Colombia has an amazing variety of fruits, some of which are endemic to the country. You should try *guanábana, lulo, curuba, zapote, mamoncillo, uchuva, feijoa, granadilla, maracuyá, tomate de árbol, borojó, mamey* and *tamarindo*, to name just a few. Refer to the Language chapter for descriptions.

## DRINKS
## Nonalcoholic Drinks
Coffee is Colombia's number-one drink – *tinto* (a small cup of black coffee) is served everywhere. Its quality, however, varies from place to place, and in some cafés it's hard to believe how such muck can be made from excellent Colombian beans. Other coffee drinks are *perico* or *pintado*, a small milk coffee, and *café con leche*, which is larger and contains more milk.

Tea is of poor quality and not very popular. On the other hand, the *aromáticas* – herbal teas made with various plants like *cidrón* (citrus leaves), *yerbabuena* (mint) and *manzanilla* (camomile) – are cheap and good. *Agua de panela* (unrefined sugar melted in hot water) is tasty with lemon.

*Gaseosas* (fizzy soft drinks) are cheap and available everywhere. Colombia is one of the world's largest consumers of soft drinks. Apart from locally produced well-known Western drinks, such as Coca-Cola, Pepsi, Sprite etc, there is a variety of Colombian drinks such as Colombiana, Uva (grape) and Manzana (apple).

## Alcoholic Drinks
Beer is popular, cheap and generally not bad. There are many local brands, including Águila, Poker, Bavaria and Club-Colombia. A bottle of beer (a third of a litre) costs about US$0.30 to US$0.40 in shops, but can easily reach US$3 in trendy nightclubs.

Colombian wine is poor, not popular and best avoided. There are some imported Chilean and Argentinian wines, which are of acceptable quality. European wines are expensive.

*Aguardiente* is the most popular spirit and is consumed in large quantities mostly by the male half of the population. It's a local alcohol flavoured with anise, and is produced by several companies throughout the country under their own brand names: Cristal and Néctar are the most popular in the Bogotá region, but Aguardiente Medellín is considered to be the best. A more refined version of aguardiente is the *mistela*, a home-made sweet liquor, produced by preserving fruit or herbs in aguardiente syrup.

*Ron* (rum) is another popular spirit, particularly on the Caribbean Coast and in Antioquia. Recommended dark rums are Ron Viejo de Caldas and Ron Medellín; the best white rums are Ron Tres Esquinas and Ron Blanco.

In some regions, mostly in rural areas, you will find *chicha* and *guarapo*. They are home-made alcoholic beverages obtained by the fermentation of fruit or maize in sugar or panela water. Most are low in alcohol, but some varieties can lay you out pretty quickly.

## ENTERTAINMENT
### Cinema
Cinema is popular in Colombia; virtually every town has a cinema and Bogotá has more than 50. Most movies are regular Hollywood fare, which arrive in Colombia a month or two after their US release. If you need something more mentally stimulating, try the *cinematecas* (arthouse cinemas), which screen quality movies. They exist in most major cities, and are most numerous in Bogotá.

Most movies are screened in their original language with Spanish subtitles. A cinema ticket costs between US$2 and US$3. Cinemas in the lowlands are air-conditioned and may sometimes be pretty cool; come prepared.

### Theatre
Most of Colombia's theatre activity is confined to the three largest cities, Bogotá, Medellín and Cali. Other cities have theatres but the choice, and usually the quality of the productions, may not be impressive. Much the same can be said about other areas of artistic expression, such as ballet, opera and classical music.

### Nightlife
Nightlife in Colombia is rich, colourful and varied. By and large, the bigger the city the wider the choice, with Bogotá, Cali and Medellín heading the league. Most cities have the so-called Zona Rosa, or the area of night-time entertainment, packed with nightclubs, discos and bars.

Colombians love to dance and are good dancers, and there are plenty of discos everywhere. The usual fare of many places is a mixed bag of Western rock, reggae, salsa and merengue (which they call 'crossover'), but some discos focus on more specific rhythms. Of these, *salsotecas*, which play salsa and Cuban *son*, are the most numerous, but there are also venues playing hip-hop, techno, rap, heavy metal etc. Some places have live music on weekends.

Some discos open most of the week (usually except Sunday and Monday, which are the slowest days), while others operate Thursday to Saturday only. Discos open their doors around 9pm, but the action doesn't usually begin before 11pm. There may be an entry fee on weekends, but rarely on other days of the week. Music is usually played at a volume that limits any conversation significantly or prevents it entirely.

There are plenty of bars and pubs, although they may not remind you of classic English or Irish pubs. They open late into the night and have a variety of drinks. Bottles are emptied quickly, so if you keep up with your Colombian friends, you may have some problems returning safely to your hotel.

## SPECTATOR SPORTS
Soccer and cycling are the most popular spectator sports. Colombia regularly takes part in international events in these two fields, such as the World Cup and the Tour de France, and has recorded some successes. The national soccer league has matches most of the year.

### Tejo – Colombia's Traditional Game

The *tejo* is a popular local game, which has been played for centuries in towns, villages and the countryside. Its origins date back to pre-Hispanic times, when it was played by the indigenous people and called *turmequé* in the Chibcha language. It's still referred to as turmequé in some regions, particularly in Boyacá.

The players throw metal disks (called *tejos*) towards a large wooden tray filled with soft earth, sand or clay, and traditionally placed 18m away. In the middle of the tray is a *bocin* (metal bowl), with a small envelope of *mecha* (gunpowder) placed inside. The aim is to throw the tejo in such a way that it hits the mecha and makes it explode. A tejo session may last for hours and is invariably accompanied by huge amounts of beer.

Colombians are passionate about *corrida* (bullfighting), which was introduced by the Spaniards. Most cities and towns have *plaza de toros* (bullrings). The bullfighting season usually peaks in January, when top-ranking matadors are invited from Spain.

Cockfighting is another cruel, thrilling 'sport'. It's popular in Colombia and much of South America. *Galleras* (cockfight rings) can be found in most cities.

## SHOPPING

Colombia is famous for its emeralds, but if you aren't knowledgeable about these gemstones you are unlikely to strike a good deal. See the boxed text 'The Bewitching Green Gem' in the earlier Facts about Colombia chapter, and Shopping in the later Bogotá chapter.

Colombian handicrafts vary region by region. Some areas and towns are famous for particular local crafts. Boyacá is the largest handicraft manufacturer, producing excellent handwoven items, basketry and pottery. The basketwork of the Pacific Coast is also interesting; the best selection is in Cali. Pasto is noted for decorative items covered with the *barniz de Pasto*, a kind of vegetable resin. Ceramic miniatures of *chivas* (traditional buses) have become a popular souvenir, and can be found in every craft shop.

Hammocks are another tempting buy and come in plenty of regional variations, from the simple, practical hammocks made in Los Llanos to the elaborate *chinchorros* of the Guajiro Indians. Another well-known Indian product is the *mola* (rectangular cloth with coloured designs) made by the Cuna Indians, sold in plenty of craft shops.

*Ruanas* (Colombian woollen ponchos) are found in the colder parts of the Andean zone, where the climate justifies it. In many villages they are still made by hand with simple patterns and natural colours. Bogotá and Villa de Leyva are good places to buy them.

The best and most fashionable *mochilas* (a kind of woven handbag) are those of the Arhuaco Indians from the Sierra Nevada de Santa Marta. They are not cheap, but are beautiful and usually of good quality.

Colombian leather goods are relatively cheap and are among the best in South America. There are leather bags and suitcases of every shape, size and style. Bogotá has the widest choice, but you can find a good selection in other cities. Leather boots are an attractive purchase.

Colombia publishes an assortment of both well-edited and illustrated coffee-table books about the country's flora and fauna, art and architecture. The best choice is in bookshops of large cities. If you're interested in local music, there are lots of CDs (US$10 to US$15). Bogotá has the widest selection.

# Getting There & Away

## AIR

Colombia is certainly not the world's major tourist destination, but sitting at the northern edge of South America, it has relatively cheap air links with both Europe and North America.

### Airports & Airlines

Bogotá is Colombia's major international air hub, and most visitors arrive at Bogotá's El Dorado airport. Other cities servicing international flights include Cartagena, Barranquilla, San Andrés, Medellín and Cali. Charter flights bringing international package tourists fly into Cartagena.

The country is serviced by a number of major intercontinental airlines including British Airways, Air France, American Airlines and Iberia. As for the Colombian carriers, Avianca is the country's flagship, with flights to Europe (Madrid), North America (New York, Los Angeles, Miami and Mexico City), Central America (San José and Panama City) and South America (Caracas, Quito, Guayaquil, Lima, Santiago, Buenos Aires, São Paulo and Rio de Janeiro). A few other Colombian carriers also operate international flights within the Americas.

### Onward Ticket Requirements

Colombia requires, technically at least, that visitors have an onward ticket before they're allowed into the country. This is quite strictly enforced by airlines and travel agents, and probably none of them will sell you a one-way ticket unless you already have an onward ticket. Upon arrival in Colombia, however, hardly any immigration official will ask you to present your onward ticket.

### Travellers with Special Needs

If you have special needs of any sort – you're vegetarian, travelling in a wheelchair, taking a baby or terrified of flying – you should let the airline know as soon as possible so that it can make appropriate arrangements. You should remind it of your needs when you reconfirm your booking and again when you check in at the airport. It may be worth ringing around the airlines before you make your booking to find out how they can handle your particular requirements.

Children under two travel for 10% of the standard fare (or free on some airlines), as long as they don't occupy a seat. They don't get a baggage allowance either. Skycots should be provided by the airline if requested. Children between two and 12 can usually occupy a seat for half to two-thirds of the full fare, and do get a baggage allowance.

### Departure Tax

The airport tax on international flights out of Colombia is US$28 if you have stayed in the country up to 60 days, and US$45 if you have stayed longer. The tax is payable either in US dollars or pesos at the exchange rate of the day, but can't be paid by credit card.

### The USA

Two of the most reputable discount travel agencies in the USA are STA Travel and Council Travel. Although they both specialise in student travel, they may offer discount tickets to nonstudents of all ages. Their national head offices are:

Council Travel (☎ 1800-226 8624, 212-822 2700, fax 212-822 2719; W www.counciltravel .com) 205 East 42nd St, New York, NY 10017

**STA Travel** (☎ 1800-777 0112, 213-937 8722, fax 213-937 2739; W www.sta-travel.com) 5900 Wiltshire Boulevard, Los Angeles, CA 90036

Both Council Travel and STA have offices in Boston, Chicago, Los Angeles, Miami, Philadelphia, New York, San Diego, San Francisco and other cities. Check their websites for addresses. For more discount travel agencies, check the Sunday travel sections in newspapers such as the *Los Angeles Times, San Francisco Examiner, Boston Globe, Chicago Tribune* and *New York Times*.

The major US gateway for Colombia is Miami, from where several carriers, including American Airlines, Avianca and Aces, fly to Bogotá. A 90-day Apex return ticket normally costs about US$400 to US$500 depending on the season.

Another important gateway to Colombia is New York, from where American Airlines and Avianca have flights to Bogotá. A 30-day Apex return ticket is around US$550 to US$650 depending on the season.

On the West Coast, the major departure point is Los Angeles, but flights to Bogotá can be expensive. The cheapest 60-day return fares will be probably somewhere between US$700 and US$800.

You can also fly from the USA to Colombia via Central America or Venezuela, and these indirect routes may work out cheaper than direct USA–Colombia flights. For example, the Panamanian carrier Copa may have competitive air fares for its flights from Miami to Colombia via Panama City. Similarly, Venezuelan carriers (Aeropostal, Servivensa) may offer good fares for their Miami–Caracas–Bogotá route. Your travel agent should know the best deals.

## Canada

There are no direct scheduled flights from Canada to Colombia. Anyone flying from Canada will have to fly via the usual US transit points such as Los Angeles or Miami. Another possibility is to fly via Central America, but flights to Central America are only slightly less expensive than flights to Colombia, so it will not be any cheaper going this way.

The cheapest flights from Canada to Colombia are from Toronto or Montreal via Miami. Prices vary according to the length of your stay and the season – expect return tickets from Toronto to cost somewhere

between C$1100 and C$1400. From Vancouver on Canada's west coast it is usually cheaper to fly to Toronto or Montreal, and then go on via Miami, rather than flying via Los Angeles. The following agencies may offer good air-fare deals:

**Flight Centre** (☎ 604-739 9539) 3030 Granville St, Vancouver, BC V6H 3J8
**Nouvelles Frontières** (☎ 514-526 8444) 1001 Sherbrook East, Suite 720, Montreal PQ H2L 1L3
**Travel CUTS** (☎ 888-838 2887, 416-979 2406) 187 College St, Toronto, Ontario M5T 1P7

Scan budget travel ads in weekend editions of the *Toronto Globe & Mail, Toronto Star, Montreal Gazette* and the *Vancouver Sun*.

## Europe

A number of airlines, including British Airways, Air France and Iberia, link Bogotá with European cities. Colombia is one of the cheapest South American destinations to reach from Europe, and many travel agents will offer flights to Bogotá.

London, where bucket shops are by the dozen, usually has the cheapest fares to Bogotá. Other major cities which have long-standing ticket-discounting traditions include Amsterdam, Brussels, Frankfurt and Paris. Elsewhere, special deals come and go, but there is usually less to choose from and air fares are generally higher.

**The UK**  London is Britain's major hub for discounted tickets. You'll find plenty of deals listed in the travel sections of weekend editions of London newspapers. Advertisements for many travel agents appear in the travel pages of the weekend broadsheets, such as the *Independent* on Saturday and the *Sunday Times*. Look out for free magazines, such as *TNT*, which are widely available in London.

Following is a list of recommended agencies selling discounted tickets to South America:

**Flynow.com** (☎ 020-7835 2000; W www.gofly .com) 125A Gloucester Rd, London SW7 4SF
**Journey Latin America** (JLA; ☎ 020-8747 3108, fax 8742 1312; W www.journeylatinamerica .co.uk) 12–13 Heathfield Terrace, Chiswick, London W4 4JE
**Scott Dunn Latin America** (☎ 020-8767 8989, fax 8767 2026) Fovant Mews, 12 Noya Rd, London SW17 7PH

**South American Experience** (☎ 020-7976 5511, fax 7976 6908) 47 Causton St, Pimlico, London SW1P 4AT

**STA Travel** (Telesales Europe ☎ 020-7361 6161, Telesales Worldwide ☎ 0207-7361 6262, Head Office ☎ 0207-7361 6100; W www.statravel .co.uk)

**Trailfinders** (☎ 020-7938 3366) 42-48 Earls Court Rd, London W8 6FT (☎ 020-7938 3939) 194 Kensington High St, London W8 7RG

Apart from selling tickets, some of these travel agencies offer other services. JLA, consistently recommended by travellers, will arrange itineraries for both independent and escorted travel. Ask for its helpful free magazine *Papagaio*. The equally reputable Trailfinders publishes a free quarterly magazine, *Trailfinder*, packed with useful information on tickets, vaccinations, visas etc.

Prices for discounted flights from London to Bogotá start at around UK£250 one way and UK£400 return. Bargain hunters may find lower prices, but make sure you use a travel agent affiliated with the ABTA (Association of British Travel Agents). If you have bought your ticket from an ABTA-registered agent who then goes out of business, ABTA will guarantee a refund or an alternative. Unregistered bucket shops are sometimes cheaper, but can be riskier.

**France** The Paris–Bogotá route is serviced directly by Air France, but travel agents may offer cheaper indirect routes on board other carriers (eg, via Madrid with Iberia). Following is a list of selected travel agencies selling discounted tickets in Paris. Many have branch offices in other major French cities.

**Forum Voyages** (☎ 01 55 26 71 60, fax 01 55 26 71 74) 114 Rue de Flandres, 75019 Paris

**FUAJ** (Fédération Unie des Auberges de Jeunesse; ☎ 01 48 04 70 30, fax 01 44 89 87 10; W www.fuaj.org) 9 Rue Brantôme, 75003 Paris

**Usit Connect Voyages** (☎ 01 42 44 14 00, fax 01 42 44 14 01; W www.usitconnect.fr) 14 Rue Vivienne, 75002 Paris

**Voyageurs en Amérique du Sud** (☎ 01 42 86 17 70, fax 01 42 86 17 92; W www.vdm.com) 55 Rue Sainte-Anne, 75002 Paris

The cheapest Paris–Bogotá return tickets can be bought for about 5000FF. Some agencies offer cheaper fares for students.

## Australia & New Zealand

To start with, travel between Australasia and Colombia is arduously long – at least 20 hours in the air alone. Add to this the need for several stopovers as there are no direct flights. Secondly, there are a number of alternative routes, none of which is clearly better or cheaper than the others. Lastly, fares are high and there is not much in the way of budget tickets in Australia or New Zealand.

In theory, there are four air routes to Colombia. Many travellers first think about the route through Los Angeles as the seemingly best option, but getting from there to Colombia is expensive (see The USA earlier in this chapter). Even a couple of days in the USA would eat up all the savings in air fares, so it's only good value if you want to visit the USA anyway or if you go through without stopping. A return ticket is likely to cost somewhere between A$2500 and A$3000, depending on the season, length of stay etc.

The route through Europe is the longest, but not as absurd as it may sound. Given the discounted air fares to various European cities, including London and Paris, and interesting fares on to Bogotá, the total fare may be comparable or even lower than travelling via Los Angeles.

The shortest route between Australasia and South America goes over the South Pole. Aerolíneas Argentinas flies three times a week between Auckland and Buenos Aires, and has arrangements with other carriers which cover the Auckland–Australia leg. It may be an interesting proposition if you plan on beginning your overland trip from Argentina, but note that Colombia is at the opposite end of the continent. Aerolíneas Argentinas can fly you to Bogotá, but the total fare will be pretty high; expect to pay between A$2500 and A$3000 for the Sydney–Bogotá return flight, depending on the length of stay and the season. The Auckland–Bogotá fare will be only marginally lower.

Finally, you can fly right across the southern Pacific to Santiago de Chile. Lan Chile flies from Sydney via Auckland to Santiago, and has flights on to Bogotá. The Sydney–Bogotá return fares of Lan Chile cost much the same as those of Aerolíneas Argentinas.

Unless you are really interested in any of the four above-mentioned routes, it's worth thinking about a RTW ticket. RTW tickets with various stopovers can still be found for A$2200, but they tend to include only northern hemisphere stopovers; RTWs which include Latin America or the South Pacific will cost at least an additional A$1000. Alternatively, look for a cheap northern hemisphere RTW which includes Miami, then make a side trip to Colombia.

The Saturday editions of major newspapers, the *Sydney Morning Herald* and the *Age*, carry travel sections which have discount air fare ads, but very few of them include South American destinations. It may be worth getting a copy of some of the Spanish-language newspapers published in Australia such as *El Español* or *Extra Informativo*, which list travel agents specialising in South America.

**STA Travel** (☎ *131 776 Australia-wide;* Ⓦ *www.statravel.com.au)* has offices around Australia – call or visit its website for the location of your nearest branch. In New Zealand, **STA Travel** (☎ *09-309 0458; 10 High St, Auckland)* has branches in Auckland, Christchurch, Dunedin, Hamilton, Palmerston North and Wellington.

**Flight Centre** (☎ *131 600 Australia-wide;* Ⓦ *www.flightcentre.com.au; 82 Elizabeth St, Sydney)* has dozens of offices throughout Australia. In New Zealand, **Flight Centre** (☎ *09-309 6171; National Bank Towers, Queen St at Darby St, Auckland)* has many branches throughout the country.

### Central America
Colombia has regular flight connections with most Central American capitals. Sample fares include: Guatemala City–Bogotá US$356, San José–Bogotá US$312 (US$377 60-day return) and Panama City–Bogotá US$151 (US$274 60-day return).

It may work out cheaper to go via the Colombian island of San Andrés and then get a domestic flight to the Colombian mainland. See the later San Andrés & Providencia chapter for details. Also, check out the Colombian airline West Caribbean Airways, which may have interesting fares. As we went to press it was offering a San José–Medellín service for US$278 return, and a Panama City–Medellín service for US$210 return.

### Venezuela
There are several flights daily between Caracas and Bogotá, with Avianca, Aeropostal and Servivensa. The regular one-way fare is US$258; a discount 30-/60-day return ticket costs US$219/299. There may be some lower promotional fares (eg, Aeropostal was offering a US$150 return) but they come and go.

### Ecuador
There are a dozen flights a week between Quito and Bogotá (US$162 one way, US$229 for a 30-day return). Tame (an Ecuadorian carrier) has flights between Cali and Tulcán in Ecuador (US$84 one way) and between Cali and Quito (US$118 one way).

### Peru & Brazil
Direct flights between these countries and Colombia are expensive. It will be cheaper to fly through Leticia in the Colombian Amazon. See Leticia in the later Amazon Basin chapter for details.

### LAND
Colombia borders Panama, Venezuela, Brazil, Peru and Ecuador, but has road connections with Venezuela and Ecuador only. These are the easiest and the most popular border crossings.

### Venezuela
There are four border crossings between Colombia and Venezuela. By far the most popular with travellers (and probably the safest) is the route via San Antonio del Táchira (Venezuela) and Cúcuta (Colombia), on the main Caracas–Bogotá road. See Cúcuta in the later North of Bogotá chapter for details.

Another reasonably popular border crossing is the one at Paraguachón, on the Maracaibo (Venezuela) to Maicao (Colombia) road. Take this if you plan on heading from Venezuela straight to Colombia's Caribbean Coast and it's reasonably safe. There are buses and shared taxis between Maracaibo and Maicao, and direct buses between Caracas/Maracaibo and Santa Marta/Cartagena. Your passport will be stamped by both Colombian and Venezuelan officials on the border. See the Santa Marta and Cartagena sections in the later Caribbean Coast chapter.

Not so popular is the border crossing between Colombia's Puerto Carreño and either Puerto Páez or Puerto Ayacucho (both in Venezuela). Still less useful is the crossing from El Amparo de Apure (Venezuela) to Arauca (Colombia), a guerrilla-ridden region.

## Ecuador

Virtually all travellers use the Carretera Panamericana border crossing through Tulcán (Ecuador) and Ipiales (Colombia). See Ipiales in the later Southwest Colombia chapter for information. Parts of the Panamericana (particularly the section between Pasto and Popayán) may be at times unsafe to travel; check for news when you come. If you find the road too risky for travel, consider flying to Cali from Ipiales or Pasto.

## Panama

The Darién Gap effectively separates Colombia from Panama. There are no through roads, and it's unlikely that one will be built to complete the missing 150km link in the Carretera Panamericana anytime soon. The trek through the jungle is extremely dangerous these days due to Colombian guerrillas, so don't even think about it.

## Brazil & Peru

The only viable border crossing from these two countries into Colombia is via Leticia in the far southeastern corner of the Colombian Amazon. Leticia is reached from Iquitos (Peru) and Manaus (Brazil). See Leticia in the later Amazon Basin chapter for details. The area around Leticia is safe.

## SEA

Sailboats operate between Colón in Panama and Cartagena in Colombia. See Cartagena in the Bolívar section of the later Caribbean Coast chapter for details.

## ORGANISED TOURS

Tours to South America have become popular, and there are plenty of companies in the USA, the UK and elsewhere organising them. Some of the recommended US and UK tour operators are listed in the following sections. Check their offer, though don't expect many tours including Colombia in their itineraries due to current safety problems.

## The USA

The USA has plenty of tour companies specialising in South America. They are advertised in travel and outdoor magazines such as *Outside*, *Escape* and *Ecotraveler*, as well as magazines of a more general nature, including *Natural History* and *Audubon*. Here is a list of some reputable operators:

**Eco Voyager** (☎ 617-769 0676 or toll-free ☎ 1800-326 7088, fax 617-769 0667; W www.ecovoyager.com) 79 Parkingway, Suite 10, Quincy, MA 02169

**International Expeditions** (☎ 205-428 1700 or toll-free ☎ 1800-633 4734, fax 205-428 1714; W www.ietravel.com) One Environs Park, Helena, AL 35080

**Lost World Adventures** (☎ 404-373 5820 or toll-free ☎ 1800-999 0558, fax 404-377 1902; W www.lostworldadventures.com) 112 Church St, Decatur, GA 30030

**Mountain Travel Sobek** (☎ 510-527 8100 or toll-free ☎ 1888-687 6235, fax 510-525 7710; W www.mtsobek.com) 6420 Fairmount Ave, El Cerrito, CA 94530

**Southwind Adventures** (☎ 303-972 0701 or toll-free ☎ 1800-377 9463, fax 303-972 0708; W www.southwindadventures.com) PO Box 621057, Littleton, Colorado 80162

**Wilderness Travel** (☎ 510-558 2488 or toll-free ☎ 1800-368 2794, fax 510-558 2489; W www.wildernesstravel.com) 1102 Ninth St, Berkeley, CA 94710

**Wildland Adventures** (☎ 206-365 0686 or toll-free ☎ 1800-345 4453, fax 206-363 6615; W www.wildland.com) 3516 NE 155th, Seattle, WA 98155

## The UK

Following is a list of some overland operators offering tours in South America:

**Dragoman** (☎ 01728-861 133, fax 861 127; W www.dragoman.co.uk) Camp Green, Kenton Rd, Debenham, Suffolk IP14 6LA

**Encounter Overland** (☎ 020-7370 6845, fax 7244 9737; W www.encounter.co.uk) 267 Old Brompton Rd, London SW5 9JA

**Exodus Travels** (☎ 020-8673 0859, fax 8673 0779; W www.exodus.co.uk) 9 Weir Rd, London SW12 0LT

**Guerba Expeditions** (☎ 01373-826 611, fax 858 351; W www.guerba.co.uk) Wessex House, 40 Station Rd, Westbury, Wiltshire BA13 3JN

**Last Frontiers** (☎ 01296-658 650, fax 658 651; W www.lastfrontiers.co.uk) Fleet Marston Farm, Aylesbury, Buckinghamshire HP18 0QT

**Top Deck** (☎ 020-7244 8641, fax 7373 6201; W www.topdecktravel.co.uk) Top Deck House, 131/135 Earls Court Rd, London SW5 9RH

Also see the travel agencies listed in the Air section earlier in this chapter; some of these, including JLA, South American Experience and Scott Dunn Latin America, offer tours to South America and may have Colombia in their programmes.

# Getting Around

## AIR

Colombia was the first country in South America to have an airline. The Colombian-German company SCADTA (Sociedad Colombo Alemana de Transporte Aéreo) was founded in 1919 and later became Avianca. Today, the country has a well-developed airline system and one of the most dense domestic-flight networks in Latin America.

Air travel in Colombia is no longer cheap, but you may want to use it because it's safer and faster than bus travel. The time saving is considerable, especially on long-distance routes, eg, a bus between Bogotá and Cartagena takes about 20 hours, while a flight is just 1½ hours.

The question of safety is a bit more complex. Firstly, it's relative; what is risky for one traveller, may be perfectly safe for another, and it's ultimately up to you to judge. Secondly, it's very dynamic; a road notorious for being unsafe in the past may be quite safe today, and vice versa. Check the current situation upon arrival.

### Airlines

Colombia has more than half a dozen main passenger airlines and another dozen smaller carriers. **Avianca** (W www.avianca.com) has long been Colombia's principal domestic airline, with the widest network of both domestic and international routes. **Aces** is much younger, but has developed into a major domestic carrier and also has some international flights. It has been Colombia's most reliable airline in recent years, and has had the best service. The Medellín-based **Sam** has also plenty of flights all around the country, plus some international routes. In 2002, the three airlines entered into an alliance, **Alianza Summa** (W www.summa.aero), which now controls about 75% of domestic air traffic.

The other major players include **Aero-República** (W www.aerorepublica.com.co) and **Intercontinental de Aviación** (W www.inter.com.co), popularly known as Inter, both founded in the mid-1990s and flying between some major cities in large jets. **Aires** (W www.aires.com.co) uses mostly turbo planes and travels to smaller localities. **Satena** (W www.satena.com) is the commercial carrier of the

FAC (the Colombian Air Force) and services flights to the vast areas of the Amazon, Los Llanos and the Pacific Coast; it lands at 50 small towns and villages that would be otherwise virtually inaccessible.

**West Caribbean Airways** (W www.wca.com.co) is the most recent addition to the fleet of passenger airlines and has flights focussed on northern Colombia and San Andrés and Providencia.

Colombian airlines operate an enormous variety of aircraft, ranging from light turbo types with few seats to jumbo jets. The planes of the major companies are relatively new and, on the whole, they are in acceptable condition.

The on-board service of the major carriers is OK. As flight time is usually not much longer than an hour, don't expect any gastronomic treats; on most flights you get no more than a snack. Smoking is banned on domestic flights.

### Air Fares

In general, Colombian air fares are higher than those in neighbouring Venezuela and Ecuador. Prices are adjusted frequently to account for the depreciation of the peso against hard currencies.

Fares vary significantly between carriers, so if the route you're flying is serviced by several airlines, compare fares before buying your ticket. The Alianza Summa is normally more expensive than the remaining airlines, but occasionally has good deals.

Additionally, every airline may offer different fares on the same route, depending on a number of factors such as what season it is, how much in advance you book, if it's a weekday or a weekend etc, and there may be various promotional and discounted fares. Travel agencies, where you are most likely to buy your tickets, will know who is flying which route and how much it costs.

Some airlines offer discount fares for students and/or senior citizens, but these change frequently and may only apply to Colombians. Check with the airlines or agencies for news.

Make sure to reconfirm your flight at least 72 hours before departure (preferably in person rather than by phone). Remember,

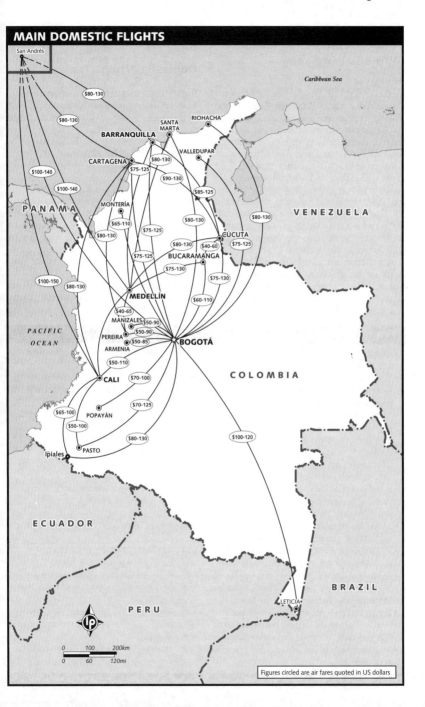

# MAIN DOMESTIC FLIGHTS

Caribbean Sea

San Andrés

$80-130

$80-130

$100-140

$100-140

PANAMA

RIOHACHA

SANTA MARTA

BARRANQUILLA

VALLEDUPAR

CARTAGENA

$80-130

$75-125

$90-130

$85-125

MONTERÍA

$80-130

VENEZUELA

$65-110

$75-125

$80-130

$80-130

CÚCUTA

$75-125

$80-130

$40-60

$75-125

BUCARAMANGA

$75-130

$100-150

$80-130

$75-130

MEDELLÍN

$60-110

$40-65

MANIZALES

$50-90

PEREIRA

$50-90

$50-85

BOGOTÁ

ARMENIA

COLOMBIA

$50-110

CALI

$70-100

$70-125

$65-100

POPAYÁN

$50-100

$80-130

$100-120

PASTO

Ipiales

PACIFIC OCEAN

ECUADOR

BRAZIL

PERU

LETICIA

0   100   200km

0    60   120mi

Figures circled are air fares quoted in US dollars

not all flights depart on time, so be patient and have a flexible itinerary, particularly if you have flight connections.

## Air Passes
Until recently, visitors who flew into Colombia with Avianca could take advantage of the 30-day Avianca air pass. It could only be purchased outside the country and allowed for five domestic stopovers of your choice serviced by Avianca and Sam. There were different versions of the pass, ranging from about US$180 to US$300, and you were allowed to buy up to three additional stopovers for US$40 each. The pass was suspended in 2002 when Alianza Summa was founded, but may be reintroduced, possibly incorporating Aces routes into the scheme. Check with Avianca offices abroad or online.

AeroRepública and Intercontinental de Aviación have domestic air passes which can be bought locally. They are not great deals, but will save you some money if you commit yourself to flying with one or the other airline. Inquire at their offices when you arrive in Colombia.

## Domestic Airport Tax
There's a US$4 airport tax on domestic flights departing from all major airports. This tax is included in the air fares listed in this book. You usually pay this tax when buying the ticket in the airline office or travel agency. If not, you'll be charged at the airport while checking in.

## BUS
As there are almost no passenger-train services in Colombia, buses are the main means of getting around. The bus transport system is well developed and extensive, reaching even the smallest villages. There are dozens of bus companies, each owning buses ranging from archaic pieces of junk to the most recent models.

All intercity buses depart from and arrive at a *terminal de pasajeros* (bus terminal). Every city has such a terminal, usually outside the

---

### Ten Road-Tested Getting-Around Tips

- Check air fares as soon as you arrive in Colombia. Some tickets bought in advance or for weekend flights may be attractively cheap and a tempting alternative to long bus trips.
- Some airlines may offer packages to major tourist destinations (Cartagena, San Andrés), which can cost not much more than you'd pay for air tickets only. Check as soon as you can because good deals sell quickly.
- Flights do not always depart on time, and sometimes are rescheduled, suspended or cancelled. It's a good idea to call the airport and ask for your scheduled departure before going there. In any case, be prepared to spend some time at the airport and don't plan on any immediate connections.
- Air fares tend to rise significantly in the holiday seasons, approximately from mid-December to late January and from mid-June to late July. Flights fill up fast during these periods and you may need to book well in advance.
- Avoid bus or air travel between Christmas and early January and during Semana Santa (Easter Week). Colombians get crazy about travelling in these periods so buses and flights are completely full and traffic is chaotic.
- Most long-distance buses are air-conditioned and some may be as cold as freezers. Have a lot of warm clothing at hand, just in case.
- At the bus terminal, if several companies have buses to your destination departing around the same time, go and view the buses and select the best option before buying your ticket.
- Because of fierce competition between bus companies servicing main routes, some companies may offer discount fares, sometimes much lower than others. Be sure to shop around bus offices at the terminal before buying your ticket.
- If your budget is not completely rock bottom, always consider colectivo (shared taxi; see Colectivo later in this chapter) as a faster and usually more comfortable means of road transport than bus, especially an ordinary bus which usually makes many stops.
- Taxis are cheap in Colombia, so don't be afraid of using them in cities for safety, comfort and to save time.

## Bussing about, Chiva-style

The *chiva* is a Disneyland-style vehicle that was Colombia's principal means of road transport several decades ago. Also called *bus de escalera* in some regions, the chiva is a piece of popular art on wheels. The body is made almost entirely of wood and has wooden benches rather than seats, with each bench accessible from the outside. The body of the bus is painted with colourful decorative patterns, each different, with a main painting on the back. There are homebred artists who specialise in painting chivas. Ceramic miniatures of chivas are found in just about every Colombian handicraft shop.

Today, chivas have almost disappeared from main roads, but they still play an important role on back roads between small towns and villages. There are still a few thousand of them and they are most common in Antioquia, Huila, Nariño and on the Caribbean Coast. Chivas take both passengers and any kind of cargo, animals included. If the interior is already completely packed, the roof is used for everything and everybody that doesn't fit inside. Chivas usually gather around markets, from where they depart for their journeys along bumpy roads. They are rare guests at the bus terminals.

Night city tours in chivas are organised by travel agents in most large cities and have become a popular form of entertainment. There is normally a band on board playing local music, and a large stock of *aguardiente* to create the proper atmosphere. The tour usually includes some popular nightspots and can be great fun.

city centre, but always linked to it by local transport. Bogotá is the most important bus transport hub in Colombia, handling buses to just about every corner of the country.

On the main roads buses run frequently, so there is no need to buy tickets in advance. You usually just go to the terminal, find which company has the next bus due to depart, buy your ticket and board the bus. On some minor routes, where there are only a few departures a day, it's worth considering buying your ticket several hours before the scheduled departure. The only times you really need to book well in advance are during and around Christmas and Easter, when Colombians rush to travel.

## Classes

There are three principal classes of buses: ordinary (called *corriente*, *sencillo* or *ordinario*), 1st class (which go by a variety of names such as *pullman*, *metropolitano* or *directo*) and air-conditioned buses (known as *climatizado* or *ejecutivo*).

The corriente buses are usually old crates and mostly service side (back) roads. They often stop for every passenger on the road, which sometimes results in the bus being packed far beyond its capacity. The pullmans are more modern and comfortable. They ply both side roads and main routes.

Climatizados are the best. They have plenty of legroom, reclining seats and large luggage compartments, and some have toilets. They are predominantly long-distance buses covering main routes, and many travel at night. They are the fastest and most comfortable way of travelling. They normally depart and arrive on schedule, stop only in a few main towns en route and won't pick up passengers elsewhere. They almost never take more passengers than they have seats. They are the dominant means of intercity transport, but carry warm clothes – some drivers have the air-conditioning going full blast.

Smoking in buses is not allowed, although in corrientes people often smoke and nobody seems to care. The long-distance buses stop for meals, but not necessarily at mealtimes; it seems to depend on when the driver is hungry or when the bus gets to a restaurant that has an arrangement with the bus company. Don't leave any hand luggage in the bus when you get off for your meal.

The traditional bus entertainment is music (anything from vallenato to ranchera to salsa) chosen according to the driver's taste. The volume is also at the whim of the driver and you may experience an entire night of blaring music – not necessarily great fun.

A newer form of entertainment is the video movie. Most buses, including some corrientes, are now equipped with video equipment. Bloody US action movies interlaced with sweet Mexican love stories – two Colombian favourites – played most of the night and often at full volume can be a form of torture. The technical quality, too, often leaves a bit to be desired.

## Bus Fares

Bus travel is reasonably cheap in Colombia. As a rule of a thumb, the climatizado costs roughly US$4 for every 100km. Pullmans cost about 20% less than climatizados and the corrientes 20% less than the pullmans.

If various companies service the same route, the comparative fares are much the same (though some may offer temporary promotions). However, standards may differ from one company to the next and you'll soon become familiar with choosing the best option.

When you get on a bus out on the road, you pay the fare to the *ayudante* (driver's sidekick) and rarely get a ticket. Ayudantes have been known to charge gringos more than the actual fare or at least round the price up. Ask other passengers beforehand to be sure of the correct fare.

## COLECTIVO

Quite widespread in Colombia, the *colectivo* is a cross between a bus and a taxi. They are usually US-made large cars of 1960s and '70s vintage, less often vans, minibuses, jeeps or pick-up trucks. They ply fixed routes and depart when all the seats are filled rather than to a set schedule. The colectivo service came into being on roads where bus service was deficient and slow. Although colectivos mainly cover short-distance routes, there are some medium- and long-distance services.

Colectivos charge roughly 30% to 60% more than buses, but are faster and usually more comfortable. They are a good option if you have a long wait for a bus, and a saviour if the last bus is gone. In some cities they depart from and arrive at the bus terminal, but in smaller towns they are usually found in the main square. The frequency of service varies largely from place to place. At some places there may be a colectivo every five minutes, but elsewhere you can wait an hour or longer until the necessary number of passengers has been collected.

## CAR & MOTORCYCLE

Travelling by an independent means of transport is a comfortable and attractive way of getting around the country. Some advantages are schedule flexibility, access to remote areas and the ability to seize fleeting photographic opportunities.

Unfortunately, Colombia is not the best country for travelling by car or motorcycle. The major problem is security. Car theft is a well-established business and thieves usually steal accessories and anything of value left inside. More importantly, roads can be unsafe due to guerrillas, paramilitaries or common criminals – and cars are an obvious target. You may pass through unsafe regions undisturbed if you travel by public transport, but a nice jeep won't get through unnoticed.

In the cities, on the other hand, traffic is heavy, chaotic and mad. Driving 'manners' are wild and unpredictable. It takes some time to get used to the local style of driving, but even if you master it, the risk of an accident remains high.

There has been quite a confusing legal issue regarding motorcycles. Since *sicarios* (paid killers) began to use them as the most suitable means of transport to and from their crimes, authorities set about introducing new rules. The regulations included a ban on carrying a passenger, prohibiting the use of crash helmets (intended to make it easier to recognise the rider) and a ban on riding at night. In most departments these regulations have been abandoned, but given the volatile situation you can't rule out further changes.

All of these internal problems aside, note that there is no way of bringing your vehicle to South America other than by sea or air. This involves time and substantial costs and there's a lot of paperwork involved. You'll probably spend less on (and be safer) travelling in Colombia by air and using taxis. To sum up, driving in Colombia can be unsafe and is not recommended, and bringing in your own car or motorcycle is not a good idea at all.

Renting a car might be a better solution. Firstly, it saves you the money you would spend on getting your own car to Colombia (but obviously adds car-rental costs). Secondly, your rental vehicle will have Colombian registration plates so it won't stand out from local vehicles as much and attract unwanted attention. However, given the convenience of public transport, you may still be better off and safer using planes and taxis, rather than driving a rented car.

Should you be hell-bent on renting a car, it's best to contact major international rental companies such as Avis, Hertz or Budget at home before your trip to check what they can offer in Colombia (they all have offices in major Colombian cities), and possibly to prebook, which is likely to be cheaper than renting a car after arrival.

Car rental is not cheap in Colombia and there are seldom any discounts. Carefully check clauses pertaining to insurance and liability before you sign a rental contract. Pay close attention to any theft clause, as it may load a large percentage of any loss onto the hirer.

This book doesn't feature specific information about car-rental companies, but it's easy to find. They normally have offices at the airports and in the best city hotels. Any top-class hotel, tourist office or travel agent can tell you where to find them.

## BICYCLE

Colombia is certainly not a paradise for bikers. Bike tracks in the cities are few and far between, and bike-rental facilities are almost nonexistent. Cycling is unsafe because of chaotic traffic and Colombia's endemic security problems. Foreign travellers with their own bikes are virtually unknown.

On a positive note, there has been some development in the cities, including new bike tracks and *ciclovías* (weekend closures for cars and buses of selected streets, making them tracks for bikers and skaters instead).

## HITCHING

Predictably, hitchhiking in Colombia is uncommon and difficult. Given the complex internal situation, drivers don't want to take risks and simply don't stop on the road. As intercity buses are fast, efficient and relatively cheap, it's not worth wasting time on hitching and taking a potentially serious risk.

## BOAT

With some 3000km of Pacific and Atlantic coastline, there is a considerable amount of shipping traffic, consisting almost exclusively of irregular cargo boats, which may also take passengers. They are of little interest to travellers except, perhaps, boats from Buenaventura to Isla de Gorgona.

Rivers are important transport routes in regions such as the Chocó and the Amazon where there is no other way of getting around. Unfortunately, both these regions are noted for guerrilla and paramilitary activities and are not recommended for tourists, except for the area around Leticia.

The Río Magdalena was once the principal waterway of the central part of the country, but no longer has much importance as far as river transport goes. The only boats you are likely to use on the Magdalena are in the Mompós area.

## LOCAL TRANSPORT
### Bus

Buses are the main means of getting around the cities. Almost every urban centre of over 100,000 inhabitants has a bus service, as do many smaller towns. The standard, speed and efficiency of local buses vary from place to place, but on the whole they are slow and crowded. City buses have a flat fare, so the distance of the ride makes no difference. You get on by the front door and pay the driver or his assistant, if any, on entering. You never get a ticket.

In some cities or in some streets there are bus stops (*paraderos* or *paradas*), while in most others you just wave down the bus. To let the driver know that you intend to get off you simply say, or shout, *por aquí, por favor* (here, please), *en la esquina, por favor* (at the next street corner, please) or *el paradero, por favor* (at the coming bus stop, please).

There are lots of different types of local buses, ranging from old wrecks to modern air-conditioned vehicles. One common type is the *buseta* (small bus), a dominant means of urban transport in cities such as Bogotá and Cartagena. The bus fare is somewhere between US$0.25 and US$0.40, depending on the city and type of bus.

Some cities (Bogotá being one) also have minibuses called colectivos (see that entry earlier in this chapter). They ply main city routes, are faster than buses and charge about US$0.40.

A bus or buseta trip, particularly in large cities such as Bogotá or Barranquilla, is not a smooth and silent ride but rather a sort of breathtaking adventure with a taste of local folklore thrown in. You'll have an opportunity to be saturated with loud tropical music, learn about the Colombian meaning of road rules, and observe your driver desperately trying to make his way through an ocean of vehicles.

A special, new kind of bus is the Trans-Milenio, which has recently been introduced in Bogotá. It's fast, clean and efficient, and has no musical entertainment. See the later Bogotá chapter for details.

## Taxi

Taxis are an inexpensive and convenient means of getting around, especially if you are travelling with a few companions. The price will usually be the same, regardless of the number of passengers, though some drivers may demand more if you have a lot of luggage. Taxis are particularly useful when you arrive in an unfamiliar city and want to get from the bus terminal or the airport to the city centre to look for a hotel.

A taxi may also be chartered for longer distances. This is convenient if you want to visit places near major cities that are outside local transport areas but too near to be covered by long-distance bus networks.

In most cities, taxis are painted yellow or yellow and black. In major cities they have meters, though drivers are not always eager to switch them on, preferring to charge a gringo fare, obviously far higher than the normal metered fare. It's always advisable to ask a few people beforehand (eg, a bus terminal official or hotel receptionist) what the usual taxi fare to your destination would be. Then, ask the taxi driver for the expected fare, and if they quote a significantly higher fare, bargain and agree on a price. If you are not satisfied, try another taxi.

While taxis are officially obliged to display the current legal tariff, due to regular price rises their meters are not always adjusted to the latest tariff amount and the driver can legitimately ask more than is shown on the meter.

In provincial towns metered taxis are rare. Instead there are commonly accepted fares on given routes so always fix the price beforehand.

Don't use taxis with a driver and somebody else inside. Taxi drivers sometimes have a friend along for company or for security reasons, but it may be insecure for you; some cases of robbery have been reported.

## Metro

Over the past 30 years Bogotá has drawn and redrawn plans for building a metro system. The project was ultimately abandoned and instead the city recently built a fast bus system called TransMilenio.

Meanwhile, Medellín began constructing its metro in 1985 and opened it in 1995. It was the first (and currently the only) Colombian city to have a fast metropolitan train system.

## ORGANISED TOURS

There are very few genuine tour companies in Colombia, so don't expect many adventure tours. Some travel agencies organise tours, but these are mostly conventional affairs such as city tours, one-day excursions to nearby attractions and night chiva trips around the city discos. Longer, more adventurous tours to remote regions are thin on the ground, due to both safety fears and a lack of demand. Information about tours has been included in relevant sections throughout regional chapters in this book.

# Bogotá

☎ 1 • pop 7 million • elevation 2600m • temp 14°C

The capital of the country, Bogotá is the quintessence of all things Colombian. It's a city of brilliant museums, splendid colonial churches, futuristic architecture, renowned universities and intellectuals and artists, offering a vibrant and diverse cultural life. Yet, it is also a city of vast shantytowns, street urchins, beggars, thieves, itinerant vendors, wild traffic and graffiti. It's a huge Latin American city, which offers just about every modern Western convenience yet suffers from every developing-world problem.

The spontaneous architecture, with makeshift shacks sitting next to ultramodern towers, seems to have evolved beyond all rational rules of urban planning. Streets are the battlefields of wild traffic. Everything from mules to Maseratis all struggle to impose their own right of way. The pavements are crammed with a human mosaic crawling between countless street stalls and vendors selling just about everything. Although the population is essentially mestizo, every colour of skin can be found in this huge cosmopolitan melting pot.

Over the past 50 years, Bogotá has grown 20-fold to its present population of about seven million. The size and status of the capital city makes Bogotá the major focus of political, economic, cultural and intellectual life. It's a bustling, noisy and aggressive metropolis – amazing but awful, fascinating but dangerous. You may love it or hate it, but it won't leave you indifferent.

## HISTORY

Long before the Spanish Conquest, the Sabana de Bogotá, a fertile highland basin which today has been almost entirely taken over by the city, was inhabited by one of the most advanced pre-Columbian Indian groups, the Muisca. The Spanish era began when Gonzalo Jiménez de Quesada and his expedition arrived at the Sabana.

Quesada set off from Santa Marta in April 1536 with about 750 men and reached the Sabana one year later, accompanied by only 166 soldiers. On 6 August 1538 he founded a town near the Muisca capital, Bacatá. The town was named Santa Fe de Bogotá,

## Highlights

- Tour the Museo del Oro, arguably the world's best gold museum
- Stroll around La Candelaria, Bogotá's charming historic quarter
- Go for a weekend night crawl around the pubs and discos of Zona Rosa
- Explore Bogotá's magnificent colonial churches
- Visit the Donación Botero, a world-class painting collection

Bogotá
page 79
✪ Central Bogotá
pages 88-89
Northern Bogotá
pages 94-95

a combination of the traditional name and Quesada's hometown in Spain, Santa Fe. Nonetheless, throughout the colonial period the town was simply referred to as Santa Fe.

At the time of its foundation Santa Fe consisted of 12 huts and a chapel where a mass was held to celebrate the town's birth. The Muisca religious sites were destroyed and replaced by churches. By 1600, 13 religious buildings were constructed, among them five churches.

During the early years Santa Fe was governed from Santo Domingo (on the island of Hispaniola, the present-day Dominican

Republic), but in 1550 it fell under the rule of Lima, the capital of the Viceroyalty of Peru and the seat of Spain's power for the conquered territories of South America. In 1717, Santa Fe was made the capital of the Virreynato de la Nueva Granada, the newly created viceroyalty comprising the territories of present-day Colombia, Panama, Venezuela and Ecuador.

Inspite of its political importance, the town's development was hindered by earthquakes, and smallpox and typhoid epidemics that plagued the region throughout the 17th and 18th centuries. The first census of 1778 showed only 16,002 inhabitants (52% of whom were whites). The Indian Chibcha language was banned in 1783.

After independence the Congress of Cúcuta shortened the town's name to Bogotá and decreed it the capital of Gran Colombia. The town developed steadily and by the middle of the 19th century it had 30,000 inhabitants and 30 churches. In 1884, the first tramway began to operate in the city and soon after railway lines were constructed to La Dorada and Girardot, giving Bogotá access to the ports on the Magdalena River. At the beginning of the 20th century the population had reached 100,000, and by 1938 the 400-year-old city had 330,000 inhabitants.

Rapid progress came only in the 1940s with industrialisation and the consequent peasant migrations from the countryside into the city. On 9 April 1948, the popular leader Jorge Eliécer Gaitán was assassinated, sparking the uprising known as El Bogotazo. The city was partially destroyed; 136 buildings in central Bogotá were burnt to the ground and 2500 people died. In recent decades the city has continued to expand rapidly to become a vast metropolis.

## CLIMATE

Bogotá is the third-highest capital in South America, after La Paz and Quito. It sits at an altitude of about 2600m, and at this height altitude sickness can occur. You may feel a bit dizzy when you arrive. Take it easy for a day or two – it should soon go away.

The main dry season lasts from December to March, and there is also a second, less dry period with only light rainfall from July to August. The wettest months are April and October. The mean annual rainfall is about 1020mm.

The city's average temperature is 14°C year-round, dropping to about 9°C at night and rising to around 18°C (higher on sunny days) during the day. In the rainy season there is less difference between day and night-time temperatures.

## ORIENTATION

Bogotá has grown along its north–south axis and is bordered to the east by a mountain range topped by the two peaks of Monserrate and Guadalupe. Having expanded up the mountain slopes as far as possible, Bogotá is now developing to the west and north.

The city centre divides the metropolis into two very different parts. Bogotá's northern sector consists mainly of upmarket residential districts, while the city's southern part is a vast spread of undistinguished lower-income suburbs, culminating in the vast shantytowns on the southernmost outskirts. Western Bogotá is the most heterogeneous and industrial. This is where the airport and the bus terminal are located.

The central area is not uniform either and can be roughly divided into three parts. The southern one (south of Av Jiménez), La Candelaria, is the partly preserved colonial sector, the heart of the original town. The northern part (north of Calle 26), the Centro Internacional, is a small Manhattan where most of the city's skyscrapers have sprung up. Sandwiched between these two is the proper city centre, the area full of office buildings, banks, restaurants, shops and cinemas.

Carrera Séptima (Carrera 7) is one of the main streets running parallel to the mountains along the entire length of the city. In the centre it links Plaza de Bolívar with the Centro Internacional.

Av Jiménez is a business and financial street with a mishmash of architecture and, unusually, it is curved as a result of it having been built over a riverbed. Carrera Décima (Carrera 10) is the busiest traffic artery of the centre, crowded with busetas and countless street vendors. It roughly cuts the centre into the less dangerous area to the east and the 'heavy' zone to the west. Finally, Av Caracas (Carrera 14) is the major road linking the centre with the north and south, the principal bus route.

Bogotá has enough tourist sights to keep you busy for several days. It's particularly renowned for its museums and colonial

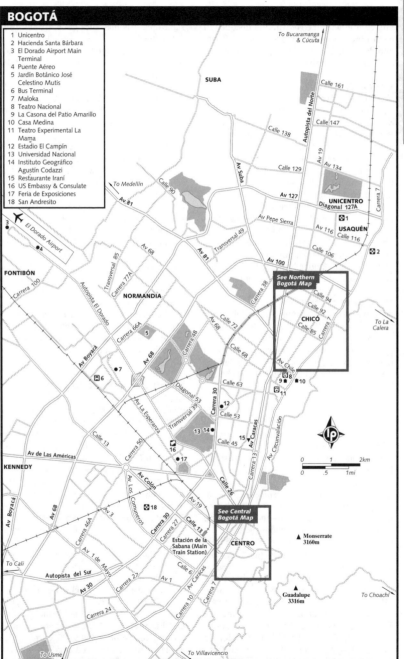

# BOGOTÁ

1 Unicentro
2 Hacienda Santa Bárbara
3 El Dorado Airport Main Terminal
4 Puente Aéreo
5 Jardín Botánico José Celestino Mutis
6 Bus Terminal
7 Maloka
8 Teatro Nacional
9 La Casona del Patio Amarillo
10 Casa Medina
11 Teatro Experimental La Mama
12 Estadio El Campín
13 Universidad Nacional
14 Instituto Geográfico Agustín Codazzi
15 Restaurante Iraní
16 US Embassy & Consulate
17 Feria de Exposiciones
18 San Andresito

churches. Most major attractions are in the city centre, within easy walking distance of each other. Bogotá has a far more vibrant and diversified cultural and artistic life than any other city in the country.

## INFORMATION
## Tourist Offices

The city tourist office, **Instituto Distrital de Cultura y Turismo** (☎ 334 6800; Carrera 8 No 9-83; open 8am-noon & 2pm-4.30pm Mon-Fri, 8.30am-5.30pm Sat & Sun) is in the western corner of Plaza de Bolívar. The Instituto operates information desks at the bus terminal (☎ 295 4460) and El Dorado airport (☎ 413 9053).

The **Oficina de Ecoturismo** (☎ 243 3095, 243 1634; Carrera 10 No 20-30, Piso 4; open 8am-4.30pm Mon-Fri) provides information about national parks, and issues permits and books accommodation in the parks (see National Parks under Flora & Fauna in the earlier Facts about Colombia chapter).

### Visa Extensions

A 30-day extension can be obtained from the **DAS office** (☎ 610 7315; Calle 100 No 11B-27; open 7.30am-3.30pm Mon-Fri). Only your passport is required (no photos, no onward tickets). Arrive early, as you have to pay the US$25 fee at the bank. You then get the extension on the spot.

### Money

Bogotá's banks keep different hours than banks elsewhere in the country – they work without a lunch break, 9am to 3pm Monday to Thursday, and 9am to 3.30pm Friday. However, some of them only handle foreign exchange operations until noon or 1pm.

**Lloyds TSB Bank** (Carrera 8 No 15-46) changes travellers cheques at possibly the best rate in town. **Banco Unión Colombiano** (Carrera 8 No 14-45) is perhaps the next best place for cashing cheques. **Bancolombia** (Carrera 8 No 12-55) is also good and the service is quick.

These banks also change cash, but check the *casas de cambio* beforehand, which may offer the same rates and do things much quicker. Central casas de cambio include **Titán Intercontinental** (☎ 336 0549; Carrera 7 No 18-42), **Casa de Cambio La Candelaria** (☎ 342 1184; Av Jiménez No 5-81) and **Casa de Cambio Unidas** (341 0537; Carrera 6 No

14-72), and there are several others in the same area. Another three casas are at Carrera 7 No 26-62.

All banks shown on the Central Bogotá map give cash advances on Visa and/or MasterCard. Most banks have ATMs.

The **Expreso Viajes & Turismo** (☎ 593 4949; Calle 85 No 20-32) represents American Express (see Money in the earlier Facts for the Visitor chapter).

## Post & Communications

The post office of **Avianca** (Carrera 7 No 16-36) has poste restante. If you want letters sent to you, they should be addressed care of Lista de Correos Avianca, Edificio Avianca, Carrera 7 No 16-36, Bogotá. The mail is kept for one month. Note that courier companies do not accept mail sent to Lista de Correos.

The main post office of **Adpostal** (Carrera 7 at Calle 13) is in Edificio Murillo Toro. Attractive and colourful post stamps can be bought on the 1st floor of this building. There's another office of **Adpostal** (Carrera 7 No 27-54) in the Centro Internacional.

The main office of **Telecom** (Calle 23 No 13-49) is in the city centre, but you can make long-distance calls and send faxes from branch offices scattered throughout the city.

### Email & Internet Access

Central Bogotá has plenty of facilities, including **Café Internet Doble-Click** (☎ 334 9865; Calle 19 No 6-68), which is one of the largest (about 100 computers) and cheapest options. Other central Internet cafés include **OfficeNET** (☎ 282 6560; Carrera 4 No 19-16, Oficina 112), **mes@net.com** (☎ 380 2900; Calle 19 No 4-42) and **K@binas** (☎ 334 4992; Av Jiménez No 5-61). There are perhaps a dozen other Internet cafés in the same area. **Biblioteca Luis Ángel Arango** (☎ 343 1212; Calle 11 No 4-14) in La Candelaria has the Sala de Internet. Also, Platypus (see Places to Stay later) offers online services to guests and nonguests.

In the northern sector of the city, one of the cheapest options is **El Café de Bogotá** (☎ 217 5395; Carrera 15 No 72-63). Other Internet facilities in the north include **Café Olé Internet** (☎ 691 3823; Carrera 15 No 95-55) and **hp invent** (☎ 531 9090; Carrera 12 No 82-31). Any of the listed services will cost US$1 to US$1.50 per hour.

## Travel Agencies

**Trotamundos** (☎ 285 8070; Carrera 6 No 34-62) represents STA Travel and may have attractive discounted air fares for students and young people. There's another, more central office of **Trotamundos** (☎ 341 7167; Carrera 6 No 14-48, Oficina 404). Alternatively, try **Educamos Viajando** (☎ 620 5359; Calle 108A No 18-64) or **Viajes Vela** (☎ 635 3389; Calle 100 No 19-61, Oficinas 210 & 211).

## Cultural Centres

All the listed centres have their own libraries with a selection of books and press in their own language.

**Alianza Colombo Francesa** (☎ 341 1348)
Carrera 3 No 18-45
**British Council** (☎ 236 3976) Calle 87 No 12-79
**Centro Colombo Americano** (☎ 334 7640) Calle 19 No 3-05
**Goethe Institut** (☎ 254 7600) Carrera 7 No 81-57

## Laundry

Most hotels provide this service for their guests. Budget hotels will usually wash your clothes in their washing machine (or send them for washing elsewhere) and charge per kilogram or per load, whereas upmarket establishments will probably offer dry cleaning only and will charge by item.

If your hotel doesn't have laundry service, there are several budget *lavanderías* in the centre, including **Lavandería Espumas** (Calle 19 No 3A-37, Local 104).

## Medical Services

Many minor health problems, such as mild diarrhoea, cold, cough, pain, and small cuts and wounds, can be solved by just applying a proper remedy, which you can buy in a *droguería* (pharmacy). Bogotá has a wide array of pharmacies, and there's always one in every suburb of the city that takes its turn and stays open the whole night. They are listed in the local press. Some drugs that can be bought only with a prescription in Western countries (eg, antibiotics) are readily available over the counter in local pharmacies. Always make sure you buy the proper drug (it may appear under a different name here) and check the expiration date.

If you happen to get really sick, seek qualified medical help promptly. Your embassy or consulate may recommend doctors or clinics, but if you can't get that advice, act on your own without delay. Fortunately, Bogotá has a number of public hospitals, private clinics, specialist medical centres and dental surgeries.

If you're insured, it's preferable to use private clinics rather than government-owned institutions, which are cheaper but may not be as well equipped. Most private clinics offer inpatient and outpatient services, carry out laboratory tests and have specialist doctors, some of whom speak English.

**Clínica de Marly** (☎ 343 6600; Calle 50 No 9-67) is a recommended outpatient clinic with doctors covering most specialities you might need. It also has an inpatient section.

**Fundación Santa Fe de Bogotá** (☎ 629 0766; Calle 116 No 9-02) is considered to have the most developed and sophisticated medical equipment in South America. It provides excellent services at prices to match and it boasts both outpatient and inpatient facilities.

**Hospital San Ignacio** (288 8188; Carrera 7 No 40-62) is a university hospital with a high level of medical expertise, but long queues.

**Centro de Atención al Viajero** (☎ 215 2029, 612 0272; Carrera 7 No 119-14) is a travellers medical centre which offers various vaccinations (including yellow fever and hepatitis A and B). Other facilities which provide vaccination services include **Cruz Roja Colombiana** (☎ 437 5330; Av 68 No 66-31) and **Instituto Nacional de Salud** (☎ 220 7700; Av 26 No 51-60).

Bogotá's tap water is chlorinated and is said to be safe to drink, but it's better to avoid it. Bottled water is readily available from most food shops, supermarkets, cafés, restaurants etc.

## Emergency

The services listed below operate 24 hours a day, except for the Tourist Police (7am to 7pm). Don't expect the attendants to speak English, so if your Spanish is not up to scratch, try to get a local to call on your behalf.

| | |
|---|---|
| **Ambulance** | ☎ 125 |
| **Fire** | ☎ 119 |
| **Police** | ☎ 112 or ☎ 156 |
| **Red Cross** | ☎ 132 |
| **Tourist Police** | ☎ 337 4413 |
| **Traffic Police** | ☎ 127 |

## Dangers & Annoyances

Bogotá is not a perfectly safe place: violent crime, theft, armed robbery, rape and traffic accidents are all common. On a more positive note, however, it appears that parts of the city centre, including La Candelaria, are safer now than they once were. The centre has been largely restored over recent years and vigilance has improved. The northern districts are generally regarded as safer, but it's best to observe some security precautions there as well. Heed the precautions under Dangers & Annoyances in the earlier Facts for the Visitor chapter.

There's no need to panic when strolling about during the daytime, but try to keep night-time walks to a minimum and don't carry money or other valuables. However, don't get paranoid about going out at night. Simply use common sense and use taxis where appropriate.

Bogotá's street traffic is heavy, fast and wild – be careful! Drivers don't obey traffic rules as they usually do in the West, and may run red lights or crawl against the flow on a one-way street if they feel like doing so. This is simply the land of the strong, and pedestrians are at the bottom of the pecking order. Crossing the street may involve some effort and risk; take it as a rule that no driver will stop to give way to you.

## PLAZA DE BOLÍVAR & AROUND

The usual place to start discovering Bogotá is Plaza de Bolívar, the heart of the original town. In the middle of the square is a bronze statue of Simón Bolívar (cast in 1846), the work of an Italian artist, Pietro Tenerani. This was the first public monument erected in the city.

The square has changed considerably over the centuries and is no longer lined by colonial buildings; only the Capilla del Sagrario (see that entry under Churches later for a description) dates from the Spanish era. Other buildings are more recent and are in different architectural styles.

On the northern side of the square is the **Palacio de Justicia**, a massive, rather styleless edifice serving as the seat of the Supreme Court. The Palace of Justice has had quite a tragic history. The first court building, erected in 1921 on the corner of Calle 11 and Carrera 6, was burnt down by a mob during El Bogotazo in April 1948.

A modern building was then constructed on Plaza de Bolívar, but in 1985 it was taken by M-19 guerrillas and gutted by fire in a fierce 28-hour offensive by the army in an attempt to reclaim it. The ruin stood untouched for four years until authorities decided to take it down altogether and construct a new building in a completely different style.

The whole western side of the plaza is taken over by the French-style **Edificio Liévano**, which is now home to the Alcaldía (mayor's office). The building was erected between 1902 and 1905.

On the southern side of the plaza stands a monumental stone building in neoclassical style, the **Capitolio Nacional**, the seat of Congress. It was begun in 1847, but due to numerous political uprisings it was not completed until 1926. The facade facing the square was designed by English architect Thomas Reed.

Beyond the Capitolio is the **Casa de Nariño**, a neoclassical palace-like building erected at the beginning of the 20th century. It was the official home of presidents from 1908, but in 1948 it was sacked after the assassination of Jorge Eliécer Gaitán and only restored in 1979.

Between the Capitolio and the Casa are spacious formal grounds where the change of the presidential guard is held at 5pm on Monday, Wednesday, Friday and Sunday. On the western edge of the grounds is the **Observatorio Astronómico**, commissioned by José Celestino Mutis and constructed in 1803. This is reputedly the first astronomical observatory built on the continent. It's closed to the public.

## LA CANDELARIA

East of Plaza de Bolívar stretches the colonial barrio of La Candelaria, the oldest part of the city. Some of the houses have been carefully restored, others are in a dilapidated state, but on the whole the neighbourhood preserves an agreeable old-time appearance, even though a number of modern edifices have replaced the original buildings. Possibly the best preserved part of the quarter is between Calles 9 and 13 and Carreras 2 and 5. It's a pleasant area for a stroll.

The largest modern building in La Candelaria is the **Biblioteca Luis Ángel Arango** (☎ 343 1212; Calle 11 No 4-14), which occupies the whole block between Carreras 4 and 5 and Calles 11 and 12. The building houses a library, a concert hall, some small auditoriums for video and music, a small exhibition of musical instruments, and a cafeteria on the top floor.

One block west is the Italian-style **Teatro Colón** (☎ 341 0475; Calle 10 No 5-32), begun in 1885 and opened in 1892 for the fourth centenary of the discovery of America. It was designed by Italian architect Pietro Cantini and is lavishly decorated inside. It is only open for performances. Concerts, opera and ballet are performed here.

Opposite the theatre is the massive edifice of **Palacio de San Carlos** (Calle 10 No 5-51), originally a Jesuit college, now the seat of the Ministry of Foreign Affairs (it's not open to the public).

One block south is another fine colonial building, **Camarín del Carmen** (☎ 283 1780; Calle 9 No 4-96), which was originally a Carmelite convent. It's now a cultural centre with its own 500-seat auditorium, which features theatre, cinema and other performances.

Stroll about the streets of the district to discover other interesting sights. Make sure that you include some of the museums and churches described in the following sections.

## MUSEUMS

Bogotá has about 50 museums. The following sections cover some of the most important ones, all of which are in the city centre and within walking distance from each other. Contact the tourist office if you need more information about these or other museums. Even if you hate museums, you shouldn't miss the Museo del Oro and the Donación Botero.

The last Sunday of each month is a free-admission day to the museums – be prepared for big crowds.

### Museo del Oro

Housed in a modern building facing Plaza de Santander, the Gold Museum (☎ 343 0545; Calle 16 No 5-41; adults Tues-Sat US$1.50, Sun US$0.75, students US$0.10 all days; open 9am-4.30pm Tues-Sat, 10am-4.30pm Sun) houses more than 34,000 gold pieces from all the major pre-Hispanic cultures in Colombia. It is arguably the most important gold museum in the world.

Most of the gold objects are displayed in a large strongroom on the top floor – a breathtaking sight. Don't miss the famous Balsa Muisca and ponder the genius of the people who created that mysterious golden world long before Columbus crossed the Atlantic. It is worth planning more than one visit to the museum, as it's impossible to appreciate it all in one go.

Apart from the strongroom, the museum has a big exhibition on the historical, geographical and social aspects of pre-Columbian cultures, which are well illustrated by artefacts including objects in stone, bone, clay, gold and textiles. You'll also find here explanations of gold production methods and the importance of gold in these cultures.

Guided tours in English are conducted twice daily (at 10am and 2pm at the time of writing), or you can rent headphones with English commentary (US$2.50) and do your own audio tour. Videos featuring various pre-Columbian cultures are shown five times daily (including two with an English soundtrack) and the film of the month is screened every Wednesday. Check the programme and times when you come to plan your visit accordingly.

### Donación Botero

Opened in 2000 in a restored colonial mansion known as Casa Luis López de Mesa, the Botero collection (☎ 343 1331; Calle 11 No 4-41; admission free; open 10am-8pm Mon & Wed-Fri, 10am-7pm Sat, 10am-4pm Sun) is Bogotá's other museum highlight. It's a permanent exhibition of works of art donated by Fernando Botero, Colombia's most famous artist, to the Banco de la República.

The 208-piece collection contains 123 of Botero's own works, including his paintings, drawings and sculptures, plus 85 works by European artists such as Picasso, Chagall, Miró, Dali, Renoir, Matisse, Léger and Monet. In effect, this is easily one of South America's richest art collections. Botero has made another impressive gift to his native city – see Medellín under Antioquia in the later Northwest Colombia chapter.

### Casa de la Moneda

Next door to Donación Botero, another historic building which served as the Mint (☎ 343 1212; Calle 11 No 4-93; admission free; open 10am-8pm Mon & Wed-Fri,

*10am-7pm Sat, 10am-4pm Sun)* gives room to several permanent exhibitions.

Most of the rooms are taken up by a numismatic collection, which includes coins and bills and some related matters such as presses and strong boxes. Other rooms feature paintings by renowned Colombian artists including Guillermo Wiedemann (1905–69) and Luis Caballero (1943–95).

A strongroom at the back of the building shelters a collection of religious objects which includes two extraordinary *custodias* (monstrances). The larger one, known as La Lechuga, dates from the early 18th century and comes from Bogotá's Iglesia de San Ignacio. It is 4902g of pure gold, encrusted with 1485 emeralds, one sapphire, 13 rubies, 26 diamonds, 168 amethysts, one topaz and 62 pearls. The other one, which has been brought from the Iglesia de Santa Clara La Real of Tunja, dates from a slightly later period and has a marginally shorter list of precious stones.

## Museo Arqueológico

The Archaeological Museum *(☎ 243 1048; Carrera 6 No 7-43; adult/student US$1.50/ 0.75; open 8.30am-5pm Tues-Fri, 9.30am- 5pm Sat, 10am-4pm Sun)* features an extensive collection of pottery from the country's major pre-Columbian groups, confirming the high technical level and artistic ability achieved by local Indian cultures. The museum is housed in the Casa del Marqués de San Jorge, a beautifully restored 17th-century mansion and an outstanding piece of local colonial architecture known as *arquitectura santafereña*.

## Museo de Arte Colonial

The Museum of Colonial Art *(☎ 284 1373; Carrera 6 No 9-77; adult/student US$1/0.75; open 9am-5pm Tues-Fri, 10am-4pm Sat & Sun)* was inaugurated in 1942 in a great 17th-century building, which was originally a Jesuit college. It features paintings, carvings, furniture, silverware, books and documents from the colonial era.

The museum's pride and joy is a collection of 76 oil paintings and 106 drawings (not all of which are on display) by Gregorio Vásquez de Arce y Ceballos (1638–1711), the most important painter of the colonial era. This is the largest collection of the artist assembled in one place.

## Museo de Artes y Tradiciones Populares

Housed in an old Augustine convent, the Museum of Popular Arts and Traditions *(☎ 342 1266; Carrera 8 No 7-21; adult/student US$1.25/0.50; open 8.30am-5pm Tues-Sat)* features crafts representing 20 major indigenous cultures currently living in Colombia (of a total of about 80 that exist in the country). The collection is pretty small, but gives some idea about the diversity and richness of Colombia's indigenous craftwork. There is a craft shop attached (see Shopping later) and a restaurant, Claustro de San Agustín (see Places to Eat later). Both the shop and the restaurant are also open on Monday.

## Museo del 20 de Julio

The Museum of Independence *(☎ 282 6647; Calle 11 No 6-94; adult/student US$2/1.50; open 9am-4.30pm Tues-Fri, 10am-3.30pm Sat & Sun)* is in a colonial house called the Casa del Florero, on the corner of Plaza de Bolívar. It was here on 20 July 1810 that the Creole rebellion against Spanish rule broke out. The museum has memorabilia (documents, paintings, personal objects etc) recalling that important event, a milestone in the struggle for independence which was achieved nine years later.

## Museo de Arte Moderno

Opened in the mid-1980s in a modern, spacious building, the Museum of Modern Art *(☎ 286 0466; Calle 24 No 6-00; adult/student US$1.50/1; open 10am-6pm Tues-Sat, 10am- 3pm Sun)* focuses on various forms of visual arts (painting, sculpture, photography) from the beginning of the 20th century until the present. There are no permanent collections on display; all rooms are given to frequently changing exhibitions by national and sometimes foreign artists.

## Museo Nacional

The National Museum *(☎ 334 8366; Carrera 7 No 28-66; adult/student US$1.50/1; open 10am-5.30pm Tues-Sat, 10am-3.30pm Sun)* is in an unusual building known as El Panóptico. It was designed as the city prison by Thomas Reed (the same English architect who planned the Capitolio) and built of stone and brick on a Greek cross floor plan in the second half of the 19th century. The jail, which housed over 200 cells for both rhen and women, was closed in 1946 and after considerable internal reconstruction was transformed into a museum in 1948.

The well-prepared exhibition gives an insight into Colombian history from the first settlers to the modern times, through a wealth of exhibits including historic objects, photos, maps, artefacts, paintings, documents and weapons, all displayed in several halls over the museum's three floors.

There's also a modern art section featuring paintings by some of the best Colombian artists including Guillermo Wiedemann, Alejandro Obregón and Fernando Botero. The museum also puts on temporary exhibitions.

## Quinta de Bolívar

The Quinta (☎ 336 6419; Calle 20 No 2-91 Este; adult/student US$1.50/1; open 9am-5pm Tues-Sat, 10am-4pm Sun) is a country mansion set in a garden, built in 1800 at the foot of the Cerro de Monserrate and donated to Simón Bolívar in 1820 in gratitude for his services. Bolívar used it as a retreat on various occasions.

The Quinta was acquired by the government, declared a national monument and turned into a museum. The house has been furnished in the style of Bolívar's day and filled with his possessions, documents, weapons, maps, uniforms and medals. Don't miss a stroll in the lovely, sloping garden.

## Other Museums

The Museo de Trajes Regionales (☎ 282 6531; Calle 10 No 6-36) displays costumes from different regions of Colombia. Museo Militar (☎ 281 3131; Calle 10 No 4-92) traces the evolution of Colombia's armed forces. Museo del Siglo XIX (☎ 281 9948; Carrera 8 No 7-93) focuses on the culture and art of the 19th century. Museo de Desarrollo Urbano (☎ 281 4150; in Planetario Distrital, Calle 26 No 6-07) provides an insight into the urban development of Bogotá through old maps, photos, drawings, models, antiques etc.

In northern Bogotá, you can visit the Museo El Chicó (☎ 623 1066; Carrera 7 No 93-01; adult/student US$1.50/1; open 9am-12.30pm & 2pm-5pm Mon-Fri, 9am-noon Sat) housed in a fine 18th-century casona (large, rambling, old house) surrounded by what was once a vast hacienda, now little more than a garden. It features a collection of historic objects of decorative art, mostly from Europe.

## CHURCHES

Having been the capital since the early days of Spanish rule and a centre of evangelisation of a vast colony, Bogotá boasts a good collection of colonial churches, most dating from the 17th and 18th centuries. Unlike the outwardly ornate churches of the other viceroyalties' capitals, such as Lima or Mexico City, those of Bogotá have usually quite austere exteriors, though internal decoration is often quite elaborate.

Two elements of decoration are particularly noticeable: the influence of the Spanish-Moorish style known as the Mudéjar style (mainly in the ceiling ornamentation), and paintings by Gregorio Vásquez de Arce Y Ceballos, the best-known painter of the colonial era, who lived and worked in Bogotá.

## Iglesia Museo de Santa Clara

Today open as a museum, the Church of Santa Clara (☎ 337 6762; Carrera 8 No 8-91; adult/student US$2/1.50; open 9am-5pm Tues-Fri, 10am-4pm Sat & Sun) is probably the most representative of Bogotá's colonial churches. Built between 1629 and 1674 as a part of the Poor Clares Convent, the church is a single-nave construction topped with a barrel vault painted with floral motifs. The walls are entirely covered with paintings (more than 100 of them), statues of saints and altarpieces, all dating from the 17th and 18th centuries. The wooden figure of Santa Clara in the high altar is the oldest piece of artwork in the church.

## Catedral Primada

The cathedral (☎ 243 9794; Plaza de Bolívar; open 9am-10am Mon-Sat, 9am-2pm Sun) is a monumental building in the neoclassical style. It stands on the site where the first mass was celebrated after Bogotá had been founded in 1538. (Some historians argue that the first mass was celebrated on Plazoleta del Chorro de Quevedo, Carrera 2 at Calle 13.) Understandably, the original church where the event took place was just a small thatched chapel. A more substantial building was erected in 1556–65, but soon after collapsed because of poor foundations. In 1572, the third church went up, but the earthquake of 1785 turned it into ruins. Only in 1807 was the massive building that stands to this day initiated and it was successfully completed by 1823. Today, it's Bogotá's largest church. The interior is spacious and solemn but has relatively little ornamentation. The tomb of Jiménez de Quesada, the founder of Bogotá, is in the largest chapel off the right-hand aisle.

## Capilla del Sagrario

The Sagrario Chapel (☎ 243 9794; Plaza de Bolívar; open 8am-noon & 1pm-4pm Mon-Fri), on the same side of the plaza as the cathedral, was built in the second half of the 17th century and has preserved its mannerist–baroque facade, which is considered to be one of the best examples of arquitectura santafereña. The chapel boasts a Mudéjar vault and six large paintings by Gregorio Vásquez.

## Iglesia de San Ignacio

The Church of San Ignacio (☎ 342 1639; Calle 10 No 6-35; open 9am-noon & 3pm-6pm Mon-Fri, 9am-noon Sat & Sun) was begun by the Jesuits in 1610 and although opened for worship in 1635, it was not completed until their expulsion in 1767. It was the largest church during the colony and perhaps the most magnificent. Today it's one of the most richly decorated churches that houses a wealth of artwork, including numerous colonial paintings. It has a typical Mudéjar vault and a fine main altarpiece (carved in 1749 by Pedro Laboria), plus a dozen elaborate side altarpieces, each different, lining both aisles.

## Iglesia de San Francisco

Completed in 1556, the Church of San Francisco (☎ 341 2357; Av Jiménez at Carrera 7; open 7am-7pm Mon-Fri, 7am-1pm & 6pm-7pm Sat & Sun) is Bogotá's oldest surviving church. It is rather sober from the outside, but the interior is elaborately decorated. Of particular interest is the extraordinary 17th-century gilded main altarpiece, which is Bogotá's largest and most elaborate piece of art of its kind. Also of note are the Mudéjar ornamentation of the ceiling under the organ loft and a collection of side altarpieces. The church is always full with worshippers.

## Iglesia de la Veracruz

The Veracruz Church (☎ 342 1343; Calle 16 No 7-19; open for mass only at 8am, noon and 6pm) is known as the National Pantheon because many of the heroes of the struggle for independence have been buried here. Of the 80 patriots executed by the Spaniards in

Bogotá between 1810 and 1819, most have found their resting place in La Veracruz.

The church has a rather simple interior, topped with a panelled Mudéjar vault. There are four richly decorated historic altarpieces in the right-hand aisle, of which the impressive Señor de la Buena Esperanza, which has sat at the back of the aisle since colonial times, attracts the major number of faithful.

The tomb of the martyrs is in the nave in front of the high altar. In the niche in the left-hand wall, left of the tomb, is Cristo de los Mártires. This small Christ figure on the cross witnessed all the executions of the heroes buried in the church.

## Other Churches

There are a dozen other interesting historic churches in the centre.

The Iglesia La Tercera (Carrera 7 at Calle 16) is remarkable for its fine stone facade and, inside, for altarpieces carved in walnut and cedar.

Iglesia de La Concepción (Calle 10 No 9-50) is the second-oldest existing church in Bogotá (after San Francisco) and is noted for its extraordinary Mudéjar vault, brought from Seville and installed in the presbytery.

Iglesia de San Diego (Carrera 7 No 26-37) is a lovely whitewashed church built as part of a Franciscan monastery at the beginning of the 17th century. At that time it was well outside the town; today it is surrounded by the forest of high-rise buildings that form the Centro Internacional.

Iglesia del Carmen (Carrera 5 No 8-36) is the most recent church in Bogotá's colonial quarter, inaugurated in 1938. It's an impressive piece of architecture, resembling a colourful wedding cake. The interior boasts fine stained-glass windows and a mosaic of the Virgen del Carmen over the high altar.

## CERRO DE MONSERRATE

This is one of the peaks (3160m) in the mountain range flanking the city to the east and overlooking the Sabana de Bogotá. It's easily recognisable by the church crowning its top. Monserrate has become a mecca for pilgrims, due to the statue of the Señor Caído (the Fallen Christ), dating from the 1650s, to which many miracles have been attributed. The church was erected after the original chapel had been destroyed by an earthquake in 1917.

Several cafés, restaurants and stalls selling food and crafts have sprung up around the church, and are particularly busy on Sunday when most pilgrims and tourists come.

The view of the city from the top is superb. On a clear day you can even spot Los Nevados, the volcanic range in the Cordillera Central, 135km away, noted for a symmetrical cone of the Nevado del Tolima.

There are three ways to get to the top: by *teleférico* (cable car), funicular railway or on foot along a path.

Both the cable car and funicular run from the lower station (☎ 284 57 00; Carrera 2E No 21-48) at the foot of the Cerro. It's close to the city centre, but the access road leads through a poor suburb, so don't walk; instead take the bus marked 'Funicular' or a taxi.

The cable car operates every 15 minutes 9.30am to midnight Monday to Saturday, 6am to 5pm Sunday. The funicular normally only operates on Sunday and public holidays, 6am to 6pm. The return fare by either is US$4.

If you want to do the trip on foot (one hour uphill), do it only on Sunday, when crowds of pilgrims go; on weekdays, take it for granted that you will be robbed along the way.

## MIRADOR TORRE COLPATRIA

For another impressive bird's-eye view of the city, although quite different, go to the top of the Colpatria Tower (☎ 283 6697; Carrera 7 No 24-89; admission US$1.25; open 11am-5pm Sat, Sun & holidays). The 360° lookout atop this 48-storey 162m-high skyscraper (built from 1975 to 1979) provides excellent views in all directions.

At night, the tower is illuminated by a hi-tech light system composed of 36 reflectors placed around the top of the building. It features filters of different colours operated by a computer.

## JARDÍN BOTÁNICO JOSÉ CELESTINO MUTIS

The botanical gardens (☎ 630 0949; Calle 57 No 61-13; adult/student US$1.50/1; open 8am-4pm Tues-Fri, 9am-4pm Sat & Sun) have a variety of national flora from different climatic zones, some in gardens and others in greenhouses. To get there take a bus running along the Autopista El Dorado (the bus to the airport will let you off near the gardens).

## MALOKA

Maloka (☎ 427 2707; Carrera 68D No 40A-51; adult/student US$3.50/2; open 9am-6pm Tues-Sun) is an interactive centre of science and technology, possibly the continent's largest and best. It features a variety of thematic exhibitions such as the universe, human being, technology, life, water and biodiversity, plus a hi-tech Cine-Domo cinema. Set aside at least three hours for your visit.

## LANGUAGE COURSES

Bogotá's best-known school of Spanish language is the **Universidad Javeriana's Centro Latinoamericano** (☎ 320 8320; Carrera 10 No 65-48), which offers regular one-year courses and three-week intensive courses. Other providers to check include the **Universidad Nacional** (☎ 316 5335), **Universidad de los Andes** (☎ 286 9211) and **Universidad Externado de Colombia** (☎ 282 6066).

## ORGANISED TOURS

**Eco-Guías** (☎ 347 5736, 212 1423; W www.ecoguias.com; Carrera 7 No 57-39, Oficina 501) is an adventure travel company which focuses on ecotourism and offers individualised tours to various regions of the country, including some national parks. It also organises reasonably priced Sunday walks in the environs of Bogotá.

**Sal Si Puedes** (☎ 283 3765; Carrera 7 No 17-01, Oficina 639) is an association of outdoor-minded people who organise weekend walks in the countryside. These are mostly one-day excursions to Cundinamarca, though longer trips to other regions are also arranged during holiday periods and long weekends. Other associations of this type include **Colombia Ecoturística** (☎ 241 0065, 366 3059; Carrera 3 No 21-46, Apto 802B), **Andarines del Senderismo** (☎ 617 8857; Transversal 48 No 96-48) and **Viajar y Vivir** (☎ 211 1368, 211 1205; Carrera 13 No 61-47, Local 125).

## SPECIAL EVENTS

Bogotá has its **Feria Taurina**, or bullfighting season, when the major *corridas* take place. It's celebrated in January and February, with bullfights held on most Sundays. Famous international matadors are invited, mostly from Spain and Mexico. The Feria is held at the city's 13,600-seat, Moorish-style bullring, Plaza de Toros de Santamaría, built between 1927 and 1931.

**BOGOTÁ**

# CENTRAL BOGOTÁ

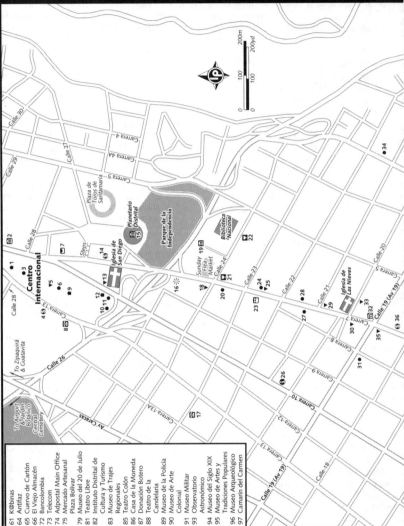

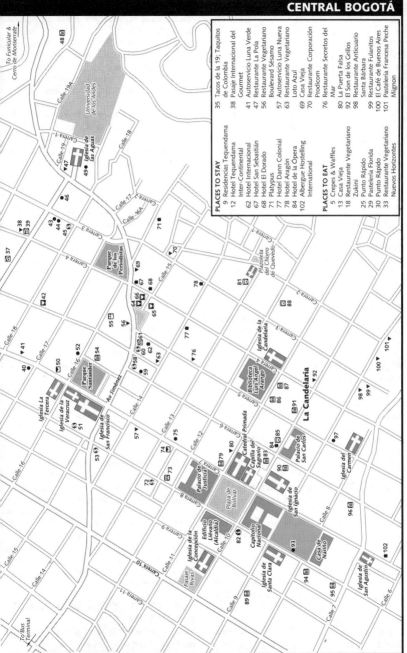

**PLACES TO STAY**

9  Residencias Tequendama
12  Hotel Tequendama Inter-Continental
62  Hotel Internacional
67  Hotel San Sebastián
68  Hotel El Dorado
71  Platypus
77  Hotel Dann Colonial
78  Hotel Aragón
84  Hotel de la Opera
102  Albergue Hostelling International

**PLACES TO EAT**

5  Crepes & Waffles
13  Casa Vieja
18  Restaurante Vegetariano Zúkini
25  Punto Rápido
29  Pastelería Florida
30  Punto Rápido
33  Restaurante Vegetariano Nuevos Horizontes
35  Tacos de la 19; Taquitos de Colombia
38  Pasaje Internacional del Gourmet
41  Autoservicio Luna Verde
47  Restaurante La Pola
56  Restaurante Vegetariano Boulevard Sésamo
57  Autoservicio Luna Nueva
63  Restaurante Vegetariano Loto Azul
69  Casa Vieja
70  Restaurante Corporación Prodicom
76  Restaurante Secretos del Mar
80  La Puerta Falsa
92  El Son de los Grillos
98  Restaurante Anticuario Santa Bárbara
99  Restaurante Fulanitos
100  El Café de Buenos Aires
101  Pastelería Francesa Peche Mignon

The **Festival Iberoamericano de Teatro**, a theatre festival featuring groups from all of Latin America and beyond, takes place in March/April of every even year. Many of the local groups present their latest achievements, so it's a good time to taste what's going on in Colombian theatre.

The international book fair, **Feria Internacional del Libro**, is attended by publishers from all over the world and is held annually in late April and early May.

The **Feria Internacional de Bogotá** is an international fair featuring industrial and consumer goods. It takes place in July and/or August of every even year.

Organised by the Teatro Libre in September, the **Festival de Jazz** features some local and other Latin jazz artists, plus an occasional US or European star.

With a 20-year history, the **Festival de Cine de Bogotá**, the city's film festival, attracts films from all around the world, including a usually strong Latin American selection. It's held in October.

A crafts fair, **Expoartesanías**, is organised in December and gathers together artisans and their products from all around the country. Crafts are for sale and it's an excellent place to buy them.

## PLACES TO STAY

Bogotá has loads of places to stay in every price bracket. A good share of hotels is concentrated in the city centre. This is the most convenient area to stay in, as most tourist attractions are here.

The alternative area is the northern part of the city, but there are virtually no budget hotels here.

## PLACES TO STAY – BUDGET

The accommodation listed in this section includes anything that costs up to about US$15 for a double. Most hotels that fall into this price category are in the city centre.

### Central Bogotá

The historic suburb of La Candelaria is the most popular area with foreign travellers and it has a reasonable choice of budget accommodation.

**Platypus** (☎ 341 2874, 341 3104; W www .platypusbogota.com; Calle 16 No 2-43; dorm beds US$5, singles/doubles without bath US$8/11) is by far the most popular budget place among backpackers. It has no sign on the door, just a picture of the platypus, so don't be confused. The hostel has three four-bed dorms and several singles and doubles. Although conditions are quite simple and only a couple of rooms have private baths, the place is safe, clean and pleasant and has hot water. The hostel offers book exchange, Internet access, laundry and kitchen facilities, and there's a cosy dining room where you can relax and have a *tinto* (a small cup of black coffee), which is provided free of charge. The friendly owner, Germán (pronounced Hermann), a long-time traveller himself, speaks several languages and is an excellent source of practical information.

If the Platypus is full, you can try one of the following places in the same area, though none of these provides such a wide range of facilities or extensive information.

**Hotel Aragón** (☎ 284 8325; Carrera 3 No 14-13; US$5 per person) is one of the cheapest places around. It has bright rooms with large windows (which is not common in Bogotá's budget hotels), but it only has shared baths.

**Hotel El Dorado** (☎ 334 3988; Carrera 4 No 15-00; doubles with/without bath US$12/10) is another convenient option. It has fairly small rooms, but most of them have private baths.

**Hotel Internacional** (☎ 341 8731; Carrera 5 No 14-45; singles/doubles/triples without bath US$5/10/13, with bath US$6/11/15) is a favourite haunt among Israeli travellers. It provides Internet access and the use of a kitchen.

**Albergue Hostelling International** (☎ 280 3202; Carrera 7 No 6-10; dorm beds with/ without bath US$5/4.50) is a 105-bed youth hostel, actually the only genuine youth hostel in Colombia. Located four blocks south of Plaza de Bolívar, it's not ideally convenient but sometimes hosts foreign travellers. It has six- and eight-bed dorms, most with shared bath (hot water in the morning only). An HI membership card will save you US$1 on the listed prices.

## PLACES TO STAY – MID-RANGE & TOP END

Most of upmarket hotels are in the northern districts of the city, but there are also some interesting options in the centre.

## Central Bogotá

**Hotel San Sebastián** (☎ 480 0503; Av Jiménez No 3-97; singles/doubles/triples US$18/25/32) is one of the few reasonable central mid-range establishments. It provides fairly good, airy rooms which all have TV and private bath, and is well situated just a couple of blocks from the Gold Museum.

**Hotel Dann Colonial** (☎ 341 1680; Calle 14 No 4-21; singles/doubles US$26/36) sits in La Candelaria. Despite its name it's a modern building, not a colonial one. This 30-year-old, 80-room hotel has seen better days and is in need of refurbishment, yet it's still probably worth its moderate rates. There may be some discounted room rates for students.

**Residencias Tequendama** (☎ 286 8111; W www.residenciastequendama.com.co; Carrera 10 No 27-51; singles/doubles/triples/quads US$45/50/70/90) is in two 30-storey towers in the middle of the Centro Internacional (don't confuse it with Hotel Tequendama just a few steps away). It has 274 mini-apartments equipped with a bathroom, kitchen and one or two bedrooms, suitable for one to five persons. You can stay just one night (at the rates listed above), but the longer you stay the cheaper the price per day becomes.

**Hotel Tequendama Inter-Continental** (☎ 382 0300; W www.inter-tequendama.com .co; Carrera 10 No 26-21; doubles US$100-140) is the top-notch option in the Centro Internacional. This establishment provides comfortable rooms and most facilities you might need, including a gym, sauna, Internet access, two restaurants and two bars. With 525 rooms, it's Bogotá's largest accommodation option.

**Hotel de la Ópera** (☎ 336 2066; W www .hotelopera.com.co; Calle 10 No 5-72; double rooms/suites US$95/115) is by far the best accommodation option in La Candelaria. Housed in two meticulously restored historic buildings right next door to the Teatro Colón, this five-star hotel has much charm and character, and a rooftop restaurant with views over red-tiled roofs of the surrounding colonial houses. The atmosphere and service are great, and the place is small enough that you receive personal attention. If you need a classy hotel in the historic centre this is the place to go.

## Northern Bogotá

**La Casona del Patio Amarillo** (☎ 212 8805; Carrera 8 No 69-24; singles/doubles/triples without bath US$12/20/24, with bath US$14/24/33) is one of the cheapest options in the area. It's in a quiet residential neighbourhood with good transport to the centre. The rooms are spotlessly clean and airy, and the place offers various services, including breakfast (US$2), laundry and Internet.

**Hotel Saint Simon** (☎ 621 8188; Carrera 14 No 81-34; double rooms/suites US$40/45) is the cheapest accommodation in the Zona Rosa, an attractive suburb noted for its nightlife. Take a suite – they are significantly better than standard rooms and the price difference isn't great.

**Hotel Los Urapanes** (☎ 218 1188; Carrera 13 No 83-19; double rooms/suites US$60/70) is the smallest (32 rooms) and perhaps the quietest option throughout the Zona Rosa. Here again, suites are considerably larger than rooms and are equipped with a fridge and a kitchenette.

**Hotel La Bohème** (☎ 644 7100; W www .hotelesroyal.com; Calle 82 No 12-35; double rooms/suites US$70/85) is a top-end choice in the Zona Rosa. It has a bit of European style and flavour and offers a satisfactory range of facilities, including air-conditioning and Internet access. Breakfast is included in the hotel rates.

**Casa Medina** (☎ 217 0288; W www.hoteles -charleston.com; Carrera 7 No 69A-22; suites US$160-240) is one of Bogotá's finest and most atmospheric places to stay. Housed in a restored historic building, it combines old-time charm and beauty with modern facilities. In 1993, a large extension was built, adding 32 new suites to the 26 existing ones. The hotel belongs to the international chain of Charleston Hotels and can be easily booked worldwide.

## PLACES TO EAT

The Bogotá phone directory lists about 1000 restaurants and that's not all: there are markets, food stalls and other establishments serving meals, such as hotels, supermarkets, transport terminals, universities, clubs and societies. Almost every foreign cuisine is available and, of course, a full range of regional Colombian dishes. On the whole, the city centre is better for budget eating while the north takes pride in fine dining.

If you are on a tight budget you will be stuck with the regular set meals – *almuerzo* (lunch) and *comida* (dinner) – which are the staple offerings of hundreds of cheap restaurants scattered throughout the city. They cater for office employees and do much of their business at lunch time, between noon and 2pm. Some of them also serve a set dinner, roughly between 6pm and 8pm. A set meal costs somewhere between US$1.50 and US$3, rarely more.

## Central Bogotá

There are so many places serving set lunches all over the centre that it's hard to make any reasonable selection. Possibly the best way to choose is to drop into one, see what people are eating and stay or move on to the next one.

**Restaurante Corporación Prodicom** *(Calle 15A No 2-21; set lunches US$1.50-2)* is relatively new, but has already become popular with locals for its tasty lunches, which are great value.

**Pasaje Internacional del Gourmet** *(Carrera 4 No 19-44/56; lunches US$1.50-4)* shelters nearly a dozen restaurants, so you have quite a choice under one roof.

There's also a good choice of vegetarian restaurants in the city centre. They are all simple, virtually without decor, and serve inexpensive, straightforward food, including set lunches for around US$2. Most of them operate from Monday to Friday only, and close late afternoon. They include **Restaurante Vegetariano Loto Azul** *(Carrera 5A No 14-00)*, **Restaurante Vegetariano Boulevard Sésamo** *(Av Jiménez No 4-64)*, **Restaurante Vegetariano Zukini** *(Calle 24 No 7-12)* and **Restaurante Vegetariano Nuevos Horizontes** *(Calle 20 No 6-37)*.

There are a number of barbecued-chicken restaurants in the centre, mainly on Carreras 7 and 10. A half-chicken with potatoes or chips makes a really filling meal for US$3 to US$4. Should you prefer pizza, there are plenty of pizzerias – several of these are conveniently grouped on Calle 19 between Carreras 3 and 7. There are also plenty of delicatessens, mostly on Calle 19 and Carrera 7, which serve inexpensive sandwiches.

**Pastelería Francesa Peche Mignon** *(Calle 9 No 1-95; breakfast US$2-3)* has good, fresh bread and pastries and also provides great breakfasts.

**Pastelería Florida** *(Carrera 7 No 20-82; snacks US$0.50-1.50)* is the place for the famous chocolate santafereño (hot chocolate with cheese and local bread).

**La Puerta Falsa** *(Calle 11 No 6-50; snacks US$0.50-1.50)*, in a 370-year-old house beside the cathedral, is Bogotá's (and Colombia's for that matter) oldest operating place to eat. It serves local snacks (including tamales and chocolate santafereño) and sweets as it has done since 1816.

**Tacos de la 19** and **Taquitos de Colombia** *(Carrera 7 at Calle 19; snacks US$0.30-1)* are two minuscule snack bars next door to each other, serving beautiful tacos Mexicanos and other snacks.

**Crepes & Waffles** *(Carrera 10 No 27-91, Piso 2, Local 2-33; crepes US$2-5)* in the Centro Internacional has delicious crepes with a range of fillings and great salads. There are several outlets of this chain in the north (see the following Northern Bogotá section).

**Punto Rápido** *(Carrera 7 No 19-53 • Carrera 7 No 22-60; meals US$2-4)* is a chain of self-service budget cafeterias open 24 hours, with two convenient central locations at Carrera 7. Similar and even marginally cheaper (but open till 9pm only) are **Autoservicio Luna Nueva** *(Carrera 7 No 13-55)* and **Autoservicio Luna Verde** *(Carrera 7 No 17-48)*.

**Restaurante Secretos del Mar** *(Carrera 5 No 13-20; mains US$2-5)* looks basic but has delicious food typical of the Pacific Coast. For more Pacific cuisine try one of several budget *pescaderías* (fish restaurants) on Carrera 4 between Calles 20 and 21.

**El Son de los Grillos** *(Calle 10 No 3-60; mains US$2.50-5)* is a charming, cosy place that serves good food at reasonable prices.

**Claustro de San Agustín** *(☎ 342 1803; Carrera 8 No 7-21; mains US$3-5)*, in the Museo de Artes y Tradiciones Populares, has delicious regional dishes at lunch time (until about 3pm). It has a different menu every day of the week.

**Restaurante La Pola** *(☎ 566 5654; Calle 19 No 1-85; mains US$4-7)* is another place to go and try some of Bogotá's specialities such as the *ajiaco* (soup with chicken, corn on the cob and three varieties of potato, served with cream and capers) or *puchero sabanero*.

**Casa Vieja** *(☎ 342 6752; Av Jiménez No 3-63; mains US$6-9)* is yet another address for traditional local cuisine, but it's more expensive. It's open for lunch only, but there's another **Casa Vieja** (☎ 336 0588; Carrera 10 No 26-60) in the building adjoining San Diego church, which is open for dinner as well. There's a third Casa Vieja in the north (see the following Northern Bogotá section). All three have the same menu and prices, and the decor is old-fashioned.

**Restaurante Fulanitos** (☎ 352 0173; Carrera 3 No 8-61; mains US$4-7) is a beautifully arranged, informal place which offers food typical of the Valle del Cauca in southern Colombia.

**El Café de Buenos Aires** (☎ 561 3282; Calle 9 No 2-17; mains US$6-10) is in a charming colonial house that provides several different ambiences. It offers fine Argentine steaks and some international fare.

**Restaurante Anticuario Santa Bárbara** (☎ 243 3691; Calle 9 No 3-27; mains US$6-10) offers typical Bogotá food prepared according to traditional recipes and served in a part of a private home adorned with antiques that feels warm and cosy. Booking is essential.

## Northern Bogotá

There are hundreds of restaurants in Bogotá's northern suburbs, and a thorough exploration would take months. The north is particularly renowned for fine (and consequently expensive) dining, but budget eating is no problem either. Plenty of restaurants, particularly those located in the areas that feature many offices, provide reasonably priced lunches. They are usually easily recognised by boards with the menu and prices, which they place at the door.

The north also shelters some outlets of the restaurant chains mentioned in the previous section, including another **Pastelería Francesa Peche Mignon** (Carrera 13 No 83-21), **Crepes & Waffles** (Carrera 9 No 73-33 • Carrera 12A No 83-40 • Carrera 11 No 85-79 • Calle 93B No 12-10) and **Casa Vieja** (☎ 236 3421; Carrera 11 No 89-08).

Here are some other options in the northern suburbs:

**Restaurante Vegetariano El Integral Natural** (☎ 256 0899; Carrera 11 No 95-10; meals US$2-4) is one of the better budget options for vegetarians. This small restaurant offers set lunches and a menu which changes daily.

**La Esquina de la Mona** (Calle 82 No 14-32; mains US$2-3) is one of the cheapest

restaurants in the Zona Rosa and is open till late. Take note of this in case you get hungry at midnight while bar-hopping, as the Zona doesn't abound in budget eateries.

**Ventura Soup & Salad** (Calle 90 No 16-36; salads US$2-5) has excellent salads.

**Restaurante Iraní** (Carrera 16 No 48-79; mains US$3-5) provides solid, reasonably priced Middle Eastern food.

**Café & Crêpes** (☎ 236 2688; Carrera 16 No 82-17; mains US$3-6) is a charming, informal place which offers good food, including crepes and salads, plus plenty of drinks.

**Restaurante Wok** (☎ 218 9040; Carrera 13 No 82-74; mains US$5-10) is one of the Zona Rosa's better options for Asian cuisine.

**La Casa de la Paella** (☎ 610 4242; Calle 93 No 13A-46; mains US$6-10) is a fine, moderately priced Spanish restaurant, offering tapas, paellas and other typical fare.

**Restaurante Las Cuatro Estaciones** (☎ 218 0745; Carrera 8A No 98-38; mains US$6-12) has a varied international menu, mostly French and Spanish, including a mouthwatering paella.

## ENTERTAINMENT

Bogotá has far more cultural activities than any other city in Colombia. Have a look at the entertainment columns of leading local paper El Tiempo. Its Friday edition carries a what's-on section called Eskpe, which gives brief descriptions of selected coming events, including music, theatre, cinema and exhibitions, along with short reviews of some restaurants, nightspots etc.

You can also check the new what's-on monthly magazine Informativo Cultural del Altiplano Quira (US$0.50).

Go online and check W www.terra.com.co/bogota, which covers cinemas, theatres, nightclubs, cultural events and more.

## Cinema

Bogotá has about 60 cinemas offering the usual Hollywood fare. For something more thought-provoking, check the programme of the cinematecas (art cinemas). Regular cinemas of that type include **Cinemateca Distrital** (☎ 334 3451; Carrera 7 No 22-79), **Museo de Arte Moderno** (☎ 286 0466; Calle 24 No 6-00) and **Auditorio de la Antigua Calle del Agrado** (☎ 281 4671; Calle 16 No 4-75). Major universities have cineclubes (film clubs) which show films

BOGOTÁ

# NORTHERN BOGOTÁ

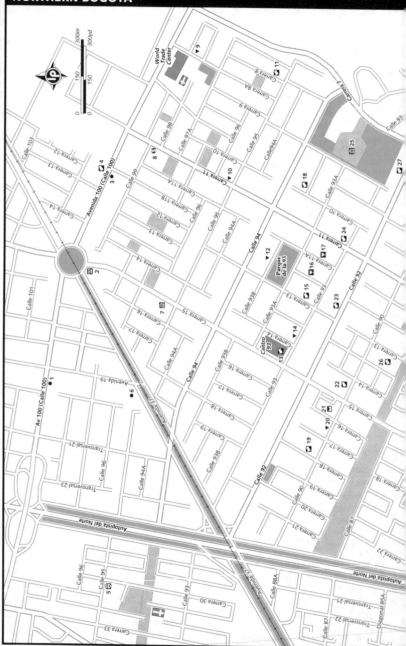

# NORTHERN BOGOTÁ

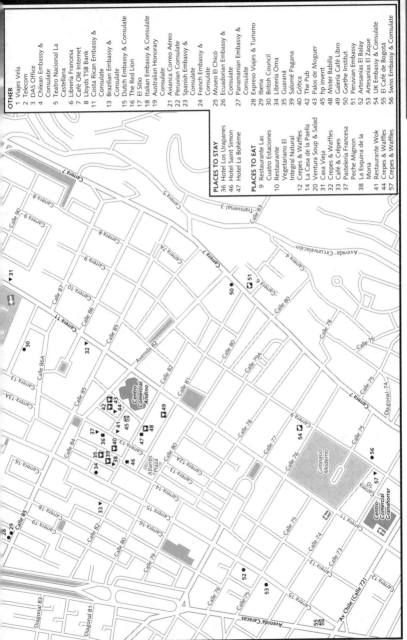

**OTHER**
1 Viajes Vela
2 Telecom
3 DAS Office
4 Chilean Embassy & Consulate
5 Teatro Nacional La Castellana
6 Librería Francesa
7 Café Olé Internet
8 Lloyds TSB Bank
11 Costa Rican Embassy & Consulate
13 Brazilian Embassy & Consulate
15 Dutch Embassy & Consulate
16 The Red Lion
17 El Sito
18 Italian Embassy & Consulate
19 Australian Honorary Consulate
21 Avianca Correo Aéreo
22 Peruvian Consulate
23 Spanish Embassy & Consulate
24 French Embassy & Consulate
25 Museo El Chicó
26 Ecuadorian Embassy & Consulate
27 Panamanian Embassy & Consulate
28 Expreso Viajes & Turismo
29 Iberia
30 British Council
34 Librería Oma
35 Guaraná
39 Salomé Pagana
40 Gótica
42 The Pub
43 Palos de Moguer
45 hp invent
48 Mister Babilla
49 Galería Café Libro
50 Goethe Institut
51 Peruvian Embassy
52 Artesanías El Balay
53 Artesanías El Zaque
54 UK Embassy & Consulate
55 El Café de Bogotá
56 Swiss Embassy & Consulate

**PLACES TO STAY**
36 Hotel Los Urapanes
46 Hotel Saint Simon
47 Hotel La Bohème

**PLACES TO EAT**
9 Restaurante Las Cuatro Estaciones
10 Restaurante Vegetariano El Integral Natural
12 Crepes & Waffles
14 La Casa de la Paella
20 Ventura Soup & Salad
31 Casa Vieja
32 Crepes & Waffles
33 Café & Crêpes
37 Pastelería Francesa Peche Mignon
38 La Esquina de la Mona
41 Restaurante Wok
44 Crepes & Waffles
57 Crepes & Waffles

on campus or utilise commercial cinemas or auditoriums of some institutions. They are accessible to anybody.

Cinematecas and cineclubes often offer interesting programmes, featuring films that are not seen elsewhere – such as local and other Latin American films which rarely make it to commercial cinemas. All films are shown with the original soundtrack and almost all have Spanish subtitles (except, of course, Spanish-language films).

## Theatre

There are a dozen regular groups with their own theatres, and many more that put on their productions wherever they can.

Over the past three decades, **Teatro de la Candelaria** (☎ 281 4814; Calle 12 No 2-59) has been one of the most inspiring venues in town. Another place to check is **Teatro Libre** (☎ 281 4834; Calle 13 No 2-44), although most of its productions are now presented in a new branch of **Teatro Libre** (☎ 217 1988; Calle 62 No 10-65) in Chapinero. **Teatro Experimental La Mama** (☎ 211 2709; Calle 63 No 9-60) can also have something interesting on offer.

**Teatro Colón** (☎ 341 0475; Calle 10 No 5-32) is the venue for large-scale productions, mostly by invited foreign groups. The historic auditorium is a piece of art in itself. **Teatro Nacional** (☎ 217 4577; Calle 71 No 10-25) focuses on mainstream fare and is another popular venue for visiting groups. The theatre has an offshoot, **Teatro Nacional La Castellana** (☎ 618 1252; Calle 95 No 30-13).

## Classical Music

Check the programme of the **Biblioteca Luis Ángel Arango** (☎ 343 1212; Calle 11 No 4-14), which runs concerts in its own concert hall. Concerts by international artists are usually presented on Wednesday (tickets are rather expensive) while young local artists are scheduled on Monday (nominal fee).

Another regular stage for invited orchestras is the Auditorio León De Greiff in the campus of the **Universidad Nacional** (☎ 316 5562; Carrera 30 at Calle 45), which usually has concerts on Saturday (tickets cost US$1.50).

## Nightlife

Bogotá is alive 24 hours a day and there's a lot of activity going on at night. There are plenty of nightspots, including nightclubs, bars and discos, offering a variety of ambience and musical rhythms, such as rock, reggae, rap, tango, samba, techno, hip-hop and salsa. The last-named is perhaps the most popular among hot-blooded city dwellers, and a worthwhile experience for travellers. There are plenty of disco-type places called *salsotecas*, which play salsa predominantly or exclusively. Don't miss trying one, if only to listen to the music and watch people dancing.

Many discos are open every night except on Sunday and Monday, though Thursday, Friday and Saturday, especially around midnight, are when things are hottest. On weekends there may be live music in some places. There's usually no cover charge on weekdays but there may be on the weekend. Bars and discos don't usually serve any snacks or meals, so arrive after your dinner.

The nightlife in Bogotá (and in the whole of Colombia for that matter) is very dynamic and volatile. Venues mushroom like spring flowers and often close down soon after. They also frequently change names, owners, decor and music. And they are very dependent on the fashion of the day; an extremely trendy place one month can suddenly be deserted the next.

**Central Bogotá** The city centre has revived over recent years and nightspots have mushroomed, particularly in La Candelaria. Most are reasonably cheap, offering a bottle of beer for less than US$1.

**Quiebra Canto** (☎ 243 1630; Carrera 5 No 17-76) is one of the most popular nighttime hang-outs in the centre. This pleasant double-level disco features various music beats on different days and has groups playing on some weekends.

**Antifaz** (☎ 281 0113; Calle 15 No 4-34) is a salsoteca with a large dance floor, playing a ragbag of old salsa and mostly Spanish rock. It's open Thursday to Saturday and has a young clientele.

**Cuervo de Cartón** (Calle 15 No 4-15) is a small bar which has good salsa music. It has no dance floor as such, but people rush to dance between the tables.

**El Viejo Almacén** (☎ 284 2364; Calle 15 No 4-18) is a tango bar with a tradition going back to the 1960s. It has 4000 old tango vinyls (many of which are of 78rpm vintage), which provide a nostalgic backdrop to cheap beer.

**Terraza Pasteur** *(Carrera 7 No 23-56)* is a shopping mall, but shops were gradually replaced by bars. Today, you'll find 30-something bars spread over three floors and open most of the week from afternoon till late. They all are tiny places, usually split over two levels, and each plays its favourite musical genre – from salsa to vallenato and rock to reggae – so you can choose the music that suits you.

**La Bodeguita del Centro** *(☎ 599 9314; Calle 24 No 5-81)* is another salsa bar that has a choice of good music and gets crowded on Friday and Saturday nights.

**Northern Bogotá** Here you'll find various areas of night entertainment. Zona Rosa is the largest and most popular playground among Bogotá's youth. The area sits between Carreras 11 and 15, and Calles 81 and 84, Calle 82 being its main axis. There's a maze of music spots, bars, restaurants, cafés and snack bars that become particularly vibrant on weekend nights. This is the best time to come, hang around and see Bogotá's more affluent revellers in action. Many of the Zona Rosa's nightspots keep going till 3am or even longer. On a less pleasant note, most of these nightspots are expensive, especially drinks and cover charges.

**Galería Café Libro** *(☎ 256 8018; Calle 81 No 11-92)* is one of the best salsotecas, with great music and atmosphere. It's consistently popular and packed with salsa fans despite rather high prices.

**Salomé Pagana** *(☎ 218 4076; Carrera 14A No 82-16)* is another recommended salsoteca, with possibly the best *son cubano* in town, as it's run by the renowned collector and connoisseur of that genre, César Pagano.

**Mister Babilla** *(☎ 236 5426; Calle 82 No 12-15)* is one of the best-known discos presenting a ragbag of musical rhythms, including rock, merengue and salsa.

**Gótica** *(☎ 218 0730; Calle 14 No 82-50)* is a large place offering different musical ambiences on different levels, including salsa, techno and trance. It's one of the most popular places around.

**Guaraná** *(☎ 623 7811; Calle 83 No 14-13)*, just a few steps from the Gótica, is another new, attractive spot for trance and related rhythms.

**The Pub** *(☎ 691 87 11; Carrera 12A No 83-48)* is a new Irish addition to the Zona Rosa, which has become hugely popular with some more affluent locals and expats.

**Palos de Moguer** *(☎ 218 8376; Calle 84 No 12-09)* is a bar that serves beer straight from its own brewery, and you can see brass vats used in the production process. The beer is made according to traditional European recipes. Several kinds are available, including ales and lagers, dark and light.

Another area which has recently become trendy with beautiful people is the Parque de la 93, between Calles 93A and 93B and Carreras 11A and 13. It's getting increasingly packed with a variety of restaurants and night bars. It's also an expensive area for dining or drinking, probably even more so than the Zona Rosa.

**The Red Lion** *(☎ 691 7938; Carrera 12 No 93-64)*, owned by the same English guy who has The Pub in the Zona Rosa, is one of the most popular bars around.

**El Sitio** *(☎ 530 5050; Carrera 11A No 93-52)* is another trendy bar which runs discos Wednesday to Saturday.

## Gay & Lesbian Venues

Most gay and lesbian hang-outs are in northern Bogotá. They include **Café Village** *(Carrera 8A No 64-29)* and **Bianca** *(Calle 72 No 16-48)*. A new place, **Theatrum** *(Calle 58 No 10-34)* was very much the 'in' disco venue for the gay community as we went to press.

## SPECTATOR SPORTS

Soccer is Colombia's national sport. The principal venue is the **Estadio El Campín** *(Carrera 30 at Calle 55)*. Matches are played on Wednesday nights and Sunday afternoons. Tickets can be bought at the stadium before the matches (US$4 to US$40). For local games, tickets can also be bought at **Millonarios** *(Carrera 24 No 63-68)* and **Santa Fe** *(Calle 64A No 38-08)*. For international matches (Selección Colombia), you can buy tickets in advance at **Federación Colombiana de Fútbol** *(Av 32 No 16-22)*.

Bullfighting is invariably popular, with fights held at the **Plaza de Toros de Santamaría** *(Carrera 6 at Calle 27)* on most Sundays in January and February. Tickets are available from the bullring's box office (US$10 to US$100). The events bring the area around the bullring to a standstill, whereas the bullring itself invariably fills to capacity, or beyond, with men, women and children.

## SHOPPING
### What to Buy

There are a number of craft shops and markets in the city centre and you'll also find outdoor equipment suppliers, music shops, leather-goods suppliers, bookshops and good opticians. Colombia is famous for its emeralds and it seems there is no better or cheaper country on the planet for buying these stones.

**Crafts & Souvenirs** A good place to start is the craft shop at the **Museo de Artes y Tradiciones Populares** (Carrera 8 No 7-21). You can also check the **Artesanías de Colombia** (Carrera 3 No 18-60), next to the Iglesia de las Aguas.

There are several cheap craft and souvenir markets on or just off Carrera 7, the best of which seems to be **Galería Artesanal de Colombia** (Calle 16 No 5-70). Other markets include **Mercado Artesanal Plaza Bolívar**

(Carrera 7 No 12-52/54), **Centro Colombiano de Artesanías** (Carrera 7 No 22-66/78) and **Galería Artesanal Colombia Linda** (Carrera 7 No 23-49). **Pasaje Rivas** (Carrera 10 at Calle 10) is a nontouristy craft market, good for cheap buys, particularly for hammocks and ruanas (Colombian ponchos).

There are more craft and souvenir shops in the northern districts, several of which are on Carrera 15 between Calles 72 and 85. **Artesanías El Balay** (Carrera 15 No 75-63) and **Artesanías El Zaque** (Carrera 15 No 74-73) are among the largest and arguably the best craft shops in this area.

Flea markets (see that entry later in this chapter) are also good places to shop for crafts and souvenirs.

**Emeralds** These precious stones can be bought in plenty of joyerías (jewellery shops) scattered throughout the city centre and the northern districts. In the centre, the main emerald area is at Carrera 6 between Calles 12 and 13, where you'll find more than 40 jewellers, plus another 40 in the adjacent streets. There are some good (but expensive) jewellers in the Centro Internacional.

---

### So You Wanna Do a Great Emerald Deal?

Yes, you've heard about these wonderful and cheap Colombian emeralds and you'd like to buy some, perhaps with the hope of reselling them at home for a profit. Colombia is cheap, emeralds abound, so by any common logic you would make some good money. Right? Not necessarily. Think twice.

To start with, it's extremely difficult to judge the value of an emerald because minute differences in the colour, cut and clarity of a stone can mean extraordinary differences in its worth. It's virtually impossible for an amateur to make even a rough estimate, and even specialists would probably evaluate the same stone quite differently.

Secondly, there are various techniques used to make stones look better. One of the most common is oiling – the gems are bathed in clear oil, which seeps into the stones' surface fractures and improves their clarity. However, the oil dries out after a few years leaving the stones looking worse than before oiling. More recently, merchants have began to bathe emeralds in resins to seal small fissures, but this too, is only a temporary remedy. The resin changes colour over time, making stones' imperfections only more noticeable. Furthermore, you should know that there are synthetic emeralds, which are chemically, physically and optically identical to the natural stone.

Forget about any local seller giving you the right price of the stone you want to buy. You are likely to be asked for far more than the stone's real value, and even if you succeed in bargaining the price down significantly, you'll still be paying perhaps more than the retail price of the stone in your home country.

Finally, keep in mind that quality emeralds are expensive, even in Colombia, so if you want to buy anything serious enough that might bring a reasonable profit, you'll be playing with big money. And this can be risky.

So, if you are not an expert, take it easy. Go to see the stones, learn about them, talk to jewellers and enjoy your time, but be wary of purchasing, unless it's just a cheap souvenir.

The cheapest place is a flourishing emerald street market at the southwestern corner of Av Jiménez and Carrera 7, where dozens of *negociantes* buy and sell stones. However, it can be a trap for the uninitiated.

Before you head off on your emerald-shopping spree, read the boxed text 'So You Wanna Do a Great Emerald Deal?'

**Camping & Outdoor Equipment** While imported camping and trekking gear is increasingly available, it can be expensive. Locally produced gear is cheaper and often of reasonable quality. Gas canisters for common camping stoves (such as Gas Bluet) are available without major problems.

A good place to start is **Almacén Aventura** (☎ 248 1679; *Carrera 13 No 67-26)*. It makes backpacks, and also sells sleeping bags, jackets, stoves, tents and other hiking gear.

Other places to check out include **Montaña Accesorios** (☎ 236 6734; *Calle 77A No 13-27)*, **Extremo** (☎ 530 0645; *Calle 83 No 12-63)* and **Camping Vive** (☎ 235 7265; *Calle 57 No 9-29, Local 301)*.

**Music** All varieties of Colombian music, including salsa, vallenato, cumbia and musica llanera, can be bought in CD stores, which are everywhere. Virtually every shopping mall has at least a few of them. San Andresito (see below) has plenty of CD stalls.

In the centre, CD stores include **Mercado Mundial del Disco** (☎ 342 67 12; *Carrera 7 No 21-41/43)* and **La Música** (☎ 281 1188; *Carrera 7 No 21-64)* and each has plenty of branches all over town. Also check **Centro Comercial Omni 19** (*Calle 19 at Carrera 8)*, which has a dozen small CD shops and is one of the cheapest places in the centre.

**Books** There are plenty of bookshops both in the centre and in the northern part of the city. Most of the books are in Spanish. Imported books in foreign languages are available but expensive and the choice is limited.

**Librería Buchholz** (☎ 342 5337; *Calle 26 No 10-18 • ☎ 235 1249; Calle 59 No 13-13)* has a choice of foreign books. For imported books also check **Librería Oma** (☎ 610 3200; *Carrera 15 No 82-54)*.

**Librería Francesa** (☎ 636 0143; *Calle 95 No 19-30)* has a selection of books in both French and English, and also offers French and English weekly magazines.

**Leather Goods** For quality leather goods try shops on Calle 19 between Carreras 4 and 7; more shops of that kind are on Carrera 10 in the centre, in the Centro Internacional and further north. Shopping malls (see that entry later) are also worth checking out.

**Spectacles** Should you need a pair of spectacles, Bogotá is a good and cheap place to order them. There are about 80 *ópticas* tightly packed on Calle 19 between Carrera 8 and Av Caracas, where you can get reasonable glasses for as little as US$10.

## Where to Shop

There are plenty of shopping areas, including the centre, Chapinero, the north and beyond, all packed with shops, shopping malls and markets. Generally, the centre is cheaper than the north.

**Shopping Malls** Bogotá has many shopping malls and, despite the precarious economic situation of recent years, new ones keep appearing. Malls are not the cheapest places to shop, but are convenient because everything is under one roof. They are likely to feature a variety of shops with clothing, shoes, books and CDs. Apart from these, you can generally expect that most malls will include a collection of fast-food outlets, a casa de cambio, an Internet café and a multiplex cinema.

**Unicentro** (☎ 213 8800; *Av 15 No 123-30)* was the first large shopping mall in Bogotá and remains popular and busy. **Centro Comercial Granahorrar** (☎ 312 7077; *Calle 72 No 10-34)* is another older-generation centre which is always packed with shoppers. More recent and stylish is the **Hacienda Santa Bárbara** (☎ 612 0388; *Carrera 7 No 115-60)* built around a colonial casona, making the place a fine combination of historic and modern architecture.

The Zona Rosa is home to the **Centro Comercial Andino** (☎ 621 3111; *Carrera 11 No 82-71)*. Nearby is the more recent, attractive **Atlantis Plaza** (*Calle 81 No 13-05)*, which has Bogotá's most modern cinema complex.

**Hypermarkets** These huge supermarkets offer food and a wide range of everyday products such as clothing, shoes, toiletries, household appliances and stationery. They have appeared relatively recently, mainly in the outer suburbs and on the city outskirts. The quality of the products they sell is nothing extraordinary, but their main weapon is low pricing.

The major local player on the market is the Medellín-born chain Éxito, which means 'success', and it really has been so. After having conquered its native city, Éxito opened stores in other major cities, including six outlets in Bogotá. The most convenient are the **Éxito Norte** *(☎ 592 7100; Carrera 43 No 173-98)*, opposite the northern terminus of TransMilenio (Portal del Norte), and **Éxito Ochenta** *(☎ 660 5300; Carrera 59A No 79-30)*, also easily accessible by TransMilenio (Parada Av 68).

Of the international chains, the closest to the centre is the **Carrefour** *(Carrera 30 at Calle 19)*.

**San Andresito** This is a huge shopping area which spreads over several city blocks, centred at Carrera 38 between Calles 8 and 9. It's packed with a couple of thousand stalls that have almost everything that can be bought in Colombia. It's open daily from around 9am to 6pm. San Andresito is one of the cheapest places to buy video, hi-fi and TV equipment, computers, film and photographic gear, watches, cassettes and CDs, and clothing and footwear. Urban buses and busetas go there from the centre and you can catch them on Calle 19.

**Flea Markets** The main central flea market, Mercado de San Alejo, is held on Sunday from 9am to 5pm at the parking lot on Carrera 7 between Calles 24 and 26. Northern Bogotá has a flea market at Usaquén.

## GETTING THERE & AWAY
### Air
Bogotá's airport, Aeropuerto El Dorado, which handles all domestic and international flights, is 13km northwest of the city centre and has two terminals. The principal one, **El Dorado** *(☎ 425 1000; Av El Dorado)*, offers plenty of facilities, including snack bars and restaurants, tourist information, Internet access and money exchange.

The terminal houses two tourist information stands, in the international and domestic arrival areas, where you pick up your luggage. They are only accessible by passengers arriving at El Dorado by air.

Internet access (7am to 7pm daily) is provided by Telecom in its office on the upper floor.

Three casas de cambio (Aerocambios, City Exchange and Cambios Country), next to each other on the ground floor (open 24 hours), change cash. The Banco Popular (also open 24 hours), next to the casas, changes both cash and travellers cheques, but rates for cheques are a bit lower than those at banks in the city centre. There are a dozen ATMs on the upper level.

The other terminal, **Puente Aéreo** *(☎ 413 9511; Av El Dorado)*, is 1km before El Dorado. It handles some of Alianza Summa's international and domestic flights. Make sure to check which terminal your flight departs from.

There are a lot of international departures (see the earlier Getting There & Away chapter for details). There are also plenty of domestic flights to destinations all over the country. Some of the major routes and their approximate air fares are given below. They include the US$3.50 domestic airport tax, which you pay when buying your ticket.

| destination | fare (US$) |
| --- | --- |
| Armenia | 50 to 85 |
| Barranquilla | 75 to 125 |
| Bucaramanga | 60 to 110 |
| Cali | 50 to 110 |
| Cartagena | 75 to 125 |
| Cúcuta | 70 to 130 |
| Leticia | 100 to 120 |
| Manizales | 50 to 90 |
| Medellín | 50 to 110 |
| Pasto | 70 to 125 |
| Pereira | 50 to 90 |
| Popayán | 70 to 100 |
| San Andrés | 100 to 140 |
| Santa Marta | 80 to 130 |

### Bus
The **bus terminal** *(☎ 295 1100; Calle 33B No 69-13)* is situated a long way west of the city centre. You can either take a bus or a *colectivo* marked 'Terminal' from Carrera 10, or a taxi (US$4).

The bus terminal is large, functional and well organised. It has a tourist office, restaurants, cafeterias, showers and left-luggage rooms plus a number of well-dressed thieves who will wait for a moment's inattention to grab your stuff and disappear, so watch your bags closely.

The terminal has three departure halls: Norte (from which all buses towards the north depart), Oriente & Occidente (handling all buses towards the east and west) and Sur (servicing southbound buses). If one bus company operates buses in various directions, it has separate offices in the relevant halls. The terminal handles buses to just about every corner of the country, except for some short-distance regional buses, which depart from other points of the city.

On the main roads, buses run frequently almost round the clock. For example, for Medellín, Cali or Bucaramanga, you can expect departures every half-hour throughout most of the day, by one or another of several companies that operate these routes. The usual type of bus on long-distance routes is the *climatizado*, which is air-conditioned.

The main destinations, distances, average fares and approximate times of journeys are given in the following table. All fares are for air-conditioned buses, the dominant kind of bus used on long-distance routes.

| destination | distance (km) | fare (US$) | time (hr) |
| --- | --- | --- | --- |
| Armenia | 296 | 13 | 8 |
| Barranquilla | 999 | 36 | 18 |
| Bucaramanga | 429 | 19 | 10 |
| Cali | 481 | 20 | 12 |
| Cartagena | 1127 | 40 | 20 |
| Cúcuta | 630 | 29 | 16 |
| Ipiales | 948 | 35 | 23 |
| Manizales | 292 | 13 | 8 |
| Medellín | 440 | 17 | 9 |
| Neiva | 309 | 10 | 6 |
| Pasto | 865 | 32 | 21 |
| Pereira | 340 | 15 | 9 |
| Popayán | 617 | 24 | 15 |
| San Agustín | 529 | 15 | 12 |
| Santa Marta | 966 | 32 | 16 |
| Tunja | 147 | 5 | 3 |

## GETTING AROUND
### To/From the Airport
Both El Dorado and Puente Aéreo terminals are accessible from the centre by busetas and colectivos marked 'Aeropuerto'. In the centre you catch them on Calle 19 or Carrera 10. At the airport they park next to the El Dorado terminal. They all pass by Puente Aéreo en route. Urban transport to the airport stops at about 8pm.

If going by taxi (US$6), you pay a *sobrecargo* (surcharge) of US$1.

El Dorado terminal has a special taxi service aimed at protecting passengers from overcharging by taxi drivers. At the exit from the baggage-claim area there's a taxi booth where you get a computer printout indicating the expected fare to your destination. You then take the taxi, which waits at the door and shows the printout to the driver. The fare is paid upon arrival at your destination.

### To/From the Bus Terminal
There are both buses and colectivos running between the bus terminal and the city centre, but the service is relatively infrequent and stops around 9pm. During rush hours the bus trip between the terminal and the city centre may take up to an hour.

From the centre, take the northbound colectivo marked 'Terminal' from Carrera 10 anywhere between Calles 19 and 26. You can also take a bus or colectivo from Calle 13 west of Av Caracas but this is an unsafe area best avoided.

The best and fastest way is a taxi (US$4). The same applies if you are going from the terminal to the city centre; you can take a bus or colectivo but it's best to go by taxi.

The bus terminal has a similar taxi service to that at the airport. Upon arrival, follow the 'Taxi' signs, which will lead you to a taxi booth where you'll get a computer printout indicating the expected fare to your destination.

### TransMilenio
TransMilenio has revolutionised Bogotá's public transport. After numerous plans and studies drawn up over 30 years to build a metro, the project was eventually buried and a decision to introduce a fast urban bus service called TransMilenio was taken instead.

Inaugurated in 2000 on Av Caracas, the system employs large buses which run on their own street lines, uninterrupted by other vehicles. The service is cheap (US$0.40), frequent and fast, and operates from 5am to 11pm. Buses get very crowded at rush hour.

The main TransMilenio route is Av Caracas, which cuts the city south to north, linking the centre to both southern and northern suburbs. The system is being extended by introducing the buses on other streets. In the centre, there's already a side line along Av Jiménez up to Carrera 3. Some other cities are interested in building a similar system.

## Bus & Buseta

TransMilenio apart, Bogotá's public transport is operated by buses and busetas (small buses). They all run the length and breadth of the city, usually at full speed if traffic allows.

There are 613 routes serviced by 22,000 buses and busetas, which transport an average of 7.2 million passengers a day.

Except on a few streets, there are no bus stops – you just wave down the bus or buseta wherever you happen to be. You board via the front door, pay the driver or the assistant but you don't get a ticket. In buses you get off through the back door, where there's a bell to ring to let the driver know to stop. In busetas there's usually only a front door through which all passengers get on and off. When you want to get off tell the driver *'por acá, por favor'* ('here, please') or *'la esquina, por favor'* ('on the corner, please').

Each bus and buseta displays a board on the windscreen indicating the route and number. For locals they are easily recognisable from a distance, but for newcomers it can be difficult to decipher the route description quickly enough to wave down the right bus. It will probably take you several days to learn to recognise busetas and buses.

The fare ranges from US$0.30 to US$0.50 depending on the class and generation of the vehicle, and is slightly higher at night (after 8pm) and on Sunday and holidays. The fare is always posted by the door or on the windscreen. The fare is flat, so you will be charged the same to go one block as to go right across the city.

There are also minibuses called colectivos which operate on major routes. They are faster and cost about US$0.50.

## Taxi

Bogotá's taxis are mostly of recent vintage. They all have meters and drivers usually use them, though occasionally the sight of a gringo can make them reluctant to do so. Insist on having the meter running or take another taxi. Taxis also should have stickers displaying day and night-time fares.

Taxis are a convenient and inexpensive means of getting around. A 10km ride (eg, from Plaza de Bolívar to Calle 100 in northern Bogotá) shouldn't cost more than US$4. There's a US$1.25 surcharge on rides to the airport.

You can either wave down a taxi on the street or request one by phone from numerous companies that provide radio service, eg, **Taxis Libres** (☎ *311 1111*), **Taxi Express** (☎ *411 1111*), **Radio Taxi** (☎ *288 8888*) or **Taxi Real** (☎ *333 3333*). They all have a fixed *recargo* (surcharge) of about US$0.40 for this service, and will usually arrive at the requested address within 15 minutes (this may take longer on weekend nights).

A word of warning – when taxiing from the bus terminal or the airport to a budget hotel, be wary of any driver who insists that your chosen hotel no longer exists, that it's now a brothel and/or has security problems then offers you a seemingly better option. Some taxi drivers may have agreements with hotel owners and may be paid to take tourists to certain establishments.

# Around Bogotá

Thanks to its varied topography, Cundinamarca, the department surrounding Bogotá, provides every kind of environment, from hot lowlands in the west to freezing *páramos* (open highlands) in the east. Within a two-hour bus ride from Bogotá you may experience significant differences in temperature and landscape. You will find lakes, waterfalls, forests, mountains and a maze of small towns and villages, many of which have preserved some of their colonial fabric.

The western slopes of the Cordillera Oriental, running gently down to the Magdalena River, are dotted with old market towns and are very picturesque. The area east of Bogotá, by contrast, where the Cordillera reaches its greatest heights, is rugged and sprinkled with tiny lakes, many of which were once sacred ritual centres of the Muisca Indians.

## ZIPAQUIRÁ

☎ 1 • pop 70,000 • elevation 2650m
• temp 14°C

Zipaquirá, 50km north of Bogotá, is noted for its salt mines, which are in the mountain just to the west of town. The mines date back to the Muisca period and have been intensively exploited, but they still contain vast reserves; they tap into virtually a huge mountain of rock salt.

In the heart of the mountain an underground salt cathedral has been carved out and was opened to the public in 1954. It was closed in 1992 for safety reasons, but a new **salt cathedral** (☎ 852 4035; admission US$4, half-price Wed; open 10am-4pm Tues-Sun) was scooped out 60m below the old one and opened for visitors in 1995. It is 75m long and 18m high and can accommodate 8400 people.

Visits are by guided tours which take an hour (English-speaking guides are sometimes available). You can also visit the adjacent **salt museum** (admission US$1; open 10am-4pm Tues-Sun), which features the history of salt exploitation and a model of the local mine.

The salt cathedral and museum apart, you can have a quick glance at Zipaquirá's central plaza with its church and chapel. Founded in 1606, the town still shelters some colonial buildings around the main square.

### Getting There & Away

Buses to Zipaquirá (US$0.80, 1¼ hours) run from Bogotá every 10 minutes, departing from the northern terminus of TransMilenio, known as Portal del Norte, on Autopista del Norte at Calle 170. TransMilenio from Bogotá's centre will take you there in 40 minutes. The mines are a 15-minute walk uphill from Zipaquirá's centre.

### LAGUNA DE GUATAVITA
elevation 3000m • temp 11°C

The Laguna de Guatavita is a small, perfectly circular lake about 50km northeast of Bogotá. It was the sacred lake and ritual centre of the Muisca Indians and came to be the cradle of the myth of El Dorado. It was here half a millennium ago that the Zipa, the Muisca cacique coated with gold dust, would throw precious offerings into the lake from his ceremonial raft and then plunge into the waters to obtain god-like power.

The famous golden piece representing the ceremonial raft, Balsa Muisca, is evidence of the elaborate Indian rituals held in the lake. You can see the raft in the Gold Museum in Bogotá. There are supposedly many other precious gold objects at the bottom of the lake (see the boxed text 'The Treasures of Laguna de Guatavita'). However, don't bring along scuba gear or diving equipment; instead, enjoy the beauty of this charming lake with its emerald waters, nestled in a crater-like ring covered with greenery.

If you come to see Laguna de Guatavita you may want to visit the town of Guatavita (see the following section) during the same trip from Bogotá, as the lake and town are close to each other.

### Getting There & Away

To get to the lake from Bogotá, take a bus to the town of Guatavita (see Getting There & Away under the following Guatavita section for transport details) and get off 11km before reaching the town (6km past Sesquilé), where there is a sign directing you to the lake. It's best to ask the driver and he will let you off at the right place.

From the road, it's a 7km walk uphill to the lake. The first half of the way goes along a partly paved road, until you reach the Escuela Tierra Negra. At this point take a dirt track branching off to the right and leading to the lake. There are several farms around so ask for directions if in doubt. On weekends it's possible to hitch a lift with tourists in their jeeps. You will arrive at the lake shore after passing through a deep, V-shaped cut in the lake's bank that is the legacy of ill-fated efforts to drain it. Don't miss the walk around the lake.

### GUATAVITA
☎ 1 • pop 2600 • elevation 2680m
• temp 14°C

Guatavita, also called Guatavita Nueva, is a town designed in its entirety and built in one go in the late 1960s. It was constructed to provide a home for the inhabitants of the old, colonial Guatavita, dating from 1542, which was flooded by the waters of a hydroelectric reservoir, the Embalse de Tominé.

The new Guatavita is somewhat artificial, but impressive. Architects took the best of the colonial style and added modern designs to obtain an interesting blend of old and new. Among the things to see are the museum of religious art, the bullring, the church (don't miss its beautiful altar) and the market on Sunday, which is best visited during the morning.

Although the town is an innovative architectural creation, it has failed as a social experiment. A traditional rural mentality has not accepted the radical leap into modernity; the inhabitants of old Guatavita were reluctant to settle in modern homes. As only a handful of peasants live in town,

## The Treasures of Laguna de Guatavita

The Muiscas had many sacred lakes such as Tota, Siecha, Iguaque and Chingaza, but Guatavita was presumably the most important, supposedly because of its astral origins. Everything seems to suggest that the lake was formed by a giant meteor, which fell some 2000 years ago and left a huge circular hole shaped like a volcanic crater. The Indians interpreted the phenomenon as the arrival of a golden god who lived thereafter at the bottom of the lake. The lake became an object of worship, where gold pieces, emeralds and food were offered to ensure abundant crops and protection against misfortunes.

When the Spaniards saw the Indians throwing gold into the lake, they believed incalculable treasures were to be found at the bottom and they made numerous attempts to salvage the riches. In fact, no other lake in Colombia, and perhaps on the whole continent, experienced as many desperate efforts to get to its bottom as did Laguna de Guatavita.

One of the best-known early expeditions was directed in the 1560s by a rich merchant, Antonio de Sepúlveda, who succeeded in getting a permit from the Crown to drain the lake. With a large Indian labour force, he cut into one side of the crater to drain off the water. The result of this enormous effort was 232 pesos and 10g of fine gold. Sepúlveda died bankrupt.

In the 19th century, after Colombia achieved independence, attempts to retrieve the legendary treasures intensified. Initially, the most viable way to do so appeared to be to enlarge the former cut in the ridge to drain the lake. Several successive operations succeeded in lowering the water level (though not in draining the lake completely), but the gold didn't materialise as expected. Other methods were then tried such as a siphon construction and an underground channel, but all in vain.

Despite these failures, the lake continued to draw in new challengers. By the late 19th century an English company, Contractors Ltd, arrived with a load of machinery including the new high-tech invention of the day, a steam pump. The company managed to drain the lagoon almost completely and even washed out most of the mud from the bottom. However, the 20-odd gold objects plus some emeralds and ceramics found during eight years of exploration didn't compensate for the £40,000 invested in the whole operation. The company went broke.

The rains refilled the muddy basin and peace and quiet returned to the lake. Not for long, however, as new treasure hunters began to search the lake with more determination. In the 1940s, a Colombian miner, Gustavo Jaramillo Sánchez, set about installing a dragline. Soon after North American divers arrived with sophisticated metal detectors. Yet, as so often like before, very little was found.

Yet another attempt was planned in 1965 by a US–Colombian company. By that time, however, the Colombian authorities decided to ban further excavations in the lake. Thus, after four centuries of digging, draining, dragging, pumping and diving, the lagoon was finally left in peace.

Legend has it that the bottom still retains its treasure, but more cautious historians have some doubts. First of all, there are no historic records of the amount of gold the Indians actually deposited in the lake. By all rational estimates there couldn't have been much; the Muiscas had emeralds and salt, but no gold mines of their own. Given the number of sacred lakes, the gold offerings are likely to have been distributed over plenty of ritual sites, and not lakes alone. Caves, for example, were also places where ritual sacrifices were made.

Furthermore, it's not quite clear whether it was the Laguna de Guatavita that served as the major centre of gold-offering. It was simply the lake where the Spaniards had the opportunity to witness the Muisca ceremony. Some sceptics believe that the Indians were play-acting in front of the Spaniards in order to confuse them and divert their attention from the places where genuine rituals were held.

The Balsa Muisca, considered to be the Muiscas' most elaborate gold object and ultimate proof of their ceremonies, was found (in 1856) in Laguna de Siecha, not in Guatavita. Another Balsa (the one displayed today in Bogotá's Gold Museum), only found in 1969, doesn't come from Guatavita either, but from a cave near the village of Pasca.

Regardless of whether Laguna de Guatavita contains Muisca treasures, it is certainly full of mystery and beauty.

it has become a weekend haunt for tourists, mostly from Bogotá, who come to look at its architecture.

There are a couple of simple places to stay and eat in Guatavita. More restaurants open on Sunday when tourists come.

## Getting There & Away

Buses from Bogotá to Guatavita (US$2, two hours) depart every half-hour from the northern terminus of TransMilenio, on Autopista del Norte at Calle 170. TransMilenio from Bogotá's centre will take you there in 40 minutes.

## PARQUE NATURAL CHICAQUE

Chicaque (☎ 368 3114 in Bogotá; admission US$2.50; open 8am-4pm daily) is a private nature reserve about 20km west of Bogotá. Most of its 3-sq-km area is covered with bosque de niebla (cloudforest). Walks along the paths of the reserve (about 8km long altogether) give an opportunity to enjoy the forest's flora and fauna, particularly the

birds. The reserve provides accommodation in a cabaña (cabin) for US$5 per dorm bed or you can camp for US$2 per person. You can go horse riding for US$5 per hour.

## Getting There & Away

The reserve is a few kilometres off the Soacha–La Mesa road. To get there from Bogotá's centre, take a bus or colectivo to the plaza in Soacha, and negotiate a taxi to the administrative centre of the reserve (about US$8 per taxi, up to four passengers). There may be some colectivos on weekends.

Eco-Guías (see Organised Tours earlier in this chapter) can organise tours to Chicaque on request. The five-hour trip costs about US$10 per person with a minimum of four persons required; the price includes return transport, admission fee to the reserve and guided walks.

From the reserve you can walk along a camino de herradura (old Spanish path) to the small village of San Antonio de Tequendama. Ask the management for details.

# North of Bogotá

This chapter covers part of the Cordillera Oriental to the north of Bogotá, between the Magdalena River in the west and Los Llanos in the east. Administratively, the region falls into three departments: Boyacá, Santander and Norte de Santander. Like all other parts of the Andean region, the topography varies widely, from verdant lowland valleys to snowy peaks. While travelling around, you'll enjoy a variety of landscapes and attractive views.

Once the territory of the Muiscas (Boyacá) and the Guane Indians (Santander), the region was one of the first to be conquered and settled by the Spaniards. Many colonial towns have been preserved to this day in remarkably good shape. Villa de Leyva, Barichara and Girón are among the finest examples.

Boyacá and the Santanders were also the cradle of Colombia's independence. Socorro (Santander) was the site of one of the first rebellions against Spanish rule, and Simón Bolívar fought decisive battles at Pantano de Vargas and Puente de Boyacá (both in Boyacá). The first constitution was signed in Villa del Rosario (Norte de Santander), and there are many more reminders of that turbulent period.

Of the three departments, Boyacá is perhaps the safest and most pleasant in which to travel. Boyacá is also the most traditional province, widely known for handicrafts, particularly pottery, basketwork and weaving. Boyacá's craftwork has a long tradition dating back to pre-Columbian times. The Muisca forms and patterns, developed by their descendants and backed by techniques introduced by the Spaniards, have resulted in a wide variety of good-quality crafts.

## Boyacá

### TUNJA
☎ 8 • pop 140,000 • elevation 2820m
• temp 13°C

Tunja, the capital of Boyacá, was founded by Gonzalo Suárez Rendón in 1539 on the site of Hunza, the pre-Hispanic Muisca settlement. The town developed as the starting point for expeditions to Los Llanos, where the Spaniards hoped to find the legendary El

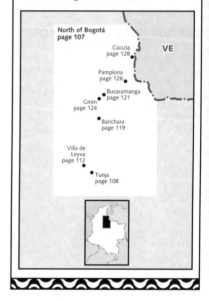

### Highlights

• Stroll about the charming colonial streets of Villa de Leyva
• Go hiking in the Santuario de Iguaque
• Explore Tunja's splendid colonial churches
• Enjoy the historic architecture and old-time atmosphere of Barichara
• Take a rafting tour in San Gil

North of Bogotá page 107
Cúcuta page 128
VE
Pamplona page 126
Bucaramanga page 121
Girón page 124
Barichara page 119
Villa de Leyva page 112
Tunja page 108

Dorado. Within a short time Tunja became an important religious centre.

Though almost nothing is left of the indigenous legacy, much colonial architecture remains. The central sector has been restored for the town's 450th anniversary and many historic public buildings have recovered their original splendour. Tunja is particularly noted for its colonial churches; several imposing examples dating from the 16th century stand almost untouched by time.

Tunja is the highest and coldest departmental capital in the country. It has a mountain climate, characterised by a considerable difference between day and night-time temperatures. Make sure that you bring enough warm clothing.

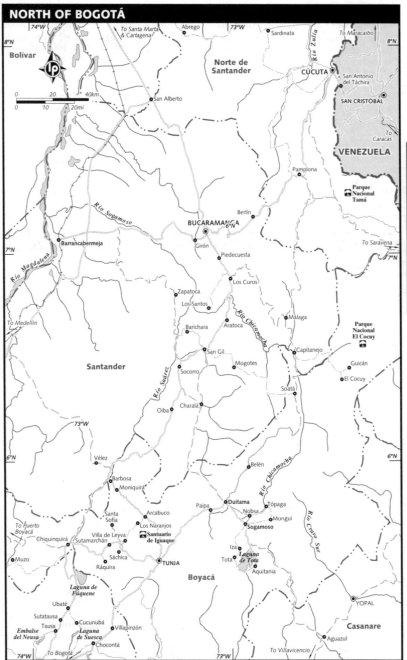

# NORTH OF BOGOTÁ

## Information

**Tourist Offices** The municipal tourist office, the **Secretaría de Educación, Cultura y Turismo** (☎ 742 3272; Carrera 9 No 19-68; open 8am-noon & 2pm-6pm Mon-Fri), is in the Casa del Fundador on Plaza de Bolívar.

**Money** Bancolombia (Carrera 10 No 22-43) is likely to change travellers cheques and perhaps cash as well. **Banco de Bogotá** (Calle 20 No 10-60) may also exchange travellers cheques but not cash. Other banks marked on the map are only useful for cash advances on Visa and/or MasterCard. If you can't change your cash in a bank, go to **Giros & Finanzas** (Carrera 10 No 16-81), a casa de cambio nestled at the back of the Supermercado Comfaboy.

**Email & Internet Access** There are several convenient facilities on or just off Plaza de Bolívar, including **Internet Cibertienda** (Carrera 10 No 19-83), **Café Internet** (Calle 20 No 8-94) and **Internet Orbitel** (Calle 20 No 10-26).

## Historic Houses & Museums

Tunja has some great historic mansions, which have been opened as museums. The **Casa del Fundador Suárez Rendón** (☎ 742 3272; Carrera 9 No 19-68; admission US$1; open 8am-noon & 2pm-6pm daily) is the original home of the founder of Tunja. Built in the mid-16th century on the eastern side of Plaza de Bolívar (previously called Plaza de Suárez Rendón), it's a fine example of a magnificent aristocratic residence from the

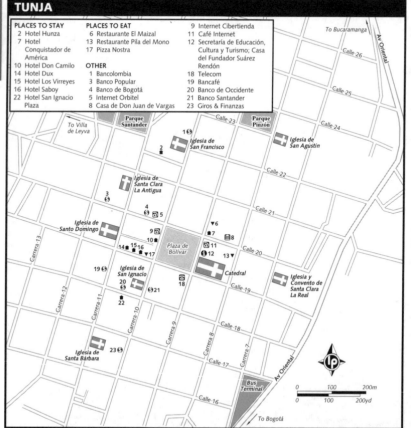

**TUNJA**

PLACES TO STAY
2 Hotel Hunza
7 Hotel Conquistador de América
10 Hotel Don Camilo
14 Hotel Dux
15 Hotel Los Virreyes
16 Hotel Saboy
22 Hotel San Ignacio Plaza

PLACES TO EAT
6 Restaurante El Maizal
13 Restaurante Pila del Mono
17 Pizza Nostra

OTHER
1 Bancolombia
3 Banco Popular
4 Banco de Bogotá
5 Internet Orbitel
8 Casa de Don Juan de Vargas

9 Internet Cibertienda
11 Café Internet
12 Secretaría de Educación, Cultura y Turismo; Casa del Fundador Suárez Rendón
18 Telecom
19 Bancafé
20 Banco de Occidente
21 Banco Santander
23 Giros & Finanzas

## Tunja's Enigmatic Ceiling Paintings

Several colonial mansions in Tunja, including the Casa del Fundador Suárez Rendón and the Casa de Don Juan de Vargas, have their ceilings adorned with unusual paintings featuring a strange mishmash of motifs taken from very different traditions. They include mythological scenes, human figures, animals and plants, coats of arms and architectural details. You can spot Zeus and Jesus amid tropical plants or an elephant under a Renaissance arcade – you've probably haven't seen anything like that before. In fact, there's nothing similar anywhere in Latin America.

The key to the explanation of this bizarre decoration seems to be Juan de Vargas, the owner and resident of one of these mansions. He was a scribe and had a large library with books on European art and architecture, ancient Greece and Rome, religion and natural history. It all appears to suggest that the illustrations in the books were the source of motifs for the anonymous painters of the ceiling decoration in the houses.

It's interesting to note that the original illustrations were in black and white, so the colour is the product of the imagination of the unknown artisans. Curiously enough, they also introduced elements of local origin, particularly the native flora and fauna.

The paintings are not frescoes, as was initially thought. They are all painted *al temple* (in tempera) on dry plaster. Even though this technique doesn't usually assure extreme durability, the paintings remain in remarkably good shape and colour, despite the 400 years since their creation.

NORTH OF BOGOTÁ

times of the Spanish Conquest. Today, it is a museum containing some colonial artefacts, but the star attractions are the ceilings which are covered with intriguing painted compositions of humans, animals and plants, coats-of-arms, architectural elements etc (see the boxed text 'Tunja's Enigmatic Ceiling Paintings'). The paintings were created after the town founder's death in 1583, most likely between 1585 and 1605.

The **Casa de Don Juan de Vargas** (☎ 742 6611; Calle 20 No 8-52; admission US$1; open 9am-noon & 2pm-5pm Tues-Fri, 10am-4pm Sat & Sun) is another splendid 16th-century residence. Once home to Juan de Vargas, it also has been converted into a museum and has a collection of colonial artworks on display. However, here again, most captivating are the ceilings, which are also covered with paintings, similar to those in the Casa del Fundador, and equally enigmatic.

### Churches

Tunja has some of Colombia's best colonial churches. They are noted for their Mudéjar art, an Islamic-influenced style, which developed in Christian Spain between the 12th and 16th centuries. It is particularly visible in the ornamented coffered vaults. Even if churches are not your cup of tea, don't forget to enter Santa Clara La Real and Santo Domingo – you'll hardly find more impressive interiors anywhere in the country.

The **Iglesia y Convento de Santa Clara La Real** (☎ 742 5659; Carrera 7 No 19-58; admission US$1; open 8am-noon & 2pm-6pm daily) was founded in 1571 and is thought to be the first convent in Nueva Granada. In 1863 the nuns were expelled and the convent was used for various purposes, among them as a hospital. The church, however, continued to provide religious services. In the 1980s the church and a part of the convent were extensively restored and opened as a museum.

The single-naved church interior shelters a wealth of colonial artwork distributed over the walls, most of which comes from the 16th to 18th centuries. The vault is, typically, in the Mudéjar style and the splendid, three-tier, 17th-century main retable is an excellent example of local baroque woodcarving. Note the golden sun above it, a Spanish trick to help the Indians convert to Catholicism (the sun was the principal god of the Muisca people). The pulpit is reputedly one of the oldest objects, dating back to around 1572.

Interesting wall paintings have been discovered in the church choir during the restoration, after the outer plaster layer was removed. Some of them are preserved in admirable shape. They reveal similar features to those made in the Casa del Fundador and other historic houses, and they may have been executed by the same team of artisans. Next to the choir is the cell where Madre Francisca Josefa, a mystic nun looked upon as Colombia's St Teresa, lived for 53 years (1689–1742).

The mid-16th-century **Iglesia de Santo Domingo** (Carrera 11 No 19-55) is pretty undistinguished from the outside, but has one of the most richly decorated interiors in Colombia. To the left as you enter is the large Capilla del Rosario, dubbed 'La Capilla Sixtina del Arte Neogranadino' (Sistine Chapel of New Granada's Art). Decorated by Fray Pedro Bedón from Quito, the chapel is exuberantly rich in gilded woodcarving and wonderful in every detail – a magnificent example of Hispano-American baroque art. The statue of the Virgen del Rosario in the altar niche is encrusted in mother-of-pearl and clad with mirrors, another typical Spanish trick to attract Indians.

The **Iglesia de San Francisco** (Carrera 10 No 22-23) is yet another masterpiece of colonial religious art. Built between 1550 and 1572, it boasts a splendid main retable, framed into an elaborate gilded arch at the entrance to the presbytery. At the beginning of the left-hand aisle is an impressively realistic sculpture of Christ (carved in 1816), *Cristo de los Mártires*.

At the other end of the same aisle you'll come to the Capilla de la Virgen de las Angustias, with a filigree-carved black-cedar altar, made in Quito and brought to Tunja by the Franciscans. It's known as the Altar de los Pelícanos, after the carved birds on both sides.

The **Catedral** (Carrera 9 No 19-28) is on Plaza de Bolívar and is Tunja's largest church and stylistically the most complex. Its construction was begun in 1554, but many interruptions delayed its completion until the end of the 19th century. It was started in Gothic style, but every fashion since has left its mark. The interior shelters a fine high altar, plus a collection of side chapels dating from different periods. The large Capilla de la Hermandad del Clero, from 1647, is perhaps the most magnificent. It is the second chapel to the right after you enter the church and it boasts a gold-plated baroque retable and colonial paintings on both sides.

The **Iglesia de Santa Bárbara** (Carrera 11 No 16-62) was completed in 1599. The highlight here is the Capilla de la Epístola with its outstanding Mudéjar ceiling. The chapel is to the right of the main altar.

The late-16th-century **Iglesia de San Agustín** (Carrera 8 at Calle 23) facing the Parque Pinzón (thought to be the place where the heart of Hunza, the Muisca capital, once was) is now a library. You may want to pop in anyway, to see the uncovered fragments of old frescoes.

The 17th-century Jesuit **Iglesia de San Ignacio** (Carrera 10 No 18-15) no longer serves religious purposes either; it's now an auditorium for concert and other performing acts.

## Special Events

Boyacá is one of the most traditional departments, so religious celebrations such as **Semana Santa**, held in the countryside and Tunja itself, are observed with due solemnity. Processions circle the city streets on Maundy Thursday and Good Friday.

The **Festival Internacional de la Cultura** is a cultural event which takes place in September and includes theatre performances, musical concerts (held, among other sites, in the Iglesia de San Ignacio) and art exhibitions.

The popular **Aguinaldo Boyacense** religious feast runs for a week in December just before Christmas. It features contests, fancy dress parades, a procession of floats, music, dances and the like.

## Places to Stay

There are a number of hotels close to the bus terminal, but they are mostly basic and often overpriced. It's more pleasant to stay in the heart of the city, around Plaza de Bolívar.

**Hotel Saboy** (☎ 742 3492; Calle 19 No 10-40; rooms without/with bath per person US$4/5) is one of the cheapest options in the heart of the city and is good value. In a historic building with a glass-roofed patio, it's basic but clean and pleasant and has hot water in the morning.

If Saboy can't accommodate you, you may want to check its two neighbours, **Hotel Los Virreyes** (☎ 742 3556; Calle 19 No 10-64; rooms without/with bath per person US$5/6) and **Hotel Dux** (☎ 742 5736; Calle 19 No 10-78; rooms without/with bath per person US$5/7). Each of them offers much the same as the Saboy, but both are a bit more expensive.

**Hotel Don Camilo** (☎ 742 6574; Carrera 10 No 19-57; rooms without/with bath per *person US$4/6)* is right on Plaza Bolívar, but none of its windows overlooks the plaza. It's another convenient budget shelter, but it's basic and slightly unkempt.

**Hotel Conquistador de América** *(☎ 742 3534; Calle 20 No 8-92; singles/doubles/triples US$12/17/22)*, in a colonial-style building at the corner of Plaza Bolívar, has 20 ample rooms, all with private baths. The Conquistador is good for those who need somewhere that's more than basic yet still a low-budget option.

**Hotel San Ignacio Plaza** *(☎ 743 7583; Calle 18 No 10-51; singles/doubles/triples US$20/26/32)* is well kept and has cosy rooms with bath, making it another good, affordable choice in the city's heart.

**Hotel Hunza** *(☎ 742 4111; Calle 21A No 10-66; singles/doubles/triples/suites US$30/40/50/60)* is Tunja's top offering. It's a modern hotel with a small swimming pool and sauna, and comfortable rooms which have been refurbished in recent years.

### Places to Eat
Plenty of restaurants serve inexpensive set lunches for US$1.50 to US$2. There are also a number of outlets serving snacks, fast food and chicken.

**Restaurante El Maizal** *(Carrera 9 No 20-30; mains US$3-5)* doesn't look very elegant, but has long been popular with the locals for its tasty food, including regional dishes. It doesn't serve set meals.

**Restaurante Pila del Mono** *(Calle 20 No 8-19; mains US$5-7)* is one of the better dining options and it also has some regional dishes.

**Pizza Nostra** *(Calle 19 No 10-36; pizza US$3-8)* is a reasonable pizzeria, conveniently located just off Plaza de Bolívar.

### Getting There & Away
The bus terminal is on Av Oriental, a short walk southeast of Plaza de Bolívar. Buses to Bogotá (US$5, 2½ to three hours) depart every 10 to 15 minutes. If you're going to the centre, get off at Portal del Norte at Calle 170 and change for TransMilenio.

Buses to Bucaramanga (US$14, seven hours) run every hour or less. They all travel from Bogotá and pass through San Gil (US$9, 4½ hours).

Minibuses to Villa de Leyva (US$1.50, 45 minutes) depart regularly until about 6pm.

## VILLA DE LEYVA
☎ 8 • pop 4000 • elevation 2140m
• temp 18°C

Villa de Leyva is a small colonial town almost untouched by the 20th century. The town was declared a national monument in 1954, so it has been extensively restored, and is virtually free of modern architecture. It is one of the finest gems of colonial architecture in the country.

The town was founded in 1572 by Hernán Suárez de Villalobos and was named Nuestra Señora de la Villa Santa María de Leyva. Ever since its early days, it attracted politicians, artists and clergymen who came and settled here. It continues to draw people, and many Colombians and some foreigners have chosen to live here. The town enjoys a healthy, dry and mild climate, far warmer than Tunja, just 39km away but 700m higher.

Since Villa de Leyva lies reasonably close to the capital, it has become a trendy weekend spot for people from Bogotá. This has made the town somewhat artificial, with a noticeably split personality – on weekdays it is a sleepy, lethargic village, but on weekends and holidays it comes alive, crammed with tourists and their cars. It's up to you to choose which of the town's faces you prefer, but don't miss it.

### Information
The tourist office, **Oficina de Turismo** *(☎ 732 0232; Carrera 9 at Calle 13; open 8am-1pm & 3pm-6pm Mon-Sat, 9am-1pm & 3pm-6pm Sun)*, is at the east corner of the main plaza.

Travellers cheques are useless in Villa de Leyva. Probably the only place you can change cash (at a poor rate) is at the photocopier's business, five doors up from the parish church. The **Banco Popular**, on the main plaza, gives cash advances on Visa cards.

**Servientrega**, nine doors from the church (four doors past the photocopier), offers access to the Internet (US$3 per hour).

### Plaza Mayor
You are likely to start your tour from the Plaza Mayor, an impressive central square paved with massive cobblestones and lined with whitewashed colonial houses and a charmingly simple parish church. Measuring nearly 120m by 120m, this is reputedly the

largest main square in the country. The vast expanse is only interrupted by a small Mudéjar fountain in its middle, which provided water to the village inhabitants for almost four centuries. Unlike all other Colombian cities and towns where the main squares have been named after historic heroes, most often Bolívar, the one in Villa de Leyva is traditionally and firmly called Plaza Mayor.

## Historic Houses & Museums

Small as it is, the town has half a dozen museums, most of which are in old colonial buildings.

**Casa Museo de Luis Alberto Acuña** (*Plaza Mayor; admission US$0.80; open 10am-1pm & 3pm-5pm Tues-Sun*) has been set up in the mansion where Acuña (1904–93) lived for

the last 15 years of his life. It features works by this painter, sculptor, writer and historian who was inspired by influences ranging from Muisca mythology to contemporary art.

**Casa Museo de Antonio Nariño** (*Carrera 9 No 10-19*) is the house where Nariño lived until his death in 1823. Known as the forefather of Colombia's independence, he was a fierce defender of human rights. He's also revered for translating Thomas Paine's *Rights of Man* into Spanish. The house has been converted into a museum containing colonial objects and memorabilia related to this great man. It was closed for refurbishing as we went to press.

**Casa Museo de Antonio Ricaurte** (*Parque Ricaurte; admission US$0.80; open 9am-noon & 2pm-5pm Wed-Fri, 9am-1pm & 2pm-6pm*

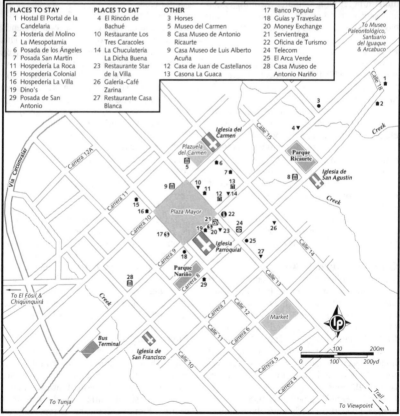

## VILLA DE LEYVA

**PLACES TO STAY**
1 Hostal El Portal de la Candelaria
2 Hostería del Molino La Mesopotamia
6 Posada de los Ángeles
7 Posada San Martín
11 Hospedería La Roca
15 Hospedería Colonial
16 Hospedería La Villa
19 Dino's
29 Posada de San Antonio

**PLACES TO EAT**
4 El Rincón de Bachué
10 Restaurante Los Tres Caracoles
14 La Chuculatería La Dicha Buena
23 Restaurante Star de la Villa
26 Galería-Café Zarina
27 Restaurante Casa Blanca

**OTHER**
3 Horses
5 Museo del Carmen
8 Casa Museo de Antonio Ricaurte
9 Casa Museo de Luis Alberto Acuña
12 Casa de Juan de Castellanos
13 Casona La Guaca

17 Banco Popular
18 Guías y Travesías
20 Money Exchange
21 Servientrega
22 Oficina de Turismo
24 Telecom
25 El Arca Verde
28 Casa Museo de Antonio Nariño

*Sat & Sun)* is the house where Ricaurte was born in 1786. He fought under Bolívar and is remembered for his heroic act of self-sacrifice in the battle of San Mateo (near Caracas in Venezuela) in 1814. Defending an armoury and closely encircled by the Spaniards, he let them in, then set fire to the gunpowder kegs and blew up everybody including himself. The battle was won. The house is now a museum, which displays furniture and weapons of the period as well as some related documents.

**Museo del Carmen** *(Plazuela del Carmen; admission US$0.80; open 10am-1pm & 2pm-5pm Sat, Sun & holidays)*, in the convent of the same name, is one of the best museums of religious art in the country. It contains valuable paintings, carvings, altarpieces and other religious objects dating from the 16th century onward.

**Museo Paleontológico** *(Vía Arcabuco; admission US$0.80; open 10am-1pm & 3pm-5pm Tues-Sun)*, about 1km northeast of town on the road to Arcabuco, has a collection of locally found fossils dating from the period when the area was a seabed (100 to 150 million years ago).

## Churches
Villa de Leyva has four churches, all of which date back to the town's early years. The **Iglesia Parroquial**, the parish church facing the main square, was built in 1608 and has hardly changed since. It boasts a marvellous baroque main retable. The only other church in religious service, the **Iglesia del Carmen**, has interesting paintings in the chancel and the wooden structure supporting the roof. The two remaining churches, **Iglesia de San Francisco** and **Iglesia de San Agustín**, no longer serve religious purposes and can't be visited.

## Other Attractions
Villa de Leyva is a leisurely place in which to wander around charming white-washed cobbled streets, enjoying the lazy rhythm of days gone by. It's still a very traditional place, where locals greet strangers in the street with *buenos días* or *buenas tardes*. Be sure to return the greeting.

As you stroll about, pop into the **Casa de Juan de Castellanos** and **Casona La Guaca**, two meticulously restored colonial mansions on Carrera 9 just off Plaza Mayor.

They have beautiful patios and house cafés and craft shops.

Go and see the colourful **market** held on Saturday on the square three blocks southeast of Plaza Mayor. It's best and busiest early in the morning. Walk further southeast and climb the hill behind the Hospedería Duruelo for a marvellous bird's-eye view of the town.

## Activities
The environs of Villa de Leyva are a pleasant area for **hiking**, and you can visit some of the nearby attractions on your way (see Around Villa de Leyva later in this chapter), or go trekking in the Santuario de Iguaque (see that entry later in this chapter). The region abounds in fossils, so you can combine walking with fossil hunting.

The region is also good for **cycling** and you can hire a bicycle in Villa de Leyva – see the following Organised Tours section.

**Horse riding** has become another popular activity, with up to 200 horses offered to tourists in Villa de Leyva. Many locals rent out horses – your hotel may be one of these – or go to the corner of Carrera 9 and Calle 16, where horses with their owners wait for tourists, especially on weekends. Horse rental costs around US$2.50 per hour plus another US$2.50 for the guide per group.

Of the more unusual activities, you might try **canyoning**, reputedly the only place in Colombia where you can do it – see the following Organised Tours section for details.

## Organised Tours
The local tour agency, the **Guías & Travesías** (☎ 732 0742; Calle 12 No 8A-31), managed by Enrique Maldonado, can show you around the region, organising transport, guides and accommodation if needed. The agency also rents out bicycles (US$1.50/5/9 per hour/half day/full day), and will give you maps of the recommended cycling routes.

**El Arca Verde** (☎ 732 0177; Calle 13 at Carrera 8), run by a Frenchman, Pierre, organises various ecological walks, taking from two hours to a full day. He also offers canyoning tours for beginners (US$12, four hours) and the experienced (US$18, full day).

Taxis parking in front of the bus terminal offer return taxi trips around the surrounding sights. The standard routes include El Fósil, El Infiernito and Convento del Santo Ecce

Homo (US$20) and Ráquira and La Candelaria (US$25). Prices are per taxi for up to four people and include stops at the sights.

## Special Events

The **Festival de las Cometas** (Kite Festival) is held in August. Locals and some foreign kite fans compete in this colourful event. The **Festival de Luces** (Firework Festival) takes place in December, usually on the first or second weekend of the month.

## Places to Stay

The town has a good choice of places to stay, and most hotels, particularly the upmarket ones, are stylish and charming. If you're looking for a place to splurge in Colombia, Villa de Leyva is one of the best places, and is good value.

There are more than 40 hotels in town, yet accommodation may become limited on weekends, and can fill up completely on *puentes* (long weekends) and during Easter week, despite the fact that the prices tend to rise, sometimes significantly, at these times. Prices listed below are weekday rates. Prices appear to be negotiable in some places, especially the cheaper ones, if you come in a larger party on weekdays.

**Dino's** (☎ 732 0803; Plaza Mayor; camping US$2, rooms per person US$5), next to the parish church on the main plaza, is one of the cheapest places. It has six neat rooms, all with private baths, or you can camp in the garden at the back and use the hotel facilities.

**Hospedería La Villa** (☎ 732 0848; Calle 12 No 10-11; rooms per person US$5), on the west corner of the main plaza, is also cheap but more basic and not all rooms have private baths.

**Hospedería Colonial** (☎ 732 1364; Calle 12 No 10-81; rooms per person US$5-6), just a block off the plaza, is another basic but acceptable option. It has 20 rooms, some of which have private baths.

**Hospedería La Roca** (☎ 732 0331; Plaza Mayor; rooms per person US$7.50), on the main plaza, is a bit better than the Colonial. All the rooms have baths and are arranged around two fine patios.

**Posada San Martín** (☎ 732 0428; Calle 14 No 9-43; rooms per person US$7.50) is a new, small place set up in a beautiful old-fashioned house. It has just five rooms, all with private bath.

There is a range of more upmarket and charming hotels, most of which are set in restored colonial mansions.

**Posada de los Ángeles** (☎ 732 0562; Carrera 10 No 13-94; rooms per person US$12) is one of the cheapest of these hotels. Overlooking El Carmen Church, it has nine rooms distributed over two storeys of this historic house.

**Hostal El Portal de la Candelaria** (☎ 732 0534; Calle 18 No 8-12; doubles/triples US$25/40) is another excellent establishment offering a lot of old-time charm and atmosphere. It has just seven rooms, each different.

**Posada de San Antonio** (☎ 732 0538; Carrera 8 No 11-90; doubles US$35-45, suites US$50-60) is another wonderful place, with a choice of comfortable rooms and good service.

**Hostería del Molino La Mesopotamia** (☎ 732-0235; Carrera 8 No 15A-265; singles/doubles/triples US$38/44/55) is in a lovely flour mill, the oldest building in town, erected in 1568 (four years before the town was founded). If you want to sleep in a canopied bed, request the old section. The rooms are a bit dim and the beds are hard, but you are, after all, in a legendary 435-year-old place. Even if you don't stay there, the management is friendly and will allow you to look around the grounds and the public areas.

## Places to Eat

Villa de Leyva has plenty of restaurants, possibly more than 50, though some don't open on weekdays.

**Restaurante Casa Blanca** (Calle 13 No 7-16; set meals US$2.50, mains US$4-5) is one of the best budget restaurants in town. Apart from set meals, it offers a choice of tasty à la carte dishes.

**Restaurante Star de la Villa** (Calle 13 No 8-85; set meals US$2.50, mains US$4-5) can be your alternative choice to the Casa Blanca, with reasonable food and prices.

**El Rincón de Bachué** (Carrera 9 at Calle 15A) is yet another address for a budget set meal and some typical regional dishes in pleasant surroundings.

**La Chuculatería La Dicha Buena** (Carrera 9 No 13-41; dishes US$2-5) is a cosy place offering something for just about everyone, including salads, soups, crepes, tortillas, spaghetti and trout.

Galería-Café Zarina *(Calle 14 No 7-67; mains US$5-6)* is an arty place that serves vegetarian and Middle Eastern dishes.

Restaurante Los Tres Caracoles *(Plaza Mayor; mains US$6-10)*, on the main square, offers rich, if not very cheap, Spanish food.

Most hotels listed in the previous section have their own restaurants, and you'll find more places to eat at Casa Juan de Castellanos and Casona La Guaca.

## Shopping

Villa de Leyva has a number of handicraft shops noted for fine basketry and good-quality woven items such as sweaters and *ruanas* (ponchos). There are some artisan shops on Plaza Mayor and more in the side streets, particularly on Carrera 9. A number of weavers have settled in town and their work is of excellent quality and their prices are reasonable. Most craft shops only open on weekends when tourists come.

The locals and their children offer fossils for sale. Prices are a matter of negotiation and usually drop considerably.

## Getting There & Away

The bus terminal is three blocks southwest of the Plaza Mayor, on the road to Tunja. Minibuses run regularly to Tunja (US$1.50, 45 minutes) until around 6pm. There are only two direct buses daily to Bogotá (US$6, four hours), or go to Tunja and change. For transport information to El Fósil, Convento del Santo Ecce Homo, Santuario de Iguaque and Ráquira, see those entries later in this chapter.

## AROUND VILLA DE LEYVA

Villa de Leyva is a good jumping-off place for excursions around the surrounding region, which is noted for a variety of attractions, both cultural and natural, including arqueological relics, colonial monuments, petroglyphs, caves, lakes and waterfalls. It is also a great place for fossil hunting.

And it's one of Colombia's safest regions in which to travel.

You can walk to some of the nearest sights, or go by bicycle or on horseback (see Activities under Villa de Leyva earlier in this chapter). You can also use local buses or go by taxi, or arrange a tour with Villa de Leyva's tour operators (see Organised Tours under Villa de Leyva earlier in this chapter).

## El Fósil

This is a reasonably complete fossil of a kronosaurus *(admission US$1; open 9am-noon & 2pm-5pm Fri-Wed)*, a 120-million-year-old prehistoric marine reptile vaguely resembling a crocodile. The fossil is 7m long (the animal was about 12m long but its tail hasn't survived). It's a baby kronosaurus (the adult animals were far larger) and it remains in the place where it was found.

The fossil is off the road to Chiquinquirá, 6km east of Villa de Leyva. You can walk there by path in a bit more than an hour, or take the Chiquinquirá or Ráquira bus, which will drop you off 1km from the fossil.

## El Infiernito

Nicknamed El Infiernito (literally 'the little hell'), this is the Muisca astronomic observatory *(admission US$1; open 9am-noon & 2pm-5pm Tues-Sun)*, dating from the early centuries AD. It contains 30-odd cylindrical stone monoliths sunk vertically into the ground about 1m from each other in two parallel lines 9m apart.

By measuring the length of shadow the Indians were able to determine the season of the year and thus to plan their agricultural and other activities accordingly. The complete lack of shadow (corresponding to the sun's zenith), which occurred for a short instant twice a year, on a day in March and September, is thought to have been the time for great festivities. The place was also a ritual site, noted for a number of large, phallic stone monoliths, which are scattered around the grounds.

El Infiernito is 2km north of El Fósil. There's no public transport all the way to the site, but you can walk there from the fossil in 25 minutes.

Bicycle, horse and taxi are other possible means of transport.

## Convento del Santo Ecce Homo

The convent *(admission US$1; open 9am-noon & 2pm-5pm Tues-Sun)*, founded by the Dominican fathers in 1620, is a large stone and adobe construction with a lovely courtyard. The floors are paved with stones quarried in the region, so they contain ammonites and fossils, including petrified corn and flowers. There are also fossils in the base of a statue in the chapel. The chapel boasts a magnificent gilded main retable with a small image of Ecce Homo and the original wooden ceiling.

The convent is 13km from Villa de Leyva. The morning bus to Santa Sofía will drop you off a 15-minute walk from the convent.

A return taxi trip (for up to four people) from Villa de Leyva to El Fósil, El Infiernito and Ecce Homo will cost about US$20, including waits allowing for visiting the three sights.

## SANTUARIO DE IGUAQUE

Iguaque is a 67.5-sq-km nature reserve northeast of Villa de Leyva. It covers the highest part of the mountain range that stretches up to Arcabuco. There are eight small mountain lakes in the northern part of the reserve, which sit at an altitude of between 3550m and 3700m. The Laguna de Iguaque, which gave its name to the whole reserve, is the most important lake, mostly because it was a sacred lake for the Muiscas (see the boxed text 'Legend of Laguna de Iguaque').

Today the lake is the prime destination for visitors to the reserve. It's perhaps not the most beautiful lake you would have seen in your life, but the scenery and the frailejón patches on the way certainly justify the trip. You can visit some of the other lakes by the way, most of which are no more than an hour's walk away.

Although these side trails may be faint, it's pretty easy to get around.

Keep in mind that it can get pretty cold here, so come prepared. The average temperature at these altitudes ranges between 10°C and 12°C.

The mean annual rainfall in the area is about 1700mm and the wettest months are April, October and November. However, March and September are not ideal months for hiking either. It's best to come here between January and February or between July and August.

### Places to Stay & Eat

The visitor centre is at an altitude of 2950m, 3km off the Villa de Leyva–Arcabuco road. It offers accommodation in dorms (US$8 per person), serves meals (US$8 per three meals) and collects the reserve's entrance fee (US$3). If you plan on staying here overnight, check the availability of the beds in advance at Bogotá's park office.

### Getting There & Away

The usual starting point for the reserve is Villa de Leyva. Take a bus to Arcabuco (there are four buses a day, at 7am, 10am, 1.30pm and 4pm), get off 12km from Villa at a place known as Los Naranjos, where a rough road branches off to the right and leads uphill to the visitor centre (3km). The walk from the centre uphill to the Laguna de Iguaque takes between two and three hours. A leisurely return trip is likely to take four to six hours, unless you plan on visiting some other lakes as well.

### RÁQUIRA

☎ 8 • pop 1500 • elevation 2150m
• temp 18°C

A small village 25km southwest of Villa de Leyva, Ráquira is known countrywide for its quality pottery – everything from kitchen utensils to copies of indigenous pots. There are a number of small pottery workshops in the village itself and on its outskirts, where you can watch the production process and buy some products if you want. Plenty of craft shops around the main square sell, apart from pottery, other crafts such as hammocks, ponchos, baskets, woodcarving etc. Many facades have been painted in bright colours, which gives the village much life and charm.

### Places to Stay & Eat

There are several hotels and restaurants in the village.

---

### Legend of Laguna de Iguaque

Laguna de Iguaque is small and perhaps not overwhelmingly impressive, yet it was reputedly one of the most sacred lakes for the Muiscas. After all, Iguaque means 'the cradle of humankind' in Chibcha language.

According to Muisca legend a beautiful woman, Bachué, walked out from the lake holding a three-year-old child in her arms. She built a house where they lived. When the boy was an adult they married and had many children, and that is how the earth was populated. When they reached old age, they returned to the lake, turned themselves into snakes and dived into its waters forever.

**Hotel Suaya** (☎ 735 7029; rooms per person US$5), a block off the main plaza, is the cheapest option. It has nine rooms, all with private baths, but no restaurant.

**Hostería La Candelaria** (☎ 735 7259; rooms with bath per person US$7), near the Suaya, has 10 rooms that sleep from two to six persons, plus a restaurant.

**Hostería Nemqueteba** (☎ 735 7083; doubles/triples with bath US$15/20), on the corner of the main plaza, is perhaps the best choice, with its fine patio and a restaurant.

### Getting There & Away

Ráquira is 5km off the Tunja–Chiquinquirá road, down a side road branching off at Tres Esquinas. Only two buses daily travel along this road to Ráquira (and continue on to La Candelaria). Both come from Bogotá, one through Tunja, the other one through Chiquinquirá.

Three or four minibuses run daily from Villa de Leyva to Ráquira (US$1.50, 35 minutes) and back, plus the occasional *colectivo* if there's demand.

### LA CANDELARIA

This tiny hamlet set amid arid hills, 7km beyond Ráquira, is noted for the **Monasterio de La Candelaria** (open 9am-5pm daily). The monastery was founded in 1597 by Augustine monks and completed about 1660. Part of it is open to the public. Monks will show you through the chapel (note the 16th-century painting of the Virgen de la Candelaria over the altar), a small museum, the library, and the courtyard flanked by the cloister with a collection of 17th-century canvasses hanging on its walls. Some of them were allegedly painted by Gregorio Vásquez de Arce y Ceballos and the Figueroa brothers.

### Getting There & Away

Only two buses a day call at La Candelaria, both of which come from Bogotá. Otherwise, walk by a path from Ráquira (one hour). It begins in Ráquira's main plaza, winds up a hill to a small shrine at the top and then drops down and joins the road to La Candelaria.

You can also go by taxi. A return taxi trip from Villa de Leyva to Ráquira and La Candelaria can be arranged for around US$25 (up to four people), allowing some time in both villages.

# Santander

## SAN GIL

☎ 7 • pop 33,000 • elevation 1110m • temp 22°C

San Gil is a 300-year-old town which is situated on a bank of the Río Fonce, on the main Bogotá–Bucaramanga road in the department of Santander. The town's major attraction is the riverside Parque El Gallineral, and this sight alone probably justifies a stop if you are passing this way.

If you happen to stop in San Gil, be sure to take the short trip to Barichara (see that entry later in this chapter), a beautiful small colonial town. You may also take a trip to the village of Curití, 12km northeast of San Gil, noted for its 17th-century church and the Quebrada Curití, a mountain-like river with waterfalls and ponds to swim in. Finally, San Gil is the place to go rafting with some of the local tour companies.

### Information

The tourist office, the **CAI de Turismo** (☎ 724 3433; Malecón at Calle 7; open 7am-noon & 1pm-6pm daily), is near the entrance to the Parque El Gallineral.

The town has a collection of banks including **Bancolombia** (Calle 12 No 10-44) and **Bancafé** (Carrera 10 No 11-16).

If you're seeking Internet access you can try **Compugu@nes** (Carrera 10 No 12-37, Piso 2) in the Centro Comercial El Edén on the main plaza.

### Things to See

The town's showpiece is the **Parque El Gallineral** (☎ 724 4372; Malecón at Calle 6; admission US$1.50; open 8am-6pm daily). The four-hectare (10-acre) park is set on a triangle-shaped island between two arms of the Quebrada Curití and Río Fonce. Almost all of its 1867 trees are covered with *barbas de viejo*, long silvery fronds of tillandsia that form spectacular transparent curtains of foliage. The park is on the road to Bucaramanga, a 10-minute walk from the town centre.

San Gil has a rather pleasant main plaza, **Parque La Libertad**, with huge old ceibas and a handsome 18th-century stone **Catedral Santa Cruz** (Carrera 9 at Calle 13). One block uphill from the plaza is the **Museo de Arte Religioso** (☎ 724 6986; Calle 12 No

10-31; admission US$1; open 9am-11.30am & 2.30pm-5pm Sat-Mon) featuring a collection of religious artefacts.

## Organised Tours
Three tour operators – **Ríos y Canoas** (☎ 724 7220), **Rafting Club Brújula** (☎ 723 7000) and **Planeta Azul** (☎ 724 0000) – have their desks at the entrance to the Parque El Gallineral and operate together. About 100m away, next to the tourist office, is the stand of the fourth tour agency, **Aventura Total** (☎ 723 8888).

The major product of all four companies is white-water rafting on local rivers. A standard 10km run on Río Fonce (grades 1 to 3) costs US$12 per person and takes 1½ hours, but longer, more adventurous trips on Río Chicamocha (grades up to 4) can be organised on request.

Most operators also offer horse riding, caving, paragliding, abseiling, rock climbing and ecological walks.

## Places to Stay
San Gil has plenty of hotels, predominantly budget ones, all across the centre.

**Hotel San Carlos** (☎ 724 2542; Carrera 11 No 11-25; singles/doubles/triples US$2.50/ 4.50/6, with bath US$5/7/10) is one of the cheapest acceptable places and is friendly.

**Hotel El Viajero** (☎ 724 1965; Carrera 11 No 11-07; singles/doubles US$3.50/6, with bath US$6/8), next door to San Carlos, is marginally better and a bit more expensive.

**Hotel Victoria** (☎ 724 2347; Carrera 11 No 10-40; singles/doubles/triples with bath US$5/9/11) has 15 rooms, all with baths, arranged around a large central courtyard.

**Hotel Villa del Oriente** (☎ 724 5089; Calle 10 No 10-47; singles/doubles with bath US$5/9) is another reasonable, if rather mundane, budget choice.

**Hotel Mansión del Parque** (☎ 724 5662; Calle 12 No 8-71; singles/doubles/triples with bath US$18/26/36), set in a colonial mansion at the corner of Parque Central, has large rooms, some with balconies overlooking the plaza.

## Places to Eat
A good number of budget restaurants are along Carrera 11 between Calles 10 and 15, and on Calle 10 between Carreras 9 and 11. **Restaurante El Maná** (Calle 10 No 9-12; set meals US$2) is one of the best among them.

## Getting There & Away
The bus terminal is 2km west of the town centre on the road to Bogotá. Urban buses shuttle regularly between the terminal and the centre, or take a taxi (US$1).

Frequent buses travel south to Bogotá (US$15, 7½ hours) and north to Bucaramanga (US$5, 2½ hours). There are also half-hourly minibuses going to Bucaramanga (US$5, 2¼ hours). Buses to Barichara (US$1, 40 minutes) leave every 45 minutes from the Cotrasangil bus company office at Carrera 10 No 14-82, in the town centre.

## BARICHARA
☎ 7 • pop 3000 • elevation 1340m • temp 22°C
Barichara is a small, old town, set amid arid hills on the rim of the canyon of Río Suárez, 20km northwest of San Gil. Founded in 1705 as Villa de San Lorenzo de Barichara, Barichara's streets were paved with massive, flat slabs and lined with modest single-storey adobe houses. Four stone churches were built, including a massive cathedral.

Despite the nearly 300 years that have passed since its foundation, Barichara is almost untouched by time; its paved streets, adobe houses and stone churches are all still there, as is its sleepy, old-world atmosphere. In 1975 the town was decreed a national monument, and much work has gone into its restoration.

Authentic, well-preserved and clean, this is one of the most beautiful small colonial towns in Colombia.

The name Barichara comes from Barachalá, a Guane Indian word (the original inhabitants of this territory) which means 'a good place for a rest' – absolutely true! Whether you are going to sightsee this small colonial pearl or just want a place to rest, Barichara won't fall short of your expectations. Don't miss it.

## Things to See
As you stroll about the streets take a look at the churches. The 18th-century sandstone **Catedral de la Inmaculada Concepción** (Parque Principal) is the largest and most elaborate single piece of architecture in town, looking somewhat too big for the town's needs. Its golden stonework (which turns deep orange at sunset) contrasts with the whitewashed houses surrounding it. The

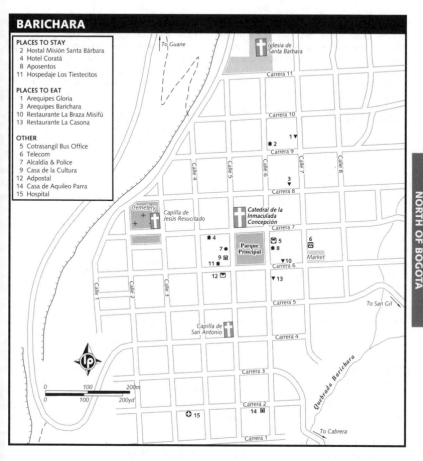

**BARICHARA**

PLACES TO STAY
2  Hostal Misión Santa Bárbara
4  Hotel Coratá
8  Aposentos
11  Hospedaje Los Tiestecitos

PLACES TO EAT
1  Arequipes Gloria
3  Arequipes Barichara
10  Restaurante La Braza Misifú
13  Restaurante La Casona

OTHER
5  Cotrasangil Bus Office
6  Telecom
7  Alcaldía & Police
9  Casa de la Cultura
12  Adpostal
14  Casa de Aquileo Parra
15  Hospital

To Guane

Iglesia de
Santa Bárbara

Carrera 11

Carrera 10

Carrera 9

Carrera 8

Carrera 7

Carrera 6

Carrera 5

Carrera 4

Carrera 3

Carrera 2

Carrera 1

Calle 4
Calle 5
Calle 6
Calle 7
Calle 8

Cemetery
Capilla de
Jesús Resucitado

Catedral de la
Inmaculada
Concepción

Parque
Principal

Market

Calle 1
Calle 2
Calle 3

Capilla de
San Antonio

To San Gil

To Cabrera

Quebrada Barichara

0    100    200m
0    100    200yd

**NORTH OF BOGOTÁ**

doorframe of the main entrance is designed so that when open it appears that the arched entrance has no doors, giving an impression of space and airiness. The building has a clerestory (a second row of windows high up in the nave) which is unusual among Spanish colonial churches.

The **Iglesia de Santa Bárbara** *(Carrera 11 at Calle 6)* at the northern end of town has been carefully reconstructed in the 1990s (only the facade survived). The cemetery chapel, the **Capilla de Jesús Resucitado** *(Carrera 7 at Calle 3)*, unfortunately lost a part of its bell tower when it was damaged by lightning. Do visit the cemetery, next to the chapel, noted for interesting tombs elaborated in stone. Also have a look at the **Capilla de San Antonio** *(Carrera 4 at Calle 5)*,

the youngest of the town's churches, dating from 1831.

The **Casa de la Cultura** *(☎ 726 7002; Calle 5 No 6-29; admission US$0.25; open 8am-noon & 2pm-6pm Wed-Sat, 9am-1pm Sun)*, in a colonial house laid out around a fine patio, on the main square, features a small collection of fossils and pottery of the Guane Indians.

The **Casa de Aquileo Parra** *(Carrera 2 No 5-60)* is a small, humble house where an ex-president lived, but there's not much to see inside. If you want to check it out, *la señora* in the house around the corner will open it for you.

Barichara is a good jumping-off point for some short excursions, particularly a trip to the tiny old village of **Guane**, 10km to the northwest, where time seems to have been frozen a century or two ago. It has a fine rural church and a museum with a collection of fossils and Guane cultural artefacts.

## Places to Stay
Barichara has half a dozen hotels, plus some locals who rent rooms in their homes.

**Aposentos** *(☎ 726 7294; Calle 6 No 6-40; rooms per person US$5)* is one of the cheapest hotels, and very good value. This small, friendly place, right on the main plaza, has just five rooms, all with private baths.

**Hospedaje Los Tiestecitos** *(☎ 726 7224; Carrera 6 No 4-57; rooms per person US$5)*, just off the plaza, has six simple rooms, all with bath. The rooms upstairs are brighter.

**Hotel Coratá** *(☎ 726 7110; Carrera 7 No 4-08; rooms per person US$7)* is a likeable historic house with neat, ample rooms with baths.

**Hostal Misión Santa Bárbara** *(☎ 726 7163, in Bogotá ☎ 1-288 4949; Calle 5 No 9-12; singles/doubles/triples US$22/36/48)* is set in a meticulously refurbished beautiful colonial mansion. It has comfortable, old-fashioned rooms with bath, a restaurant and a swimming pool. Room prices include breakfast.

## Places to Eat
There are quite a number of simple, budget restaurants around the plaza and neighbouring streets, including **Restaurante La Braza Misifú** *(Carrera 6 No 6-31)* and **Restaurante La Casona** *(Calle 6 No 5-68)*. They have cheap set meals and some typical regional dishes. If you need somewhere a bit more upmarket, the restaurant of **Hostal Misión Santa Bárbara** provides tasty home-cooked meals.

The specialities of the region include *cabro* (grilled goat), *mute* (tripe and vegetable soup) and the famous *hormiga culona*, a giant fried ant which appears mainly in March and April. Barichara is also well-known for its *arequipe* (thick milk pudding). There are a number of arequipe shops, including **Arequipes Barichara** *(Carrera 8 No 5-51)* and **Arequipes Gloria** *(Calle 6 No 9-29)*. The local drink is the *chicha de maíz* (an alcoholic maize drink).

## Getting There & Away
Buses shuttle between Barichara and San Gil every 45 minutes (US$1, 40 minutes).

They depart from the Cotrasangil bus company office on the main plaza.

Two buses a day (except Saturday) go to Guane, or you can walk there by an old Spanish trail in about 1½ hours. The trail was declared a national monument in 1997 and has been extensively restored.

## BUCARAMANGA
☎ 7 • pop 550,000 • elevation 960m • temp 23°C

Bucaramanga, the capital of Santander, is a fairly modern, busy commercial and industrial centre with an agreeable climate. It is noted for its numerous parks, cigars and the famous *hormiga culona*, a large ant which is fried and eaten.

The city was founded in 1622 and developed around what is today the Parque García Rovira, but very little of its colonial architecture remains. Over the centuries, the city centre moved eastwards, and today Parque Santander marks the heart of Bucaramanga. Further east are newer districts, peppered with upmarket hotels, restaurants and nightspots.

This is one of the trendiest and most pleasant sectors of the city, and it's safer than the centre.

There is not much to see or do in Bucaramanga, but it may be a stopover on the long route between Bogotá and the coast or Cúcuta. If you do stop here, don't miss taking a side trip to Girón (see that entry later in this chapter), 9km away.

## Information
The tourist office, the **Corporación Mixta de Promoción de Santander** *(☎ 630 7589; Carrera 19 No 35-02, Oficina 215; open 8am-noon & 2pm-6pm Mon-Fri)* is in the building of Universidad Industrial de Santander, on the corner of Parque Santander.

The central branch offices of the major banks are marked on the map. They are all packed within a small central area. Most of the banks also have branches in the eastern sector.

Internet access in the city centre is provided by **Click and Play** *(Calle 34 No 19-46)* in the Centro Comercial La Triada. In the eastern sector of the city there are a number of facilities including **Mundo Internet** *(Carrera 33 No 34-45)* and **SAI Telecom** *(Carrera 33 No 45-86)*.

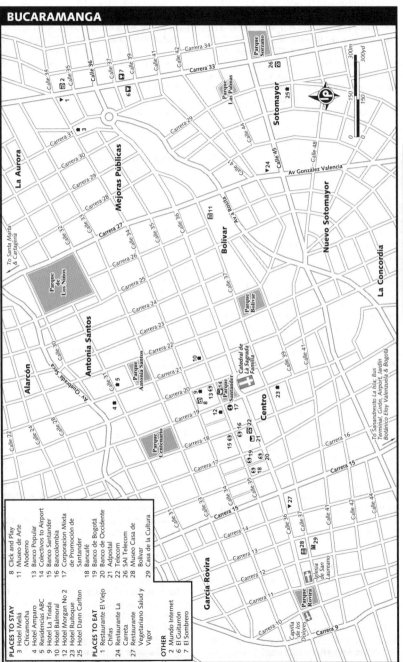

# BUCARAMANGA

PLACES TO STAY
3  Hotel Meliá
    Chicamocha
4  Hotel Amparo
5  Residencias ABC
9  Hotel La Triada
10 Hotel Balmoral
12 Hotel Morgan No 2
23 Hotel Ruitoque
25 Hotel Dann Carlton

PLACES TO EAT
1  Restaurante El Viejo
    Chifas
24 Restaurante La
    Carreta
27 Restaurante
    Vegetariano Salud y
    Vigor

OTHER
2  Mundo Internet
6  El Guitarrón
7  El Sombrero

8  Click and Play
11 Museo de Arte
    Moderno
13 Banco Popular
14 Colectivos to Airport
15 Banco Santander
16 Bancolombia
17 Corporación Mixta
    de Promoción de
    Santander
18 Bancafé
19 Banco de Bogotá
20 Banco de Occidente
21 Adpostal
22 Telecom
26 SAI Telecom
28 Museo Casa de
    Bolívar
29 Casa de la Cultura

## Things to See

Bucaramanga has several museums. The **Museo Casa de Bolívar** (☎ 630 4258; Calle 37 No 12-15; admission US$0.50; open 8am-noon & 2pm-5.50pm Mon-Fri) is housed in a colonial mansion with two patios, where Bolívar stayed for two months in 1828. The museum has a ragbag of historic and archaeological exhibits, including old weapons, documents, paintings, and mummies and artefacts of the Guane Indians which inhabited the region before the Spaniards arrived.

Diagonally opposite, the **Casa de la Cultura** (☎ 630 2046; Calle 37 No 12-46; admission US$0.25; open 8am-noon & 2pm-6pm Mon-Fri, 8am-noon Sat), in another historic building, features a collection of paintings donated by the local artists.

Fourteen blocks east along the same street is the **Museo de Arte Moderno** (☎ 645 0483; Calle 37 No 26-16; admission US$0.50; open 9am-noon & 3pm-6pm Tues-Sat). It has temporary exhibitions of modern art.

Of the city churches, the **Catedral de la Sagrada Familia** (Calle 36 No 19-56), facing Parque Santander, is the most substantial piece of religious architecture. Constructed for nearly a century (1770–1865), it's a massive, eclectic edifice with fine stained-glass windows and a ceramic cupola brought from Mexico.

The **Capilla de los Dolores** (Carrera 10 at Calle 35), in the Parque García Rovira, is Bucaramanga's oldest surviving church, erected in stone in 1748–50. It's no longer operating as a church and is seldom open.

The city has pleasant botanical gardens, the **Jardín Botánico Eloy Valenzuela** (☎ 648 0729; admission US$0.25; open 8am-5pm daily), featuring a variety of fine trees, a small pond and a replica of a Japanese garden. The gardens are on the old road to Floridablanca, in the suburb of Bucarica. To get there, take the Bucarica bus from Carrera 15 in the city centre.

## Places to Stay

Budget hotels are centred around the Parque Centenario, particularly on Calle 31 between Carreras 19 and 22. They are mostly basic, but many have private baths.

**Residencias ABC** (☎ 633 7352; Calle 31 No 21-44; singles/doubles/triples US$3/5/6) and **Hotel Amparo** (☎ 630-4098; Calle 31 No 20-29; singles/doubles/triples US$4/6/7) are among the cheapest in the area. They both have rooms with private baths and fans.

**Hotel Balmoral** (☎ 630 4663; Carrera 21 No 34-75; singles/doubles/triples US$12/15/20) is a bit flashier and better located, and has hot water.

**Hotel Morgan No 2** (☎ 630 4226; Calle 35 No 18-83; singles/doubles US$12/17), just off Parque Santander, is another reasonable, very central and affordable place. It has ample rooms with baths and fans; choose one with a window facing the street.

**Hotel Ruitoque** (☎ 633 4567; Carrera 19 No 37-26; singles/doubles/triples US$20/28/35) is one of the cheapest places that provide air-conditioning. The prices include breakfast.

**Hotel La Triada** (☎ 642 2410; e netriada@col1.telecom.com.co; Carrera 20 No 34-22; singles/doubles/triples US$50/60/70) is the best central choice, with air-conditioning, free Internet access and buffet breakfast included in the price.

**Hotel Meliá Chicamocha** (☎ 634 3000; w www.solarhoteles.com.co; Calle 34 No 31-24; singles/doubles US$50/65) is in the eastern sector, in the Zona Rosa, and provides a range of facilities comparable to La Triada.

**Hotel Dann Carlton** (☎ 643 1919; e reservas@hoteldanncarltonbucaramanga.com.co; Calle 47 No 28-83; doubles US$90) is at the top of Bucaramanga's luxuries, providing a gym, sauna and a rooftop swimming pool with a panoramic view over the city.

## Places to Eat

There are plenty of cheap restaurants around, or attached to, the budget hotels, where you can grab a set meal for less than US$2. Vegetarians can have inexpensive lunches at **Restaurante Vegetariano Salud y Vigor** (Calle 36 No 14-24).

A better area for dining is the eastern sector of the city, particularly on and around Carreras 27 and 33 where you'll find plenty of snack bars, fast foods, cafés and restaurants for every budget, including some of the city's best eateries.

**Restaurante El Viejo Chiflas** (Carrera 33 No 34-10; mains US$3-6; open 24hr) is one of the good budget options. It serves typical local food, including *mute* (traditional soup; US$2.50) and *cabrito* (grilled goat; US$6).

**Restaurante La Carreta** (Carrera 27 No 42-27; mains US$6-12) is housed in a historic mansion and has a 40-year-old tradition and a good address for a fine dinner.

Typical regional dishes include *mute* and *cabro* or *cabrito*. The legendary *hormiga culona* is not a dish you order in restaurants but a kind of snack you buy by weight in shops (about US$30 per kilogram). The ants only appear in season (roughly March to May) and are sold in delicatessens and in the shopping mall of **Sanandresito La Isla** *(Diagonal 15 between Calles 55 & 56)*.

### Entertainment
Most of the night entertainment revolves around the eastern sector, with the Zona Rosa being its major focus. The Zona Rosa proper is centred on Carrera 31 between Calles 33 and 34, and Calle 33 between Carreras 31 and 33, but bars and discos spread along Carrera 33 up to Calle 45. Here is also the city's most famous mariachi venue, **El Guitarrón** *(Carrera 33 No 37-34)*, which has live music by mariachi groups nightly 10pm to 2am. Across the road is another mariachi affair, **El Sombrero** *(Carrera 33 No 37-13)*.

### Getting There & Away
**Air** The Palonegro airport is on a *meseta* (plateau) high above the city, off the road to Barrancabermeja. The landing here is breathtaking. Local buses marked 'Aeropuerto' link the airport and the city centre every hour or so; you catch them on Carrera 15. It's faster to go by colectivo (US$2), which park in Parque Santander. There are flights to some major Colombian cities, including Bogotá (US$60 to US$110) and Medellín (US$75 to US$130).

**Bus** Bucaramanga's bus terminal is situated southwest of the centre, midway to Girón; frequent city buses marked 'Terminal' go there from Carrera 15. Buses depart regularly to Bogotá (US$19, 10 hours), Cartagena (US$27, 12 hours) and Santa Marta (US$20, nine hours).

There are also a number of buses to Cúcuta (US$10, six hours). A scenic road winds up to the *páramo* (open highland) at 3400m and then drops down to Cúcuta. If you sit on the right-hand side of the bus, you will have a splendid view as you leave Bucaramanga and again when you arrive at Pamplona. Travel by day if possible and have a sweater handy.

## GIRÓN
☎ 7 • pop 45,000 • elevation 780m
• temp 24°C

A beautiful, colonial town 9km southwest of the city centre, San Juan de Girón is today a distant suburb of Bucaramanga. It was founded in 1631 on the banks of the Río de Oro, and in 1963 it was declared a national monument. Its central area has been largely restored and preserves much of its historic character.

The town has become a trendy place, and some artists and intellectuals have settled here giving it a bit of a bohemian flavour. Due to its proximity to Bucaramanga, Girón has become a popular weekend getaway for city dwellers.

### Information
The tourist office, the **Secretaría de Cultura y Turismo** *(☎ 646 1337; Calle 30 No 26-64; open 8am-noon & 2pm-6pm daily)*, is in the Casa de la Cultura.

There are two ATMs (Cajero Automático Servibanca and Cajero Automático ATH) and two banks (Banco Popular and Banco Sudameris) on the eastern side of the Parque Principal.

Internet facilities include **Café Arles** *(Calle 31 No 23-48)* and **el port@l.net** *(Calle 30 No 25-03)*.

### Things to See
You'll find that Girón is an agreeable place. Take time to stroll about its narrow cobbled streets, looking at whitewashed old houses, shaded patios and half a dozen small stone bridges, which are reputed to have been built by slaves.

The **Catedral del Señor de los Milagros** on the main plaza was begun in 1646 but not completed until 1876, so it's stylistically eclectic.

Also on the main square is the **Mansión del Fraile** *(Calle 30 No 25-27)*, a beautiful colonial mansion which is 350 years old. It now houses a restaurant (see the following Places to Stay & Eat section) as well as a craft shop.

While wandering around the streets, don't miss the **Plazuela Peralta**, which is one of the most charming spots in town.

Just as enchanting is the **Plazuela de las Nieves** which features a simple, but noble, 18th-century **Capilla de las Nieves**.

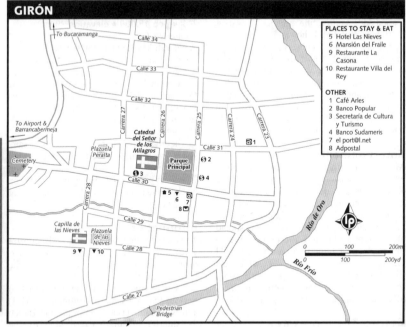

**GIRÓN**

To Bucaramanga

Calle 34

Calle 33

Calle 32

To Airport & Barrancabermeja

Carrera 27

Carrera 26

Carrera 25

Carrera 24

Carrera 23

Catedral del Señor de los Milagros

Plazuela Peralta

Cemetery

Calle 31

Parque Principal

Calle 30

Carrera 28

Calle 29

Capilla de las Nieves

Plazuela de las Nieves

Calle 28

Calle 27

Pedestrian Bridge

Río de Oro

Río Frío

0 100 200m
0 100 200yd

**PLACES TO STAY & EAT**
5 Hotel Las Nieves
6 Mansión del Fraile
9 Restaurante La Casona
10 Restaurante Villa del Rey

**OTHER**
1 Café Arles
2 Banco Popular
3 Secretaría de Cultura y Turismo
4 Banco Sudameris
7 el port@l.net
8 Adpostal

**NORTH OF BOGOTÁ**

## Places to Stay & Eat

Girón is just a half-day trip from Bucaramanga, but if you wish to stay longer there is the pleasant **Hotel Las Nieves** (☎ 646 8968; Calle 30 No 25-71; singles/doubles/triples US$8/15/22) on the main plaza. It has large, comfortable rooms, all with private baths. Three rooms have balconies overlooking the plaza, so you may be lucky enough to grab one of these. The hotel has a budget restaurant serving set meals and regional dishes.

You can also dine out in any of several finer restaurants which include **Mansión del Fraile** (Calle 30 No 25-27; mains US$4-6), **Restaurante Villa del Rey** (Calle 28 No 27-49; mains US$3-6) and **Restaurante La Casona** (Calle 28 No 28-09; mains US$5-8). All three serve hearty, typical food in charming, colonial-style surroundings. On Sunday, when people from Bucaramanga come, riverside stalls open and offer a choice of regional dishes and snacks.

## Getting There & Away

Frequent city buses from Carreras 15 and 33 in Bucaramanga will deposit you at Girón's main plaza in half an hour.

# Norte de Santander

## PAMPLONA
☎ 7 • pop 44,000 • elevation 2290m
• temp 16°C

Pamplona, 124km northeast of Bucaramanga and 72km southwest of Cúcuta, is spectacularly set in the deep Valle del Espíritu Santo in the Cordillera Oriental. It's the only town of note on the Bucaramanga–Cúcuta road, and is actually one of the very few towns of importance in the Norte de Santander department.

Pamplona was founded by Pedro de Orsúa and Ortún Velasco in 1549, making it the oldest town in the region. Soon after its foundation, five convents were established, and the town swiftly developed into an important religious and political centre.

The only Spanish dot on the map for hundreds of kilometres around, Pamplona became the base for various expeditions that set off to conquer the region and to found new cities. Bucaramanga, Cúcuta, San Cristóbal and Mérida (the last two in present-day Venezuela) were all founded from Pamplona and, ironically, they are all far larger and more important than their mother town today.

On 4 July 1810 Pamplona heeded the Grito de Independencia (Cry for Independence) proclaimed by Agueda Gallardo de Villamizar, which made it one of the forerunners in the move for independence. By then, it was a stately, fair-sized town, dotted with churches and noble mansions.

Unfortunately, an earthquake in 1875 wiped out a good part of the colonial architecture. The most representative buildings were restored or reconstructed in their original style but most of the houses were replaced by new ones. Since then the construction of modern buildings has affected the colonial character of the town even further.

Pamplona was a schooling and catechistic centre from its early days, and the traditions have not been lost. Today the town is home to the Universidad de Pamplona, and the large student population is very much in evidence. Pamplona has a distinctly cultured air, and boasts more museums than Cúcuta and Bucaramanga combined.

## Information

The tourist office has closed. The Banco de Bogotá in the Parque Agueda Gallardo (the main plaza) gives cash advances on Visa credit cards.

## Historic Houses & Museums

Pamplona has quite a collection of museums and almost all are set in restored colonial houses.

**Museo de Arte Moderno Ramírez Villamizar** (☎ 568 2999; Calle 5 No 5-75; admission US$0.50; open 9am-noon & 2pm-6pm Tues-Fri, 9am-6pm Sat & Sun) is in a 450-year-old mansion known as the Casa de las Marías. The museum features about 40 works by Eduardo Ramírez Villamizar, one of Colombia's most outstanding artists, who was born in Pamplona in 1923. The collection gives an insight into his artistic development from expressionist painting of the 1940s to geometric abstract sculpture in recent decades. The museum also presents works by other Colombian artists.

**Museo Arquidiocesano de Arte Religioso** (☎ 568 1814; Carrera 5 No 4-53; admission US$0.25; open 10am-noon & 3pm-5pm Wed-Sat, 10am-noon Sun) features religious art, comprising paintings, statues, altarpieces and the like, collected from the region.

**Casa Anzoátegui** (Carrera 6 No 7-48; admission free; open 9am-noon & 2pm-5.30pm daily) is named after General José Antonio Anzoátegui. This Venezuelan hero of the independence campaign fought under Bolívar and his strategic abilities largely contributed to the victory in the Battle of Boyacá of 1819. He died in this house just three months after the battle, at the age of 30. The house has been restored and turned into a museum presenting a modest collection of arms and other exhibits related to the crucial historical events of the period.

**Casa Colonial** (Calle 6 No 2-56; admission by donation; open 8am-noon & 2pm-5pm Mon-Sat) is one of the oldest buildings in town, dating from the early Spanish days. The collection on display includes some pre-Columbian pottery, colonial sacred art, artefacts of several indigenous communities including the Motilones and Tunebos (the two Indian groups living in Norte de Santander department) plus a variety of antiques and old photos.

**Museo Fotográfico** (Carrera 7 No 2-44) is a curiosity rather than a museum, but do go in to see hundreds of old photos. Don't be put off by coffins at the entrance because this is primarily a funeral parlour.

Have a look at the **Casa de las Cajas Reales** (Carrera 5 at Calle 4), a great colonial mansion, and at **Casa de Mercado** (Carrera 5 at Calle 6), the 19th-century market building, just off the main square.

## Churches

There are some 10 old churches and chapels in town, reflecting Pamplona's religious status in colonial days, though not many of them have preserved their old splendour.

The 17th-century **Catedral** was seriously damaged during the earthquake of 1875 and altered in the reconstruction. The wide, five-nave interior (the two outer aisles were added at the beginning of the 20th century) is rather austere except for the magnificent main retable that somehow survived the disaster. The central figure of San Pedro was made in Spain in 1618.

The **Iglesia del Humilladero**, at the entrance to the cemetery, boasts the famous *Cristo del Humilladero*, an impressively

**PAMPLONA**

OTHER
1 Museo Fotográfico
2 Casa de las Cajas Reales
4 Casa Colonial
5 Bus Offices
6 Mueseo Arquidiocesano de Arte Religioso
7 Cotranal
9 Museo de Arte Moderno Ramírez Villamizar
11 Extra Rápido Los Motilones
12 Banco de Bogotá
14 Telecom
15 Casa Anzoátegui

PLACES TO STAY
8 Hotel Orsúa
10 Hotel Imperial
13 Hotel El Álamo
18 Hotel Cariongo

PLACES TO EAT
3 Restaurante Vegetariano Govinda's
16 Restaurante La Casona
17 Restaurante Delicias del Mar

realistic sculpture of Christ brought from Spain in the 17th century.

## Special Events

The town is known nationwide for its solemn **Semana Santa** celebrations (the week before Easter Sunday). Another important annual event is the **Fiestas del Grito de Independencia**, also called the Fiestas de Pamplona. The feast is celebrated for about two weeks preceding 4 July, and features concerts, exhibitions, bullfights and – never to be missed on such occasions – the beauty pageant.

## Places to Stay

The **Hotel Orsúa** (☎ 568 2470; Calle 5 No 5-67; singles/doubles/triples US$5/9/12) on the main plaza is one of the cheapest places to stay. It's pretty basic, but all its rooms have private baths.

**Hotel El Álamo** (☎ 568 2137; Calle 5 No 6-68; singles/doubles/triples US$7/12/17) is slightly better and it too, has rooms with bath attached. Much in the same class is the **Hotel Imperial** (☎ 568 2571; Carrera 5 No 5-36; singles/doubles/triples US$7/12/17) on the main plaza.

**Hotel Cariongo** (☎ 568 1515; Calle 9 at Carrera 5; singles/doubles/triples US$25/30/40), three blocks southwest of the plaza, is Pamplona's top-end accommodation option.

## Places to Eat

There are quite a number of restaurants scattered throughout the central area. Some of the cheapest set meals can be had in the restaurant of **Hotel Orsúa**, which is as simple as the hotel itself. For cheap vegetarian food go to **Restaurante Vegetariano Govinda's** (Calle 4 No 5-77; set meals US$2). As almost everywhere in the country, the market serves cheap local food.

**Restaurante La Casona** (Calle 6 No 7-58; mains US$4-6) and **Restaurante Delicias del Mar** (Calle 6 No 7-60; mains US$4-7) are just two examples of better restaurants.

## Getting There & Away

Pamplona doesn't have a bus terminal. Bus companies have their own offices, all packed on Carrera 5 just off the main plaza, from where their buses depart.

Pamplona's on the Bucaramanga–Cúcuta road, and buses pass by regularly to both

Cúcuta (US$3.50, 1¾ hours) and Bucaramanga (US$6, 4½ hours).

Two colectivo companies, Extra Rápido Los Motilones and Cotranal, both situated on the main plaza, operate shared taxis to Bucaramanga (US$6, 3½ hours) and Cúcuta US$3.50, 1½ hours).

## CÚCUTA
☎ 7 • pop 550,000 • elevation 320m
• temp 27°C

The capital of Norte de Santander, Cúcuta was founded in 1733, but completely destroyed by an earthquake in 1875. The town was rebuilt and has evolved into a busy commercial city, fuelled by its proximity to Venezuela, just 12km away. The city has a modern, if rather uninspiring, centre and vast poor suburbs. The climate is hot and dry.

Cúcuta doesn't have significant tourist attractions, so unless you're en route to or from Venezuela, there's little reason to visit. Even if you're coming this way, you may prefer to stay overnight in Pamplona (see that entry earlier in this chapter) rather than Cúcuta, as some travellers do.

## Information
**Tourist Offices** In the town centre is the **Corporación Mixta de Promoción de Norte de Santander** (☎ 571 3395; Calle 10 No 0-30; open 8am-noon & 2pm-6pm Mon-Fri).

**Immigration** The DAS immigration post (where you have to get an exit/entry stamp in your passport) is just before the border on the Río Táchira, on the left side of the road going towards Venezuela. There's also a DAS post at Cúcuta's airport – convenient if you're coming or leaving by air.

According to the most recent news, you no longer need to visit the Venezuelan consulate in Cúcuta to get the tourist card – it's issued directly by the DIEX office in San Antonio del Táchira, on Carrera 9 between Calles 6 and 7. If you want to confirm this anyway, the **Venezuelan consulate** (☎ 579 1956; Av Camilo Daza) is on the road that goes to the airport, about 3km north of the centre. You can get there by local buses marked 'Consulado' from the bus terminal or from Calle 13 in the centre.

**Money** No banks in Cúcuta will probably change cash dollars, but there are plenty of casas de cambio, including two dozen at the bus terminal and a number in the centre. They all change dollars, pesos and bolívares. There's also a rash of casas de cambio in San Antonio (on the Venezuela side of the border), paying much the same as those in Cúcuta.

Only a few of Cúcuta's banks, including **Bancolombia** (Av 5 No 9-80 • Av 0 No 14-50), change travellers cheques. Other banks marked on our map give advances on Visa and/or MasterCard, and most have ATMs.

**Email & Internet Access** The largest and cheapest (US$0.80 per hour) Internet facility is at the **Biblioteca Pública Julio Perez Ferrero**. The library takes almost the whole block between Av 1 and 2 and Calles 12 and 13; the access to its Internet café is from Av 1.

**OpinoNet** (Centro Comercial Gran Bulevar, Piso 6, Oficina 606B, Av 0 at Calle 11) is another budget place. Other facilities include **SIS Café Internet** (Calle 14 No 4-47); **cafe-rock.com** (Av 0 No 11-43), across the road from Gran Bulevar; **Café Cadena Internet** (Edificio Domus Center, Local 105, Av 0 No 12-66); and **Café Internet Telecom** (Av 0 No 10-55) in the Telecom office.

## Things to See
With time to spare, visit **Casa de la Cultura** (☎ 571 6689; Calle 13 No 3-67; open 8am-noon & 2pm-6pm Mon-Fri), noted for its impressive clock tower, which has temporary exhibitions. **Banco de la República** (☎ 575 0131; Av Diagonal Santander at Calle 11; open 8am-noon & 2pm-6pm Mon-Fri) also stages temporary exhibitions in its Area Cultural.

You can also take a short trip to Villa del Rosario (see that entry later in this chapter), 10km from Cúcuta.

## Places to Stay
There are a number of cheapies just south of the bus terminal, particularly along Av 7, but they range from basic to ultra-basic and most double as love hotels or brothels. The area is not attractive and may get unsafe at night. It's safer and more pleasant to stay further south, in the city centre, though hotels there are not as cheap.

**Hotel Internacional** (☎ 571 2718; Calle 14 No 4-13; singles/doubles/triples US$6/12/16) is one of the cheapest acceptable central

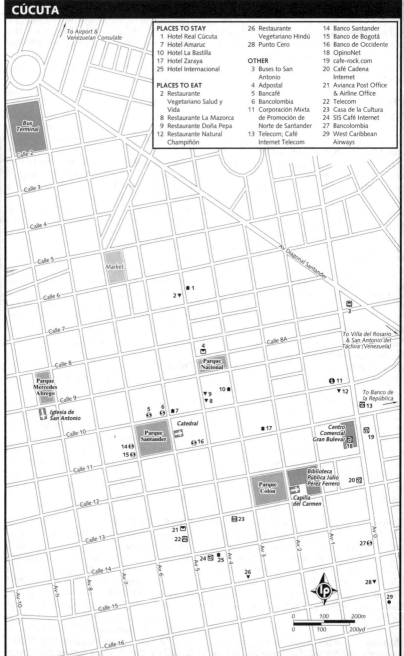

# CÚCUTA

**PLACES TO STAY**
1 Hotel Real Cúcuta
7 Hotel Amaruc
10 Hotel La Bastilla
17 Hotel Zaraya
25 Hotel Internacional

**PLACES TO EAT**
2 Restaurante Vegetariano Salud y Vida
8 Restaurante La Mazorca
9 Restaurante Doña Pepa
12 Restaurante Natural Champiñón

26 Restaurante Vegetariano Hindú
28 Punto Cero

**OTHER**
3 Buses to San Antonio
4 Adpostal
5 Bancafé
6 Bancolombia
11 Corporación Mixta de Promoción de Norte de Santander
13 Telecom; Café Internet Telecom

14 Banco Santander
15 Banco de Bogotá
16 Banco de Occidente
18 OpinoNet
19 cafe-rock.com
20 Café Cadena Internet
21 Avianca Post Office & Airline Office
22 Telecom
23 Casa de la Cultura
24 SIS Café Internet
27 Bancolombia
29 West Caribbean Airways

options. Just three blocks south of Parque Santander, the hotel has a spacious patio, a swimming pool and rooms come with bath and fan.

**Hotel La Bastilla** (☎ *571 2576; Av 3 No 9-42; singles/doubles/triples US$7/11/15)* is another central budget establishment offering rooms with private facilities, though it's not as pleasant as the Internacional.

**Hotel Real Cúcuta** (☎ *571 6841; Av 4 No 6-51; singles/doubles/triples with fan US$7/11/14, with air-con US$11/14/17)* is one of the cheapest options providing air-conditioning. It has rooms with bath, but is otherwise undistinguished.

**Hotel Amaruc** (☎ *571 7625; Calle 10 at Av 3; singles/doubles with fan US$17/25, with air-con US$22/30)* is a bit more decent and very central, overlooking Parque Santander, yet it has seen better days.

**Hotel Zaraya** (☎ *571 9436; Calle 11 No 2-46; singles/doubles/triples with air-con US$25/36/46)* is a new addition to Cúcuta's options and a good one. It has just 14 rooms, all with bath and air-conditioning.

### Places to Eat
**Restaurante La Mazorca** *(Av 4 No 9-67; set meals US$2; mains US$5-7)* and **Restaurante Doña Pepa** *(Av 4 No 9-57; set meals US$2; mains US$4-6)* serve tasty budget *almuerzos* (set lunches) and typical Colombian dishes à la carte.

Vegetarians can choose between **Restaurante Vegetariano Salud y Vida** *(Av 4 No 6-60)*, **Restaurante Natural Champiñón** *(Calle 10 No 0-05)* and **Restaurante Vegetariano Hindú** *(Calle 15 No 3-48)*, all of which serve budget set lunches on weekdays.

The 24-hour **Punto Cero** *(Av 0 No 15-60; mains US$4-5)* offers typical food, such as *bandeja paisa* (a traditional Antioquian dish) and *sancocho* (traditional soup). There are some more upmarket restaurants further south on Av 0.

### Getting There & Away
**Air** The airport is 4km north of the city centre. Minibuses marked 'El Trigal Molinos' (from Av 1 or Av 3 in the centre) will drop you 350m from the terminal. A taxi between the airport and the centre costs US$3.

The airport handles flights to most major Colombian cities (either direct or with a connection) including Bogotá (US$70 to US$130 one way), Medellín (US$80 to US$130), Cali (US$90 to US$140) and Cartagena (US$90 to US$130).

There are no direct flights to Venezuela (you must go to San Antonio del Táchira, the Venezuelan border town, 12km from Cúcuta, from where there are flights to Caracas and other domestic destinations).

**Bus** The bus terminal is on Av 7 at Calle 1 and is very dirty and very busy – one of the

---

## Hide Your Dollars in Your Shoes

Cúcuta's bus terminal is a playground for a well-organised and efficient gang of con men. It has been operating with impunity for years and it seems that nothing can be done about it. The con men target foreign travellers, principally those who've just arrived from Venezuela and may be unfamiliar with the ingenious practices of Colombian criminals.

The scenario is more or less like this: Upon arrival at the terminal you're approached by a well-dressed character and politely asked (usually in good English) if you want to buy a bus ticket. If you do, you're invited to a small room which you take to be the bus ticketing office. Your ticket is issued (though they actually just go round the corner to buy it from the true bus company office).

You are then told that the bus company has an insurance scheme for your money, since so many buses have been robbed. They show you a huge record book of people's names, signatures, nationalities, and the amount of money each had, so the whole thing appears completely genuine. They ask you to show your money, then they count the notes out, put them into a small plastic bag and return it to you. You are then instructed to place the bag in your shoe 'for security'.

It's all done right before your eyes so you see the whole process and nothing arouses your suspicion. What you don't realise is that while they count your money, they skilfully remove some of the notes from the bundle. You then take the bus to your destination and feel yourself protected and insured, until the moment you count the notes out...

poorest in Colombia. Watch your belongings closely. If you are arriving from Venezuela, you could be approached by some English-speaking individuals who will kindly offer their help in buying bus tickets and insuring your money (see the boxed text 'Hide Your Dollars in Your Shoes'). Ignore them – they are con men. Buy tickets directly from bus company offices.

There are frequent buses servicing Bucaramanga (US$10, six hours). At least two dozen buses daily run to Bogotá (US$29, 16 hours).

To Venezuela, take one of the frequent buses or shared taxis that run from Cúcuta's bus terminal to San Antonio del Táchira (US$0.30 or US$0.50 respectively, paid in either pesos or bolívares). You can also catch colectivos and buses to San Antonio from the corner of Av Diagonal Santander and Calle 8, in the centre. Don't forget to get off just before the bridge to have your passport stamped at DAS.

There's one hour's time difference between Colombia and Venezuela. Move your watch one hour forward when crossing from Colombia into Venezuela.

From San Antonio's bus terminal you can easily proceed further into Venezuela. There are half a dozen departures daily direct to Caracas; they all depart in the late afternoon or early evening for an overnight trip. There are no direct buses to Mérida; go to San Cristóbal and change. Colectivos to San Cristóbal leave frequently.

## VILLA DEL ROSARIO
☎ 7 • pop 45,000 • elevation 280m
• temp 27°C

Villa del Rosario, 10km southeast of Cúcuta on the road to the Venezuelan border, is the town where the constitution of Gran Colombia was drawn up and passed in 1821. Gran Colombia, the union of Venezuela, Colombia and Ecuador, was brought to life in Angostura (today Ciudad Bolívar in Venezuela) in 1819. It was largely a concept of Simón Bolívar, who insisted on creating

a strong, centralised republic made up of the provinces he was liberating. In practice this didn't happen; Gran Colombia was, since its birth, a weak, vast state incapable of being governed by a central regime. It gradually disintegrated before splitting into three separate countries in 1830. Bolívar's dream came to an end before he died.

### Things to See
The site of this important event in Colombia's history has been converted into a park, the **Parque de la Gran Colombia**. Its central feature is the ruin of the **Templo del Congreso**, the church (built in 1802) where the sessions of the congress were held. The congress debated in the sacristy of the church from May to October, before agreeing on the final version of the bill. Then the inauguration ceremony of Bolívar and Santander as president and vice-president of Gran Colombia took place in the church.

The church was almost completely destroyed by the 1875 earthquake and although some efforts were made to reconstruct it, only the dome was rebuilt (in quite a different style from the original). A marble statue of Bolívar has been placed in the rebuilt part of the church.

The park's other major sight is the **Casa Natal de Santander** (☎ 570 0741; admission US$1; open 9am-11.30am & 2pm-5.30pm Mon-Fri), a large country mansion which was the birthplace of Francisco de Paula Santander and his home for the first 13 years of his life. The house was also damaged by the earthquake of 1875 and restored in a partly altered style. It now houses a modest exhibition of documents and photos relating to Santander's life and to the congress.

### Getting There & Away
To get to the Parque de la Gran Colombia from Cúcuta, take the bus to San Antonio del Táchira, which passes next to the park on the way to the border. Don't take buses marked 'Villa del Rosario' – they won't bring you anywhere near the park.

# Caribbean Coast

The Colombian Caribbean Coast stretches 1760km from the dense jungles of the Darién Gap on the border with Panama, in the west, to the desert of La Guajira near Venezuela, in the east. The region extends south to the foot of the Andes. Administratively, the area falls into the departments of La Guajira, Cesar, Magdalena, Atlántico, Bolívar, Sucre and Córdoba, plus the northern tips of Antioquia and Chocó.

The Caribbean Coast was inhabited by various Indian communities long before the arrival of the Spaniards. Two of these groups evolved into highly developed cultures: the Tayrona in the Sierra Nevada de Santa Marta, and the Sinú in what are now the Córdoba and Sucre departments. Neither of the two cultures survived the Spanish Conquest, but other Indian groups today live in the region: the Cunas in the northwestern tip of the coast (though most of them live in Panama), the Kogis and Arhuacos in the Sierra Nevada de Santa Marta and the Guajiros (or Wayú) in La Guajira.

The coast was the first region conquered by the Spaniards. Santa Marta (founded in 1525) and Cartagena (1533) are the oldest surviving Colombian cities. Halfway between them sits Barranquilla, which is much younger but which has developed into the largest city on the coast and Colombia's second biggest port.

El Caribe, as the Caribbean region is locally known, is steeped in sun, rum and tropical music. Its inhabitants, the *costeños*, are easy-going, fun-loving folks with much of the hot African spirit who give the coast a touch of carnival atmosphere. The coast hosts one of the most colourful and wild Colombian feasts, the Carnaval de Barranquilla. The Carnaval de Cartagena is only marginally less mad.

## Magdalena

### SANTA MARTA
☎ 5 • pop 300,000 • elevation 2m
• temp 28°C

Founded in 1525 by Rodrigo de Bastidas, Santa Marta is the oldest surviving colonial town in Colombia. The site was deliberately

## Highlights

• Enjoy Cartagena, one of Latin America's most beautiful colonial cities

• Bask in the sun on the marvellous beaches in Parque Nacional Tayrona

• Visit the town of Mompós, a small gem of colonial architecture

• Take a tour to Ciudad Perdida, a great pre-Hispanic city of the Tayronas

• Join the crowds at the Carnaval de Barranquilla, one of Colombia's maddest festivals

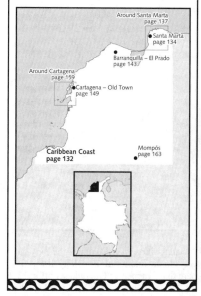

Around Santa Marta page 137

● Santa Marta page 134

Barranquilla – El Prado page 143

Around Cartagena page 159

Cartagena – Old Town page 149

Caribbean Coast page 132

Mompós page 163

chosen at the foot of the Sierra Nevada de Santa Marta to serve as a convenient base for the reputedly incalculable gold treasures of the Tayronas. Bastidas had previously briefly explored the area and was aware of the Indian riches to be found.

As soon as the plundering of the Sierra began, so did the natives' resistance, and clashes followed. By the end of the 16th century the Tayronas were eventually wiped out and many of their extraordinary gold objects (melted down for rough material by the Spaniards) were in the Crown's coffers.

CARIBBEAN COAST

131

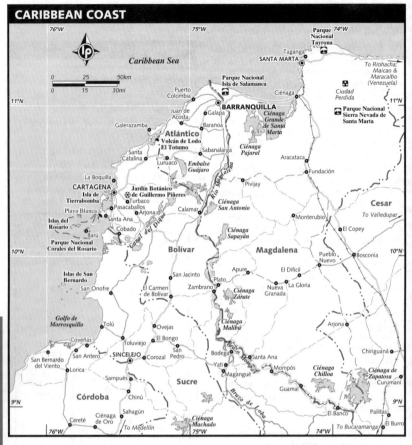

## CARIBBEAN COAST

Santa Marta was also one of the early gateways to the interior of the colony. It was from here that Jiménez de Quesada set off in 1536 for his strenuous march up the Magdalena Valley, to found Bogotá two years later.

Engaged in the war with the Tayronas and repeatedly ransacked by pirates, Santa Marta didn't have many glorious moments in its colonial history, and was soon overshadowed by its younger, more progressive neighbour, Cartagena. If there's an important date remembered nationwide in Santa Marta's history, it's 17 December 1830, the day when Simón Bolívar died here, after bringing independence to six Latin American countries.

Today, Santa Marta is Colombia's third largest seaport and the easy-going, pleasant capital of Magdalena. It still has some fine historic buildings, even though its colonial character has largely disappeared.

Santa Marta has become a popular tourist centre mostly because of its surroundings rather than for the city itself. El Rodadero, just to the south (today within the city limits), is a fashionable beach resort. North of Santa Marta is the attractive fishing village of Taganga, and further northeast, the beautiful Parque Nacional Tayrona. Santa Marta is also a jumping-off point for Ciudad Perdida, Tayrona's great pre-Hispanic city.

The climate is hot, but the sea breeze, especially in the evening, cools the city and makes it pleasant to wander about, or to sit over a beer in any of the numerous open-air waterfront cafés.

## The Tayrona – Another Lost Civilisation of Pre-Hispanic America

In pre-Columbian times, the Sierra Nevada de Santa Marta on the Caribbean Coast was home to various indigenous communities, of which the Tayronas, belonging to the Chibcha linguistic family, were the dominant and most developed group. The Tayronas (also spelt Taironas) are believed to have evolved into a distinctive culture since about the 5th century AD. A millennium later, shortly before the Spaniards came, the Tayronas had developed into an outstanding civilisation, based on a complex social and political organisation and advanced engineering.

The Tayronas lived on the northern slopes of the Sierra Nevada where they constructed hundreds of settlements, all of a very similar pattern. Due to the rugged topography, a large number of stone terraces supported by high walls had to be built as bases for their thatched wooden houses. The groups of terraces were linked by a network of paths and stairways, all made of stone slabs. Ingenious technical know-how and an enormous amount of physical effort were required in the construction of their stone terraces, paths, stairways, bridges, irrigation canals and drainage systems.

Recent surveys have pinpointed the location of about 300 Tayrona settlements scattered over the slopes, once linked by stone-paved roads. Of all these, the Ciudad Perdida (Lost City), discovered in 1975, is the largest and is thought to have been the Tayrona 'capital'.

Tayrona was the first advanced indigenous culture encountered by the Spaniards in the New World, in 1499. It was here, in the Sierra Nevada, that the conquerors were for the first time astonished by Indian gold, and the myth of El Dorado was born. An obsessive search for gold took off and became the principal driving force behind the Spanish Conquest for at least the following century.

The Spaniards crisscrossed the Sierra Nevada, but met with brave resistance from the Indians. The Tayronas defended themselves fiercely, but were almost totally decimated in the course of 75 years of uninterrupted war. A handful of survivors abandoned their homes and fled into the upper reaches of the Sierra. Their traces have been lost forever.

## Orientation

In Santa Marta's centre, Av Rodrigo de Bastidas (Carrera 1C) lining the beach is the principal tourist boulevard, alive until late at night. It provides a nice view over the bay with a small rocky island, El Morro, in the background.

Most tourist activity occurs between the waterfront and Av Campo Serrano (Carrera 5), the main commercial street.

Another hub of tourist activity, principally for the Colombian holidaymakers, is the beach resort of El Rodadero, 5km south of the centre. Buses shuttle frequently between the centre and El Rodadero and the trip takes just 15 minutes.

## Information

**Tourist Offices** The city tourist office, **Etursa** *(☎ 421 1833; Calle 17 No 3-120; open 8am-noon & 2pm-6pm Mon-Fri)* is diagonally opposite the cathedral.

**Money** Of the local banks, probably only **Bancolombia** *(Carrera 3 No 14-10)* will change your travellers cheques and cash. Before you change there, however, check

the *casas de cambio*, which may provide comparable rates and have quicker service. There are plenty of them in the bank area, especially on Calle 14 between Carreras 3 and 5. The two casas with a good reputation are **Todo Arte** *(Calle 14 No 4-45, Local 25)* in the Centro Comercial Royal Plaza, and **Titán Intercontinental** *(Calle 14 No 3-08)*. Both change cash and travellers cheques. All banks marked on the map give advances on Visa and/or MasterCard, and most of them have ATMs.

**Email & Internet Access** In the Centro Comercial San Francisco Plaza, **DialNet** *(Calle 13 No 3-13, Local 205; open daily)* is convenient and cheap. Hotel Miramar and Casa Familiar (see Places to Stay later) have their own Internet facilities.

## Museo Tayrona

The Tayrona Museum *(☎ 421 0953; Calle 14 No 2-07; admission free; open 8am-11.45am & 2pm-5.45pm Mon-Fri)* is in the fine colonial mansion known as the Casa de la Aduana (Customs House). It has an interesting collection of Tayrona objects,

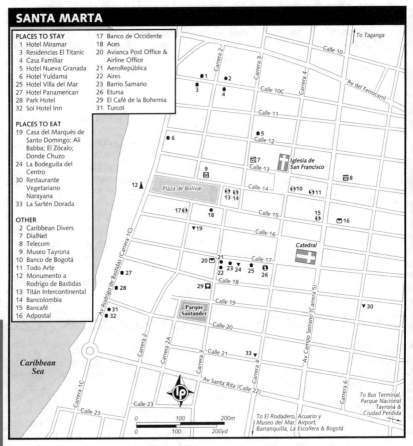

SANTA MARTA

PLACES TO STAY
1 Hotel Miramar
3 Residencias El Titanic
4 Casa Familiar
5 Hotel Nueva Granada
6 Hotel Yuldama
25 Hotel Villa del Mar
27 Hotel Panamerican
28 Park Hotel
32 Sol Hotel Inn

PLACES TO EAT
19 Casa del Marqués de
Santo Domingo; Ali
Babba; El Zócalo;
Donde Chuzo
24 La Bodeguita del
Centro
30 Restaurante
Vegetariano
Narayana
33 La Sartén Dorada

OTHER
2 Caribbean Divers
7 DialNet
8 Telecom
9 Museo Tayrona
10 Banco de Bogotá
11 Todo Arte
12 Monumento a
Rodrigo de Bastidas
13 Titán Intercontinental
14 Bancolombia
15 Bancafé
16 Adpostal

17 Banco de Occidente
18 Aces
20 Avianca Post Office &
Airline Office
21 AeroRepública
22 Aires
23 Barrio Samario
26 Etursa
29 El Café de la Bohemia
31 Turcol

mainly pottery and gold, as well as artefacts of the Kogi and Arhuaco Indians. Don't miss the impressive model of Ciudad Perdida, especially if you plan on visiting the real thing.

**Catedral**

This massive whitewashed cathedral *(Carrera 4 at Calle 17)* claims to be Colombia's oldest church, but work was not actually completed until the end of the 18th century, and thus reflects the influences of various architectural styles. It holds the ashes of the town's founder, Rodrigo de Bastidas (just to the left as you enter the church). Simón Bolívar was buried here in 1830, but in 1842 his remains were taken to Caracas, his birthplace.

**Quinta de San Pedro Alejandrino**

This is the hacienda where Simón Bolívar spent his last days and died. The hacienda was established at the beginning of the 17th century and was engaged in cultivating and processing sugarcane. It had its own *trapiche* (sugarcane mill) and a *destilería* (distillery).

During the Bolívar era, the hacienda was owned by a Spaniard, Joaquín de Mier, a devoted supporter of Colombia's independence cause. He invited Bolívar to stay and take a rest at his home before his intended journey to Europe.

Today it's a national monument, open to the general public (☎ 433 0589, 433 2994; admission US$4; open 9.30am-4.30pm daily).

The central feature is the mansion which has been furnished in the style of Bolívar's days. Next to the house are the mill and distillery, both of which can be visited.

Several monuments have been built on the grounds in remembrance of Bolívar, the most imposing of which is a massive central structure called the Altar de la Patria. Just to the right of the Altar is the Museo Bolivariano, which features works of art donated by Latin American artists, particularly those from Colombia, Venezuela, Panama, Ecuador, Peru and Bolivia, the countries liberated by Bolívar.

The Quinta is in the far eastern suburb of Mamatoco, about 4km from the city centre. To get there, take the Mamatoco bus from the waterfront (Carrera 1C); it's a 20-minute trip to the hacienda. The Quinta may be closed on Monday and/or Tuesday in the off season – check with the tourist office before setting off.

## El Rodadero

El Rodadero, Santa Marta's distant southern suburb, is a beach resort popular with Colombian tourists. It has a wide beach lined with high-rise apartment blocks and upmarket hotels, plus a collection of restaurants, bars and discos.

Colombians come here en masse during their holiday seasons turning the beach into a human swarm.

El Rodadero is some 5km south of Santa Marta's centre and is linked by frequent bus service. Since there are virtually no cheap hotels here, you may prefer to stay in Santa Marta's centre and make a day trip to El Rodadero.

## Acuario y Museo del Mar

The aquarium and museum (☎ 422 7222; admission US$5; open 9am-4pm daily) are on the seashore 2km northwest of El Rodadero. The aquarium has sharks, dolphins, turtles, seals and other marine species, and a dolphin show is held when tourists come. The attached museum displays an odd variety of objects, ranging from copies of Inca ceramics to the propeller of an aeroplane which crashed nearby.

Transport to the aquarium is provided by boats operated from the beach in El Rodadero; tickets can be bought from the stands on the beach (US$3 return).

## Activities

Santa Marta is an important centre of scuba diving. Most dive schools have settled in nearby Taganga (see that entry later in this chapter), but there are also some operators in the city centre, including the French-run **Caribbean Divers** (☎ 431 1568; W www.caribbeandiverscol.com; Calle 10C No 2-11).

There's some good hiking around Santa Marta, including walks in the Parque Nacional Tayrona, though if you're after some longer and more adventurous tramping, the hike to Ciudad Perdida (see that entry later in this chapter) is the region's showpiece.

## Organised Tours

Santa Marta's tour market mainly revolves around Ciudad Perdida. Tours are organised by **Turcol** (☎ 421 2256, 433 3737; Carrera 1C No 20-15). You can book and pay for the tour through some hotels (eg, the Hotel Miramar or Casa Familiar), which will then transfer your application and payment to Turcol. See Ciudad Perdida later in this chapter.

## Places to Stay

There are plenty of hotels in the city centre. All places listed here have rooms with fan, unless specified otherwise.

**Hotel Miramar** (☎ 423 3276, 421 4756; Calle 10C No 1C-59; hammocks/dorm beds US$1/2, doubles without/with bath US$4/5) provides some of the cheapest accommodation in town. The place has long been the archetypal gringo hotel, with a noisy, hippie-type atmosphere, but it's very basic and unkempt. It has a café serving budget meals, snacks, soft drinks and beer.

**Residencias El Titanic** (☎ 421 1947; Calle 10C No 1C-68; singles/doubles US$4/6), right across the street from the Miramar, can be a better and quieter alternative. It has 10 rooms, all of which have private baths and cable TV.

**Casa Familiar** (☎ 421 1697; Calle 10C No 2-14; dorm beds/singles/doubles/triples US$3/4/7/9), a few steps away, is another popular backpacker shelter. Rooms have private baths, but dorms have shared facilities. A good breakfast is available on request.

**Hotel Nueva Granada** (☎ 421 1337; Calle 12 No 3-17; dorm beds/singles/doubles/triples US$3/6/11/14) is both quiet and well kept, and has rooms with bath overlooking a spacious flowered patio.

For somewhere with a view over the sea (particularly attractive at sunset), there are several modern hotels on the waterfront (Carrera 1C). In ascending order of price and standard they are **Sol Hotel Inn** (☎ 421 1131; Carrera 1C No 20-23; singles/doubles/triples US$10/15/18); **Park Hotel** (☎ 421 1215; Carrera 1C No 18-67; singles/doubles/triples US$13/18/22); **Hotel Panamerican** (☎ 421 3932; Carrera 1C No 18-23; singles/doubles/triples US$17/23/28, with air-con US$23/30/38); and **Hotel Yuldama** (☎ 421 0063; Carrera 1C No 12-19; singles/doubles/triples with air-con & breakfast US$30/38/46).

**Hotel Villa del Mar** (☎ 421 1556; Calle 17 No 3-96; singles with air-con US$12-22, doubles with air-con US$18-36) is a decent option a couple of blocks back from the beach. It has a variety of rooms of different standard, including some cheaper rooms with fan.

Should you want to escape from heat and people and relax for a while, there are two lovely places high on the slopes of the Sierra Nevada de Santa Marta. The Belgian-run **Finca Carpe Diem** (hammocks/beds US$3/5) is an ecological farm at 400m above sea level, 15km southeast of Santa Marta by a partly rough road. It provides budget accommodation and meals (made principally from products raised on the farm) and a base for walking, horse riding and bird-watching. There's no public transport all the way to the farm; you need to go by colectivo and then walk for 1½ hours, or take a taxi.

Inquire at Hotel Miramar in Santa Marta or La Casa de Felipe in Taganga (see that entry later in this chapter) for details on how to get there.

The other place, **Jungle Lodge Sans Souci** (☎ 423 9898; e ronnimeib@yahoo.de; rates US$3-5), is German-run and at an elevation of 600m in Minca, a village southeast of Santa Marta. Pick-up trucks depart hourly from Santa Marta's market (US$1.25, 40 minutes), or take a taxi (US$8). The lodge offers budget hammocks, dorms and rooms, plus meals and the use of the kitchen. It's a good place to relax, walk, rent a mountain bike or ride horses or mules. Further information is available from the popular backpackers' hotels found in Santa Marta (Hotel Miramar, Casa Familiar), in Taganga (La Casa de Felipe) and in Cartagena (Casa Viena, Hotel Holiday).

## Places to Eat
There are a lot of cheap restaurants around the budget hotels, particularly on Calles 11 and 12 near the waterfront, where you can get an unsophisticated set meal for at most US$2. The restaurant of the **Hotel Miramar** serves reasonable budget breakfasts, lunches and dinners. For vegetarians there are tasty lunches in **Restaurante Vegetariano Narayana** (Carrera 6 No 18-15; set meals US$3).

The waterfront is packed with cafés and restaurants offering almost anything from burgers and pizzas to local cuisine and seafood. It's a pleasant area for an evening stroll and a dinner or just a snack.

**Casa del Marqués de Santo Domingo** (Calle 16 No 2-08) is a beautiful colonial mansion. It has an ample courtyard and shelters three restaurants: **Donde Chuzo** (mains US$5-8), which serves seafood, **El Zócalo** (dishes US$3-6), serving Mexican food, and **Ali Babba** (dishes US$3-6), offering Middle Eastern fare.

**La Sartén Dorada** (Carrera 4 at Calle 21; mains US$4-7) is one of the cheaper restaurants that does good seafood.

**La Bodeguita del Centro** (Calle 17 No 3-38; mains US$5-9) is one of the best restaurants in the centre, serving beautiful seafood and beef, plus a choice of wines.

## Entertainment
The best known nightspot in the area is **La Escollera** (☎ 422 95 90; Calle 5 No 4-107), a trendy disco on a small islet in the northern end of El Rodadero.

There are also some establishments in Santa Marta's centre.

**El Café de la Bohemia** (Calle 18 No 2-82; open until midnight Mon-Sat) is an enjoyable arty café-bar.

**Barrio Samario** (Calle 17 No 3-36; open until late Tues-Sun) is a popular central bar run by a Belgian. It has cheap beer and plays a ragbag of music.

## Getting There & Away
**Air** The airport is 16km south of the city on the road to Barranquilla/Bogotá. City buses marked 'El Rodadero Aeropuerto' will take you there in 45 minutes from Carrera 1C. Alianza Summa, AeroRepública and Aires service Santa Marta. Flights include Bogotá (US$80 to US$130 one way) and Medellín (US$80 to US$130).

CARIBBEAN COAST

**Bus** The terminal is on the southeastern outskirts of the city. Frequent minibuses go there from Carrera 1C in the centre.

Half a dozen buses run daily to Bogotá (US$32, 16 hours) and roughly the same number travel to Bucaramanga (US$20, nine hours). Buses to Barranquilla (US$4, 1¾ hours) depart every 15 to 30 minutes. Some of them go direct to Cartagena (US$8, four hours), but if not, there are immediate connections in Barranquilla.

Half-hourly buses leave for Maicao (US$9, four hours), where you change for a colectivo to Maracaibo (Venezuela). Colectivos depart regularly from about 5am to 3pm (US$10, 2½ hours) and go as far as Maracaibo's bus terminal. From there, Venezuelan bus companies operate buses further inside the country,

including Caracas, Coro and Mérida. Note that Maicao is widely and justifiably known as a lawless town and can be unsafe – stay there as briefly as possible and don't move outside the bus terminal.

There are also three buses daily from Santa Marta direct to Maracaibo (US$25, seven hours), operated by Expreso Brasilia, Expresos Amerlujo and Unitransco/Bus Ven. They come through from Cartagena, go to Maracaibo and continue to Caracas.

All passport formalities are done in Paraguachón on the border. Change Colombian pesos to Venezuelan bolívares in Maicao or Paraguachón. They will be extremely difficult to change beyond Maracaibo. Wind your watch one hour forward when crossing from Colombia to Venezuela. Expect

AROUND SANTA MARTA

a search of your luggage by Venezuelan officials in Paraguachón or at the military checkposts on the road to Maracaibo.

## TAGANGA

Taganga is a small fishing village set in a beautiful, deep, horseshoe-shaped bay, 5km northeast of Santa Marta. The village's beach is packed with boats and open-air restaurants and bars blasting out music at full volume. Locals offer boat excursions along the coast or you can walk around the surrounding hills, which provide splendid views.

Go to Playa Grande, a magnificent bay northwest of the village. Either walk there (20 minutes) or take a boat from Taganga (US$1). The beach is lined with palm-thatched restaurants serving good fried fish.

### Scuba Diving

Taganga is a popular scuba-diving centre, with half a dozen dive schools offering dives and courses. Local services are among the cheapest you can find in Colombia (some say in the world). A four-day open-water PADI/NAUI course including six dives is advertised for US$160 and a mini-course with two dives for US$40. The best local schools include **Centro de Buceo Tayrona** (☎ 421 9195; **w** www.buceotayrona.net; Calle 18 No 1-45) and **Centro de Buceo Poseidon** (☎ 421 9224; **w** www.poseidondivecenter.com; Calle 18 No 1-69).

**BD Diving** (☎ 421 9140; **e** charudive55@hotmail.com; Carrera 1 No 18-43), run by a Canadian and a Brit, also offers diving trips but takes a different approach. It doesn't operate from land as do the other agencies, but from its *Charu* boat, equipped with kitchen and berths. It offers diving trips of different length (from one to five days), which include accommodation and all meals on the boat, and can include fun diving, fishing and/or PADI courses, depending on what you want. It can access more remote dive sites and beaches than other companies which just take short trips out of Taganga.

### Places to Stay & Eat

Taganga has quite a reasonable choice of accommodation.

**La Casa de Felipe** (☎ 421 9101; **w** www.lacasadefelipe.com; Carrera 5A No 19-13; beds in rooms/suites US$4/6) is a few blocks

uphill from the beach past the soccer pitch. Run by a friendly Frenchman, Jean-Philippe, it's a quiet and pleasant place that offers four rooms with bath and three suites with bath and kitchenette, and you can have breakfast if you wish for an extra US$2.

**Casa Blanca** (☎ 421 9232; **e** barbus85@latinmail.com; Carrera 1 No 18-161; rooms per person US$5) is right on the beach. Each of its 10 rooms has a private bath and a balcony with a hammock overlooking the bay. Guests can use the kitchen, fridge and washing machine free of charge.

**Pelikan Hostal** (☎ 423 3736; Carrera 2 No 17-04; rooms per person US$5) can be an alternative if you want to stay close to the beach on a low budget and the Casa Blanca is full.

**Chalet Suizo** (☎ 421 9070; Calle 4 No 1B-12; rooms per person US$5) is a Swiss-run hostel, tucked away from the beach. It has five double rooms with baths.

There are a string of open-air budget **restaurants** along the waterfront, where a fresh fried fish with rice and salad shouldn't cost more than US$5.

### Getting There & Away

Taganga is easily accessible by frequent minibuses (US$0.25, 15 minutes) from Carrera 1C in Santa Marta.

## PARQUE NACIONAL TAYRONA

One of Colombia's most popular national parks, Tayrona is set on the jungle-covered coast at the foot of the Sierra Nevada de Santa Marta. The park stretches along the coast from the Bahía de Taganga near Santa Marta to the mouth of the Río Piedras, 35km to the east.

The scenery varies from sandy beaches along the coast in the north to rainforest at an altitude of 600m on the southern limits of the park. The extreme western part is arid, with light-brown hills and xerophytic plant species such as cacti. The rainfall here is low, restricted mostly to little rains in October and November. The central and eastern parts of the park are wetter and more verdant, largely covered by rainforest. May to June and September to November are the wettest periods. Many animals live in the park but most stay out of sight, deep in the forest.

The region was once the territory of the Tayrona Indians, and some archaeological remains have been found in the park. The most important of these are the ruins of the pre-Hispanic town of Pueblito (called Chairama in the indigenous language), considered to have been one of Tayrona's major settlements.

For many travellers, the park's biggest attraction is its beaches, set in deep bays and shaded with coconut palms. In fact, Tayrona beaches are among the loveliest and most picturesque on Colombia's coast. They are not wide or long, but are spectacular thanks to the huge boulders scattered all around the place. Some of the beaches are bordered by coral reefs providing reasonable snorkelling and scuba-diving opportunities.

## Orientation

Tayrona's eastern part features most of the park's attractions and tourist facilities, and is by far the most popular and visited area of the park. Its main gateway is El Zaíno, 34km east of Santa Marta on the coastal road to Riohacha, where you pay the US$3 park admission fee.

From El Zaíno, a 4km paved side road goes northwest to Cañaveral, on the seaside. Here is the park's administrative centre, car park, a campground, *cabañas* (cabins), a restaurant and a small Museo Arqueológico Chairama, which displays some archaeological finds excavated in Pueblito. The beaches in Cañaveral are good, but there is no shade and swimming can be dangerous because of treacherous offshore currents.

From Cañaveral, most visitors take a 45-minute walk west along a trail to Arrecifes, where there are budget lodging and eating facilities and the coast is very spectacular, dotted with massive boulders both on and off the shore. Remember, however, that sea currents here are just as dangerous as those in Cañaveral.

From Arrecifes, a 20-minute walk northwest along the beach will bring you to La Piscina, a deep bay partly cut off from the open sea by an underground rocky chain. As a result, it has quiet waters and is reasonably safe for swimming and snorkelling. This is actually the best place in the eastern part of the park for snorkelling.

Another 20-minute walk by path will take you to the Cabo San Juan de la Guía, a beautiful cape with good beaches and views. A local family provides simple meals but no accommodation.

From the Cabo, a scenic path goes inland uphill to Pueblito, providing some splendid tropical forest scenery. It will get you to Pueblito in a bit more than an hour. Not much of Pueblito's urban tissue has survived, apart from small fragments of the stone paths and foundations of houses, but nonetheless it's worth seeing, especially if you aren't planning a trip to Ciudad Perdida.

From Pueblito, a path continues southwest to Calabazo on the main road, but it may be better not to walk this way for your safety – some cases of robbery have been reported here. Check the current safety situation with the park rangers if you want to do this trip anyway.

There are two other tourist areas in Tayrona – Bahía Concha in the western part of the park and Bahía Neguanje in the central sector – but they are nowhere near as popular or visited as the Cañaveral–Arrecifes area. They are accessible by separate roads from Santa Marta, but there's no road or path linking the two bays within the park. Both bays have snorkelling and scuba-diving sites. Tourist facilities are scarce on both beaches.

## Places to Stay & Eat

In Cañaveral, the park's management operates a colony of cabañas known as the **Eco-habs** *(3-bed/6-bed cabins US$25/30)*. They are made in the style of Tayrona huts and are spectacularly set on a coastal hill. There are 11 six-bed cabañas and three three-bed cabañas. Rates rise in the tourist season by about 20%. Another, larger cabaña at the foot of the hill houses a **restaurant**.

The park's authorities also run a **camp site** *(sites US$15)* in Cañaveral during the tourist season. It's run-down, unkempt and largely overrated. You need to book both cabañas and tent sites through the **national park office** (☎ 420 4505; Calle 15 No 21-63) in Santa Marta. You can also do it through Oficina de Ecoturismo in Bogotá (see that chapter earlier for details).

In Arrecifes, there are three places to stay and eat, the cheapest of which is **Rancho Lindo** *(camp sites per person US$1.50, hammocks US$2)*, the first business you get to when coming from Cañaveral. It offers a camp site, rents out hammocks under the roof and has a restaurant (meals US$4 to US$6), but it doesn't provide accommodation in beds.

**Finca El Paraíso** *(camp sites per person US$2, hammocks US$2.50, 2-bed/4-bed/6-bed cabins US$15/25/35)*, just behind the Rancho Lindo, offers cabañas, under-cover hammocks, camp sites and a restaurant with meals ranging from US$5 to US$7.

A 10-minute walk further west along the beach is **Bucarú**, an offspring of El Paraíso, offering similar facilities for marginally less. Both El Paraíso and Bucarú can be booked through their **Barranquilla office** *(☎ 358 8086; Carrera 43 No 79-188)*.

### Getting There & Away

Cañaveral is easy to get to on your own from Santa Marta. Take a minibus to Palomino and get off in El Zaíno (US$1.25, one hour); Palomino minibuses depart every 20 to 30 minutes from Santa Marta's market (Carrera 11 at Calle 11). From El Zaíno, walk for 50 minutes to Cañaveral or catch the jeep that shuttles regularly between the two (US$0.60, 10 minutes).

Bahía Concha and Bahía Neguanje are accessible by unsurfaced roads but there's no public transport on these roads. In the tourist season, jeeps go to both bays from Santa Marta; they park on Carrera 1C near Turcol.

Inquire at the tourist office and backpackers hotels (Hotel Miramar, Casa Familiar), which may know about other options.

## CIUDAD PERDIDA

Ciudad Perdida (literally the 'Lost City') is one of the largest pre-Columbian towns discovered in the Americas. Known by its indigenous name of Teyuna, it was built by the Tayrona Indians on the northern slopes of the Sierra Nevada de Santa Marta, and was most probably their biggest urban centre. During the Conquest, the Spaniards wiped out the Tayronas, and their settlements disappeared without trace under lush tropical vegetation. So did Ciudad Perdida for four centuries, until its discovery in 1975 (see the boxed text 'The Discovery of Ciudad Perdida').

Ciudad Perdida was built between the 11th and 14th centuries, though its origins are much older, going back to perhaps the 7th century. It's estimated that its population was somewhere between 2000 and 4000 people, but it could have been far larger in its heyday. Spreading over an area of about 2 sq km, it is the largest Tayrona city found so far, and it appears to be their major political and economic centre.

---

## The Discovery of Ciudad Perdida

Ciudad Perdida was found in 1975 by the *guaqueros*, treasure hunters who earned their living by seeking and plundering Indian tombs for gold and other antique objects. It was Florentino Sepúlveda, together with his sons Julio César and Jacobo, who discovered the Lost City. He was born in the Norte de Santander department but, like many other colonists, had come to the Sierra Nevada and settled in the 1950s with dreams of a better life. He divided his time between trading with the Indians and hunting for gold.

Life was not easy. The guaqueros were numerous and it became necessary to penetrate further and further into the Sierra to make new finds. During one such expedition, a long, strenuous march up the Buritaca River, the Sepúlvedas stumbled upon the city. They were astonished by the long stone stairways, which they had to climb to get to the dozens of terraces, all buried beneath lush tropical vegetation. It was the tombs that primarily interested them, but they didn't find the gold they were after, only some necklaces made of colourful stones which they sold on their return to Santa Marta.

The news spread like wildfire. Other treasure hunters soon pinpointed the ruins and the Indian tombs fell victim to looting. A war for the Lost City broke out, with shooting between rival gangs of grave robbers. Not without reason the guaqueros named the place the Infierno Verde or the Green Hell.

The government woke up to the guaqueros' find in 1976 and sent out an expedition to examine it. Soon after, an archaeological base was established on the site, as well as an army post to protect the ruins. Nevertheless, the looting of graves continued and gangs of guaqueros fought for supremacy. In one of these clashes, Julio César was killed and buried at the foot of the Infierno. Four years later his father brought his son's remains down to Guachaca where he lived.

The man credited with one of the greatest archaeological discoveries of our times, Sepúlveda died in his mid-70s in misery and oblivion. Actually, he never found any gold in Ciudad Perdida.

Ciudad Perdida lies on the relatively steep slopes of the upper Buritaca River valley at an altitude of between 950m and 1300m. The central part of the city is set on a ridge from which various stone paths lead down to other sectors on the slopes. Although the wooden houses of the Tayronas are long gone, the stone structures, including terraces and stairways, remain in remarkably good shape.

There are about 150 terraces, most of which once served as foundations for the houses. The largest terraces are set on the central ridge and these were used for ritual ceremonies. Originally, the urban centre was completely cleared of trees, but it has been reclaimed by the jungle. Today, the city is quite overgrown, which gives it a somewhat mysterious air.

Archaeological digs have uncovered some Tayrona objects (fortunately, the guaqueros didn't manage to take everything), mainly various kinds of pottery (both ceremonial and utensil), goldwork and unique necklaces made of semiprecious stones. Some of these objects are on display in the Museo Tayrona in Santa Marta and the Museo del Oro in Bogotá. It's a good idea to visit the museum in Santa Marta before going to Ciudad Perdida.

### Getting There & Away
Ciudad Perdida lies about 40km southeast of Santa Marta as the crow flies. It's hidden deep in the thick forest amid rugged mountains, far away from any human settlement, and without access roads. The way to get there is by foot and the return trip takes six days.

There are two trails leading to the Lost City: through La Tagua and Alto de Mira; and through El Mamey and up along the Río Buritaca. The former trail was abandoned years ago. Now visitors take the Buritaca trail, which is shorter and easier but perhaps less spectacular. The section between Santa Marta and El Mamey is done by vehicle.

Access to Ciudad Perdida is by tour only, organised by Turcol in Santa Marta. You cannot do the trip on your own or hire an independent guide. The price is about US$150 per person for the all-inclusive six-day tour. This includes transport, food, accommodation (in hammocks), porters, guides and all necessary permits. You carry your own personal belongings. Take a flashlight, water container and insect repellent.

Tours are in groups of four to 12 people, and depart year-round as soon as a group is assembled. In the high season, expect a tour to set off every few days. In the off season, there may be just one tour a week.

The trip takes three days uphill to Ciudad Perdida, one day at the site and two days back down. The hike may be tiring due to the heat, and if it's wet (as it is most of the year) the paths are pretty muddy. The driest period is from late December to February or early March. There are several creeks to cross on the way; be prepared to get your shoes wet and carry a spare pair.

# Atlántico

## BARRANQUILLA
☎ 5 • pop 1,100,000 • elevation 10m • temp 28°C
Barranquilla is Colombia's fourth biggest city and the capital of the Atlántico department. It's the most important industrial and commercial centre on the Caribbean Coast and Colombia's second largest seaport (after Cartagena). It has a hot, damp, often windless climate.

Barranquilla is a vast concrete sprawl without many tourist attractions. Numerous industrial estates don't add much to its grace (more to its pollution), while sweltering heat doesn't encourage strolling about the streets. The sticky, still air is frequently refreshed by torrential rains which invariably turn most streets into rushing rivers, washing out litter, garbage, people and cars alike. This seems to be the only regular form of city cleaning.

While foreigners may find it a bit hard to feel Barranquilla's beauty and vibrant pulse, for many Colombians (not just the city's inhabitants) the city does have great style and character. It embodies the costeño nature at is best (some would say craziest), and this is palpable in the city's ardent atmosphere and in the animated temperament of its dwellers. It all explodes during the four-day Carnaval de Barranquilla, the maddest of all Colombian fiestas.

### History
The town was founded in 1629, but did not gain importance until the middle of the 19th century. Despite its potential as a port on the country's main fluvial artery, navigation

CARIBBEAN COAST

problems at the mouth of the Magdalena River hindered development. Most of the merchandise moving up and down the Magdalena passed through Cartagena, using the Canal del Dique which joins the river about 100km upstream from its mouth.

Only at the end of the 19th century did progress really begin. The opening of Puerto Colombia, Barranquilla's port built on the coastline 15km west of the town, and later, the regulation of the river mouth by the construction of breakwaters, boosted the development of the city, both as a fluvial and sea port.

By the early 20th century, Barranquilla was one of the major ports from which local goods, primarily coffee, were shipped overseas. It also came to be the gateway through which foreign influences and innovations first arrived in the country. It was here that Colombian aviation was born when the Sociedad Colombo-Alemana de Transporte Aéreo (SCADTA) was founded in 1919. South America's first commercial airline commenced scheduled flights into the interior in 1920. Twenty years later, it became Avianca, Colombia's national airline.

Progress attracted both Colombians from other regions and foreigners, mainly from the USA, Germany, Italy and the Middle East. This, in turn, gave the city an injection of foreign capital and accelerated its growth. It also brought about the city's cosmopolitan character.

## Orientation

Barranquilla sits on the left (west) bank of the Río Magdalena, about 10km upstream from its mouth. The city plan is roughly oval, 12km long from north to south and 8km wide. Its limits are marked by a ring road, Vía Circunvalación. The city centre (where the town was originally settled) is along the Paseo Bolívar, close to the river. Most of this sector, especially the area between the Paseo and the river, is inhabited by wild street commerce – it's actually one vast market. It's busy, noisy and unbelievably littered.

About 3km to the northwest is El Prado, Barranquilla's new centre, and possibly the most pleasant district of the city. The bus terminal is off the southern edge of the oval, beyond Vía Circunvalación. The airport is still further south.

## Information

**Tourist Offices** The tourist office, the **Comité Mixto de Promoción Turística del Atlántico** (☎ 370 3870; Vía Cuarenta No 36-135; open 8am-noon & 2pm-6pm Mon-Fri) is in the Antiguo Edificio de Aduana. It's within reasonable walking distance north of the centre.

**Money** In the centre, most major banks have nestled along the Paseo Bolívar and Carrera 44. In El Prado, many banks can be found in the area of Calles 70 and 72, two important commercial streets of the district. There's also a sufficient supply of casas de cambio, including **Giros & Finanzas** (Carrera 54 No 72-80, Locales 22-24), which changes cash, travellers cheques and represents Western Union. Directly across the road is another casa de cambio, **Cambiamos**.

**Email & Internet Access** There are plenty of Internet cafés in El Prado, including **Orbitel** (Carrera 54 No 72-17), **Call Center** (Carrera 48 No 70-218) and **Chalupa.com** (Calle 72 No 56-20).

## Things to See

The two areas you might want to visit are the city centre and El Prado. They are just a few kilometres away, but a world apart from each other.

The central sector is cut in two by Paseo Bolívar. Halfway along is the mock-Gothic **Iglesia de San Nicolás** (Paseo Bolívar at Carrera 42), worth entering for its main altarpiece and pulpit. To the east of the church is the sprawling market that spreads down to the river. Contraband items, presumably coming here from Maicao, are plentiful.

El Prado is quite a different story. It's cleaner, greener and safer than the centre, and has a far calmer atmosphere. Calle 72 is the district's principal shopping street, lined with restaurants, snack bars, shops and supermarkets – a hell of a difference to the shabby street stands of Paseo Bolívar.

Strolling around, you'll find some architectural relics from the late 19th and early 20th centuries, the time when El Prado began to develop. Note the buildings in the Islamic-influenced Moorish style – you'll find some of them on and just off Carrera 54. Include in your trip the following attractions, most of which are in El Prado or its vicinity.

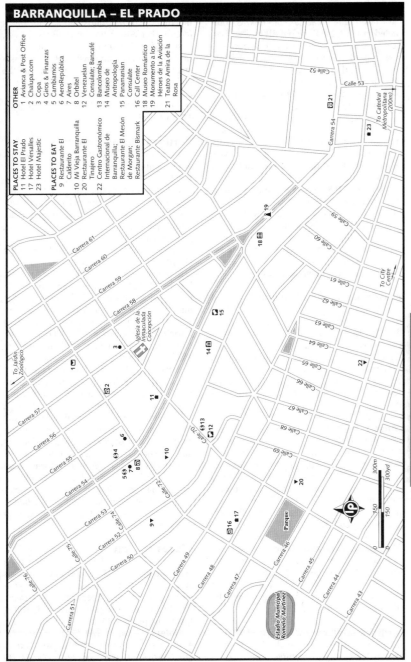

## BARRANQUILLA – EL PRADO

**PLACES TO STAY**
11  Hotel El Prado
17  Hotel Versalles
23  Hotel Majestic

**PLACES TO EAT**
9  Restaurante El Calderito
10  Mi Vieja Barranquilla
20  Restaurante El Tinajero
22  Centro Gastronómico Internacional de Barranquilla; Restaurante El Mesón de Morgan; Restaurante Bismark

**OTHER**
1  Avianca & Post Office
2  Chalupa.com
3  Copa
4  Giros & Finanzas
5  Cambiamos
6  AeroRepública
7  Aires
8  Orbitel
12  Venezuelan Consulate; Bancafé
13  Bancolombia
14  Museo de Antropología
15  Panamanian Consulate
16  Call Center
18  Museo Romántico
19  Monumento a los Héroes de la Aviación
21  Teatro Amira de la Rosa

CARIBBEAN COAST

**Catedral Metropolitana** The modern cathedral (*Calle 53 at Carrera 46*) was completed in 1982. Don't be put off by its squat, heavy, somewhat bunker-like exterior – go inside. It's likely to be open around 4.30pm to 8pm, but if you knock on the door of the adjoining building to the left (south) at any other reasonable time of the day, someone will probably let you in.

The interior features a number of large stained-glass windows in the side walls and over the main entrance. There are two mosaics on the side walls: of María Reyna y Auxiliadora (patron saint of the cathedral) and of San José. Each mosaic is composed of about 400,000 pieces of coloured glass imported from Germany. Both the stained-glass windows and the mosaics are the work of Mario Ayala, a Cali artist.

Over the high altar is a 16m-high bronze sculpture of Cristo Libertador, a 16-tonne work by Rodrigo Arenas Betancur, Colombia's pre-eminent monument designer.

**Museo Romántico** Confusingly named the Romantic Museum (*☎ 344 4591; Carrera 54 No 59-199; adult/student US$2/1; open 8.30am-11.30am & 2pm-5pm Mon-Fri, 9am-noon Sat*), it is actually a museum of the city's history, featuring exhibits related to Barranquilla's past. Some rooms are dedicated to migrant communities – German and Jewish among others – that have influenced the region.

**Museo de Antropología** The Museum of Anthropology (*☎ 358 8488; Calle 68 No 53-45; admission free; open 8am-noon & 2.30pm-5pm Mon-Fri*), on the 1st floor of the building of the Universidad del Atlántico, displays a small collection of pre-Columbian pottery from different regions, including pieces from the Calima, Tumaco and Nariño cultures.

**Museo de Arte Moderno** The Museum of Modern Art (*☎ 379 6610; Vía Cuarenta No 36-135; admission free; open 9am-5pm Mon-Fri, 9am-1pm Sat*) is in the Antiguo Edificio de Aduana, the same building where the tourist office is located.

**Jardín Zoológico** The zoo (*☎ 353 0605; Calle 76 No 68-40; admission US$2.50; open 9am-5.30pm daily*) features some 2000 animals belonging to about 300 species, including plenty of birds and several ligers (a cross between a lion and a Bengal tiger, first bred in Colombia). Some cages look far too small for their inhabitants. There is a small Museo de Historia Natural within the zoo grounds. To get to the zoo from the city centre, take the bus marked 'Vía Cuarenta' from Plaza de Bolívar. From El Prado, it's a 10- to 15-minute walk.

### Carnaval de Barranquilla

With a century-long official history (but with traditions dating back much further), this four-day fiesta preceding Ash Wednesday (February or March) is when the whole city goes wild. All normal city activities such as urban transport and commerce are totally paralysed by street dances, music, parades and masquerades.

The Carnaval begins on Saturday with La Batalla de Flores (the Battle of Flowers), a float parade. It continues on Sunday with La Gran Parada, when thousands of people put on fancy dresses and disguises and file through the streets. On Monday there is El Festival de Orquestas, a marathon concert of Caribbean music groups. The Carnaval concludes on Tuesday with a symbolic burial of Joselito Carnaval.

Apart from the official programme, it is a round-the-clock party, fuelled by large quantities of spirits. An estimated 100,000 cases of rum and aguardiente are sold. Although it is getting more commercialised and lacks some of the spontaneity of years ago, it is still probably the most colourful and maddest of all of Colombia's festivals. Unfortunately, as at all such crowded events, it's a focus for all sorts of local and visiting thieves and robbers. Be on guard, especially if you plan to photograph or film the event. Think twice before accepting drinks or smokes from strangers or new 'friends'.

### Places to Stay

The centre of budget accommodation is on and around Paseo Bolívar (Calle 34). This area is not that safe at night, so limit your evening strolls and keep your eyes open. Yet if you are after a genuinely cheap room, this is the place to look.

**Hotel Victoria** (*☎ 370 1242; Calle 35 No 43-140; singles/doubles/triples with bath & fan US$6/8/11, with air-con US$8/12/15*)

CARIBBEAN COAST

certainly has character. It was perhaps one of the poshest hotels half a century ago, as you can tell by its imposing balconied facade, antique lift and high, spacious corridors. These days it doesn't fly so high, but nonetheless it's still a comfortable place to stay and pretty cheap.

**Hotel Olímpico** (☎ 351 8310; Carrera 42 No 33-20; singles/doubles/triples with bath & fan US$6/8/11, with air-con US$8/12/15) is another good central option, though it doesn't have much style. It's next to the Iglesia de San Nicolás.

There's almost no budget accommodation outside the centre. El Prado is a safer and more pleasant area to stay in, but it is a rather upper-class district and the hotels there are more expensive.

**Hotel Majestic** (☎ 349 1010, 349 2002; Carrera 53 No 54-41; singles/doubles/triples/ suites with air-con US$35/45/55/65) is one of the most stylish places to stay, with a Moorish air. The hotel has a small swimming pool and a charming restaurant with impressive crystal chandeliers. Breakfast is included in the room prices.

**Hotel Versalles** (☎ 368 6970; Carrera 48 No 70-188; singles/doubles/triples with air-con US$30/40/50) is a new, modern place with 41 comfortable air-conditioned rooms and Internet facilities.

**Hotel El Prado** (☎ 368 0111; ⓦ www .cotelco.org/hotelprado; Carrera 54 No 70-10; singles/doubles/suites with air-con US$80/ 90/100) is a great place with a central swimming pool, palms and a tropical atmosphere. Built in 1928, it came to be Barranquilla's poshest and trendiest place to stay, and is still probably so today.

During the Carnaval it is unlikely you will find a room in any of the budget or mid-range hotels, despite the fact that the prices are much higher.

## Places to Eat

The central city area, along and off Paseo Bolívar, is full of cheap restaurants which offer set meals for US$1 to US$2. You can also eat in the street or in the market – the centre is actually one huge market. Many stalls sell delicious arepas de huevo (a fried maize dough with an egg inside), the local speciality. You can get good fish in the market proper, towards the river; just point to the one you want and they will fry it in front of you. Vegetarians can have tasty lunches at **Restaurante Vegetariano Vida Sana** (Carrera 44 No 44-74).

El Prado is more for finer dining, but there are a number of budget eateries to choose from as well, many of which are on Calle 70.

**Mi Vieja Barranquilla** (Carrera 53 No 70-150; mains US$5-7) is one of the more unusual places, set in a spacious open-air courtyard painted and decorated to look like a plaza of some imaginary colonial town. It serves typical local food and has live folk music on some evenings.

**Restaurante El Calderito** (Carrera 52 No 72-107; mains US$5-7) does good costeño food, while **Restaurante El Tinajero** (Carrera 47 No 69-97; mains US$5-7) offers solid Colombian fare.

**Centro Gastronómico Internacional de Barranquilla** (Carrera 46 No 64-14) houses a choice of upmarket establishments, including **Restaurante El Mesón de Morgan**, recommended for seafood, and **Restaurante Bismark** serving German and other European specialities.

All the three hotels in El Prado listed earlier have their own, good restaurants serving local and international food.

## Getting There & Away

**Air** The airport is about 10km south of the city centre and is accessible by urban buses. Almost all main Colombian carriers service Barranquilla. The principal destinations include Bogotá (US$75 to US$125 one way), Medellín (US$75 to US$125), Cali (US$90 to US$140) and San Andrés (US$80 to US$130).

**Bus** The bus terminal came into operation in 1993 on the southern outskirts of Barranquilla, about 7km from the city centre. It's not convenient, and it may take up to an hour to get to the terminal by urban bus. It's much faster to go by taxi (US$4, 20 minutes).

A dozen buses travel daily to Bogotá (US$36, 18 hours), Bucaramanga (US$23, 10 hours) and Medellín (US$28, 14 hours). Buses to Cartagena (US$4, two hours) depart every 10 to 15 minutes, as do the buses to Santa Marta (US$4, 1¾ hours).

There are three buses daily operating direct to Maracaibo and on to Caracas (both in Venezuela).

# Bolívar

## CARTAGENA

☎ 5 • pop 820,000 • elevation 5m
• temp 28°C

Cartagena de Indias is legendary for both its history and its beauty. It is Colombia's most fascinating city and unique in South America. It's a living museum of colonial Spanish architecture, and it's on Unesco's list of World Heritage Sites. You surely shouldn't miss it. Don't come here in a hurry either, as the city's charm is likely to keep you here for several days or perhaps even a week.

## History

Cartagena was founded in 1533 by Pedro de Heredia on the site of the Carib Indian settlement of Calamari. It quickly grew into a rich town, but in 1552 an extensive fire destroyed a large number of its wooden buildings. Since that time, only stone, brick and tile have been permitted as building materials.

Within a short time the town blossomed into the main Spanish port on the Caribbean Coast and the major northern gateway to South America. It came to be the storehouse for the treasure plundered from the Indians until the galleons could ship it back to Spain. As such, it became a tempting target for all sorts of buccaneers operating on the Caribbean Sea.

In the 16th century alone, Cartagena suffered five dreadful sieges by pirates, the most famous (or infamous) of which was that led by Sir Francis Drake. He sacked the port in 1586 and 'mercifully' agreed not to burn the town to the ground once he was presented with a huge ransom of 10 million pesos, which he shipped back to England.

It was in response to pirate attacks that the Spaniards decided to make Cartagena an impregnable port and constructed elaborate walls encircling the town, and a chain of forts. These fortifications made Cartagena unique in South America and helped save the city from subsequent sieges, particularly from the fiercest and biggest attack of all, led by Edward Vernon in 1741. The successful defence was commanded by Blas de Lezo (see the boxed text 'The Diminishing Saviour of Cartagena').

In spite of the high price it had to pay for the pirate attacks, Cartagena continued to flourish. The Canal del Dique, constructed in 1650 to connect Cartagena Bay with the Magdalena River, made the town the main gateway for ships to the ports upriver, and a large part of the merchandise shipped inland passed through Cartagena. The town was also granted a royal monopoly as a slave-trading port. During the colonial period, Cartagena was the most important bastion of the Spanish overseas empire and influenced much of Colombia's history.

### The Diminishing Saviour of Cartagena

If there is one man who stands out in Cartagena's heroic history it is probably Blas de Lezo. Born in Spain of noble parents, he entered the service of the king, but as a young officer he lost his left leg in the Battle of Gibraltar. He remained in service but misfortune followed him. In Toulon he lost his left eye and later on, in the Battle of Barcelona, he lost his right arm. Nevertheless, his tenacity and courage had made him a legend and when the Spaniards heard about a planned assault on Cartagena by Edward Vernon, they engaged Blas de Lezo to defend the city.

Vernon launched an offensive with a fleet of 186 ships, more than 2000 cannons and about 25,000 men. Blas de Lezo had only 2500 men, including black slaves and Indians hastily brought from the interior, and five warships. And he somehow succeeded!

The English were so sure of their imminent victory that they coined commemorative medals before the siege had ended. Such was their arrogance that one coin depicted Blas de Lezo on his knees in surrender to Vernon. The English apparently felt it ungallant to conquer half a man so they gave him back his arm and leg in the scene depicting his capitulation which never took place.

Don Blas, however, was wounded again in the battle, this time in his remaining leg, and died shortly after the withdrawal of Vernon's fleet. He was honoured posthumously with a title of nobility. The site where he was buried is unknown. His statue, with one leg and one arm, stands at the entrance to the San Felipe fortress.

The indomitable spirit of the inhabitants was rekindled again at the time of the independence movement. Cartagena was one of the first towns to proclaim independence from Spain, early in 1810, which prompted Bogotá and other cities to do the same. The declaration was signed on 11 November 1811, but the city paid dearly for it. Spanish forces under Pablo Morillo were sent in 1815 to reconquer and 'pacify' the town and took it after a four-month siege. More than 6000 inhabitants died of starvation and disease.

In August 1819, Simón Bolívar's troops defeated the Spaniards at Boyacá, bringing freedom to Bogotá. However, Cartagena had to wait for its liberation until October 1821 when the patriot forces eventually took the city by sea. It was Bolívar who gave Cartagena its well-deserved name of 'La Heroica', the Heroic City.

Cartagena soon began to recover and was shortly once again an important trading and shipping centre. The city's prosperity attracted foreign immigrants, and many Jews, Italians, French, Turks, Lebanese and Syrians settled here. Today their descendants own many businesses, including hotels and restaurants.

Over the past decades, Cartagena has expanded dramatically and is now surrounded by vast suburbs. Its population grew from about 500,000 in 1985 to nearly 800,000 in 2002. It now is Colombia's largest port and an important industrial centre specialising in petrochemicals, but the old walled town has changed little.

It is a wonderfully preserved complex of 16th- and 17th-century architecture, with narrow winding streets, palaces, churches and opulent mansions.

## Climate
Cartagena's climate is typically Caribbean, with its average annual temperature of 28°C, changing very little throughout the year. Although the days are hot, a fresh breeze blows in the evening making this a pleasant time to stroll around the city. Theoretically, the driest period is from December to April, while October and November are the wettest months. Mean annual rainfall is about 900mm.

## Orientation
The heart of the city is the old town, facing the sea to the west and almost entirely separated by water from the mainland to the east. The old town was built in two sections, an inner and outer town. Both were surrounded by walls and separated from each other by a channel, the Caño de San Anastasio. The channel was filled up to make way for the construction of the sharp, wedge-shaped, modern district, La Matuna.

The inner walled town, towards the northwest, is bigger than the outer one. It consists of El Centro in the west, where traditionally the upper classes lived, and San Diego in the northeast, an area previously occupied by the middle classes. The outer walled town, Getsemaní, once inhabited by those at the lower end of the social ladder, is smaller and poorer, with more modest architecture. Outside the walled town several monumental fortresses still stand.

Stretching south of the old town is an unusual, L-shaped peninsula, occupied by three districts: Bocagrande, Castillo Grande and El Laguito. Over the past decades, Bocagrande and El Laguito have developed into a trendy seaside resort, even though its beaches are actually not very good. This sector, packed with top-class hotels, posh restaurants, boutiques and nightspots, has become the main destination for moneyed Colombians and international charter tours. Backpackers, however, prefer to stay in the historic part of town.

## Information
**Tourist Offices** The tourist office, **Turismo Cartagena de Indias** (☎ 665 1843, 665 1391; Av Blas de Lezo; open 8am-noon & 2pm-6pm Mon-Fri) is situated in the Muelle Turístico.

Alternatively, try the **Convention and Visitors Bureau** (☎ 655 1484, 655 1517; Carrera 1; Edificio Hipocampo; open 8am-noon & 2pm-6pm Mon-Fri), next to Hotel Cartagena Plaza in Bocagrande.

**Consulates** The **Venezuelan consulate** (☎ 665 0382; Carrera 3 No 8-129) is in Edificio Centro Ejecutivo in Bocagrande. Check if you still need to get a tourist card from here or if you can head to Venezuela without one and get it on the border.

The **Panamanian consulate** (☎ 664 1433; Plaza de San Pedro Claver No 30-14) has moved from the suburb of Crespo, near the airport, to the old town.

CARIBBEAN COAST

**Money** Central banks which change travellers cheques and/or cash include the **Banco Unión Colombiano** (Av Carlos Escallón), next to Puerta del Reloj, and **Bancolombia** (Av Venezuela). **Lloyds TSB Bank** (Av San Martín No 10-21) in Bocagrande also cashes travellers cheques. Most major banks will give advances on Visa and/or MasterCard and have ATMs.

There are plenty of casas de cambio in the historic centre, many of which are around Plaza de los Coches. **Titán Intercontinental** (Av San Martín No 7-88) is in Bocagrande. **Giros & Finanzas** (Av Venezuela No 8A-87), in the old town, represents Western Union.

Cartagena is the only city in Colombia where you are likely to be propositioned (sometimes persistently) by street moneychangers. Be on guard. Heed the warning in the boxed text 'Moneychanging Magicians'.

**Email & Internet Access** There are a number of facilities in El Centro, including **CaribeNet** (☎ 664 2326; Calle Santo Domingo No 3-19), **Internet Café Colombiano** (☎ 664 2742; Plaza Santo Domingo), **Ketty Net** (Calle de la Mantilla No 3-40), **Compu Internet** (☎ 660 2034; Calle del Arzobispado No 34-18) and **Internet Discos Cartagena** (☎ 661 4017; Calle Román No 5-21). In Getsemaní, **Viena Net** (☎ 664 8387; Calle Tripita y Media No 31-29) is the major facility. Most of the listed places are open seven days a week; expect to pay US$1.50 to US$2 per hour in any of them.

## Old Town

Without doubt, Cartagena's old city is its principal attraction, particularly the inner walled town, consisting of the historical districts of El Centro and San Diego. It is a real gem of colonial architecture, packed with churches, monasteries, plazas, palaces and mansions with their overhanging balconies and shady patios.

Getsemaní, the outer walled town, is less impressive and not so well preserved, but has some charming places and is well worth exploring. It is less tourist oriented and more authentic. However, take extra precautions – this part of the city may not be safe, especially at night.

The old town is surrounded by **Las Murallas**, the thick walls built to protect it against enemies. Construction was begun towards the end of the 16th century, after the attack by Francis Drake; until that time Cartagena was almost completely unprotected. The project took two centuries to complete due to repeated damage from both storms and pirate attacks. Only in 1796 was it finally finished, just 25 years before the Spaniards were eventually expelled.

Las Murallas are an outstanding piece of military engineering preserved in remarkably good shape, except for a part of the walls facing La Matuna, which were unfortunately demolished by 'progressive' city authorities in the mid-20th century.

Most of the major tourist attractions are within the inner walled town, particularly

## Moneychanging Magicians

For some reason, Cartagena has plenty of street moneychangers, unlike any other Colombian city. They roam the streets, approach tourists and offer attractive exchange rates for your dollars, better than those in the casas de cambio. If you say 'No, thanks', they will continue to follow you and insist, offering still better rates. It all seems suspicious from the start, but nonetheless travellers have invariably been tempted and trapped by this ploy for years. If you are determined to be one of these adventurers, here's some information on how the ploy works.

The changers hand you a bundle of peso notes, supposedly the exact equivalent of the dollars you want to change. You count them, but it appears that some money is missing, sometimes just one or two small notes. They pretend to be surprised, as if it was a genuine mistake, and take the bundle back to check. They count it out again, admit you're right, and top it up with the missing notes. At the same time they skilfully remove the largest bills, and give you back the 'correct' amount of money.

It all looks so natural that few people ever count the notes out again. You obviously should do it before handing over your dollars, but remember that they may have a full range of other tricks in case you happen to be wise to this one. They operate in gangs and are very clever with their hands. They may turn violent if things don't go exactly as they expected them to go. Be warned.

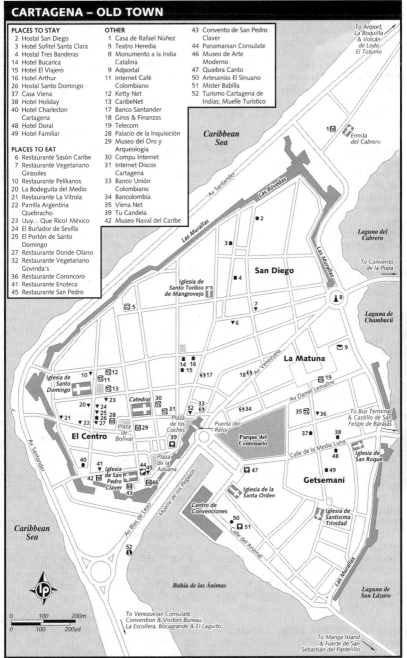

# CARTAGENA – OLD TOWN

**PLACES TO STAY**
2 Hostal San Diego
3 Hotel Sofitel Santa Clara
4 Hostal Tres Banderas
14 Hotel Bucarica
15 Hotel El Viajero
16 Hotel Arthur
26 Hotel Santo Domingo
37 Casa Viena
38 Hotel Holiday
40 Hotel Charleston Cartagena
48 Hotel Doral
49 Hotel Familiar

**PLACES TO EAT**
6 Restaurante Sasón Caribe
7 Restaurante Vegetariano Girasoles
10 Restaurante Pelíkanos
20 La Bodeguita del Medio
21 Restaurante La Vitrola
22 Parrilla Argentina Quebracho
23 Uuy... Que Rico! México
24 El Burlador de Sevilla
25 El Portón de Santo Domingo
27 Restaurante Donde Olano
32 Restaurante Vegetariano Govinda's
36 Restaurante Coroncoro
41 Restaurante Enoteca
45 Restaurante San Pedro

**OTHER**
1 Casa de Rafael Núñez
5 Teatro Heredia
8 Monumento a la India Catalina
9 Adpostal
11 Internet Café Colombiano
12 Ketty Net
13 CaribeNet
17 Banco Santander
18 Giros & Finanzas
19 Telecom
28 Palacio de la Inquisición
29 Museo del Oro y Arqueología
30 Compu Internet
31 Internet Discos Cartagena
33 Banco Unión Colombiano
34 Bancolombia
35 Viena Net
39 Tu Candela
42 Museo Naval del Caribe
43 Convento de San Pedro Claver
44 Panamanian Consulate
46 Museo de Arte Moderno
47 Quiebra Canto
50 Artesanías El Sinuano
51 Mister Babilla
52 Turismo Cartagena de Indias; Muelle Turístico

in El Centro. The best approach is to wander leisurely, savouring the architectural details, rich street life and local snacks along the way. Don't just seek out the sights detailed here – there are many other interesting places which you will find while walking around. Almost every street in the inner town is worth strolling along.

The following attractions have been listed in sequence to conveniently connect them in a walking tour.

**Puerta del Reloj** Originally called the Boca del Puente, this was the main gateway to the inner walled town and was linked to Getsemaní by a drawbridge over the moat. The side arches of the gate, which are now open as walkways, were previously used as a chapel and armoury. The republican-style tower, complete with a four-sided clock, was added in 1888.

**Plaza de los Coches** Previously known as Plaza de la Yerba, the triangular square just behind Puerta del Reloj was once used as a slave market. It is lined with old balconied houses with colonial arches at ground level. The arcaded walkway, known as El Portal de los Dulces, is today lined with confectionery stands selling local sweets. The statue of the city's founder, Pedro de Heredia, is in the middle of the plaza.

**Plaza de la Aduana** This is the largest and oldest square in the old town and was used as a parade ground. In colonial times all the important governmental and administrative buildings were here. The old Royal Customs House was restored and is now the City Hall. A statue of Christopher Columbus stands in the centre of the square.

**Museo de Arte Moderno** The Museum of Modern Art (☎ 664 5815; Plaza de San Pedro Claver; admission US$0.50; open 9am-noon & 3pm-7pm Mon-Fri, 10am-1pm Sat), housed in a part of the former Royal Customs House, presents temporary exhibitions from its own collection, including works by Alejandro Obregón, one of Colombia's most remarkable painters, born in Cartagena.

**Convento de San Pedro Claver** The convent was founded by Jesuits in the first half of the 17th century, originally as San

Ignacio de Loyola. The name was later changed in honour of Spanish-born monk Pedro Claver (1580–1654), who lived and died in the convent. Called the 'Apostle of the Blacks' or the 'Slave of the Slaves', he spent all his life ministering to the slaves brought from Africa. He was the first person to be canonised in the New World (in 1888). A statue of Pedro Claver, cast by Enrique Grau, a Cartagena artist now living in Bogotá, has recently been placed in front of the convent.

The convent is a monumental three-storey building surrounding a tree-filled courtyard, and part of it is open as a **museum** (☎ 664 4991; Plaza de San Pedro Claver; admission US$2; open 8am-6pm Mon-Sat, 8am-5pm Sun). Exhibits include religious art and pre-Columbian ceramics. You can visit the cell where San Pedro Claver lived and died, and also climb a narrow staircase to the choir loft of the adjacent church. Guides, should you need one, are waiting by the ticket office and charge US$3/4 for a Spanish/English tour for a group of up to seven people.

**Iglesia de San Pedro Claver** The church alongside the convent, completed in the first half of the 18th century, has an imposing stone facade. Inside, there are fine stained-glass windows and the high altar made of Italian marble. The remains of San Pedro Claver are kept in a glass coffin in the altar.

**Museo Naval del Caribe** Opened in 1992 on the 500th anniversary of Columbus' discovery, the Naval Museum (☎ 664 9672; Calle San Juan de Dios; admission US$1.50; open 10am-6pm Tues-Sun) occupies a great colonial building which was once a Jesuit college. It features a collection of objects related to the maritime history of Cartagena and the Caribbean.

**Plaza de Bolívar** Formerly the Plaza de Inquisición, this plaza, or rather a tiny park, is surrounded by some of the city's most elegant balconied colonial buildings. As expected, a statue of Simón Bolívar stands in the middle of the plaza.

**Palacio de la Inquisición** The Palace of the Inquisition is one of the finest buildings in the town. Although the site was the seat of the Punishment Tribunal of the Holy

Office from 1610, the palace wasn't completed until 1776. It is a good example of late colonial architecture, noted particularly for its magnificent baroque stone gateway topped by the Spanish coat of arms, and the long balconies on the facade.

On the side wall, just around the corner from the entrance, you'll find a small window with a cross on top. Heretics were denounced here, and the Holy Office would then instigate proceedings. The principal 'crimes' were magic, witchcraft and blasphemy. When culprits were found guilty they were sentenced to death in a public auto-da-fé. Five autos-da-fé took place during the Inquisition until independence in 1821. About 800 folk were condemned to death and executed. The Inquisition did not judge the Indians.

The palace is today a **museum** (☎ 664 4113; Plaza de Bolívar) displaying Inquisitors' instruments of torture, pre-Columbian pottery and historical objects from both colonial and independence times, including arms, paintings, furniture and church bells. There is also a good model of Cartagena from the beginning of the 19th century and an interesting collection of old maps of the Nuevo Reino de Granada from various periods. The museum was closed for refurbishing as we went to press.

**Museo del Oro y Arqueología** The Cartagena Gold Museum (☎ 660 0778, 660 0808; Plaza de Bolívar; admission free; open 8am-noon & 2pm-6pm Tues-Fri, 9am-noon Sat) is one of Banco de la República's six gold museums scattered around the country, and, like most of the others, it's interesting and informative. It has a collection of gold and pottery of the Sinú (also known as Zenú) Indians, who inhabited the region of the present-day departments of Bolívar, Córdoba, Sucre and northern Antioquia before the Spanish Conquest. There is also a model of a hut, complete with household utensils and artefacts, representing a dwelling of the Indians living in the region today.

**Catedral** The cathedral was begun in 1575, but in 1586, while still under construction, it was partially destroyed by the cannons of Francis Drake, and not completed until 1612. Considerable alterations were made between 1912 and 1923 by the first archbishop of Cartagena, who covered the church with

stucco and painted it to look like marble. He also commissioned the dome on the tower. Recent restoration has uncovered the lovely limestone on the building's exterior. Apart from the tower's top, the church has basically preserved its original form. It has a fort-like appearance and a simply decorated interior with three naves and semicircular archways supported on high stone columns. The main retable, worked in gold leaf, dates from the 18th century.

**Iglesia de Santo Domingo** The Santo Domingo Church, built towards the end of the 16th century, is reputedly the oldest in the city. Its builders gave it a particularly wide central nave and covered it with a heavy roof, but it seems they were not too good at their calculations and the vault began to crack. Massive buttresses had to be added to the walls to support the structure and prevent it from collapsing. The builders also had problems with the bell tower, which is distinctly crooked. However, legend has it that it was the work of a devil who knocked the tower.

The interior is spacious and lofty. The legendary figure of Christ carved in wood is set in the baroque altar at the head of the right-hand aisle. The floor in front of the high altar and in the two aisles is paved with old tombstones dating mostly from the 19th century.

**Iglesia de Santo Toribio de Mangrovejo** Compared to the other churches, this one is relatively small. It was erected between 1666 and 1732 and its ceiling is covered with Mudéjar panelling. During Vernon's attack on the city, a cannon ball went through a window into the church when it was filled with worshippers, but fortunately there were no casualties. The ball is now on display in a glassed niche in the left wall.

**Las Bóvedas** These are 23 dungeons built between 1792 and 1796 in the city walls, which are more than 15m thick in this part. It was the last major construction carried out in colonial times and was destined for military purposes. The vaults were used by the Spaniards as storerooms for munitions and provisions. Later, during the republican era, they were turned into a jail. Today they house tourist craft and souvenir shops.

**Casa de Rafael Núñez** This mansion, just outside the walls of Las Bóvedas, was the home of the former president, lawyer and poet. He wrote the words of Colombia's national anthem and was one of the authors of the constitution of 1886, which was in force (with some later changes) until 1991. The wooden mansion is now a **museum** *(admission US$1; open 8am-noon & 2pm-6pm daily)* featuring some of Núñez' documents and personal possessions. The chapel opposite the house, known as the Ermita del Cabrero, holds his ashes. The chapel only opens for mass, early in the morning and late afternoon.

**Monumento a la India Catalina** The monument, placed at the main entrance to the old town from the mainland, is a tribute to the Carib Indians, the group that inhabited this land before the Spanish Conquest. The lovely bronze statue depicts Catalina, a beautiful Carib Indian woman who served as interpreter to Pedro de Heredia upon the arrival of the Spaniards. The statue was forged in 1974 by Eladio Gil, a Spanish sculptor living in Cartagena.

**Muelle de los Pegasos** Back at the point from where you began your tour, Muelle de los Pegasos is the lovely old port of Cartagena on the Bahía de las Ánimas. It is invariably full of fishing, cargo and tourist boats. Sip a fruit juice from any of the stalls while watching the easy-going port life. The new harbour where big ships dock is on Manga Island.

## Spanish Forts

The old city is a fortress in itself, yet there are more fortifications built at strategic points outside the city. Some of the more important ones are included below.

**Castillo de San Felipe de Barajas** The Castillo (☎ 656 0590, 666 4790; Av Arévalo; admission US$3; open 8am-5pm daily) is the greatest and strongest fortress ever built by the Spaniards in their colonies. The original fort was constructed between 1639 and 1657 on top of the 40m-high San Lázaro hill, and was quite small. In 1762, an extensive enlargement was undertaken which resulted in the entire hill being covered over with this powerful bastion. It was truly impregnable

and was never taken despite numerous attempts to storm it.

The fortress is an outstanding piece of military engineering. The batteries were arranged so that they could destroy each other if the fort fell to the enemy. A complex system of tunnels connected strategic points of the fortress to distribute provisions and to facilitate evacuation. The tunnels were constructed in such a way that sounds reverberate all the way along them, making it possible to hear the slightest sound of the approaching enemy's feet, and also making it easy for internal communication.

Some of the tunnels are lit and are open to visitors – a walk not to be missed. Take a guide if you want to learn more about the curious inventions of Antonio de Arévalo, the military engineer who directed the fortress' construction.

The fortress is just a 20-minute walk from the old town, or take a local bus from the Parque del Centenario. There is a statue of Blas de Lezo in front of the fortress.

**Fuerte de San Sebastián del Pastelillo** This fort, on the western end of Manga Island, was constructed in the middle of the 16th century as one of the town's first defence posts. It's quite small and not particularly inspiring, but it's quite close to the old town – just across the bridge from Getsemaní. Today the fort is home to the Club de Pesca which has a marina where local and foreign boats anchor.

**Fuerte de San Fernando** San Fernando is on the southern tip of the Isla de Tierrabomba at the entrance to the Bahía de Cartagena through the Bocachica strait. On the opposite side of the strait is another fort, Batería de San José, and together they guarded the access to the bay. A heavy chain was strung between them to prevent surprise attacks.

Originally, there were two gateways to Cartagena Bay, Bocachica and Bocagrande. Bocagrande was partially blocked by a sandbank and two ships which sank there. An undersea wall was constructed after Vernon's attack in order to strengthen the natural barrage and to make the channel impassable to ships. It is still impassable today and all ships and boats have to go through Bocachica.

The fort of San Fernando was built between about 1753 and 1760 and was designed to withstand any siege. It had its own docks, barracks, sanitary services, kitchen, infirmary, storerooms for provisions and arms, two wells, a chapel and even a jail, much of which can still be seen today.

The fortress can only be reached by water. Boats leave daily from the Muelle Turístico between about 8am and 10am, and return in the afternoon. The tour costs US$9 including lunch and entrance to the fort. Some boats charge US$4 for the journey only, but you must pay the US$2 admission to the fort.

## Convento de la Popa

The convent *(☎ 666 2331; admission US$2.50; open 9am-5pm daily)* is perched on top of a 150m-high hill, the tallest point in the city, about 1.5km beyond the San Felipe fortress. Its name literally means the Convent of the Stern, after the hill's apparent similarity to a ship's poop, but it's actually the Convento de Nuestra Señora de la Candelaria, founded by the Augustine fathers in 1607. Initially it was just a small wooden chapel, which was replaced by a stouter construction and the hill was fortified two centuries later, just before Pablo Morillo's siege.

After independence the convent became a military headquarters, but was later abandoned for a long time. It was eventually restored by the same order of Augustine monks and today it is open for visitors. A beautiful image of La Virgen de la Candelaria, the patroness of the city, is in the convent's chapel, and there's a charming flower-filled patio. The views stretch all over the city. The patron saint's day is 2 February (see Special Events later).

There is a zigzagging access road leading to the convent on the hilltop (no public transport) and paths cutting the bends of the road. It takes half an hour to walk to the top, but it's not recommended for safety – there have been cases of armed robbery. Instead go by taxi (US$2.50).

## Manga Island

While Cartagena is principally noted for its Spanish colonial architecture, other styles have also left their mark. Walk around the residential sector on Manga Island to see some interesting houses dating mainly from the late-19th to early-20th centuries – a real hotchpotch of styles. The most noticeable feature is the Islamic influence brought by immigrants from the Middle East. You can also visit Manga's Cementerio de la Cruz, noted for many ornate old graves.

## Scuba Diving

Taking advantage of the extensive coral reefs along Cartagena's coast (particularly around the Islas del Rosario), Cartagena has grown into an important scuba-diving centre. Virtually all the local dive schools are in Bocagrande and El Laguito and include: **Dolphin Dive School** *(☎ 665 2792;* w *www.pavito.com; Edificio Costamar, San Martín No 6-105, Bocagrande)*; **Caribe Dive Shop** *(☎ 665 3517;* e *caribediveshop@ yahoo.com; in Hotel Caribe, Bocagrande)*; **Eco Buzos** *(☎ 655 1129; Edificio Alonso de Ojeda, Av Almirante Brion, El Laguito)*; and **La Tortuga Dive School** *(☎ 665 6994; Edificio Marina del Rey, Av del Retorno, El Laguito)*.

## Organised Tours

City tours in *chiva* (a colourful, traditional bus) depart daily at 2pm from Av San Martín between Calles 4 and 5 in Bocagrande. The four-hour tour includes rides around Bocagrande, Castillo Grande and the walled city, plus visits to the Convento de la Popa and Castillo de San Felipe.

You can also take a city tour in a horse-drawn carriage, which gives a glance of Bocagrande and the walled city. The carriages depart from the corner of Av San Martín and Calle 4 in Bocagrande and go along the waterfront to the old town. After a run around the main streets of the walled city they return via either Av San Martín or the waterfront, whichever you prefer. They operate daily from 5pm until midnight. The tour takes one hour and costs US$15 per coach for up to four people.

For tours to Islas del Rosario and Volcán de Lodo El Totumo, see the relevant sections in Around Cartagena later in this chapter.

## Special Events

The bullfighting season, **Feria Taurina**, takes place at the bullring on Av Pedro de Heredia during the first week of the year.

The **Fiesta de Nuestra Señora de la Candelaria** takes place on 2 February, the day of Cartagena's patron saint. A solemn

CARIBBEAN COAST

procession is held on that day at the Convento de la Popa, during which the faithful carry lit candles. Celebrations begin nine days earlier, the so-called Novenas, when pilgrims flock to the convent.

Cartagena hosts an international film festival, **Festival Internacional de Cine**, in March/April, usually a week before Easter. Winners are presented with statues of India Catalina.

The national beauty pageant, **Reinado Nacional de Belleza**, is held in November to celebrate Cartagena's independence day. Miss Colombia, the beauty queen, is elected on 11 November, the high point of the event. The fiesta, which includes street dancing, music and fancy-dress parades, strikes up several days before the pageant and the city goes wild. The event, also known as the Carnaval de Cartagena or Fiestas del 11 de Noviembre, is the city's most important annual bash.

## Places to Stay

Cartagena has a reasonable choice of accommodation and despite its touristy status, the prices of its hotels are not higher than in other large cities. The tourist peak is from late December to late January but, even then, it's relatively easy to find a budget room.

A vast majority of travellers stay in the walled city. This is Cartagena's most pleasant and convenient area to stay and the one that offers plenty of lodging options, everything from rock bottom to top notch. Within the walled city, Getsemaní is the principal area of budget accommodation, whereas El Centro and San Diego shelter the city's top-end hotels.

Another area well dotted with tourist facilities is the modern district of Bocagrande and El Laguito. However, this is essentially an upmarket sector and has little charm unless a forest of high-rise hotels is what you find atmospheric. This is mainly a destination for Colombian holidaymakers and occasional international charter packages. Very few independent foreign travellers stay here.

All hotels listed in the following sections have rooms with fans, unless specified.

**Getsemaní** If you're on a tight budget, walk to the Getsemaní area, where you'll find plenty of cheapies on Calle de la Media Luna and nearby streets. Many are dives that double as love hotels or brothels, but there are a few clean and safe options. Be careful with night walking in Getsemaní – the quarter may not be completely safe.

**Casa Viena** (☎ 664 6242; e hotel@casa viena.com; Calle San Andrés No 30-53; dorm beds with air-con US$3, singles/doubles US$4/7, doubles with bath US$9) is one of the most popular backpacker haunts. It has a variety of simple rooms, most with shared facilities, and is one of the cheapest places around. The hotel offers the usual range of Western facilities, including laundry service, Internet access, book exchange, individual strongboxes, cooking facilities, tours and tourist information.

**Hotel Holiday** (☎ 664 0948; Calle de la Media Luna No 10-47; beds in rooms without/ with bath US$3.50/4.50) is another popular and friendly travellers hangout. Its 13 neat, airy double rooms with bath are good value, and there are four smaller rooms without private facilities.

**Hotel Doral** (☎ 664 1706; Calle de la Media Luna No 10-46; beds in rooms without/with bath US$4/5) is right across the street from the Holiday. It has an attractive spacious courtyard filled with potted shrubs and flowers and umbrella-shaded tables. Rooms, distributed on two levels around the courtyard, are simple but spacious. The rooms on the 1st floor are more airy and pleasant but they don't have private baths. The ground-floor rooms do have baths.

**Hotel Familiar** (☎ 664 2464; Calle del Guerrero No 29-66; beds in rooms without/ with bath US$3.50/5) is yet another backpacker shelter. It has rather small rooms, but has new mattresses and guests can use the kitchen free of charge.

**El Centro & San Diego** Budget hotels in El Centro and San Diego, the heart of the old town, are on the whole more expensive and not always as good value as those in Getsemaní, but there are some reasonable options here as well. There is also a good supply of classier accommodation here, which includes some of Cartagena's poshest hotels. Furthermore, the sector is safer than Getsemaní and you'll feel more relaxed here while walking at night.

**Hotel El Viajero** (☎ 664 3289; Calle del Porvenir No 35-68; singles/doubles with bath US$5/10) is one of the best budget bets in the area. This new, 14-room hotel provides good beds, a spacious courtyard and free use of the kitchen.

**Hotel Bucarica** *(☎ 664 1263; Calle San Agustín No 6-08; singles/doubles/triples with bath US$7/12/17)*, just round the corner from El Viajero, is not as good or clean but can be an alternative if El Viajero can't accommodate you.

**Hostal Santo Domingo** *(☎ 664 2268; Calle Santo Domingo No 33-46; singles/ doubles/triples with bath US$14/20/25)* is quite simple and is probably not good value, yet it's small, quiet and ideally located on one of the loveliest streets in El Centro.

**Hotel Arthur** *(☎ 664 2633; Calle San Agustín No 6-44; doubles with bath & fan/ air-con US$12/15)* isn't anything particularly stylish or special, but is one of the cheapest central options with air-conditioning.

**Hostal San Diego** *(☎ 660 0986; Calle de las Bóvedas No 39-120; singles/doubles/triples with bath US$30/36/45)* in the quiet northern end of San Diego is a pleasant mock-colonial place offering 27 air-conditioned rooms.

**Hostal Tres Banderas** *(☎ 660 0160; www .caribenet.com/3band; Calle Cochera del Hobo No 38-66; doubles US$40-50)* in San Diego offers character and comfort at affordable rates. This small, family-run place has nine air-conditioned double rooms, some of which have rooftop terraces.

Until not long ago, the walled city had not a single classy hotel. Now it has not one but two world-class places to stay, both set in meticulously restored great historic buildings that were once convents. If your wallet is not thick enough to stay in any of them, it's still worth going for a drink in their verdant cloistered courtyards where you can spot parrots and toucans amid colonial surroundings.

**Hotel Charleston Cartagena** *(☎ 664 9494; e reserv-charlesctg@hoteles-charleston.com; Plaza Santa Teresa; double rooms US$120, suites US$140-180)* in the former Convento de Santa Teresa has 91 rooms and 22 suites distributed around two amazing historic courtyards straight out of a picture postcard. The rooftop swimming pool offers good views over the colonial quarter.

**Hotel Sofitel Santa Clara** *(☎ 664 6070; www.hotelsantaclara.com; Calle del Torno; double rooms US$300, suites US$360-400)* is another marvellous place in colonial style.

Housed in the former Convento de Santa Clara (dating from 1621), which in modern times served as a charity hospital, the hotel offers 144 rooms and 18 suites, a swimming pool, Internet access and two fine restaurants (French and Italian).

## Places to Eat

Cartagena is a good place to eat, particularly at an upmarket level, but cheap places are also plentiful. Dozens of simple restaurants in the walled city serve *almuerzos* (set lunches) for less than US$2, and many also offer *comidas* (set dinners). There are so many of them that it's hard to make any selection. Furthermore, these places often close, reopen and change owners and names. Some, however, have been open for many years, maintaining quality at budget prices, and have become hugely popular with the locals. They include **Restaurante Coroncoro** *(Calle Tripita y Media No 31-28)* in Getsemaní and **Restaurante Sasón Caribe** *(Calle La Tablada No 7-62)* in San Diego.

Vegetarians will get tasty budget meals at **Restaurante Vegetariano Govinda's** *(Plaza de los Coches No 7-15)* in El Centro and **Restaurante Vegetariano Girasoles** *(Calle Quero No 9-09)* in San Diego.

Plenty of snack bars all across the old town serve typical local snacks such as *arepas de huevo* (fried maize dough with an egg inside), *dedos de queso* (deep-fried cheese sticks), empanadas and *buñuelos* (deep-fried maize and cheese balls).

A dozen stalls on the Muelle de los Pegasos operate round the clock and have an unbelievable selection of fruit juices. Apart from commonly known fruit such as pineapple, banana and mandarins, they'll have plenty of exotic local fruit including *níspero, maracuyá, lulo, zapote* and *guanábana*, all of which make for delicious juices. These stalls also have plenty of local snacks.

Try typical local sweets at confectionery stands at El Portal de los Dulces on the Plaza de los Coches. Very characteristic of Cartagena are *butifarras* (small smoked meatballs), only sold on the street by *butifarreros*, who walk along with big pots, striking them with a knife to get your attention. The *peto* is a sort of milk soup made of maize, similar to Antioquian *mazamorra*, sweetened with *panela* (unrefined sugar) and served hot. It, too, is only sold by street vendors.

Plaza Santo Domingo is home to six open-air cafés which serve a varied menu of dishes, snacks, sweets and drinks. The cafés are not that cheap, but the place is trendy and fills up in the evening. Here are some of the cheaper places to eat in El Centro:

**Uuy...Que Rico! México** (☎ 660 2555; *Calle Santo Domingo No 3-30; dishes US$3-7*) is an inviting Mexican place offering pretty authentic food as well as a rich help-yourself sauce bar.

**Restaurante San Pedro** (☎ 664 5121; *Plaza San Pedro Claver No 30-11; mains US$5-8*) has a variety of cuisines, including Italian pastas, Mexican burritos and Indonesian nasi goreng. It enjoys a rather attractive location, facing the mighty San Pedro Church, and has an air-conditioned interior and tables outdoors.

**Restaurante Donde Olano** (☎ 664 7099; *Calle Santo Domingo No 33-08; mains US$6-8*) is a cosy place that cooks fine French and Creole specialities at reasonable prices.

**Restaurante Pelíkanos** (☎ 660 0086; *Calle Santo Domingo at Calle Gastelbondo; set meals US$10*) is an arty, bohemian two-level restaurant, different from any other. It has just one set menu daily, consisting of six courses (four entrees, main course and dessert), plus unlimited Chilean wine included in the price.

**La Bodeguita del Medio** (☎ 660 1993; *Calle Santo Domingo No 33-81; mains US$6-9*) is a charming place serving Cuban fare in surroundings with old Cuban photos all over the walls.

There are a number of upmarket restaurants in the old town, most of which are set in historic interiors.

**El Portón de Santo Domingo** (☎ 664 8897; *Calle Santo Domingo No 33-66; mains US$8-15*) is a new, classy place serving international food including some seafood. It has several rooms, some with air-conditioning, and live music on weekend nights.

**Restaurante La Vitrola** (☎ 664 8243; *Calle de Baloco; mains US$10-15*) is another option for international cuisine and live music (played every night). This is one of the dearer restaurants, but the place has a long tradition and the food is invariably first-class.

**Parrilla Argentina Quebracho** (☎ 664 1300; *Calle de Baloco No 2-69; mains US$8-12*) is a new kid on the block. It's easy to find, thanks to a big bull at the door. The restaurant serves Argentine cuisine, including famous juicy steaks, and has tango shows in the evening.

**Restaurante Enoteca** (☎ 664 3793; *Calle San Juan de Dios No 3-39; mains US$6-12*) is one of the best addresses in town for Italian food, prepared by an Italian chef.

**El Burlador de Sevilla** (☎ 660 0866; *Calle Santo Domingo No 33-88; mains US$7-12*) brings a bit of Spain to Cartagena, with its paellas, tapas and *jamónes* (hams) hanging over the buffet.

## Entertainment

A number of bars, taverns, discos and other venues stay open late. Plenty of them are on Av del Arsenal in Getsemaní, Cartagena's Zona Rosa. **Mister Babilla** (☎ 664 7005; *Av del Arsenal No 8B-137*) is one of the most popular discos in this area, yet also one of the most expensive. You will find cheaper venues around; just walk along the street, as everybody does, and take your pick.

**Quiebra Canto** (☎ 664 1372), overlooking the Parque del Centenario, is a good salsa spot. **Tu Candela** (☎ 664 8787; *Portal de los Dulces No 32-25*) is an informal bar on Plaza de los Coches, which serves beer and plays taped music till late.

There are several upmarket restaurants in El Centro that have bands playing Caribbean and Cuban music. Some of these restaurants are in the earlier Places to Eat section.

In Bocagrande, try **La Escollera** (*Carrera 1 at Calle 5*), a disco in a large thatched open hut, which goes wild nightly till 4am. It has three bars which serve expensive spirits and soft drinks, but there's no beer or food. The music is played at extra-high volume, so don't plan on enjoying much conversation.

You can also go on a night trip aboard a chiva, a typical Colombian bus, with a band playing *vallenato*, the popular local rhythm that has conquered virtually all the country. Chivas depart around 8pm from Av San Martín between Calles 4 and 5 in Bocagrande for a three- to four-hour trip, and leave you at the end of the tour in a discotheque – a good point to continue your party for the rest of the night.

## Shopping

Cartagena has a wide choice of tourist shops selling crafts and souvenirs, and they may be worth looking at because the quality of the goods is usually high. The biggest

## Vallenato – Musical Beat that Conquered a Country

Once you arrive on the Colombian coast, you will quickly learn that vallenato is everywhere – in bars, restaurants, discos, hotels and buses, on the street and on the beach. You may love it or hate it, but you can't escape it. The characteristic accordion sound will either drive you crazy or delight you.

Vallenato is a typical musical genre of the coast, performed by a small band and sung. A classical vallenato ensemble includes the accordion, *guacharaca* and *caja*. The guacharaca is a percussion instrument of indigenous origins. It consists of a stick-like wooden body with a row of cuts, and a metal fork. The sound is produced by rubbing the stick with the fork. The caja is a bucket-shaped wooden drum which is played by hand. It has clear African roots. The accordionist is usually also the principal vocalist of the band.

Vallenato has four major musical forms: the *paseo, merengue, puya* and *son*. They differ in their rhythmic structures and the way they are performed. Generally speaking, the paseo and *son* are slower and gentler than the puya and merengue. The paseo is the youngest and most varied of all the four forms, and it has come to be the most common vallenato species over recent decades. In other words, most of the vallenato fare you hear today are paseos.

Vallenato was reputedly born in the Valle de Upar, somewhere around the town of Valledupar, on the present-day borderland of the Cesar and La Guajira departments. It evolved into a distinct musical genre during colonial times, even though back then it was quite different to what it is today. Its melodic line was initially led by the *gaita*, a sort of simple vertical flute. This began to change when the accordion arrived in the region.

The accordion is a German invention from 1829. By the mid-19th century it started to make its way into the New World, first to the USA and Argentina. It's not exactly clear how and when the accordion appeared in Colombia, but one story has it that the first accordions were ordered for a German transport company that operated steamers on the Magdalena River. The instruments were shipped from Europe to Riohacha, then transported inland on the backs of mules. They didn't make it to their destination, however, because the mule caravan was robbed by one of the many gangs marauding throughout the region of Valledupar.

The bandits certainly expected more attractive merchandise than dozens of useless instruments, but they somehow managed to sell the gear to bars, brothels and hotels to entertain guests. Local musicians soon began experimenting with this strange newcomer and eventually succeeded in making it the leading vallenato instrument.

Vallenato began to spread beyond its native region from around the 1930s, initially along the coast. The record industry helped to propagate the music (the first recording of vallenato was made in 1943), as did broadcasting by radio and TV. The Festival de la Leyenda Vallenata, held in Valledupar annually since 1968, has become one of Colombia's major musical events.

However, it wasn't actually until the 1990s that vallenato successfully conquered virtually all of Colombia to become a national, not just regional, musical genre, and it is now making inroads into neighbouring Venezuela. Incidentally, vallenato fits snugly as a musical symbol of the country as it features the three instruments representing the three races that compose the majority of Colombia's population.

Until the 1950s, vallenato was essentially a folk rhythm of the countryside, created largely by anonymous authors. In recent decades, it made a trip from the provinces towards the cities and up the social ladder. Today it boasts famous composers, interpreters, vocalists and accordionists, and has entered concert halls. Yet it sounds more authentic and natural in the seedy, smoky taverns of popular suburbs on the coast, where it was born.

Vallenato's great composers include Rafael Escalona and Leandro Díaz, both of whom wrote many songs, now considered classics of the genre. The best-known vallenato accordionists include Alejo Durán, Nicolás 'Colacho' Mendoza, Calixto Ochoa, Alfredo Gutiérrez and Emiliano Zuleta. One of the vallenato's most remarkable innovators of recent years is Carlos Vives, who has used elements of traditional vallenato to create an attractive pop rhythm. It's partly due to him that vallenato attracted a younger audience and spread beyond national borders.

tourist shopping centre in the walled city is Las Bóvedas, offering handicrafts, clothes, souvenirs and the like. There is a small but interesting and relatively cheap **Artesanías El Sinuano** *(Av del Arsenal No 8B-55)*, opposite the Centro de Convenciones. Artisans appear during the afternoon at the Plaza de Santo Domingo and sell a variety of crafts.

## Getting There & Away

**Air** The airport is in Crespo, 3km northeast of the old city, and is serviced by frequent local buses. Also, there are colectivos to Crespo, which depart from India Catalina. By taxi, there's a surcharge of US$1.50 on airport trips. It's US$3 from the centre to the airport, but it'll be only US$1.50 if you ask the driver to leave you on Av 4 at Calle 70, just 100m before the airport. The terminal has two ATMs and the Casa de Cambio América (in domestic arrivals) which changes cash and travellers cheques.

All the major Colombian carriers operate flights to and from Cartagena. There are flights to Bogotá (US$75 to US$125 one way), Cali (US$80 to US$130), Cúcuta (US$90 to US$130), Medellín (US$75 to US$125), San Andrés (US$80 to US$130) and other major cities.

Aces flies direct to Miami, while Avianca flies to Miami via Bogotá. Copa has daily flights to Panama City.

**Bus** The bus terminal is on the eastern outskirts of the city, far away from the centre. Large green-and-white and air-conditioned Metrocar buses shuttle between the city and the terminal every 10 minutes (US$0.50, 40 minutes). In the centre, you can catch them on Av Daniel Lemaitre. Catch one with the red letters on the board, which goes by a more direct route and is faster.

There are half a dozen buses daily to Bogotá (US$40, 20 hours) and another half a dozen to Medellín (US$27, 13 hours). Buses to Barranquilla run every 15 minutes or so (US$4, two hours), and some continue on to Santa Marta; if not, just change in Barranquilla. Unitransco has one bus to Mompós, at 7am (US$11, eight hours); see Mompós later in this chapter for more details.

Three bus companies – **Expreso Brasilia** *(☎ 663 2119)*, **Expresos Amerlujo** *(☎ 653 2536)* and **Unitransco/Bus Ven** *(☎ 663 2065)* – operate buses to Caracas (US$60,

20 hours) via Maracaibo (US$35, 10 hours). Unitransco is a bit cheaper than the other two, but you have to change buses on the border in Paraguachón. Each company has one departure daily. All buses go via Barranquilla, Santa Marta and Maicao. Whereas the service is fast and comfortable, it's not that cheap. You'll save quite a bit if you do the trip to Caracas in stages by local transport, with a change in Maicao and Maracaibo.

**Boat** There is no ferry service between Cartagena and Colón in Panama, and there are very few cargo boats. More boats operate between Colón and Barranquilla, some of which will take passengers, motorcycles and even cars, but these services are irregular and infrequent.

A far more pleasant way of getting to Panama is by sailboat. There are various boats, mostly foreign yachts, that take travellers from Cartagena to Colón via San Blas Archipelago (Panama), and vice versa, but this is not a regular service. The trip takes four to six days and normally includes a couple of days at San Blas for snorkelling and spear fishing. It costs US$170 to US$200, plus about US$30 for food. It can also be organised as a return trip from Cartagena, in which case the boat doesn't go as far as Colón, but only to San Blas (about US$250, 10 days). Casa Viena and Hotel Holiday in Cartagena keep an eye on the boats and will know if there are any due to depart.

Beware of any con men attempting to lure you into amazing Caribbean boat trips (see the boxed text 'Welcome Aboard My Splendid Boat!').

### Welcome Aboard My Splendid Boat!

While strolling about Cartagena, you may be approached by men offering fabulous trips around the Caribbean in 'their boats' for a little help on board. If you seem interested, they will ask you to pay some money for a boarding permit or whatever. Don't pay a cent as you are unlikely to see the man or your money again. Don't be lured into this trick, even if they appear wearing sailor suits and speaking fluent English or French. It's amazing how innovative and skilful Colombian con men can be.

## AROUND CARTAGENA
### Islas del Rosario

This archipelago, about 35km southwest of Cartagena, consists of 27 small coral islands, including some tiny islets only big enough for a single house. The archipelago is surrounded by coral reefs, where the colour of the sea ranges from turquoise to purple. The whole area has been decreed a national park, the Corales del Rosario. The park is going to be expanded southward to cover the Islas de San Bernardo as well.

The coral reefs around the Islas del Rosario are the most extensive and magnificent on the Colombian Caribbean Coast, comparable to those around San Andrés and Providencia. The two largest islands, Isla Grande and Isla del Rosario, have inland lagoons

and some tourist facilities. The Oceanario (Aquarium) has been established on the tiny Isla de San Martín de Pajarales.

The driest period in the region is from December to March, while the wettest is from September to October.

**Organised Tours** The usual way of visiting the park is a one-day tour, and the cruise through the islands has become an established business. Tours depart year-round from the Muelle Turístico in Cartagena. Boats leave between 8am and 9am daily and return about 4pm to 6pm. The cruise office at the Muelle sells tours in big boats (US$18 per person), whereas the independent operators hanging around offer tours in smaller vessels (US$13 to US$16). Popular backpacker hotels sell

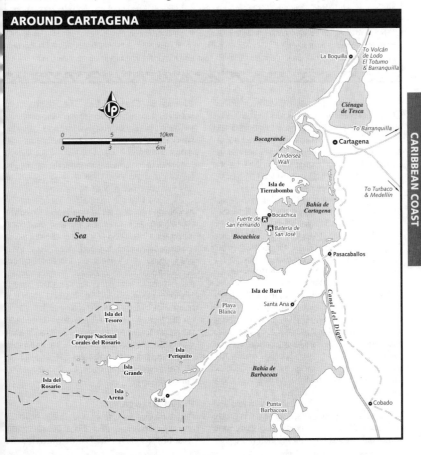

AROUND CARTAGENA

## Some Tips about Tours to Islas del Rosario

A day trip to the Islas del Rosario is by far the most popular tour organised from Cartagena. Some travellers love it, others are a bit disappointed, but at the end of the day most agree it's not a bad trip. By and large it's reasonable value and a lot of fun, and worth the time and money if only to get yourself into a sailing mood. Here are some tips on how to get the most out of what's on offer.

You can choose to go by a large boat or a small boat, and each has its pros and cons. Large boats, such as the most popular one, *Alcatraz*, take up to 150 people and are pretty slow. It takes three hours to get to the Aquarium – apparently a 'never-ending' trip – but you can freely move around the boat, having a beer at the bar downstairs, taking snaps from the upper deck, chatting to other passengers, or even dancing to the music blasting at full volume all the time. The music itself is a package of popular local fare, including vallenato, salsa and, of course, Shakira. It's great if you love these rhythms, but it can be torture if you don't. There's simply no escaping it.

Small boats don't have sound systems. They are much faster than large boats – they are actually so fast that they have enough time to include a visit to the Fuerte de San Fernando in the tour, a nice bonus. Furthermore, small vessels are able to pass nearer the islands and over the shallow coral reefs. Yet, you are stuck in your seat all the time, and if the sea is rough you may well get wet from head to toe. Here is where large boats come in handy; they will protect you from waves, wind, rain and sun much better. They are also far more suitable if you plan on shooting photos or video from the boat. And they have a toilet, just in case you need one urgently.

No matter which boat you take, however, bring along a good sunscreen, sunglasses, a hat or other protection, and a bathing suit if you plan on bathing or sunbathing at Playa Blanca. Buy a big bottle of water in Cartagena before departure; it will cost much more if you buy it during the trip.

these tours too, and may offer lower prices. Check beforehand and decide if you prefer big boats or small boats (see the boxed text 'Some Tips about Tours to Islas del Rosario'). Tours usually include lunch, but not the entrance fee to the Aquarium (US$5), Fuerte de San Fernando (US$2), port tax (US$1.50), and national park entrance fee (US$1).

The route is roughly similar with most operators, though it may differ a little between small and large boats. They all go through the Bahía de Cartagena and into the open sea through the Bocachica strait, passing between two Spanish forts: the Batería de San José and, directly opposite, the Fuerte de San Fernando.

The boats then cruise among the islands and get as far as the Aquarium, where they stop for about an hour. The admission fee is not included in the tour; you may decide to pay and visit it or just hang around waiting for the trip to continue. The Aquarium has various marine species, including sharks, turtles and rays, and runs a dolphin show for tourists. The boats then take you to Playa Blanca on the Isla de Barú to let you rest and bathe for about two hours. The beach is pretty crowded as most tour boats stop there, and some tour groups have their lunch there.

**Places to Stay & Eat** The islands have some tourist infrastructure, so you can stay longer, go sunbathing, swimming, diving, snorkelling or just take it easy in a hammock. Apart from a collection of hotels, some folk rent out their houses or bungalows on the islands and provide their own transport or have arrangements with boat owners.

The Isla Grande has half a dozen accommodation options, including **Hotel Kokomo** (☎ 673 4072; e hotelkokomo@hotmail.com; hammocks/beds US$4/10). It is the cheapest place around and not bad at all. Run by a Norwegian and a Belgian, the hotel offers accommodation in cabañas, budget meals, a salt-water swimming pool and the beach. Breakfast is included in the bed (but not hammock) rates. Diving gear can be rented on the island. The hotel provides daily boat transport to/from Cartagena for US$5 each way. Information and booking are available in Cartagena at **CaribeNet** (☎ 664 2326; e caribe@caribenet.com; Calle Santo Domingo No 3-19).

### Playa Blanca

Playa Blanca is one of the finest beaches around Cartagena. It's about 20km southwest of the city, on the Isla de Barú. It's the

Paintings by Fernando Botero, Donación Botero, Bogotá

Street performers, Plaza de Bolívar, Bogotá

Hostería del Molino La Mesopotamia, Villa de Leyva

Plaza Mayor, Villa de Leyva

Colonial architecture, Cartagena

Parque Nacional Tayrona, Magdalena

Palma de Cera (wax palm), Valle de Cocora

usual stop for the boat tours to the Islas del Rosario, so the beach may be crowded with tour participants in the early afternoon, but at other times it's pretty quiet. The place is also good for snorkelling as the coral reef begins just off the beach (take snorkel gear).

**Places to Stay & Eat** The beach has some rustic places to stay and eat. The most popular with travellers is **Campamento Wittenberg** run by a Frenchman, Gilbert, which offers hammocks with mosquito net (US$3) under a thatched roof, plus meals. It may have some beds in the future.

**Getting There & Away** The easiest way of getting to the beach is with Gilbert, who comes to Casa Viena in Cartagena once a week (usually on Wednesday or Thursday) and takes travellers in his boat (US$3, 45 minutes). If this doesn't coincide with your itinerary, go to Cartagena's main market, Mercado Bazurto, and go by boat or bus. Boats depart from about 9am to 10.30am daily except Sunday. On Sunday, there's an early morning bus direct to the beach.

## La Boquilla

This is a small fishing village 7km north of Cartagena. It sits at the northern tip of a narrow peninsula bordered by the sea on one side and the Ciénaga de Tesca on the other. Almost the entire population is black and lives off fishing. You can see locals at the *ciénaga* (lake/lagoon) working with their famous *atarrayas*, round fishing nets that are common in Colombia, particularly on the Caribbean Coast.

There's a pleasant place known as El Paraíso, a five-minute walk from the bus terminus, where you can enjoy a day on the beach. You can also arrange a boat trip with the locals along the narrow water channels cutting through the mangrove woods to the north of the village. Negotiate the price and pay upon return.

There is a collection of palm-thatched shack restaurants on the beach, which attract people from Cartagena on weekends; most are closed at other times. The fish is good and fresh, but not as cheap as you might expect given the proximity of the sea. It's usually accompanied by *arroz con coco* (rice prepared with coconut milk) and *patacones* (fried plantain).

Frequent city buses run to La Boquilla from India Catalina in Cartagena (US$0.40, 30 minutes).

## Volcán de Lodo El Totumo

About 50km northeast of Cartagena, a few kilometres off the coast, is an intriguing 15m mound, looking like a miniature volcano. It's indeed a volcano, but instead of lava and ashes it spews forth mud.

Legend has it that the volcano once belched fire but the local priest, seeing it as the work of the devil, frequently sprinkled it with holy water. He not only succeeded in extinguishing the fire, but also in turning the insides into mud to drown the devil.

The volcano sits on the bank of Ciénaga del Totumo, a shallow coastal lagoon, and is surrounded by about half a dozen shack restaurants. You can climb to the top by specially built stairs. The crater is filled with lukewarm mud with the consistency of cream. Go down into the crater and have a refreshing mud bath. It certainly is a unique experience – surely you haven't already tried volcano-dipping! The mud contains minerals acclaimed for their therapeutic properties.

**CARIBBEAN COAST**

### The Strange World of Mud Volcanoes

Mud volcanoes have little to do with traditional volcanoes. The phenomenon is due to gases emitted by decaying organic matter underground. The gases produce pressure which forces the mud upwards. It gradually accumulates to form a conical mud monticule with a crater at the top. The volcano continues to grow as long as mud is being pushed up to spill over the edge of the crater.

There are a number of mud volcanoes in Colombia, most of which are spread along the Caribbean Coast from the Golfo de Urabá in the west to the mouth of the Magdalena River in the east. The best known of all is El Totumo. It's reputedly the world's tallest mud volcano and also one of the most handsome, with its symmetrical conical shape. The majority of mud volcanoes, however, are just holes in the ground with occasional mud emissions.

Once you've finished your session, go down and wash the mud off in the lagoon, just 50m away.

The volcano is open from dawn to dusk and you pay a US$0.50 fee to have a bath. Should you like to continue your therapeutic session at home, big bottles filled with mud from the volcano can be bought at the site.

**Getting There & Away** El Totumo is on the border of the Atlántico and Bolívar departments, roughly equidistant between Barranquilla and Cartagena, which are now linked by a new coastal highway (buses are not allowed on this road). Cartagena is a far more popular jumping-off point for the volcano and has better public transport, and numerous tours.

The volcano is 52km northeast of Cartagena by the highway, plus 1km by a dirt side road branching off inland. To get to the volcano, go to Mercado Bazurto, from where hourly buses depart in the morning to Galerazamba. They go along the old Barranquilla road up to Santa Catalina and shortly after turn north onto a side road to Galerazamba. This side road crosses the coastal highway at Lomita Arena (US$1.50, 1½ hours) where you should get off. Ask the driver to let you off by the petrol station and walk along the highway 2.5km towards Barranquilla (30 minutes), then to the right 1km to the volcano (another 15 minutes). The last direct bus from Lomita Arena back to Cartagena departs at around 3pm.

A tour is a far more convenient and faster way of visiting El Totumo, and not much more expensive than doing it on your own. Several tour operators in Cartagena organise minibus trips to the volcano (US$10 transport only, US$13 with lunch in La Boquilla), which can be bought through popular backpacker hotels, including Casa Viena and Hotel Holiday.

### Jardín Botánico de Guillermo Piñeres

A pleasant half-day escape from the city rush, these botanical gardens *(admission US$2; open 9am-4pm Tues-Sun)* are on the outskirts of the town of Turbaco, 15km southeast of Cartagena. Take the Turbaco bus departing regularly from next to the Castillo de San Felipe and ask the driver to drop you at the turnoff to the gardens (US$0.75, 45 minutes).

From there it's a 20-minute stroll down the largely unpaved side road.

The 20-acre gardens feature plants typical of the coast, including two varieties of coca plant. While buying your entry ticket you get a leaflet which lists 250 plants identified in the gardens.

## MOMPÓS

☎ 5 • pop 26,000 • elevation 33m
• temp 28°C

Tucked a long way from the coast, about 200km southeast of Cartagena, Mompós is an exceptional town, with its own particular identity, unique in Colombia.

Traditionally known as Santa Cruz de Mompox, the town was founded in 1537 on the eastern branch of the Magdalena River, which in this part has two arms, Brazo Mompós and Brazo de Loba. Mompós actually lies on an island, the Isla Margarita. The town's name comes from Mompoj, the name of the last *cacique* (tribal head) of the Kimbay Indians, who inhabited the region before the Spanish Conquest.

Mompós soon became an important trading centre and active port, through which all merchandise from Cartagena passed via the Canal del Dique and the Magdalena to the interior of the colony. When Cartagena was attacked by pirates, Mompós served as a refuge for the families of the city's defenders.

The town flourished and several fair-sized churches and luxurious mansions were built. In 1810, Mompós proclaimed its independence from the Virreynato de la Nueva Granada, the first town to do so. Simón Bolívar, who stayed here for a short time during his liberation campaign, said: 'While to Caracas I owe my life, to Mompós I owe my glory'.

Towards the end of the 19th century, shipping on the Magdalena was diverted to the other branch of the river, the Brazo de Loba, bringing the town's prosperity to an end. Mompós has been left in isolation, living on memories of times gone by. Little has changed since. The town's colonial character is very much in evidence, as are the airs of a bygone era. It's fun to wander aimlessly about this tranquil town, discovering its rich architectural legacy and absorbing the old-time atmosphere.

Mompós has a long tradition in handworked filigree gold jewellery, which is of outstanding quality. Nowadays both gold and silver is used. The town's another speciality is its furniture. Despite the scarcity of timber in the region, several workshops still continue the tradition, making *muebles momposinos*, particularly rocking chairs, which are renowned nationwide.

The region around Mompós is known for the presence of guerrillas and there have been some cases of attacks on buses over recent years. Check the news before you head this way, and consider air travel if you feel uncertain.

## Information

The **tourist office** (*Plaza de la Libertad; open 8am-noon & 2pm-6pm Mon-Fri*) is in the Alcaldía building. Other possible sources of tourist information include Hotel La Casona and Hostal Doña Manuela (see Places to Stay later). They all can put you in contact with Chipi, who organises city tours and boat trips. Also, they can direct you to the artisans' workshops where you can see and buy local jewellery.

There are a couple of ATMs around Plaza de Bolívar, while the travel agency on the same plaza may change your US dollars.

**Compartel** (*Calle Real del Medio No 18-81*) is a new Internet facility. You can also try the older **Internet Café** (*Calle Real del Medio at Calle 19*), which also rents out bicycles.

## Things to See

Mompós' colonial architecture, which is in remarkable shape, has its own distinctive style known as the *arquitectura momposina*.

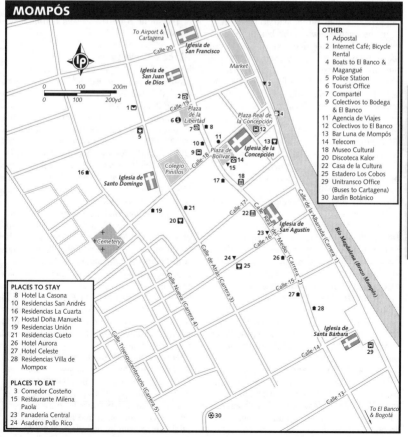

**MOMPÓS**

OTHER
1 Adpostal
2 Internet Café; Bicycle Rental
4 Boats to El Banco & Magangué
5 Police Station
6 Tourist Office
7 Compartel
9 Colectivos to Bodega & El Banco
11 Agencia de Viajes
12 Colectivos to El Banco
13 Bar Luna de Mompós
14 Telecom
18 Museo Cultural
20 Discoteca Kalor
22 Casa de la Cultura
25 Estadero Los Cobos
29 Unitransco Office (Buses to Cartagena)
30 Jardín Botánico

PLACES TO STAY
8 Hotel La Casona
10 Residencias San Andrés
16 Residencias La Cuarta
17 Hostal Doña Manuela
19 Residencias Unión
21 Residencias Cueto
26 Hotel Aurora
27 Hotel Celeste
28 Residencias Villa de Mompox

PLACES TO EAT
3 Comedor Costeño
15 Restaurante Milena Paola
23 Panadería Central
24 Asadero Pollo Rico

To Airport & Cartagena
Calle 20
Iglesia de San Francisco
Iglesia de San Juan de Dios
Market
Plaza de la Libertad
Plaza Real de la Concepción
Iglesia de la Concepción
Plaza de Bolívar
Colegio Pinillos
Iglesia de Santo Domingo
Cemetery
Iglesia de San Agustín
Calle de la Albarrada (Carrera 1)
Río Magdalena (Brazo Mompós)
Iglesia de Santa Bárbara
Calle 14
Calle 15
Calle 16 (Carrera 2)
Calle 17
Calle Real del Medio
Calle de Atrás (Carrera 3)
Calle Nueva (Carrera 4)
Calle Tresquicentenario (Carrera 5)
Calle 13
To El Banco & Bogotá

CARIBBEAN COAST

Central streets, and particularly the main thoroughfare, Calle Real del Medio, are lined with fine whitewashed colonial houses. Their characteristic feature is the elaborate wrought-iron grilles based on pedestals and topped with narrow, tiled roofs, that cover the windows. Some of the houses boast imposing carved doorways – a mark of the town's former glory and the wealth of its dwellers.

The best way to get a feel for the local architecture and atmosphere is to wander through the streets. Include in your walking tour the churches and museums listed in the following sections. Go to the market which spreads along the waterfront to the north of the Plaza Real de la Concepción, and visit the cemetery with its collection of old tombstones. And don't miss the small Jardín Botánico with lots of hummingbirds and butterflies. Knock on the gate to be let in.

In the evening, when the baking heat of day has slightly cooled, you'll see many locals relaxing in front of their homes, sitting in – of course – Mompós-made rocking chairs. Colonies of flying bats complete the scenery. At certain periods of the year there may be mosquitoes around, so have insect repellent at hand.

**Churches** Mompós has six churches, all of which date from colonial days and are fairly similar in style and construction. They are open only for mass, which may be just once or twice a week. The tourist office may be able to tell you about the churches' current opening hours.

The most interesting and unusual is the **Iglesia de Santa Bárbara**, facing the square of the same name next to the river. Built in 1630, the church has an octagonal Moorish-style bell tower circled by a balcony, unique in Colombian religious architecture.

**Iglesia de San Agustín** houses the famous, richly gilded Santo Sepulcro, which is one of the most prominent objects carried around the streets during the Holy Week processions. The statues of the saints in this church are paraded as well.

**Iglesia de San Francisco** is one of the oldest churches in town and has possibly the most interesting interior, particularly the lateral retables. **Iglesia de la Concepción** is the largest local church and is open more frequently than the others.

**Museums** There are two museums in the town, both set in colonial houses on the main street, Calle Real del Medio. **Casa de la Cultura** (admission US$0.50; open 8am-noon & 2pm-5pm Mon-Fri) displays memorabilia relating to the town's history. **Museo Cultural** (admission US$1; open 9.30am-noon & 3pm-5pm Tues-Fri, 9.30am-noon Sat & Sun), situated in the house where Simón Bolívar once stayed, features a small collection of religious art plus some objects related to Bolívar.

## Special Events

**Semana Santa**, or Holy Week, is taken very seriously in Mompós. The celebrations are very elaborate, comparable only to those in Popayán. The solemn processions circle the streets for several hours on Maundy Thursday and Good Friday nights. Many images of the saints from the town's churches are involved.

## Places to Stay

Except for Holy Week, you won't have problems finding somewhere to stay. There are a dozen hotels in town, most of them pleasant and friendly.

Among the cheapest options are the simple but well-kept **Residencias La Cuarta** (☎ 685 6040; Calle Nueva; rooms per person US$4) and the **Residencias Cueto** (Calle de Atrás; rooms per person US$4). Slightly more expensive is the **Residencias Unión** (☎ 685 5723; Calle 18 No 3-43; rooms per person US$5), in the same area.

Better accommodation options line Calle Real del Medio and they include **Residencias Villa de Mompox** (☎ 685 5208), the **Hotel Aurora** (☎ 685 5930), **Residencias San Andrés** (☎ 685 5886) and **Hotel Celeste**. Any of these will cost US$5 to US$6 per person in rooms with fan and bath.

**Hotel La Casona** (☎ 685 5307; Calle Real del Medio No 18-58; singles/doubles with fan US$7/12, with air-con US$15/25) is friendly and comfortable and has good rooms with bath.

**Hostal Doña Manuela** (☎ 685 5621; Calle Real del Medio No 17-41; singles/doubles with fan US$28/36, with air-con US$35/40) is the best place in town. It's set in a restored colonial mansion with two ample courtyards, and has a swimming pool and a restaurant. The pool can be used by nonguests (US$2.50).

## Places to Eat

Several rustic, riverfront restaurants in the market area provide cheap meals. Try the **Comedor Costeño** (*Calle de la Albarrada*), which has good *bocachico* fish and views over the river.

There are a number of restaurants in town, including the very central **Restaurante Milena Paola** (*Plaza de Bolívar*). For chicken, try **Asadero Pollo Rico** (*Calle 16 No 2-130*). **Panadería Central** (*Calle Real del Medio at Calle 16*) is good for breakfast. **Hostal Doña Manuela** has a reasonable restaurant.

## Entertainment

**Bar Luna de Mompós** (*Calle de la Albarrada*) is a great place for a drink and also organises tours. The open-air **Estadero los Cobos** (*Calle 16 No 2-133*) has cheap beer and plays good music till late. For some dancing, try **Discoteca Kalor** (*Calle de Atrás No 17-65*).

## Getting There & Away

**Air** West Caribbean Airways usually has flights between Cartagena and Mompós (US$50 one way, once a week), however, this service was suspended as we went to press. Check with travel agencies for information upon arrival.

**Bus & Boat** Mompós is well off the main routes, but can be reached relatively easily from different directions by road and river. Whichever way you come, however, the journey is time-consuming. As Mompós lies on an island and there are no bridges across Magdalena in the region, any trip involves a ferry or boat crossing.

Most travellers come to Mompós from Cartagena. Unitransco has a direct bus daily, leaving Cartagena at 7am (US$11, eight hours). It's faster to take a bus to Magangué (US$8, four hours; half a dozen departures per day with Brasilia), change to a *chalupa* (boat) to Bodega (US$2, 20 minutes, frequent departures until about 3pm) and continue by colectivo to Mompós (US$2.50, 40 minutes). There may also be direct chalupas from Magangué to Mompós.

If you depart from Bucaramanga, take a bus to El Banco (US$10, seven hours) and continue to Mompós by jeep or boat (either costs US$5 and takes about two hours); jeep is a bit faster but the trip is less comfortable.

In Mompós, Unitransco buses to Cartagena depart from near Iglesia de Santa Bárbara. Colectivos to Bodega and El Banco park on Calle 18 just off the Plaza de Bolívar. Boats to Magangué and El Banco anchor just off the Plaza Real de la Concepción.

CARIBBEAN COAST

# San Andrés & Providencia

This Colombian archipelago of small islands in the Caribbean Sea lies about 750km northwest of the Colombian mainland and only 230km east of Nicaragua. The archipelago is made up of two groups of islands: the southern group, with San Andrés as its largest and most important island; and the northern group, centred around the island of Providencia, 90km north of San Andrés. There are also several small cays away from the main islands scattered over an area of 350,000 sq km. Of these, the Cayo Bolívar, 30km southeast of San Andrés, and the Cayos de Albuquerque, 50km south of San Andrés, are the most significant.

The archipelago is a department in its own right, San Andrés y Providencia. Territorially, it's Colombia's smallest administrative unit, comprising an area of 45 sq km (57 sq km including the outer cays, reefs, atolls and sandbanks).

In 2000, the archipelago was declared the Unesco Seaflower Biosphere Reserve. The reserve includes the islands proper and a vast surrounding marine area of 300,000 sq km, which is equal to about 10% of the Caribbean Sea. The objective is to encourage conservation and environmental protection of an ecosystem of enormous biological diversity, and to foster sustainable development of the archipelago.

The islands were reputedly discovered in 1527 by Spanish explorers but they remained unsettled. The first inhabitants were probably the Dutch, who came to live on Providencia towards the end of the 16th century. In 1631, however, they were expelled by the English who effectively colonised the islands. They brought in black slaves from Jamaica and began to cultivate tobacco and cotton. By then the Spaniards seemed to realise the importance of the islands. They attacked the archipelago in 1635 and gained control, but were soon driven out.

Because of their strategic location, the islands provided convenient shelter for pirates waiting to sack Spanish galleons bound for home laden with gold and riches. In 1670, legendary pirate Henry Morgan established his base on Providencia and from here he raided both Panama and Santa Marta. Legend has it that his treasures are still on the

## Highlights

- Stay a while on Providencia, a small tropical paradise
- Go scuba diving with one of the diving schools on Providencia or San Andrés

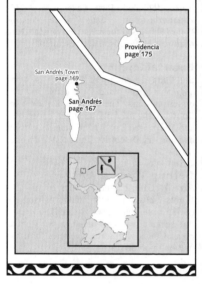

island, hidden in an underwater cave or in another secret place.

Shortly after independence, Colombia laid claim to the islands, although Nicaragua fiercely disputed its right to do so. The issue was eventually settled by a treaty in 1928, which confirmed Colombia's sovereignty over the archipelago.

However, the islands did not have any consistent form of transport or communication with the Colombian mainland until the 1950s. Until then, the English influence on the islands' language, religion and architecture remained virtually intact.

The situation began to change when a regular flight service from the Colombian mainland was established, and when San Andrés was declared a duty-free zone in 1954. Commerce and tourism attracted mainlanders to the islands, and many of them, finding conditions favourable, decided to settle, principally on San Andrés.

The population of San Andrés grew quickly, from 20,000 in 1973 to 55,000 in 1993, largely because of migration from the mainland. In the early 1990s, the local government introduced restrictions on migration to the islands in order to slow the rampant influx of people and preserve the local culture and identity. Yet, Colombian mainlanders account for two-thirds of San Andrés' population.

The native inhabitants are descendants of the Jamaican slaves and still speak thick Jamaican-English, although Spanish is now widely spoken throughout San Andrés and, to a lesser extent, in Providencia. Similarly, whereas Baptist congregations were once dominant, now Roman Catholicism is more prevalent.

The tourist and commercial boom has accelerated the process of cultural change. San Andrés has lost much of its original character and is now a blend of Latin American and English-Caribbean culture. Providencia has managed to preserve much more of its colonial culture, even though tourism is increasingly making inroads into the local lifestyle.

Nicaragua incessantly questions Colombian sovereignty over the islands. Colombia firmly rejects all such claims and at the same time does what it can to keep the *isleños* (islanders) content.

The government invests more money in the islands' development than it does on some of its other regions. Nevertheless, islanders don't seem too happy about the government flooding them with Spanish culture. Despite all this, they are friendly, patient and open to visitors.

There is virtually no local industry and agriculture is scarce. Almost everything except fish and some fruit and vegetables has to be shipped in and the islands are more expensive than mainland Colombia in terms of accommodation and most food items.

The climate is typical of the Caribbean islands, with average temperatures of 26° to 29°C. The rainy period is from September to December and (a less wet period) from May to June. Tourist season peaks are from late December to late January, during the Easter week and from mid-June to mid-July. All visitors staying more than one day are charged a local government levy of US$8 on arrival.

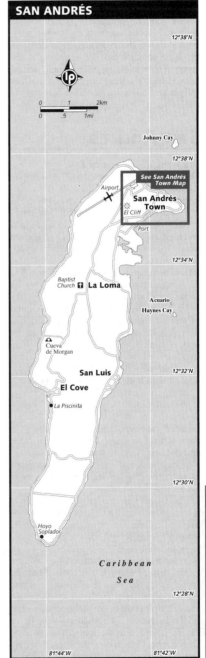

SAN ANDRÉS

The islands, especially Providencia, provide a good opportunity to experience the unique Caribbean ambience. The turquoise sea, extensive coral reefs and rich underwater life are a paradise for snorkellers and scuba divers. The easy-going pace, friendly locals, relaxed lifestyle, developed tourist facilities and general safety are other factors that make the islands an attractive destination.

# San Andrés

☎ 8 • pop 60,000 • temp 27°C

Shaped like a seahorse, the 27-sq-km San Andrés is the largest island of the archipelago, about 12.5km long and 3km wide. It is relatively flat, with a small, low range crossing the island from north to south, and reaching an altitude of 85m at the highest point. The island is largely covered with coconut palms. There are no rivers, only some intermittent streams during heavy rains. The island is surrounded by extensive *arrecifes* (coral reefs) and small cays.

The dominant urban centre and capital of the archipelago is the town of San Andrés (known locally as El Centro) at the northern end of the island. It has more than two-thirds of the island's population and is the principal tourist and commercial area, packed with hotels, restaurants and stores.

There are also two small towns: La Loma, in the central hilly region, and San Luis on the eastern coast. Both are far less tourist-oriented than San Andrés Town, and both have some fine English-Caribbean wooden architecture. A 30km scenic paved road circles the island, and several minor roads cross inland, providing sufficient infrastructure to get around the island.

The island has become one of the main tourist attractions for Colombians. Snorkelling and scuba diving are good and there are several diving schools on the island. Contrary to what might be expected, however, San Andrés is not surrounded by beaches; there are none along the western shore and those along the eastern coast are nothing special, apart from the beach in San Luis. There's a pleasant beach at the northern end of the island, in San Andrés Town, but it can be crowded in the tourist season. Possibly the best beach is on the islet of Johnny Cay just opposite San Andrés Town, though

it too fills with visitors (as tightly packed as a sardine can) in the high season.

The commercial aspect of San Andrés has been another magnet for Colombian visitors. However, measures to liberalise the economy, introduced in 1991, have caused San Andrés to lose a lot of its commercial attractiveness. Today, many products can be bought at competitive or even lower prices on the Colombian mainland. The duty-free bonanza seems to be over, and the main focus of local government now is tourism. Yet, this industry isn't in great shape either, mainly due to the political and economic crisis affecting the whole country. The number of tourists that visit the archipelago has dropped significantly over recent years.

In the past, San Andrés was often used by foreign travellers as a bridge between Central America and Colombia, but connections and air fares have changed. It's no longer a popular transit point, yet it still draws in foreign visitors seeking a taste of the Caribbean.

## Information

**Tourist Offices** The **Secretaría de Turismo Departamental** *(☎ 512 4284; Av Newball; open 8am-noon & 2pm-6pm Mon-Fri)* is in the building of the Gobernación, Piso 3. The Secretaría has a **tourist information desk** *(☎ 512 6110; open 10am-6pm daily)* on the ground floor of the airport terminal, but its opening hours can be unpredictable.

**Consulates** Both Costa Rica and Honduras have consulates in San Andrés Town. The Panamanian and Guatemalan consulates have closed. The **Honduran consulate** *(☎ 512 3235; Av Colombia)* is in the Hotel Tiuna; inquire at the reception desk. The **Costa Rican consulate** *(☎ 512 4938; Av Colombia)* is in the Novedades Regina shop, next door to the Calypso Beach Hotel. Get your visa beforehand on the mainland if you need one, as consuls do not always stay on the island and you may be stuck for a while waiting for one to return.

**Money** Some banks, including **Bancolombia** *(Av Costa Rica)* and **Banco Popular** *(Av Las Américas)*, exchange travellers cheques and cash. All banks marked on the San Andrés Town map advance cash on MasterCard and/or Visa; most have ATMs.

# SAN ANDRÉS TOWN

### PLACES TO STAY

2 Hotel Restrepo
4 Hotel Cacique Toné
5 Hotel Tiuna; Honduran Consulate
8 Calypso Beach Hotel
12 Posada Doña Rosa
13 Hotel Hernando Henry
14 Hotel Mary May Inn
23 Hotel Sol Caribe; Extasis

26 Hotel Lord Pierre; Banda Dive Shop
30 Apartahotel Tres Casitas
38 Sunrise Beach Hotel; Blue Deep
42 Hotel Aquarium Decameron; Diver's Dream

### PLACES TO EAT

1 Fisherman Place
15 Restaurante Sabor Caribe
37 Restaurante El Parqueadero
39 Restaurante La Regatta

### OTHER

3 Tourist Information Desk
6 Café Internet Sol
7 Avianca/Sam Office
9 Costa Rican Consulate
10 Avianca Post Office
11 AeroRepública
16 Banco de Bogotá
17 Bancafé; Giros & Finanzas
18 Intercontinental de Aviación
19 West Caribbean Airways
20 Cooperativa de Lancheros; Boats to Johnny Cay & Acuario; Semisubmarino Manatí
21 Internet & Coffee Island

22 Bancolombia
24 AMI
25 Centro Comercial New Point Plaza; Cambios y Capitales; Mundo Marino
27 Buzos del Caribe
28 Manolo's Bar
29 La Pollera Colorá
31 Mr Bongo's
32 Banco Popular
33 Telecom
34 Titán Intercontinental
35 Banco de Occidente
36 Islamic Centre
40 Karibik Diver
41 Biking Adventure
43 Semisubmarino Nautilus
44 Casa de la Cultura
45 Gobernación, Secretaría de Turismo Departamental; Restaurante Miss Bess
46 Adpostal

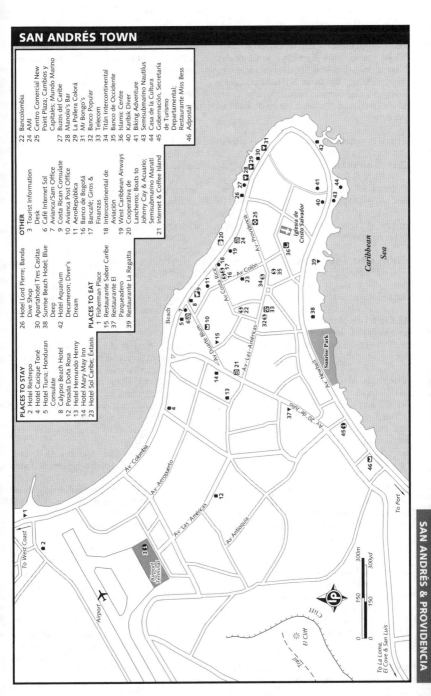

SAN ANDRÉS & PROVIDENCIA

San Andrés' *casas de cambio* include **Titán Intercontinental** *(Edificio Leda, Local 5, Av Providencia)*, **Cambios y Capitales** *(Centro Comercial New Point Plaza, Local 106, Av Providencia)* and **Giros & Finanzas** *(Centro Comercial San Andrés, Local 12, Av Costa Rica)*. Giros & Finanzas is the local agent of Western Union.

**Email & Internet Access** By Colombian standards, Internet access on San Andrés is slow and expensive. Facilities in San Andrés Town include **AMI** *(Av Colombia)*, **Café Internet Sol** *(Av Duarte Blum)* and **Internet & Coffee Island** *(Av 20 de Julio)*. Expect to be charged US$1.50 to US$2.50 per hour in any of them. Most San Andrés' Internet cafés are closed on Sunday.

## Things to See & Do

You will probably stay in San Andrés Town, but you may want to take some time to look around the island.

**El Cliff** This 50m cliff is a 20-minute walk southwest of the airport. It provides good views over the town and surrounding coral reefs.

**Cueva de Morgan** This is the cave where Welsh pirate Henry Morgan is said to have buried some of his treasure. The cave is 120m long, but it's filled with water, so you only see its mouth. You can't enter the cave and there's not much to see here anyway, yet the magic of alleged riches draws in plenty of tourists.

**La Piscinita** Also known as West View, shortly past El Cove, this is a good site for snorkelling, with calm water, plenty of fish and some facilities, including a restaurant with traditional local food and snorkel rental.

**Hoyo Soplador** At the southern tip of the island, the Hoyo Soplador is a sort of small geyser where sea water spouts into the air (up to 20m at times) through a natural hole in the coral rock. This phenomenon only occurs at certain times, when the winds and tide are right.

**La Loma** This small town, in the inner part of the island, is one of the most traditional places here. It is noted for its Baptist church, the first established on the island (in 1847). In 1896, it was largely rebuilt in pine brought from Alabama.

**San Luis** Another small town, San Luis, lies on the island's east coast and still boasts some fine traditional wooden houses. It has a nice beach, and the sea is good for snorkelling. The town is becoming pretty touristy and there's an increasing number of hotels and restaurants.

**Johnny Cay** This is a small coral islet about 1.5km north of San Andrés Town. It is covered with coconut groves and surrounded by a lovely, white-sand beach. The sunbathing is good, but be careful swimming here as there are dangerous currents. The island is a popular picnic spot and at times it can fill up far beyond capacity. Food is available. Boats to Johnny Cay go from the main San Andrés Town beach (US$3 return). If you go in the morning make sure that there's a boat to take you back in the afternoon.

**Acuario** Next to the Haynes Cay off the east coast of San Andrés, Acuario is another place frequently visited by tourists by boat (US$4 return). The surrounding sea is shallow and calm and good for snorkelling. If you forget to bring your snorkelling gear you can hire some in Acuario.

## Scuba Diving

Thanks to the beautiful coral reefs all around, San Andrés has become an important diving centre.

The water here is pleasantly warm and visibility is better than off the mainland coast. There are more than 35 different spots for diving around the island.

San Andrés has more than half a dozen diving schools. **Buzos del Caribe** *(☎ 512 8930;* **w** *www.buzosdelcaribe.com; Av Colombia)* is the oldest and largest facility. It has good equipment and a fine reputation, but it's expensive (US$250 for the open-water PADI or NAUI course).

**Karibik Diver** *(☎ 512 0101;* **e** *wernersai@ gmx.net; Av Newball)* is another reputable operator. Run by a German, this small school is also expensive (US$300), but provides quality equipment, personalised service and long dives.

## Diving on San Andrés & Providencia

San Andrés and Providencia provide excellent conditions for diving. Both islands are surrounded by extensive coral reefs with shallow reef valleys, impressive shelves, grooves and tunnels. The San Andrés barrier reef is 15km long. The Providencia reef is 32km long and encompasses an area of 255 sq km, making it Colombia's largest barrier reef.

Local coral reefs are particularly noted for sponges, which appear in an amazing variety of forms, sizes and colours. Marine life is rich and diverse, and includes barracudas, turtles, lobsters, rays, groupers and red snappers. A bonus attraction are two sunken ships off the San Andrés' shore.

Underwater visibility is remarkable, on average between 80ft and 100ft of sight throughout the year, though at some places it can be up to 150ft or even 200ft. This is largely due to the lack of currents and minimal erosion. The current-free waters also contribute to the safety of divers. The surface is also generally calm, particularly so on the west side of the islands. Last but not least, water temperature is admirably pleasant, ranging from 23° to 26°C.

Some cheaper schools include **San Andrés Divers** (☎ *513 0347, 513 0719;* Ⓦ *www.sanandresdivers.com*); **Divers Dream** (☎ *512 7701, 512 6923;* Ⓦ *www.diversdream.com; in Hotel Aquarium Decameron*) and **Banda Dive Shop** (☎ *512 2507;* Ⓔ *banda@sol.net.co; in Hotel Lord Pierre*).

### Organised Tours

The *Tren Blanco*, a sort of road train pulled by a tractor dressed up like a locomotive, departs every morning from the corner of Av Colombia and Av 20 de Julio to circle the island, stopping at several sights along the way (US$3, three hours). The same route can be done by taxi (US$18 for up to four people). Shorter or longer arrangements with taxi drivers are available.

**Cooperativa de Lancheros**, on the town's beach, provides trips to Johnny Cay (US$3) and Acuario (US$4), plus a combined tour to both cays (US$5). The Cooperativa also offers tours to the outlying islands, including Cayo Bolívar. These longer tours can also be organised through some of the diving schools.

The *Semisubmarino Manatí* is a specially designed boat with large windows in its hull. It departs once or twice daily (depending on demand) for a 1½-hour tour (US$12 per person) around the nearby reefs northeast of town. If you are not planning on scuba diving or snorkelling, this trip is probably the next best option for viewing the rich marine wildlife. Tickets for the trip can be bought from the office of the Cooperativa de Lancheros.

There's another boat, *Semisubmarino Nautilus*, which does similar trips from the wharf just west of the Casa de la Cultura (US$12, two hours). Tickets can be bought from **Mundo Marino** (☎ *512 1749; Centro Comercial New Point Plaza, Local 234*) or from the operator's desk at the wharf.

**Biking Adventure** (☎ *512 1853; Av Newball*) can organise cycling tours around the island. It offers several routes and provides good light bikes. The tours take two to three hours and cost US$14 per person, including bicycle, helmet and guide.

### Places to Stay

The overwhelming majority of the island's accommodation can be found in San Andrés Town, which has loads of hotels. Outside San Andrés Town, there are some hotels in San Luis, but elsewhere there are just a few places to stay.

San Andrés' hotels may occasionally fill up during short tourist peaks, but for most of the year there are likely to be plenty of vacancies. On the whole, accommodation on the island is more expensive than on the Colombian mainland. Prices rise during holiday seasons.

**Hotel Restrepo** (☎ *512 6744; US$5 per person*), just north of the airport terminal, is the cheapest place to stay and a favourite with foreign backpackers. It's basic, but friendly, and a bargain by San Andrés' standards. You pay US$5 per head, regardless of what room you get – some have their own bath, others don't, but all rooms have fans. Some rooms are considerably better than others, so have a look at a few before you book in and pay. There is a dining room serving breakfast, lunch and dinner (US$2 per meal).

**Posada Doña Rosa** (☎ 512 3649; Av Las Américas; singles/doubles/triples US$8/15/20) has eight rooms, all of which have baths and fans. It's good value and is handy if you need a more acceptable budget option than the Restrepo. It's also closer to the centre.

**Hotel Mary May Inn** (☎ 512 5669; Av 20 de Julio; singles/doubles/triples US$15/18/22) is small and friendly and one of the best inexpensive hotels in town. All of its eight rooms have baths, hot water and air-conditioning.

**Hotel Hernando Henry** (☎ 512 3416; Av Las Américas; singles/doubles with fan US$12/18, with air-con US$18/23) is another good affordable option, and all of its 30 rooms have private baths and balconies.

**Apartahotel Tres Casitas** (☎ 512 5873; Av Colombia; US$25 per person) is a reasonable option facing the sea. All rooms have air-conditioning and the price includes breakfast and dinner.

If money is no object, San Andrés has a wide choice of upmarket hotels, many of which offer packages that include bed and full board. This may work out reasonably cheaply if you're prepared to stick to the one place and the one kitchen.

Many of the top-end hotels are on the waterfront, which is certainly the most attractive location, providing views over the coral reefs, a fresh breeze, and a general feeling of being in the Caribbean. Hotels worth trying include the following.

**Hotel Lord Pierre** (☎ 512 7541; W www.lordpierre.com; singles/doubles/triples US$40/60/80) is a fine 60-room hotel with two swimming pools. Prices include breakfast and dinner.

**Hotel Aquarium Decameron** (☎ 512 6918; W www.decameron.com; Av Colombia; US$50-80 per person with full board) is an attractive complex of round cabañas (cabins) built on and off the shore.

**Sunrise Beach Hotel** (☎ 512 3977; W www.sunrisehotel.com; Av Newball; doubles with full board US$80-120) is the largest facility, offering 170 air-conditioned rooms which overlook the ocean, two restaurants, three bars, a disco, gym, sauna, swimming pool and tennis court.

Cheaper waterfront options include **Hotel Cacique Toné** (☎ 512 4251; doubles US$50-60), **Hotel Tiuna** (☎ 512 3235; doubles US$50) and **Calypso Beach Hotel** (☎ 512 2045; US$30 per person with breakfast & din-

ner). All are on Av Colombia overlooking the beach and the coral reefs beyond.

## Places to Eat

There are a number of simple restaurants in San Andrés Town which serve the usual set lunches and dinners for US$2 to US$3. Try **Restaurante El Parqueadero** (Av 20 de Julio). **Restaurante Miss Bess** (Av Newball), in the building of Gobernación, has budget lunches and some traditional dishes.

Meals in **Hotel Restrepo** are among the cheapest you can find in San Andrés. **Fisherman Place** (Av Colombia; open noon-5pm), near the Restrepo, offers local fare including crab soup (US$3), fried fish (US$3) and seafood stew (US$7).

**Restaurante Sabor Caribe** (Av Los Libertadores; mains US$4-5) is one of the best inexpensive restaurants serving seafood and other local specialities including rondón (a local soup prepared with coconut milk, vegetables, fish and sea snails).

San Andrés has a choice of upmarket restaurants, but they are not cheap, particularly not for seafood. Among the top-end options are **Restaurante La Regatta** (Av Newball) and **El Rincón de la Langosta** (km 7 of Carretera Circunvalar).

## Entertainment

There are several nightspots on Av Colombia between Hotel Lord Pierre and Hotel Aquarium Decameron. Popular bars with a dance floor include **Mr Bongo's**, **La Pollera Colorá** and **Manolo's Bar**, all on the waterfront.

Some of the upmarket hotels have discotheques, the most trendy (and expensive) of which is **Blue Deep** in Sunrise Beach Hotel, followed by **Éxtasis** in Hotel Sol Caribe San Andrés on Av Colón.

**Casa de la Cultura** (☎ 512 3403; Av Newball) organises Caribbean Evenings on Friday, which are folklore shows featuring live music, dance and local food.

## Getting There & Away

**Air** The airport is in San Andrés Town, a 10-minute walk northwest of the centre, or US$3 by taxi. Most major Colombian airlines service San Andrés (but no international ones). They include **Avianca/Sam** (☎ 512 3211; Av Colombia at Av Duarte Blum), **Intercontinental de Aviación** (☎ 512 2306; Av Colombia at Av Costa Rica), **AeroRepública**

(☎ 512 7325; Av Colón) and **West Caribbean Airways** (☎ 512 3184; Av Colombia).

International connections often change frequently. As we went to press, West Caribbean Airways was the only carrier flying direct between San Andrés and Central America. It has flights to and from San José (US$145/236 one way/30-day return) and Panama City (US$120/206). Both destinations are serviced three times a week, on Monday, Wednesday and Friday.

Avianca also services San José and Panama City, but its flights go via Bogotá and the air fares are considerably more expensive.

The airport tax on international departures from San Andrés is the same as elsewhere in Colombia: US$28 if you have stayed in the country less than 60 days and US$45 if you've stayed longer. You can pay in pesos or US dollars.

Avianca, Sam, Aces, AeroRepública and Intercontinental have flights to and from the major Colombian cities, including Bogotá (US$100 to US$140 one way), Cali (US$100 to US$150), Cartagena (US$80 to US$130) and Medellín (US$100 to US$140).

West Caribbean Airways operates the flights between San Andrés and Providencia (US$42 each way). There are three to seven flights daily (depending on the season) in each direction, serviced by 19-seater planes. In the high season, book in advance.

Flights between Central America and Colombia via San Andrés were once cheap and popular with travellers, but the routes and prices have changed and the flights are no longer that attractive. However, the San José–San Andrés–Cartagena route may still be worth the money, and gives you an opportunity to stay on San Andrés for a while (and perhaps visit Providencia).

If San Andrés is not a stopover on your Central–South American route, but you still fancy going there, check for package ads in weekend mainland papers. Good deals can be found in the low season.

**Boat** There are no ferries to the Colombian mainland or elsewhere. Cargo boats to Cartagena and Providencia don't take passengers.

### Getting Around

Local buses circle a large part of the island as well as ply the inland road to El Cove.

They are the cheapest way of getting around (US$0.50 per ride) unless you want to walk. They can drop you off close to all the major attractions.

A bus marked 'San Luis' goes from Av Colombia along the east-coast road to the southern tip of the island; this is the bus to take to San Luis and the Hoyo Soplador. The bus marked 'El Cove' runs along the inner road to El Cove, passing through La Loma. You can catch it on Av 20 de Julio and it will drop you in front of the Baptist church. It will also let you off within easy walking distance of Morgan's Cave and La Piscinita.

You can travel more comfortably by taxi, which can take you for a trip around the island (see Organised Tours earlier). Otherwise, hire a bicycle (from US$1.50 per hour or US$5 a day), motorcycle (from US$5 per hour or US$20 a day), scooter, car or jeep. They all can be hired at various locations throughout the town; many of the rental businesses are on Av Colombia. Shop around as prices and conditions vary.

# Providencia

☎ 8 • pop 4500 • temp 27°C

Traditionally known as Old Providence, Providencia is about 90km north of San Andrés. Covering an area of 17 sq km, it is the second-largest island of the archipelago, 7km long and 4km wide. It is a mountainous island of volcanic origin, much older than San Andrés. Its highest peak, El Pico, reaches 320m, and there are a few others slightly lower.

The island is partly covered with bushes and patches of mixed forest, whereas coconut palms grow mainly along the shores.

An 18km road skirts the island, and virtually the entire population lives along it in scattered houses or in one of several hamlets. Santa Isabel, a village at the island's northern tip, is the local administrative headquarters. Santa Catalina, a small island facing Santa Isabel, is separated from Providencia by the shallow Canal Aury, spanned by a pedestrian bridge.

Providencia is much less affected by tourism than San Andrés. English is still widely spoken and there's much English-Caribbean-style architecture to be seen. The locals are friendlier and more easy-going than those on San Andrés, and duty-free business is unknown.

Providencia has retained some of its lost paradise aura which is attracting Colombian tourists. Aguadulce on the west coast has already been converted into a tourist centre packed with hotels and restaurants. It has a diving school, motorcycle rental and several craft shops, and boat excursions are on offer. So far, the rest of the island is largely unspoiled, though the situation is changing.

## Information

There was a tourist office at the airport, but it was closed, so check whether it has reopened upon your arrival.

**Body Contact** (☎ 514 8283; Aguadulce • ☎ 514 8107; Santa Isabel) is a travel agency which can provide some tourist information and both of its branches have Internet service (but painfully slow). Another possible source of tourist information is Ecoastur, an ecological association based in Aguadulce.

Banco Agrario de Colombia in Santa Isabel gives cash advances on Visa card, whereas the ATM next door to the bank services MasterCard. The bank is open 8am to 1.30pm Monday to Thursday, 8am to 2pm Friday. There are no casas de cambio on Providencia, but some businesses (including a couple of supermarkets in Santa Isabel and Body Contact in Aguadulce) may change your dollars although we didn't find the rate attractive. It's best to bring enough pesos with you from San Andrés.

## Things to See & Do

In order to protect the habitat, a 10 sq km area in the island's northeast was declared Parque Nacional McBean Lagoon in 1995. About 10% of the park's area covers a coastal mangrove system just east of the airport, whereas the remaining 90% is an offshore belt that includes the islets of Cayo Cangrejo and Cayo Tres Hermanos. An 800m-long ecological path has been opened, enabling visitors to see different species of mangroves and the fauna that inhabits them. Access is from the sector known as Maracaibo.

The mountainous interior of the island, with its vegetation and small animal life, is attractive and provides pleasant walks. Probably nowhere else in Colombia can you see so many colourful lizards scampering through bushes. Beware of a common shrub

with spectacular horn-like thorns; ants living inside have a painful bite. Unfortunately, mosquitoes also abound on the island.

A trip to El Pico should not be missed. The most popular trail begins in Casabaja. Ask there for directions as several paths crisscross on the lower part (further up there are no problems), or ask in Casabaja for a guide. Some locals will take you up for a small charge, or take a tour (see Organised Tours later). It is a steady 1½-hour walk to the top. Carry drinking water because there is none along the way.

Snorkelling and diving are the island's other big attractions. The coral reefs around Providencia are more extensive than those around San Andrés and the turquoise sea is beautiful. You can rent snorkelling gear in Aguadulce (or better, buy some in San Andrés and bring it along). Diving trips and courses can be arranged with local operators (see Scuba Diving later).

Providencia's beaches are pleasant, but relatively small and narrow. The main ones are at Bahía Aguadulce, Bahía Suroeste and (the best) at Bahía Manzanillo at the southern end of the island. There are also some tiny, deserted beaches on the island of Santa Catalina, which is worth a look if only to see Morgan's Head – a rocky cliff in the shape of a human face, best seen from the water. There's an underwater cave at the base of the cliff. The shoreline changes considerably with the tides; the beaches during high tide get very narrow and some may totally disappear.

## Scuba Diving

Diving at Providencia is as good as at San Andrés and might be cheaper. There are three diving schools on the island: **Centro de Buceo Scuba Town** (☎ 514 8481), better known under its owner's name as Buceo Beda, in Pueblo Viejo; **Sonny Dive Shop** (☎ 514 8231) in Aguadulce; and **Sirius Dive Center** (☎ 514 8213) in Bahía Suroeste. All offer roughly similar programmes and prices, with an open-water or advance course for about US$180 to US$200. Most of the diving is done along the west side of the island.

## Organised Tours

**Body Contact** (☎ 514 8283) in Aguadulce offers tours and a range of other services including bicycle rental (US$7 a day), snorkel gear rental (US$5 a day), flight booking

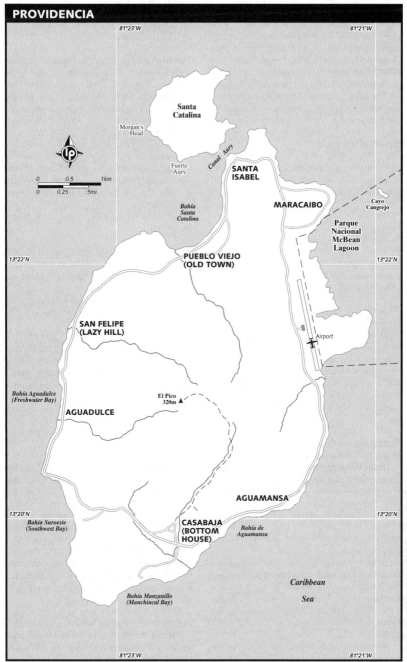

PROVIDENCIA

81°23'W
81°21'W

Santa Catalina

Morgan's Head

Canal Aury

Fuerte Aury

SANTA ISABEL

MARACAIBO

Cayo Cangrejo

Bahía Santa Catalina

Parque Nacional McBean Lagoon

13°22'N
13°22'N

PUEBLO VIEJO (OLD TOWN)

SAN FELIPE (LAZY HILL)

Airport

Bahía Aguadulce (Freshwater Bay)

AGUADULCE

El Pico 320m

13°20'N
13°20'N

Bahía Suroeste (Southwest Bay)

AGUAMANSA

CASABAJA (BOTTOM HOUSE)

Bahía de Aguamansa

Bahía Manzanillo (Manchincal Bay)

Caribbean Sea

81°23'W
81°21'W

and ticketing, Internet access and money exchange. Tours include a hike to El Pico (US$8 to US$12 per person) and boat excursions around the island (US$8 per person). Boats normally call at the Canal Aury, Morgan's Head and Cayo Cangrejo.

Horseback tours are organised by **Rodolfo** (☎ 514 8626) at Bahía Suroeste. A two-hour trip includes riding in the mountain and on the beach and costs US$7 per person.

## Special Events

The **Iguana Festival** is Providencia's major event, taking place in the last week of June. It includes music and dance, a parade of motorcycles and – you guessed it – a beauty pageant.

An annual event of a quite different nature is the crab migration in May to June, lasting for about a week or two. There may be many crabs on the move then, particularly in Aguadulce and South West Bay, and even roads can be closed to provide safe crossing for them.

## Places to Stay & Eat

Generally speaking, accommodation and food are expensive on Providencia, even more so than on San Andrés. The overwhelming majority of places to stay and eat are in Aguadulce, but there are also some lodging and eating facilities in other areas of the island, including Santa Isabel and Bahía Suroeste. They are detailed in the following sections by area, from north to south.

**Santa Isabel** There are a few reasonably cheap accommodation options here.

**Hotel Flaming Trees** (☎ 514 8049; US$12 per person) is the best choice in the area, offering nine spacious air-conditioned rooms with bath and fridge.

**Old Providence Hotel** (☎ 514 8369; beds in rooms with fan/air-con US$7/10) is really nothing stylish or special, but one of the cheapest options on the island.

Santa Isabel has a few budget eateries of which the **Restaurante El Isleñito** is perhaps the best value. Alternatively, try **Amalia's Kitchen**, which is nearly as good. Both are very rustic, but serve solid set meals for US$3, which is a bargain by Providencia's standards.

Better, but more expensive, is the open-air **Restaurante Eneida** on Santa Catalina

(just to the right off the bridge), which serves delicious fish and seafood for US$5 to US$10 a dish.

**Pueblo Viejo** Some 2km south of Santa Isabel, Pueblo Viejo is home to one of the cheapest places to stay on the island, the **Residencias Sofía** (☎ 514 8109; US$5 per person). There are very basic doubles and triples with shared facilities, and simple meals are available on request. To get there, get your driver to let you off by the SENA centre and take the rough track that branches off the main road next to the Escuela Santa Teresita del Niño Jesús and leads toward the seaside; the residencias is just 100m away, on the shore.

About 50m beyond the hotel is the Buceo Beda diving school.

**Aguadulce** This is a one-street tourist village lined with hotels, cabañas, restaurants, craft shops and tourist agencies. There are more than a dozen places to stay, with prices from about US$10 to US$40 per person. Some have their own restaurants and offer a bed-and-board package.

**Mr Mac** (☎ 514 8366; singles/doubles US$10/18), right in the middle of the village, is one of the cheapest hotels. It has just a few rooms, all of which are simple but have private baths and some overlook the beach.

**Posada del Mar** (☎ 514 8168; doubles with fan/air-con US$25/32), next to Mr Mac, is a good mid-range option. All rooms have baths and balconies with hammocks, and face the beach.

**Cabañas El Encanto** (☎ 514 8131; US$15 per person) is another affordable place and good value for money. Away a bit from the beach, it has comfortable airy rooms, all of which have bath, fan, air-conditioning and fridge. Add US$7 for breakfast and dinner in the reasonable in-house restaurant.

**Cabañas Miss Elma** (☎ 514 8229; doubles/suites US$40/60) is a bit more upmarket, particularly its spacious air-conditioned suites. It's right on the beach and has its own restaurant, which is fine but not cheap.

Eating is generally pricey in Aguadulce, though there are some basic eateries, including **Black & White** and **Estrellas del Mar**, which offer budget breakfasts (US$3), dinners (US$5) and beer (US$0.50 a bottle).

**Caribbean Place Donde Martín** is a pleasant place offering seafood and international cuisine. It is one of the best restaurants in town, but is also one of the most expensive ones.

**Bahía Suroeste** This is the second tourist destination after Aguadulce, with half a dozen places to stay and eat, plus some other facilities.

**Cabañas Miss Mary** (☎ 514 8454, 514 8206; doubles US$30) provides seven air-conditioned rooms right on the beach, plus a restaurant next door.

**South West Bay Cabañas** (☎ 514 8221; US$15 per person) on the main road, 400m back from the sea, has 16 large suites and a restaurant, and a variety of packages for up to eight days.

**Café Studio** on the main road is a three-table pleasant place that's run by a Canadian woman. It has excellent espresso and cakes, plus a full restaurant menu with some of the best food on the island (traditional local cuisine), and it's not that expensive.

**Manzanillo Bay** This beach is famous for the **Roland Roots Bar**, a charming open-air place amid coconut palms that serves fried fish (US$6) and beer, and offers hammocks under the roof (US$5). There are a few cheaper fish stalls around.

## Getting There & Away

West Caribbean Airways flies between San Andrés and Providencia several times per day (US$42 each way). You are most likely to buy a return in San Andrés before arriving. Buy your ticket in advance in the high season and be sure to reconfirm the return portion at Providencia's airport.

## Getting Around

Getting around the island is pretty straightforward as *colectivos* run along the circular road in both directions and charge US$1 for a ride of any distance. There are also pick-up trucks going around the island; they take passengers and charge the same as the colectivos.

Some pick-ups congregate at the airport waiting for incoming flights and can ask as much as US$2.50 for any distance. To avoid overcharging, walk a bit further from the airport and wave down a colectivo or pick-up passing along the road for the normal US$1 fare.

A taxi from the airport will cost US$5 to Santa Isabel and US$7 to Aguadulce.

A pleasant way of getting around the island is by bicycle, which can be rented from Body Contact (see Organised Tours earlier). You can also rent a motorcycle (US$15 a day) from a few small operators in Aguadulce and Santa Isabel.

# Northwest Colombia

In broad terms, the northwest is made up of two large regions, quite different in their geography, climate, people and culture. The first is an extensive stretch of low-lying rainforest along the Pacific Coast. This is one of the world's wettest regions, with annual rainfall reaching 10m in some areas, three times more than in the Amazon. In administrative terms it's the Chocó department, one of Colombia's poorest and least developed.

The region is sparsely populated, mainly by the black descendants of African slaves. Since there are almost no roads, transport is either by water or air and is expensive. Difficult to access, scarce in facilities and lacking any obvious tourist attractions (except for the coastal national park, Ensenada de Utría), the region has rarely been visited by Colombians, let alone foreigners.

More importantly, Chocó has suffered serious security problems over recent years due to the increasing presence of guerrillas and paramilitaries. The narrow coastal strip, including the national park, was considered the last relatively safe bit of the region, but this dramatically changed in mid-2002 when ELN guerrillas hit the area and took nearly 30 tourists hostage including, ironically, the director of the national park. Travel in the region is not recommended and we don't cover it in the book.

The other part of the northwest is comprised of the departments of Antioquia, Caldas, Risaralda and Quindío. Covering the rugged sections of the Cordillera Occidental and the Cordillera Central, it is a picturesque mountain region, crisscrossed by roads and sprinkled with little old towns with interesting architecture. The region is inhabited by the greatest proportion of whites in the country and is quite developed. Medellín, the capital of Antioquia, is the major urban centre for the whole of the northwest.

This region is attractive and relatively easy to explore due to a dense road array and good transport. Most of this land has an enjoyable mild climate and rich vegetation, and is pleasant to travel. Sadly, some areas of rural Antioquia, particularly its eastern part, can be unsafe because of the guerrilla and paramilitary presence. Check the safety conditions before you set off for the countryside.

## Highlights

- Explore Medellín – a thriving city with friendly people
- Visit Santa Fe de Antioquia, the region's oldest colonial town
- Enjoy high mountain volcano scenery in Parque Nacional Los Nevados
- Discover the fascinating world of coffee in Parque Nacional del Café
- Gaze in wonder at the stunning wax palms in the Valle de Cocora

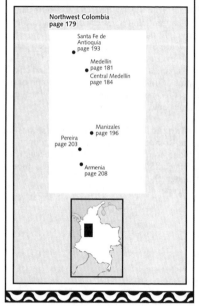

Northwest Colombia
page 179

Santa Fe de Antioquia
page 193

Medellín
page 181
Central Medellín
page 184

Manizales
page 196

Pereira
page 203

Armenia
page 208

Fortunately, the three coffee-growing departments of Caldas, Risaralda and Quindío, known collectively as the Zona Cafetera, are reasonably safe for travel.

# Antioquia

Antioquia is one of Colombia's largest, most populated and wealthiest departments. It has well-developed industry and agriculture, and some important natural resources, including gold deposits. About 70% of Colombian

To Turbo  76°W

To Cartagena
& Barranquilla

75°W

Frontino

**Antioquia**

Santa Rosa
de Osos

Yolombó

Río San Bartolomé

To Puerto
Berrio

**Parque Nacional
Las Orquídeas**

Santa Fe de
Antioquia

Entrerríos

Don Matías

Cisneros

San Pedro

Urrao

Girardota
Copacabana
Bello

**MEDELLÍN**

Itagüí   Envigado

Amagá

Caldas

Retiro

Marinilla

**Embalse
del Peñol**

Guatapé

Peñol

Rionegro

Granada

San Carlos

Río Nare

Caverna
del Nus

Río Magdalena

Puerto
Nare

Puerto
Serviez

6°N

6°N

Salgar

Concordia

Bolívar

Andes

Río Cauca

La Ceja

La Unión

Mesopotamia

Santa Bárbara

La Pintada

Abejorral

Sonsón

Argelia

Río Claro

Río Samaná Norte

Puerto
Triunfo

Puerto
Boyacá

**Chocó**

Jardín

Aguadas

Pácora

Norcasia

Marmato
Supía

Riosucio

Salamina

La Dorada

Puerto Salgar

**Risaralda**

Anserma

**Caldas**

Río La Miel

Belén de
Umbría

Neira

Honda

Apia

**MANIZALES**

Mariquita

**Parque
Nacional
Tatamá**

Marsella

Chinchiná

Santa Rosa
de Cabal

Armero

Líbano

**Parque
Nacional
Los Nevados**

Cambao

Guaduas

Andolaima

To Bogotá

5°N

5°N

La Virginia

**PEREIRA**

**Tolima**

Ambalema

**Cundinamarca**

Cartago

Filandia

**Quindío**

Salento

La Mesa

La Unión

Montenegro

**Parque
Nacional
del Café**

Armenia

Calarcá

**IBAGUÉ**

Roldanillo

Zarzal

La Tebaida

Cajamarca

Río Magdalena

To Bogotá

Sevilla

Girardot

Melgar

**Valle del Cauca**

0    15    30km

0    10    20mi

**IBAGUÉ**

Espinal

Cueva del
Cunday

4°N

Tuluá

To Cali

76°W

75°W

Guamo

To Neiva &
San Agustín

Cunday

4°N

gold comes from Antioquia, mainly from its northeastern part.

Antioquia's inhabitants, commonly known as *paisas*, have traditionally been reluctant to mix with either blacks or Indians, and the results are still noticeable today. In contrast to neighbouring 'black' Chocó, Antioquia has a high percentage of Creoles, and is popularly referred to as Colombia's 'whitest' department.

The paisas have had a more regional outlook than other Colombians, and their separatist attitudes have been expressed at various times during the region's history. They seem to have more respect for time, a notion still largely ignored in some regions. And while almost all the nation parties to salsa and *vallenato*, the paisas opt for the nostalgic tango.

The paisas are commonly regarded as being both more hard-working and entrepreneurial than their countrymen, and have good business skills. Perhaps it's no coincidence that the cocaine industry was founded and flourished in Antioquia.

Antioquia, or the *país paisa* (paisa country) as its inhabitants call it, is a picturesque rugged land, spread over parts of the Cordillera Occidental and the Cordillera Central. It's crisscrossed by roads linking little *pueblos paisa* (paisa towns) noted for their distinctive architectural style, characterised by the richly carved wooden adornments of their doors and windows.

## MEDELLÍN
**☎ 4 • pop 2,100,000 • elevation 1540m • temp 23°C**

The capital of Antioquia, Medellín, is Colombia's second largest city after Bogotá and a dynamic industrial and commercial centre. It is spectacularly set in the deep Aburrá Valley in the Central Cordillera, with a modern centre in the middle and vast slum barrios perched all over the surrounding slopes.

The Spaniards first appeared in the valley as early as 1541, but the town was not founded until 1616, when another wave of colonists arrived and decided to settle. Historians maintain that most of the group were Spanish Jews fleeing persecution.

The settlers divided the land into small haciendas which they farmed themselves, not following the common practice of using slaves. They were not really interested in having any commercial contact with their neighbouring regions, focusing instead on self-sufficiency as a way of life and development. The traditional values of the town's founders have endured till the present day.

The town was initially founded at what is now El Poblado and called San Lorenzo de Aburrá. In 1675, the name was changed to Villa de Nuestra Señora de la Candelaria de Medellín, and the settlement developed around the present-day Parque Berrío. By that time the town had 770 inhabitants.

Until the end of the 19th century there was little development, even though in 1826 Medellín replaced Santa Fe de Antioquia as the capital of the province. Only at the beginning of the 20th century did the town begin to expand rapidly, first as a result of the coffee boom in the region, and then as the centre of the textile industry. Medellín became a large metropolitan city in a relatively short period of time.

Medellín's colonial architecture – apart from a couple of historic churches – was never significant, and the precious little that did exist has virtually disappeared in the frenzy of recent growth. It's essentially a modern city, dotted with a forest of skyscrapers and a collection of brand-spanking-new shopping malls compared only to those in Bogotá.

Medellín is called the City of Eternal Spring, and the temperature is indeed very pleasant. There are, however, two rainy seasons, from March to May and September to November, and during these periods the weather is varied. The city is also known as the Capital of the Tango. It was here that Carlos Gardel, the legendary tango singer, died in an aeroplane crash in 1935.

Perhaps not a top travellers' destination, Medellín is a thriving city with an agreeable mild climate and stimulating and friendly people. It does have some good museums and other minor attractions, as well as developed tourist facilities. With its three large universities and half a dozen smaller ones, the city has a sizable student population, which gives it a vibrant and cultured air. Cultural activity is varied and interesting, surpassed only by that of Bogotá.

### Orientation
The city boasts a compact modern centre, packed with office buildings, hotels, banks and restaurants, and it's normally very busy

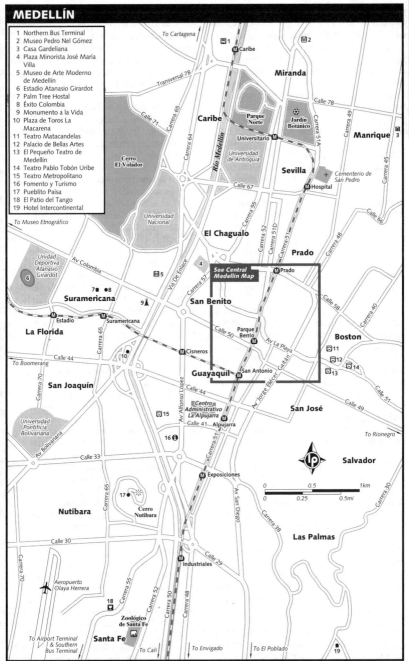

# MEDELLÍN

1 Northern Bus Terminal
2 Museo Pedro Nel Gómez
3 Casa Gardeliana
4 Plaza Minorista José María Villa
5 Museo de Arte Moderno de Medellin
6 Estadio Atanasio Girardot
7 Palm Tree Hostal
8 Éxito Colombia
9 Monumento a la Vida
10 Plaza de Toros La Macarena
11 Teatro Matacandelas
12 Palacio de Bellas Artes
13 El Pequeño Teatro de Medellin
14 Teatro Pablo Tobón Uribe
15 Teatro Metropolitano
16 Fomento y Turismo
17 Pueblito Paisa
18 El Patio del Tango
19 Hotel Intercontinental

during the daytime. Here is where you are most likely to stay and eat. About 4km south of the centre is El Poblado, an upmarket residential and commercial suburb, which has swiftly become a new flagship of the city's urban development. Here are most of the new shopping malls and the unrivalled centre of night entertainment with its clubs, bars and discos. New upscale restaurants are popping up around the place and companies are moving their offices here from the city centre.

Save for a few churches and a couple of museums in the centre, Medellín's tourist sights are scattered outside the central city area, so you need to use local transport. Fortunately, the city buses are relatively efficient and well organised, and there's also the metro, a fast city train (see Getting Around later).

In contrast to all other Colombian cities, Medellín has two bus terminals and two airports. Make sure you know which terminal you depart from. See the later Getting There & Away section for details.

Unlike in most other cities in the country, Medellín's central streets bear their proper names (not just their numbers) and are commonly known as such by the locals, especially in spoken language. In written language, in phone books or on business cards, the numerical system prevails, except for Avenidas.

## Information

**Tourist Offices** The tourist office, the **Fomento y Turismo** (☎ 232 4022; Av Alfonso López; open 7.30am-12.30pm & 1.30pm-5.30pm Mon-Fri) is in the Palacio de Exposiciones, about 1km southwest of the centre.

**Money** Banks that are likely to change travellers cheques at reasonable rates include the **Bancolombia** (Av Colombia at Carrera 52) and **Banco Santander** (Av Oriental at Av La Playa), both in the centre, and **Lloyds TSB Bank** (Calle 14 No 43-24) and **Banco Unión Colombiano** (Carrera 43A No 14-101), both in El Poblado. They may also change cash, but you will probably get similar or even better rates (and will save time) at casas de cambio.

There are half a dozen casas de cambio in Centro Comercial Villanueva, Calle 57 No 49-44; one of these, the **Giros & Finanzas**,

Local 241, is the agent of Western Union. Another collection of casas de cambio is in the Edificio La Ceiba, Calle 52 No 47-28; before changing at the Intercambio 1A on the ground floor, check the casas on the 3rd floor, which may pay better. Also check **Titán Intercontinental** (Edificio Coltejer, Local 103, Carrera 46 No 52-65), which exchanges both cash and travellers cheques.

Cash advances on credit cards are available at most of the major banks including all those marked on the map; most of them have ATMs.

**Email & Internet Access** There are plenty of Internet cafés across the centre and they are reasonably cheap, most costing around US$1 per hour. **Café Internet Doble-Click** (☎ 511 4183; Calle 50 No 43-135) is the largest facility (80 computers); it's open longer than most other places and is one of the very few that opens on Sunday.

Other central Internet cafés include **Internet Comfenalco** (☎ 511 2133; Av La Playa No 45-37), **Rapinet** (☎ 239 8435; Av La Playa No 43-51), **EMP.Net** (☎ 231 9090; Carrera 45 No 52-49) and **Internet Villanueva** (☎ 576 1110; Calle 57 No 49-44, Centro Comercial Villanueva, Local 9957).

**Dangers** Medellín has come to be known as the world's capital of cocaine trafficking, and home of Pablo Escobar and his violent Cartel de Medellín. It's no longer any of these; Escobar is long dead, the cartel is virtually dismantled and the cocaine industry has moved elsewhere. Yet Medellín isn't the safest place on the globe; like any large Colombian city, it has security problems. It is notorious for crime, but most of it happens in the poor outer suburbs. The city centre appears quite safe during the day, but keep your evening strolls to a minimum. If you're going to party at night, use taxis.

## Museums

Medellín has a dozen museums, the clear star attraction of which is the Museo de Antioquia.

**Museo de Antioquia** Founded in 1881, the Museum of Antioquia (☎ 251 3636; Carrera 52 No 52-43; adult/student US$2.50/ 1.50; open 9.30am-5pm Mon & Wed-Fri, 10am-4pm Sat & Sun) is Colombia's second oldest museum and one of the most significant. In its spacious new home, the 1932 Palacio Municipal, this museum features pre-Columbian, colonial, independence and modern art collections, spanning Antioquia's 400-year-long history.

The museum's highlight is Fernando Botero's recent donation of 92 of his own works and 22 works by other international artists. Additionally, his 23 large bronze sculptures have been placed in front of the museum, in what is known as Plazoleta de las Esculturas. Born in Medellín in 1932, Botero is the most internationally renowned Colombian contemporary artist.

**Casa Museo Pedro Nel Gómez** This museum (☎ 233 2633; Carrera 51B No 85-24; adult/student US$2/1.25; open 9am-noon & 2pm-5pm Mon-Fri, 9am-noon Sat) is dedicated to another beloved son of Medellín, Pedro Nel Gómez (1899–1984), and set in the house where the artist lived and worked. The museum has an extensive collection (nearly 2000 pieces) of his watercolours, oil paintings, drawings, sculptures and murals. Pedro Nel Gómez is said to have been Colombia's most prolific artist. The museum is 3km north of the city centre. The Aranjuez bus from the centre will drop you off at the museum's door.

**Museo de Arte Moderno de Medellín** Inaugurated in 1978, this museum, often referred to as MAMM (☎ 230 2622; Carrera 64B No 51-64; admission US$1.50; open 10.30am-7pm Mon-Fri, 10am-5pm Sat), stages changing exhibitions of contemporary art. To get there from the city centre take any bus going west along Av Colombia from Parque Berrío, or walk for 15 minutes.

**Museo Etnográfico Miguel Ángel Builes** The Ethnographic Museum (☎ 264 2299; Carrera 81 No 52B-120; admission by donation; open 8am-noon Tues-Fri) presents Indian artefacts from various regions of Colombia that were collected by missionaries. Objects from the Pacific Coast and the Amazon are best represented. The museum is about 4km west of the city centre, off the end of Av Colombia. To get there take the bus marked Circular 300/301 from Av Oriental or the Floresta–Estadio bus from Parque Berrío.

**Museo de Antropología** This university museum (☎ 210 5180; Calle 67 No 53-108; admission free; open 8am-6pm Mon-Thur, 8am-4pm Fri, 9am-1pm Sat) is in the campus of the Universidad de Antioquia, 2km north of the centre. It has a collection of pre-Columbian pottery from different regions of the country. While you're here, take a look at the Monumento al Creador de la Energía, a sculpture by Rodrigo Arenas Betancur that is also at the university (see the Public Art section).

**Museo El Castillo** This is a mock-Gothic castle built in 1930 in El Poblado. It was home to an Antioquian landowner, but after his death, it was donated to the state and opened as a museum (☎ 266 0900; Calle 9 Sur No 32-269; adult/student US$2/1; open 9am-11.30am & 2pm-5pm Mon-Fri, 9am-11.30am Sat). It contains all the original family belongings, furniture and artworks that came from all around the world. All visits are guided and take about half an hour. There may be recitals on some days in the castle's auditorium.

The museum is 5km south of the city centre. Take the El Poblado–San Lucas bus from Parque Berrío, get off at Loma de Los Balsos and follow the side street downhill for five minutes to the museum. Instead of returning the same way, you can walk further down to Carrera 43A where there are plenty of buses going to the centre.

**Museo Filatélico** The philatelic museum (☎ 251 5579; Calle 50 No 50-21; admission free; open 10am-6pm Mon-Fri) in the Banco de la República building in Parque Berrío, has a collection of Colombian and foreign stamps.

## Churches
**Catedral Metropolitana** The gigantic neo-Romanesque cathedral (Calle 56 at Carrera 48) overlooking Parque de Bolívar is thought to be the biggest South American brick church. Designed by various architects including Frenchman Charles Carré, construction began in 1875 and only in 1931 was it completed; 1,200,000 bricks were used. Its spacious but dim interior boasts Spanish stained-glass windows, a German-made organ featuring 3478 pipes and a few paintings by Gregorio Vásquez de Arce y Ceballos. Don't be misled if the cathedral's front door is locked – check the side doors.

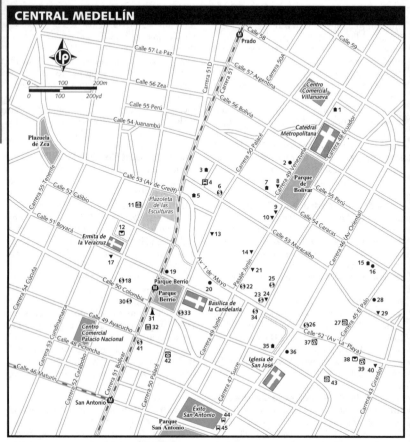

**CENTRAL MEDELLÍN**

**Basílica de la Candelaria** This basilica *(Carrera 50 at Calle 51)* facing the Parque Berrío is Medellín's most important historic church. It was built in the 1770s and did the honours as the city's cathedral from 1868 till 1931. Inside there's a much venerated figure of the Señor Caido (Fallen Christ) in the left aisle, and an interesting main retable. The image of the city's patron saint, Nuestra Señora de la Candelaria, watches over the faithful from above the high altar.

**Ermita de la Veracruz** This church *(Calle 51 at Carrera 52)* is regarded as the city's oldest. Its construction was reputedly begun in 1682, but it wasn't until 1803 that it was completed and inaugurated. It has a fine stone facade and charming interior.

**Jardín Botánico Joaquín Antonio Uribe**
The botanical garden *(☎ 233 7025; Carrera 52 No 73-182; metro Estación Universidad; admission US$1; open 9am-5pm Mon-Sat, 10am-5pm Sun)* is close to the Universidad de Antioquia and is easily accessible by metro. Opened in 1978, the garden has 600 species of trees and plants, a lake, herbarium, auditorium and the Orquideorama where an orchid display is held in March and April.

**Zoológico de Santa Fe**
Established on the grounds of an old hacienda, the zoo *(☎ 235 1326; Carrera 52 No 20-63; admission US$2; open 9am-5pm daily)* specialises in Colombian fauna and has 1350 animals and birds representing 230 species.

## CENTRAL MEDELLÍN

**PLACES TO STAY**
1   Hotel El Capitolio
3   Hotel Amarú
5   Hotel Nutibara
7   Hostal Odeón
15  Hotel Plaza Caracas
35  Hotel Gómez Córdoba

**PLACES TO EAT**
8   Restaurante La Estancia
9   El Parador de Junín
10  Salón Versalles
13  Restaurante Naturalista
    Palased
14  Restaurante Agua Clara
17  Restaurante Vegetariano
    Govinda's
21  Restaurante Hacienda Real
24  Restaurante Hatoviejo

29  Restaurante Vegetariano Trigo
    y Miel
40  Restaurante Vegetariano
    Paracelso

**OTHER**
2   Aviatur
4   Minibuses to José María
    Córdoba Airport
6   Bancafé
11  Museo de Antioquia
12  Avianca Post Office & Airline
    Office
16  Turismo Maya Londoño
18  Bancolombia
19  Murals by Pedro Nel Gómez
20  Viajes Veracruz
22  Bancolombia
23  Edificio La Ceiba

25  Titán Intercontinental
26  Banco Santander
27  EMP.Net
28  Centro Colombo Americano
30  Banco de Bogotá
31  La Gorda
32  Museo Filatélico
33  Banco Popular
34  Banco de Occidente
36  Realturs
37  Internet Comfenalco
38  Adpostal
39  Rapinet
41  Bancafé
42  Telecom
43  Café Internet Doble-Click
44  Guayabal bus stop
    (Ruta 143)
45  Trinidad bus stop (Ruta 160)

Unfortunately, some cages are too small for their residents. Casa Museo Santa Fe, in the grounds, is what once was the principal house of the hacienda. Its rooms feature some colonial objects and antiques. On Sunday the zoo is virtually besieged by families.

### Cerro Nutibara

This is an 80m-tall hill, 2km southwest of the city centre. There's a lookout on the summit, which provides good vistas over the city. The Pueblito Paisa, a miniature typical Antioquian township, has been built near the top and is home to several handicraft shops and a few food outlets.

The Parque de las Esculturas (Sculpture Park) was established in 1984 on the slopes of the hill. It contains modern abstract sculptures by South American artists, including some prominent names such as Edgar Negret, Jesús Soto and Carlos Cruz Díez. The Guayabal bus from Av Oriental in the city centre passes by the foot of the hill, or go by taxi (US$2).

### Cementerio de San Pedro

Medellín's old cemetery (Carrera 51 No 68-68; metro Estación Hospital; open 7.30am-5.30pm daily) was established in 1842. It's a collection of ornate historic tombstones, intricate sepulchral chapels and mausoleums, and it's well worth seeing if such things interest you. It's easily accessible by metro.

### Public Art

Medellín is a city of public art, particularly sculptures and murals that grace squares, streets and buildings. In fact, it has more public sculptures per area than any other Colombian city, including Bogotá.

Fernando Botero has the largest number of his works displayed outdoors. Apart from 23 sculptures in front of the Museo de Antioquia, there's a massive bronze woman's torso known as **La Gorda**, in front of the Banco de la República in Parque Berrío.

There are also three sculptures in Parque San Antonio, including the **Pájaro de Paz** (Bird of Peace). Quite ironically, this sculpture was seriously damaged by a bomb placed by guerrillas. In a symbolic response to the violent act, the damaged bird has been left untouched, however, a new one has been placed alongside.

Rodrigo Arenas Betancur (1919–95), Colombia's No 1 monument designer, has also quite a collection of his sculptures. His 14m-high **Monumento a la Vida** (Monument to Commemorate Life; Centro Suramericana, Av Colombia at Carrera 64B), unveiled in 1974, adorns a fountain. Probably even more impressive is **Monumento a la Raza** (Centro Administrativo La Alpujarra, Calle 44). Another interesting sculpture by Betancur is the **Monumento al Creador de la Energía**, in the Universidad de Antioquia.

Pedro Nel Gómez has left behind a number of murals. Probably the best known of these is the 1956 al fresco work depicting Antioquia's history, displayed in two long showcases on Carrera 51 at Calle 51, just off Parque Berrío. His other murals can be seen in the Museo de Antioquia; the Banco

Popular, Calle 51 No 50-54; the Biblioteca Pública Piloto, Carrera 64 No 50-32; and the Universidad Nacional and the Universidad de Antioquia.

## Paragliding

Medellín is regarded as the main centre of Colombian paragliding. It's home to some of the best national glide pilots, and gliding here is more popular than in any other Colombian city, Bogotá included. Thanks to the rugged topography and favourable winds, the city and the region provide good conditions for gliding.

The **Boomerang** (☎ 412 3886; e piloto_x@hotmail.com; Calle 38B No 79-16, Barrio Laureles) is one of the best local gliding schools, with highly experienced pilots and good equipment. It offers courses (about US$300 for a week-long course), equipment rental and tandem flights over the city (spectacular views) with a skilled pilot (US$25). No previous gliding experience is necessary for tandem flights.

Alternatively, you can try **Luisito Escuela** (☎ 388 0493; e luisitoescuela@hotmail.com), which is also a reputable school that offers tandem flights and courses as well as equipment rental. Its flights are in the mountainous area 30km north of Medellín. A tandem flight with a skilled pilot, taking up to 45 minutes, will cost about US$25.

## Organised Tours

There are plenty of travel agencies in the city, some of which operate tours. However, there are not many tours on offer these days because tourism (both national and international) has slumped significantly over recent years. You may need to look around to check who is currently running tours and if they already have some potential clients or fixed departure schedules. If not, they could organise a tour just for your party, but it may be costly if your group is small.

Operators to try include **Realturs** (☎ 511 6000; Carrera 46 No 50-28), **Viajes Veracruz** (☎ 511 7739; Calle 52 No 49-96), **Turismo Maya Londoño** (☎ 231 4666; Calle 54 No 45-29) and **Aviatur** (☎ 512 3899; Carrera 49 No 55-25). Their offer should include a half-day city tour (US$6 to US$10), which may be a quick and convenient way to glimpse some attractions away from the centre, such as the Pueblito Paisa and El Poblado.

One of the most popular tours out of Medellín is the so-called Circuito de Oriente (see that entry later in this chapter), to the southeast of Medellín, which includes a variety of cultural and natural attractions. The tour agents have some standard routes, or they can put together a tour to suit your interests.

It's commonly a half- or full-day trip, with lunch en route, and can be done by car or minibus, depending on the number of tourists. The price largely depends on the route and conditions; budget for US$25 to US$50 per person, including lunch.

## Special Events

**Tangovía** is tango night, which springs to life on Carrera 45 (Av Carlos Gardel) in the suburb of Manrique on the last Friday of February, May, August and December (from around 7pm until midnight), when you can listen and dance to these nostalgic rhythms.

The bullfight season, **Feria Taurina de la Macarena**, takes place in January and February at the Plaza de Toros La Macarena, the 11,000-seat, Moorish-style bullring built between 1927 and 1944. It's on Autopista Sur on the corner of Calle 44.

Still rather modest, the **Festival Internacional de Jazz** in June features several concerts presenting some local and international groups.

The **Feria Nacional de Artesanías** is a huge craft fair held in July at the Atanasio Girardot sports complex. It attracts artisans from around the country and is a good opportunity to buy crafts at bargain prices.

Held for a week in early August, the **Feria de las Flores** is Medellín's biggest event. Its highlight is the **Desfile de Silleteros** on 7 August, when up to 400 *campesinos* (peasants) come down from the mountains and parade along the streets carrying *silletas* full of flowers on their backs.

The **Alumbrado Navideño** is a colourful Christmas illumination of the city, with thousands of lights strung across the streets and parks. The lights stay on from 7 December to 6 January.

## Places to Stay

Medellín's major traveller haunt is **Palm Tree Hostal** (☎ 260 2805; w www.palmtreemedellin.com; Carrera 67 No 48D-63; metro Estación Suramericana; dorm beds US$5).

Managed by the travellers themselves, this relatively new guesthouse offers a range of facilities typical of a Western backpacker hostel, including laundry service, Internet access, bicycle rental, book exchange and the use of the kitchen, plus free coffee. It has half-a-dozen, four-bed dorms without bath and one room with bath, with a total capacity of 31 beds. The hostel is in the suburb of Suramericana, about 1.5km west of the centre, easily accessible by metro or by bus along Av Colombia. A taxi from either bus terminal is US$2.

The city centre is the main area of budget accommodation. There are plenty of cheap hotels here, though nothing as traveller-friendly or popular as the Palm Tree Hostal. Many central cheapies double as love hotels and prices double on weekends.

**Hotel Gómez Córdoba** (☎ 513 1676; Carrera 46 No 50-29; singles/doubles US$6/9) is reasonably orthodox and clean, and one of the few that attracts travellers. It has rooms with bath and hot water.

**Hostal Odeón** (☎ 511 1360; Calle 54 No 49-38; singles/doubles/triples US$9/15/22) is small, quiet, very central and inexpensive. It has rooms with bath, fan and fridge.

**Hotel El Capitolio** (☎ 512 0004; Carrera 49 No 57-24; singles/doubles/triples US$20/24/28), behind the cathedral, has recently been wholly renovated and is not a bad bet. It has rooms with bath and fan, and the prices include breakfast.

**Hotel Plaza Caracas** (☎ 512 08 36; Calle 54 No 45-17; singles/doubles/triples US$22/30/36) is a small establishment with a historic touch, providing fair-sized rooms with bath and breakfast.

**Hotel Amarú** (☎ 511 2155; Carrera 50A No 53-45; singles/doubles/triples US$30/35/40) is a good choice if you're looking for somewhere more upmarket, yet affordable. This 16-storey hotel has been fully refurbished. It has 84 comfortable, quiet, air-conditioned rooms, and the prices include breakfast.

**Hotel Nutibara** (☎ 511 5111; W www .hotelnutibara.com; Calle 52A No 50-46; singles/doubles/suites US$50/60/70) is the best central option. Built in the 1940s, it combines its historic character with modern facilities. It has 150 spacious air-con rooms, original lifts, a swimming pool, gym and two restaurants. Choose a room on one of the upper floors for better views and less

noise. A buffet breakfast is included in the room rates.

**Hotel Intercontinental** (☎ 266 0680; W www.interconti.com; Calle 16 No 28-51; doubles US$120) is the city's ultimate luxury. This five-star hotel is quite far from the city centre, in the hills of Las Palmas.

## Places to Eat

Like every big city, Medellín has hundreds of places to eat for every budget all around town. The centre is literally flooded with restaurants, snack bars and cafés and provides some of the cheapest meals.

**Restaurante La Estancia** (Carrera 49 No 54-15), in Parque de Bolívar, is one of the cheapest places to eat. It's not very clean, good or pleasant but it has set meals for just US$1. The attached bar serves *aguardiente* at extremely low prices, which makes the whole place noisy, crowded and rather bizarre.

Hunters for the cheapest snacks will probably welcome the new chain of snack bars promoted as '*todo* (everything) a $350', where any snack costs just 350 pesos. These places tend to change frequently but you'll find several of them in the centre, including **El Parador de Junín** (Pasaje Junín No 53-53), which also serves budget set meals (US$1.50) and breakfasts (US$1).

Vegetarians have several budget options, among them the **Restaurante Vegetariano Govinda's** (Calle 51 No 52-17); **Restaurante Naturalista Palased** (Carrera 50 No 52-50, Centro Comercial Unión Plaza); **Restaurante Vegetariano Trigo y Miel** (Calle 53 No 43-54); and **Restaurante Vegetariano Paracelso** (Av La Playa No 43-17). Any of these will offer a hearty set lunch for about US$2.

The pedestrian Pasaje Junín is packed with cafés and restaurants, some of which are attractively set on the 1st floor overlooking the street.

**Salón Versalles** (Pasaje Junín No 53-39) is a two-level restaurant-cum-café invariably popular with the locals. It has a varied menu including tasty set lunches (US$3), delicious Argentine and Chilean *empanadas* (US$1 each) and a wide choice of high-calorie cakes and pastries.

**Restaurante Hacienda Real** (Pasaje Junín No 52-98; mains US$4-6) serves typical local food, including the omnipresent *bandeja paisa*. It's a pleasant place for lunch or dinner or for just watching the world go by from a wide balcony while sipping a beer. It may have live music on weekends.

**Restaurante Agua Clara** (*Pasaje Junín No 52-145; mains US$4-6*) is quite similar to the Hacienda Real. It also cooks regional food and it too has a band playing local music on weekends.

**Restaurante Hatoviejo** (*Carrera 47 No 52-17; mains US$6-8*) is one of the best places in the area. Hatoviejo serves regional dishes and grilled meats.

## Entertainment

Check local dailies, *El Colombiano* and *El Mundo*, for what's going on. Alternatively, get a copy of the monthly *Opción Hoy* (US$1), which lists art exhibitions, theatre, concerts, art-house cinema, and sports and cultural events. You can read it online at w www.supernet.com.co/opcionhoy.

**Cinema** Medellín has about 20 commercial cinemas (some of them multiplexes) screening the usual Hollywood repertoire. For more thought-provoking fare, check the programmes of the *cinematecas*, the best known of which is the one in the **Museo de Arte Moderno** (☎ 230 2622; *Carrera 64B No 51-64*). Others are in the **Museo de Antioquia** (☎ 251 6888; *Carrera 52 No 52-43*) and the **Centro Colombo Americano** (☎ 513 4444; *Carrera 45 No 53-24*).

**Theatre** There are around 10 theatres in Medellín, and more theatre groups work without a permanent home.

**Teatro Matacandelas** (☎ 239 1245; *Carrera 47 No 43-47*) is one of the best experimental groups in town, whereas **Teatro Pablo Tobón Uribe** (☎ 239 2674; *Carrera 40 No 51-24*) is Medellín's major mainstream theatre. **El Pequeño Teatro de Medellín** (☎ 269 9418; *Carrera 42 No 50A-12*) has a varied repertoire, combining the traditional with the contemporary.

**Teatro Metropolitano** (☎ 232 4597; *Calle 41 No 57-30*), inaugurated in 1987, is the largest and most modern city theatre, with an auditorium to seat 1650 patrons. It's used to stage a variety of cultural acts, including concerts, opera, ballet and other presentations by local and visiting groups. It's home to Medellín's Philharmonic Orchestra.

**Teatro de la Universidad de Medellín** (☎ 256 9153; *Carrera 87 No 30-65*) is a university theatre serving as a stage for a range of student artistic presentations, not just theatre performances.

**Classical Music** Both **Teatro Metropolitano** and **Teatro de la Universidad de Medellín** present concerts of classical and contemporary music. Another regular stage for concerts and recitals is the 300-seat Sala Beethoven in the **Palacio de Bellas Artes** (☎ 239 4820; *Carrera 42 No 52-33*).

**Tango** Medellín is renowned for its tango music, with roots dating back to 1935 when the famous Argentine tango singer Carlos Gardel died here in a plane crash. The **Casa Gardeliana** (☎ 212 0968; *Carrera 45 No 76-50*) in Barrio Manrique was for years the main tango venue, hosting tango bands and dance shows. It still has them from time to time, though now it's basically a small tango museum, featuring memorabilia related to tango and Carlos Gardel.

**El Patio del Tango** (☎ 351 2856; *Calle 23 No 58-38*) is now the tango's major stage, decorated in a Buenos Aires style and serving juicy *churrascos*. Tango shows are on Friday and Saturday nights.

**Nightlife** The major scene of night-time entertainment is the Zona Rosa in El Poblado, which spreads approximately between Calles 9 and 10A, and Carreras 36 and 42, drawing in the 'beautiful people' and their cars from across the city and beyond. The area is packed with restaurants, cafés, clubs, bars, pubs and discos, which become vibrant after 10pm or later, particularly on weekend nights. A taxi from the centre will bring you to the Zona Rosa for US$2.

The best approach is to leisurely stroll about the quarter, stopping for a drink or two en route in some of the numerous open-air bars, before choosing a disco or bar and plunging into the action. There are plenty of them and the scene changes quickly. A disco that's 'in' one month can be almost dead the next. The following are just a few places that were hugely popular at the time of writing. Check if they still are and look for new crowd favourites.

**La Cantera** (☎ 314 0287; *Calle 10A No 38-20*) is new but has swiftly become one of the most popular haunts, with good, mostly Latin music and excellent sound quality.

**Sam Pués** (☎ 266 9404; Calle 10A No 40-37) is another trendy disco-bar with Caribbean music and an often great atmosphere.

**República** (☎ 266 2627; Calle 10 No 40-15) is also a primarily Latin affair, pumping with salsa, *merengue* and the like.

**Blue** (☎ 266 3047; Calle 10 No 40-20), right across the road from República, supplies rock music in a sober, decoration-free interior.

**Berlín** (☎ 266 2905; Calle 10 No 41-65) is a lively bar with pool tables, rock classics and reasonably cheap beer.

Regardless of how good the discos in the Zona Rosa are, most travellers consider that the best one is not here, but much further south, in Itagüí. It's **Mango's** (☎ 277 6123; Carrera 42 No 67A-151), on Autopista Sur, a disco with charming decor, five bars and a ragbag of good music. It's really large (1500 people can squeeze in) and expensive, but despite that it's hugely popular and often full.

If you don't want to explore Medellín by night on your own, you can go on a *chiva* tour, which can be a convenient and reasonably safe option of visiting several hot nightspots in one go. It's a three- to four-hour night trip around the city in an old traditional bus with a typical music band on board. Routes vary, but usually cover Pueblito Paisa, Envigado, Las Palmas and El Poblado. A few drinks of aguardiente and some local snacks are included. The tours are run mostly on Friday and Saturday. They cost roughly US$10 to US$15 per person.

## Shopping

The **Mercado de San Alejo** is a colourful craft market held in the Parque de Bolívar on the first Saturday of every month. It is good for cheap buys or simply to stroll around. There are many handicraft shops in the city, including a few in the Pueblito Paisa on the Cerro Nutibara.

Medellín is Colombia's major textile producer, so there's a good choice of clothes and it is generally a bit cheaper than elsewhere in the country. There are plenty of commercial centres and stores in the city centre and beyond. The centre is one of the cheapest areas for shopping.

For cheap clothing, you may start at the **Centro Comercial Palacio Nacional** (☎ 381 8144; Carrera 52 at Calle 48), a beautiful palatial building from 1925, transformed into a shopping mall. It has over 200 budget shops (most with clothing and footwear) distributed over its five floors. The area around the Palacio, nicknamed El Hueco (The Hole) by the locals, features plenty of bargain stores.

You may also try Almacenes Éxito, a Medellín-born chain of cheap stores selling food, clothing, toiletries, stationery, home appliances etc. There are seven of them in the city, including **Éxito San Antonio** (☎ 514 9400; Calle 48 No 46-115) in the centre; **Éxito Colombia** (☎ 430 6500; Carrera 66 No 49-01) in Suramericana; and **Éxito Poblado** (☎ 319 7200; Calle 10 No 43E-135) in El Poblado.

For some finer shopping, it's probably best to start off combing some of the large shopping malls. El Poblado has some of the best of these, including **El Tesoro** (☎ 321 1010; Carrera 25A No 1AS-45), **Vizcaya** (☎ 268 4822; Calle 9 No 30-382) and **Oviedo** (☎ 321 6116; Carrera 43A No 6S-15). All of them have a variety of European and American fashion stores.

**Plaza Minorista José María Villa** (Carrera 57 at Calle 55) is a huge, bustling market, which comprises more than 2500 stalls under cover, selling mostly food. It was established in 1984 to remove hawkers from the streets. It's open daily.

## Getting There & Away

**Air** Medellín has two airports. The new José María Córdoba airport, 35km southeast of the city, near the town of Rionegro, takes all international and most domestic flights, except for some flights on light planes which use the old Olaya Herrera airport right inside the city.

There are domestic flights throughout the country – to Bogotá (US$50 to US$110), Cali (US$80 to US$120), Cartagena (US$75 to US$125) and San Andrés (US$100 to US$140).

Among international flights, West Caribbean Airways has three direct flights per week (Monday, Wednesday and Friday) to Panama City (US$140/210 one way/return) and to San José (US$278 return). Copa flies daily to Panama City (US$151/268 one way/return).

**Bus** Medellín has two bus terminals. The Terminal del Norte, 3km north of the city centre, handles buses to the north, east and southeast, including Santa Fe de Antioquia

(US$3, three hours), Cartagena (US$27, 13 hours), Barranquilla (US$28, 14 hours), Santa Marta (US$32, 16 hours) and Bogotá (US$17, nine hours). It is easily reached from the centre by metro in seven minutes (Estación Caribe), or by taxi (US$2).

The Terminal del Sur, 4km southwest of the centre, handles all traffic to the west and south, including Quibdó (US$15, 10 hours), Manizales (US$10, five hours), Pereira (US$10, five hours), Armenia (US$11, six hours), Cali (US$16, nine hours), Popayán (US$20, 12 hours) and Pasto (US$28, 18 hours). It's accessible from the centre by the Guayabal bus (Ruta No 143) and the Trinidad bus (Ruta No 160), both of which you catch on Av Oriental next to the Éxito San Antonio store. Alternatively, go by taxi (US$2).

## Getting Around

**To/From the Airport** Frequent minibuses shuttle between the city centre and the new airport from the corner of Carrera 50A and Calle 53 (US$2, one hour); a taxi costs US$15. The old airport's terminal is next to the Terminal del Sur.

**Metro** Medellín is Colombia's first (and for the foreseeable future the only) city to have the metro, or fast metropolitan train. It is clean, cheap, safe and efficient, and has become the pride of the paisas. Its construction began in 1985 and after a series of setbacks it eventually opened in 1995. During its first five years in operation, 451 million passengers took the ride.

The metro consists of a 23km north–south line (Línea 1) and a 6km western leg (Línea 2), plus a 3km link between the two lines, which is part of Línea 3. The system is 32km long and has 25 stations. Trains run at ground level except for 5km through the central area where they go on viaducts above streets, providing good views.

The metro operates 5am to 11pm Monday to Saturday, 7am to 10pm Sunday and holidays, with trains running every five to 10 minutes. Tickets can be bought at any metro station and cost US$0.35/0.60 for a single/double ride, or buy a 10-ride *multiviaje* for US$2.80.

**Bus** Apart from the metro, urban transport is serviced by buses and *busetas*, and is quite well organised. All buses are numbered and display their destination point. There are bus stops on most routes, though sometimes buses will also stop in between. The majority of routes originate on Av Oriental and Parque Berrío, from where you can get to almost anywhere within the metropolitan area. Urban transport stops around 10pm, leaving only taxis plying the streets at night.

## CIRCUITO DE ORIENTE

The picturesque, rugged region surrounding Medellín is sprinkled with haciendas and lovely little pueblos paisas, looking as if the 20th century got bogged somewhere down the road. The mild climate stimulates a rich variety of flora, and indeed the region's vegetation is exuberant. Antioquia has a great variety of plants and flowers and is particularly renowned for its orchids.

The area to the southeast of Medellín is Antioquia's most touristy region because it boasts a number of tourist attractions relatively close to each other. It therefore can be easily and quickly visited, giving a taste of Antioquia in a capsule. It has quite a developed tourist infrastructure and is reasonably safe to travel in.

The most popular approach is the so-called Circuito de Oriente, a tourist loop through the sights of the area. The route covers several picturesque pueblos paisas with their distinctive architecture, and a verdant countryside with its haciendas. The standard loop usually includes Marinilla, Rionegro, Carmen de Viboral, La Ceja, Salto de Tequendamita, Retiro and the Hacienda Fizebad.

The trip can be done as a one-day tour from Medellín, or you can do it more leisurely, choosing your own route and pace. Accommodation and food are in good supply along the route, and bus transport is frequent (all buses depart from Medellín's Terminal del Norte). You may want to include El Peñol in the same trip, which doesn't usually appear on the organised tour routes because it's a bit off the track and there were some safety problems in the past on this route.

There are many other charming pueblos paisas further afield, including Abejorral, Jardín, Jericó and Sonsón. However, they require longer and less comfortable trips, as most are linked to Medellín by unpaved roads. More importantly, security conditions

## Orchids, Orchids Everywhere

An orchid is one of the most exotic and mysterious of flowers. Part of this reputation is due to the fact that orchid flowers appear in a variety of colours, shapes, sizes and fragrances virtually no other flower family can match. Their colour ranges from white to black, through literally every shade of the rainbow. The size also varies greatly, with the smallest-known flowers being not bigger than a pin-head. Their shapes too, appear in nearly every form imaginable, while their fragrances go from neutral to extremely potent, from delightful to disgusting.

Orchids form the largest flowering plant family, numbering an estimated 30,000 species. They grow almost everywhere, on every continent except Antarctica, from lowland tropics to chilling mountain tops, and from steaming rainforests to arid semi-deserts. Biologists agree that orchids are among the most evolved of flowering plants.

With an estimated 3000 species, Colombia holds the worldwide record, followed by Brazil with about 2500 species. This richness is still not the whole picture, because large parts of the country, including inaccessible parts of the Amazon and Chocó, have never been investigated by botanists. Many of Colombia's orchids are endemic, ie, they don't occur elsewhere. One of the many orchid species has been declared Colombia's national flower.

Orchids in Colombia grow in virtually all regions and all climatic zones, from sandy seaside dunes to highland *páramos* above the timber line. The greatest diversity, however, is found in montane cloud forests of the Andean region, between roughly 1000m and 2000m above sea level. The widest variety of orchids is in Antioquia, partly due to the fact that large chunks of the department lie at orchid-favoured altitudes.

are volatile due to the paramilitaries and/or guerrillas, who have a presence in the region. Always check for the latest travel safety conditions before you set off.

The following sections give a rundown of the major sights of the Circuito de Oriente.

## Marinilla

Some 46km southeast of Medellín on the road to Bogotá, Marinilla is a good example of Antioquian architecture, with a pleasant main plaza and adjacent streets. Dating from the first half of the 18th century, it's one of the oldest towns in the region, today home to 15,000 inhabitants. Stroll around the central streets and call at the **Capilla de Jesús Nazareno** *(Carrera 29 at Calle 32)*, a fine colonial church erected in the 1750s.

The Semana Santa celebration in Marinilla is one of the most elaborate in Antioquia, with processions and concerts of religious music held in the Capilla. Marinilla is also known for manufacturing top-quality stringed instruments.

There are at least half a dozen budget hotels in town, all of which are on or just off the main plaza. Buses to Medellín depart frequently from the plaza (US$1, one hour), as do *colectivos* to Rionegro (US$0.40, 15 minutes).

## El Peñol

Similar in shape to the famous Sugar Loaf of Rio de Janeiro, El Peñol (literally, the Stone) is a huge, 200m-high granite monolith. It sits on the bank of an artificial lake, the Embalse del Peñol, about 30km east of Marinilla. A staircase leads to the top of the rock; after ascending 649 steps, one gets magnificent bird's-eye views all around, with the beautiful lake at your feet. There's a snack bar on the top.

The lake has become a popular weekend getaway for Medellín's dwellers, and a number of *estaderos* (roadside restaurants) have sprung up on the road and the lakeside. They provide accommodation in rooms and/or *cabañas* and food in their own restaurants. Some of the cheapest estaderos are found at the foot of the rock, on the Peñol–Guatapé road.

Buses to and from Medellín run every one to two hours (US$2.50, 2½ hours) and they all pass via Marinilla (US$1.50, 1¼ hours).

## Rionegro

Founded in 1663, Rionegro is the oldest town in the Medellín environs. It is also the largest, today numbering 40,000 inhabitants. It's 48km southeast of Medellín and 7km southwest of Marinilla.

The town's main plaza boasts the **Monumento a José María Córdoba**, a statue of the Rionegro-born hero of the War of Independence. The allegoric figure of the naked general is one of many unconventional works by Rodrigo Arenas Betancur. The massive 200-year-old **Catedral de San Nicolás**, overlooking the plaza, has an impressive silver *sagrario* (tabernacle) in the high altar. Behind the altar is a small museum of religious art.

The **Casa de la Convención** *(Calle 51 No 47-67)* is a colonial house where the Colombian constitution of 1863 was written. This was the most liberal constitution in the country's history. The house is now a museum that features a collection of documents and period exhibits related to the event. One block from the Casa is the 1740 **Capilla de San Francisco** *(Calle 51 at Carrera 48)*, the town's oldest existing church.

Rionegro has many budget hotels and restaurants around the central streets. The town is also a busy transport hub, with frequent buses to Medellín (US$1.25, 1¼ hours) and colectivos to Marinilla (US$0.40, 15 minutes), Carmen de Viboral (US$0.50, 20 minutes) and La Ceja (US$0.70, 25 minutes).

## Carmen de Viboral

This small town of 15,000 people, 9km southeast of Rionegro, is known nationwide as a producer of hand-painted ceramics. There are a few large factories on the outskirts of the town – including Continental, Capiro and Triunfo – and several small workshops that are still largely unmechanised. In some places you'll be allowed to see the production process. Almost all tours from Medellín include a visit to one of the factories.

There are two *hospedajes* in the main plaza, as well as a few restaurants. Frequent colectivos run to Rionegro from the plaza (US$0.50, 20 minutes).

## La Ceja

La Ceja was founded in 1789 and has developed into a handsome pueblo paisa of 25,000 inhabitants. It has a pleasant, spacious main plaza lined with balconied houses, and a number of houses around the central streets have preserved their delicate door and window decoration. There are two churches on the plaza, of which the small one has an amazing interior, complete with an extraordinary baroque retable carved in wood.

Like other towns on the route, La Ceja has a choice of budget hotels and restaurants. Buses to Medellín depart frequently from the main plaza (US$1.25, 1¼ hours), as do colectivos to Rionegro (US$0.70, 25 minutes). The road to Medellín winds spectacularly through pine forests.

## Salto de Tequendamita

Tequendamita is a waterfall 9km northwest of La Ceja on the road to Medellín. There is a pleasant restaurant ideally located at the foot of the falls. Most tours organised from Medellín stop here for lunch.

## Retiro

This is a 200-year-old tiny town of 6000 souls – one of the nicest in the region. It's set amid verdant hills 33km southeast of Medellín, 4km off the road to La Ceja. The main plaza is a good example of Antioquian architecture, as are many houses lining the surrounding streets.

The **Fiesta de Los Negritos** is held annually in late December to commemorate the abolition of slavery in the region. It was here, in Retiro, that 126 slaves were liberated in the early 1810s, possibly the first case of its kind in the country's history.

Small as it is, Retiro has a choice of cheap hotels and restaurants. Buses to Medellín run every half an hour (US$1.25, one hour) along a spectacular road dotted with some lovely haciendas.

## Hacienda Fizebad

Fizebad is an old hacienda, 27km southeast of Medellín on La Ceja road. The main house dates from 1825 and has its original furniture and other period objects. A replica of a pueblo paisa, complete with chapel and shops, has been constructed, and about 150 species of orchids are grown on the grounds. One of the houses features a collection of pre-Columbian ceramics of various Colombian cultures. Many buses from Medellín to La Ceja and Retiro pass by the hacienda on their way and will let you off at the entrance.

## SANTA FE DE ANTIOQUIA

☎ 4 • pop 12,000 • elevation 550m
• temp 27°C

Founded in 1541 by Jorge Robledo, Santa Fe de Antioquia is the oldest town in the region. It became the capital of the province in

Providencia–Santa Catalina bridge

Historic building, Medellín

Santuario de las Lajas

Hotel Dann Monasterio, Popayán

Parque Arqueológico, San Agustín

*Victoria Amazonica* (a type of water lily), Leticia

1584 and was an important and prosperous centre during the Spanish days. It was from here that Medellín was settled in 1616, but it wasn't until 1826 that Medellín took over the honour as the capital of Antioquia.

The town's historic urban fabric has survived largely intact, with narrow cobbled streets, one-storey whitewashed houses and four churches. This is the only town in Antioquia that has preserved its colonial character. It is different from other towns in the region, where more recent Antioquian architecture now dominates. Santa Fe is 79km northwest of Medellín, on the road to Turbo.

### Information

The tourist office, **Oficina de Fomento y Turismo** (☎ 853 2314; Plaza Mayor; open 8am-noon & 2pm-6pm Mon-Fri) is in the Palacio Municipal on the main plaza.

### Things to See

Give yourself a couple of hours to wander about the streets to see the decorated doorways of the houses, the windows with their carved wooden guards and the patios with flowers in bloom.

Of the town's four churches, the **Iglesia de Santa Bárbara** (Calle 11 at Carrera 8) is the most interesting. Built by the Jesuits in the second half of the 18th century, the church has a fine wide baroque stone facade. The interior boasts an interesting, if time-worn, retable over the high altar. The church is open approximately 5pm to 6.30pm daily, plus for Sunday morning Mass.

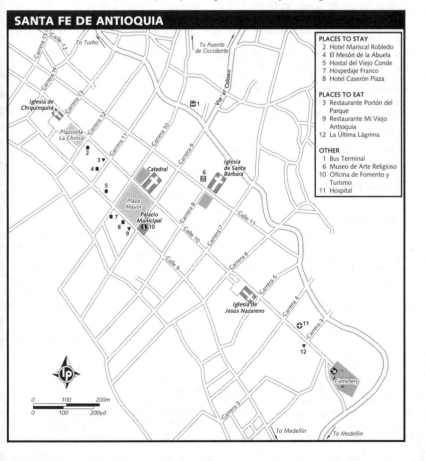

**SANTA FE DE ANTIOQUIA**

**PLACES TO STAY**
2  Hotel Mariscal Robledo
4  El Mesón de la Abuela
5  Hostal del Viejo Conde
7  Hospedaje Franco
8  Hotel Caserón Plaza

**PLACES TO EAT**
3  Restaurante Portón del Parque
9  Restaurante Mi Viejo Antioquia
12  La Última Lágrima

**OTHER**
1  Bus Terminal
6  Museo de Arte Religioso
10  Oficina de Fomento y Turismo
11  Hospital

The **Museo de Arte Religioso** (☎ 853 2345; Calle 11 No 8-12; admission US$1; open 10am-5pm Sat, Sun & holidays), next door to Santa Bárbara church, has a collection of religious objects, including paintings by Gregorio Vásquez de Arce y Ceballos.

The **Catedral** (Plaza Mayor) is sometimes referred to as the Catedral Madre, as it was the first church built in the region. However, the original church was destroyed by fire, and the large building you see today was not completed until 1837. Until that year, Iglesia de Santa Bárbara did the honours as the cathedral. Once inside, have a look at the Last Supper in the right transept and at an image of San Francisco de Borja with a skull in the opposite transept. The church is open daily for morning and evening Mass, plus an additional service on Sunday at 11am.

The two remaining churches, the mid-17th-century **Iglesia de Chiquinquirá** (Carrera 13 at Calle 10), also known as La Chinca, and the 1828 **Iglesia de Jesús Nazareno** (Carrera 5 at Calle 10) are only open for an evening Mass at 7pm daily. Admirers of funerary art may want to visit the local **cemetery** at the southeastern end of Calle 10, with a collection of historic tombstones and a 150-year-old cemetery chapel.

While you are in Santa Fe, consider a short trip to the unusual bridge, the Puente de Occidente (see that entry later).

### Special Events

Like most traditional towns dating from the early days of the Spanish Conquest, the **Semana Santa** (Easter Week) is celebrated with much solemnity and attention.

The town's main popular festival, the **Fiesta de los Diablitos**, is held annually over the last four days of the year. It includes music, dance and a craft fair, and – like almost every feast in the country – a beauty contest and bullfights.

### Places to Stay

Santa Fe is usually visited as a day trip from Medellín, but should you like to linger longer, there's no problem whatsoever. The town has a dozen hotels catering to different budgets and they are usually empty except for weekends when Medellín's city dwellers come to warm up. Most hotels raise their rates on weekends. The prices listed here are weekday rates.

**Hospedaje Franco** (☎ 853 1654; Carrera 10 No 8A-14; rooms without/with bath per person US$3/5) is basic but acceptable. It's one of the cheapest places in town and also serves some of the cheapest meals.

**El Mesón de la Abuela** (Hospedaje Rafa; ☎ 853 1053; Carrera 11 No 9-31; rooms per person US$4), also known as Hospedaje Rafa, offers much the same as the Franco. It has some rooms with bath, others without, but the price is the same. It also has its own restaurant, which offers breakfast, lunch and dinner, but it's a bit more expensive than the restaurant at Franco.

**Hostal del Viejo Conde** (☎ 853 1091; Calle 9 No 10-56; rooms with bath per person US$4) is another small budget place, much in the same class as the two above, and it too serves cheap meals.

**Hotel Caserón Plaza** (☎ 853 2040; Plaza Mayor; doubles US$25-50, triples US$40-70) is a fine upscale option. Set in a beautiful colonial mansion, the hotel provides good rooms with bath, a restaurant and a swimming pool (very useful in this climate).

**Hotel Mariscal Robledo** (☎ 853 1111; Carrera 12 No 9-70; rooms per person US$18-44) is another decent place, and it too has a swimming pool and a restaurant. The price largely depends on the kind of package (with or without meals) and the season.

### Places to Eat

Apart from the hotel restaurants listed earlier, there are a dozen other places to eat, including the budget **Restaurante Mi Viejo Antioquia** (Plaza Mayor; set meals US$2) and the **Restaurante Portón del Parque** (Calle 10 No 11-03; mains US$4-7), which is one of the finest in town.

There's one more place worth mentioning: an unremarkable looking and unmarked restaurant down Calle 10 near the cemetery, sarcastically called by the locals **La Última Lágrima** (The Last Tear), apparently because of its location between the hospital and the cemetery. It serves excellent lunches for US$2.50.

Don't miss trying pulpa de tamarindo, a local sweet made from tamarind, sold on the main plaza.

### Getting There & Away

There are half a dozen buses daily (US$3, three hours) and another half a dozen minibuses (US$4, 2½ hours) to and from Medellín's northern terminal. There are also colectivos if there's a demand (US$5, two hours). A tunnel is being constructed on this road, which should cut down the travelling time and the bus fares.

## PUENTE DE OCCIDENTE

The Puente de Occidente, or the West Bridge, is a peculiar pearl of 19th-century engineering. This 291m-long bridge over the Cauca River was designed by José María Villa and constructed in 1887–95. When built, it was one of the first suspension bridges in the Americas. It carried general traffic until 1978, when it was declared a national monument, and buses were banned (cars can still use it).

### Getting There & Away

The bridge is 5km east of Santa Fe on the road to Sopetrán. Since buses are not allowed to cross the bridge and don't go this way, you have two options: negotiate a return trip with a taxi driver in Santa Fe or walk (one hour), but avoid the unbearable midday heat.

# Zona Cafetera

Zona Cafetera, the region comprising the three small departments of Caldas, Risaralda and Quindío, lies just south of Antioquia. As its name suggests, this is Colombia's coffee-growing heartland. The region provides nearly half of the total national coffee production and covers just 1.2% of the country's total area.

The region wasn't really settled until the mid-19th century, when Antioquia began expanding southwards. It was essentially the paisas who colonised the region (the so-called *colonización antioqueña*), and they introduced the coffee plantations.

By 1905, the area had developed enough to become a department in its own right, Caldas. By the 1960s coffee accounted for half of Colombia's export earnings, and Caldas was its major producer. In 1966 conflicting economic interests within the department led to its split into three small administrative units.

Zona Cafetera has much in common with Antioquia in terms of its nature, landscape, people, culture, crafts and its cuisine. The architecture too shows direct similarities with Antioquian buildings, and one can find plenty of small towns much like pueblos paisas. The only cities in the region are the three departmental capitals: Manizales, Pereira and Armenia.

Zona Cafetera is a rugged and verdant land, with coffee plantations covering most mountain slopes between about 1300m and 1700m. The region is geologically unstable and was struck by serious earthquakes a number of times. All three departmental capitals have been repeatedly hit by quakes and the last catastrophic one, which struck in 1999, severely damaged both Armenia and Pereira.

## MANIZALES

☎ 6 • pop 420,000 • elevation 2150m
• temp 18°C

Manizales, the capital of Caldas, was founded in 1849 by a group of Antioquian colonists looking for a tranquil place to escape the civil wars that plagued the country during that period. The group was reputedly composed of 20 families, including the family of Manuel Grisales, after whom the settlement was named.

Manizales' early development was painfully slow, hindered by two serious earthquakes in 1875 and 1878. It wasn't actually until the beginning of the 20th century that the town began to grow quicker, partly because it became the capital of the newly created department, but mainly because it was a centre of coffee production. However, an extensive fire in 1925 razed the town, and construction had to start all over again.

Today, Manizales is a lively, modern city with a vibrant centre dominated by several high-rise buildings and a huge cathedral. Perched along a ridge of the Central Cordillera, Manizales has few flat streets; most are hilly, often quite steep, which gives the city additional charm. The temperature is pleasant but the rainy seasons, from March to May and September to November, can be slightly depressing.

### Information

**Tourist Offices** The tourist office, the **Instituto de Cultura y Turismo** (☎ 884 6211; Carrera 22 at Calle 33; open 8am-noon & 2pm-6pm Mon-Fri) is in the Teatro Los Fundadores.

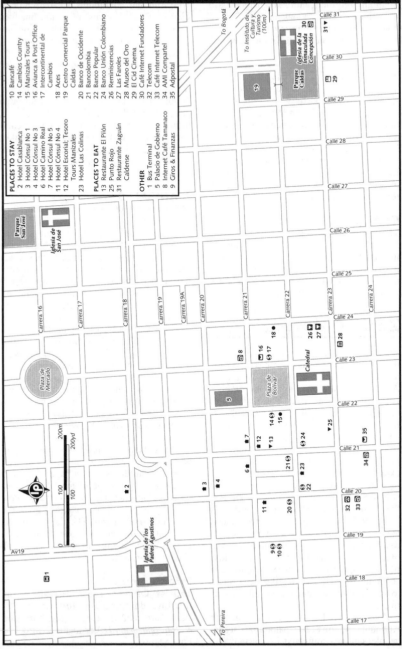

# MANIZALES

**PLACES TO STAY**
2  Hotel Casablanca
3  Hotel Cónsul No 1
4  Hotel Cónsul No 3
6  Hotel Camino Real
7  Hotel Cónsul No 5
11 Hotel Cónsul No 4
12 Hotel Escorial; Tesoro
   Tours Manizales
23 Hotel Las Colinas

**PLACES TO EAT**
13 Restaurante El Pilón
25 Punto Rojo
31 Restaurante Zaguán
   Caldense

**OTHER**
1  Bus Terminal
5  Palacio de Gobierno
8  Internet Café Tamanaco
9  Giros & Finanzas
10 Bancafé
14 Cambios Country
15 Manizales Tours
16 Avianca & Post Office
17 Intercontinental de
   Cambios
18 Aces
19 Centro Comercial Parque
   Caldas
20 Banco de Occidente
21 Bancolombia
22 Banco Popular
24 Banco Unión Colombiano
26 Reminiscencias
27 Las Faroles
28 Museo del Oro
29 El Cid Cinema
30 Café Internet Fundadores
32 Telecom
33 Café Internet Telecom
34 AMI Compartel
35 Adpostal

**Money** Bancolombia and **Banco Unión Colombiano**, both on the corner of Calle 21 and Carrera 22, change cash and travellers cheques. You can also change travellers cheques at **Lloyds TSB Bank** (Av Santander No 56-42), outside the central area.

Changing cash may be more favourable and quicker in a casa de cambio. There are plenty of these across the centre, including **Cambios Country** (Calle 22 No 21-44), **Intercontinental de Cambios** (Calle 23 No 21-25) and **Giros & Finanzas** (Calle 19 No 21-30), which is the agent of Western Union.

All the banks marked on the map give cash advances on Visa and/or MasterCard.

**Email & Internet Access** There are quite a number of Internet cafés in the city centre, including **Café Internet Fundadores** (☎ 884 2538; Carrera 23 No 30-59), **Internet Café Tamanaco** (☎ 889 6290; Calle 23 at Carrera 21), **AMI Compartel** (☎ 897 6790; Calle 21 No 23-56) and **Café Internet Telecom** (☎ 899 2000; Calle 20 No 23-42). You'll find many more Internet cafés on Av Santander, east of the centre.

## Plaza de Bolívar

The architecture around Manizales' central square is modern, except for the fine Palacio de Gobierno built in 1927, on the northern side of the plaza. In the middle of the square stands an intriguing monument known as Bolívar-Cóndor. This is another work of Rodrigo Arenas Betancur, known for his unconventional designs. Also on the plaza are two ceramic murals by Guillermo Botero, which refer to Colombia's history.

## Catedral

The Manizales' cathedral has had quite a chequered history. The existing building is the third church to be erected on this site. The first one, built in 1854, was destroyed by an earthquake in 1878. The next one, a handsome wooden church, went up in flames during the fire of 1925. There's an exact replica, the Iglesia de Nuestra Señora del Rosario, in the Chipre district, on the corner of Carrera 13 and Calle 12. The present cathedral has not escaped the misfortunes of nature either: during an earthquake in 1979 it lost one of its towers, but it has since been rebuilt.

The cathedral is a large, imposing piece of Gothic-style architecture. Its main tower

is 106m high, making it the highest church tower in the country. Begun in 1929, it took almost half a century to complete the building. It was built out of reinforced concrete and was reputedly the first church in Latin America to be constructed this way. The grey concrete exterior has been left rough, giving the cathedral an unpolished, almost unfinished look. The three front bronze doors are covered with bas-reliefs, which tell the history of the town and the cathedral. Don't be misled if these doors are locked (they are usually only open for Sunday Mass); you can enter the cathedral by either of the side doors.

The spacious interior is embellished with a number of lovely stained-glass windows in different styles. Some of them were commissioned in France and Greece, while others were made locally. The one at the back of the church over the main doors has colourful folksy, rather than religious, images. The ornate baldachin over the high altar was carved in wood and gilded in Italy. Parts of the walls in the chancel are covered with a fine cream marble, but the rest is left in rough concrete. Initially, the whole of the interior was to be laid out in marble, but the work was stopped after the engineers revealed that the structure wouldn't support such weight.

## Iglesia de la Inmaculada Concepción

This church, in the Parque Caldas, was built at the beginning of the 20th century and has a beautiful interior in which just about everything, including the columns, vault, doors, window frames, pews and pulpit, has been made of cedar.

## Museo del Oro

The Gold Museum (☎ 884 3851; Carrera 23 No 23-14, Piso 2; admission free; open 8am-11.30am & 2pm-5.30pm Mon-Fri) is in the building of the Banco de la República. It has a small collection of Quimbaya gold and ceramic artefacts.

## Other Museums

There are two museums at the Universidad de Caldas in the eastern sector of the city. The **Museo Arqueológico** (☎ 885 1374; Av Santander No 58-65; admission free; open 9am-noon & 2.30pm-6pm Mon-Fri) has Quimbaya and Calima ceramics. The

NORTHWEST COLOMBIA

**Museo de Ciencias Naturales** (☎ 886 1250; Calle 65 No 26-10; admission free; open 9am-noon & 2pm-6pm Mon-Fri) has a few thousand animal species, including an extensive butterfly collection.

## Torre de Herveo

Also called Torre El Cable, this is a 52m-tall wooden tower in the Parque Antonio Nariño on Av Santander at Calle 65, 3km east of the centre. It's a relic of a cable-way which was constructed in 1922 between Manizales and Mariquita, 73km to the east, and used to transport coffee.

## Monumento a los Colonizadores

The Monument to the Colonists (Av 12 de Octubre; admission US$1; open 2.30pm-6.30pm daily) is the most recent addition to the cityscape and the list of local attractions. It has been erected at the city's highest point, in the Chipre district 1km northwest of the centre. It's an impressive structure of 19 bronze figures designed by Guillermo Vallejo. It took five years to cast and

put together the whole thing before it was unveiled in January 2001, 15 months later than planned, to celebrate Manizales' 150th anniversary. It's easily one of the best monuments made in Colombia over recent years.

## Organised Tours

Manizales sits on the northwestern outskirts of the Parque Nacional Los Nevados, and the park is the focus of local tour activity. The most popular tour on offer is a full-day trip to the foot of Nevado del Ruiz, the highest volcano in the park. The tour (about US$18 per person) includes transport there and back, a guide, a snack, a walk up the volcano slope (but not to the top) and a bath in the hot springs of the Hotel Termales del Ruiz.

The tour can be organised through some of the city's major tour agencies. The best specialist is **Bioturismo Arte y Café** (☎ 884 4037; Centro Comercial Parque Caldas, Local PB 45), managed by Omar Vargas. The agency also offers other tours in the park (Laguna del Otún, Laguna Verde) and beyond (Valle de Cocora, Parque del Café). It

### Torre de Herveo, Relic of a Rare Cable-Way

Torre de Herveo is the only surviving tower of 376 that were part of an unusual cable-way system. It was built by a Colombian-English company, the Dorada Railway, to transport coffee from the rich coffee-growing region around Manizales to the town of Mariquita close to the Magdalena River. The coffee was then carried overland to Honda and shipped down the Magdalena to Barranquilla on the Caribbean Coast, and on to the USA and Europe.

The 73km-long cable-way was designed by an Australian director of the project, James Lindsay, and a British engineer, Franz Koppel, and was built in the early 1920s. By the time of its construction, it was the world's longest cable-way. It went across a rugged land passing over a mountain crest at 3800m then dropping to Mariquita at 500m. The towers supporting the cable differed in height from 4m to 52m.

All the towers were made of steel in England and sent piece by piece to Colombia by boat during the last years of WWI. Unfortunately, the boat which transported one of the towers was sunk in the Atlantic by a German submarine. A replacement tower was designed and built in Colombia using timber instead of steel, which wasn't easily available locally. It consisted of a 30m-tall rectangular structure topped with a 22m-high pyramid. The tower was built near the village of Herveo (hence its name), using 1470 timber blocks of various native tree species. It weighed 45 tonnes and was the tallest tower of the system.

The cable-way operated until 1961, then it was largely left to its own fate. Two decades later, the local authorities began showing interest in protecting the department's cultural and industrial heritage. In an attempt to save what was left of the cable-way, the Herveo tower was carefully dismantled piece by piece (including its 4000 screws) and transported to Parque Antonio Nariño in Manizales, where it was meticulously reassembled in 1984. In the same year it was declared a national monument. A solitary survivor of a curious engineering achievement, the timber tower still proudly overlooks the tiny park, looking a bit odd and out of place, with a growing number of high-rise office and residential buildings around.

can also arrange a licensed guide to the park, should you prefer a tailor-made route or to go mountaineering. The agency publishes a brochure featuring its offer, a list of licensed guides, prices etc.

Other tour agencies you may want to try should include **Manizales Tours** (☎ 884 1938; Calle 22 No 21-46) and **Tesoro Tours Manizales** (☎ 883 7040; Hotel Escorial, Calle 21 No 21-11).

### Special Events
With a history dating back to the 1950s, the **Feria de Manizales** is the city's major carnival, celebrated during the first weeks of the year. Costumed groups in colourful fancy dress take over the city, and the Plaza de Bolívar has nightly poetry meetings. A beauty pageant is held in which the Coffee Queen is elected, and a craft fair draws in artisans from the region and beyond. The most important *corridas* (bullfights) take place during this period.

Held since 1968, the **Festival Latinoamericano de Teatro** is one of two important theatre festivals in Colombia (the other is in Bogotá). There's always a good representation of leading Latin American theatres plus the cream of national groups. Half a dozen city theatres (including the Teatro Los Fundadores) are used for the festival performances, and free concerts are held nightly at the Plaza de Bolívar. The festival goes for a week in late September.

### Places to Stay
All the hotels included in this section are in the central city area within a short walk of the Plaza de Bolívar, and all have hot water.

There are some cheap hotels north of Carrera 18, between the bus terminal and the market, but the area is unattractive and not very safe at night. Avoid it or stay on its outskirts, for example, in the **Hotel Casablanca** (☎ 880 9098; Carrera 18 No 20-17; singles/doubles/triples US$3.50/5/7). It's very basic, but has large rooms with baths.

It's more pleasant and safer to stay south of Carrera 19, in the vicinity of the Plaza de Bolívar.

It's perhaps best to start by checking some of the Cónsul hotels, which offer good value for money. There are four of them in the chain, and all are very central and close to each other. They are all set in renovated old houses which are pretty small. All are low-budget and neat, but differ in their facilities and rates.

**Hotel Cónsul No 3** (☎ 882 2719; Carrera 20 No 20-32; singles/doubles/triples US$4/6/8) is the most rustic of the chain. It has 13 simple rooms with shared facilities, but otherwise is OK.

**Hotel Cónsul No 1** (☎ 882 3720; Carrera 20 No 20-25; singles/doubles/triples US$9/11/14) is also quite simple, however, each room has its own bath.

**Hotel Cónsul No 5** (☎ 884 4067; Carrera 21 No 21-21; singles/doubles/triples US$10/12/16) is marginally better than the No 1, and is the closest to the Plaza de Bolívar.

**Hotel Cónsul No 4** (☎ 883 1385; Calle 20 No 21-10; singles/doubles/triples US$12/15/18) is the top of the Cónsul luxuries, with airier rooms than the others.

There are also some mid-range and top-end hotels in the centre.

**Hotel Camino Real** (☎ 884 5588; Carrera 21 No 20-45; singles/doubles/triples US$25/32/40) is a reasonable mid-range place, and you may be able to bargain over the prices if paying by cash. The room rates include breakfast.

**Hotel Las Colinas** (☎ 884 2009; Carrera 22 No 20-20; doubles/triples US$50/70) is the poshest place to stay in the city centre, and breakfast is included in the room rates.

### Places to Eat
The central area is packed with mostly low- to middle-budget restaurants, snack bars and fast-food outlets. For finer, upmarket dinning, it's better to look on Av Santander in the area of El Cable.

In the centre, the main axis of gastronomic activity is Carrera 23. If you are after the cheapest set meals, you'll find a few extra low-budget eateries on Carrera 23 between Calles 30 and 32. Better budget eateries include:

**Restaurante Zaguán Caldense** (Carrera 23 No 30-64; set meals US$2, mains US$3-4) offers typical regional cuisine *(bandeja paisa, mondongo, sancocho, fríjoles)* in a charming interior laid out entirely in *guadua* (a sort of local bamboo).

**Restaurante El Pilón** (Calle 21 No 21-21; mains US$4-5) is another typical restaurant good for regional dishes. This one is laid out in *caña brava*, a common local reed.

**Punto Rojo** *(Carrera 23 No 21-39; mains US$2-4)* is a 24-hour self-service budget cafeteria, which is particularly useful if you happen to get hungry late at night.

## Entertainment

**Teatro Los Fundadores** *(☎ 884 5633; Carrera 22 at Calle 33)* is Manizales' leading theatre and also has a cinema. Another cinema, **El Cid** *(☎ 884 7017; Carrera 23 No 29-40)* is just a few blocks away, in Parque Caldas.

Most nightlife takes place outside the centre. One area noted for bars and discos is around the bullring on Av Centenario, 1km southwest of the centre. Another area is on Av Santander near El Cable.

There are two tango bars next to each other in the centre: **Reminiscencias** *(Calle 24 No 22-40)* and **Las Faroles** *(Calle 24 No 22-46)*.

## Getting There & Away

**Air** La Nubia airport is about 8km southeast of the city centre, off the road to Bogotá; take the urban bus to La Enea, then walk for five minutes the rest of the way. Aces is the only airline operating flights to and from Manizales, with seven flights a day to Bogotá (US$50 to US$90).

**Bus** The bus terminal is on Av 19 between Carreras 14 and 17, a short walk northwest of Plaza de Bolívar. Buses depart regularly to Bogotá (US$13, eight hours), Medellín (US$10, five hours) and Cali (US$10, five hours). Minibuses to Pereira (US$2.50, 1¼ hours) and Armenia (US$4.50, 2¼ hours) run every 15 minutes or so. To Salamina, there are minibuses (US$4, 2½ hours) and colectivos (US$4.50, 2¼ hours).

## PARQUE NACIONAL LOS NEVADOS

This national park, shared by the departments of Caldas, Risaralda, Quindío and Tolima, covers 583 sq km of highlands of the Cordillera Central. Altitudes in the park range from 2600m to 5325m, while average temperatures range from 14°C at the lower reaches to 3°C on the highest peaks.

The park's axis is formed by a volcanic range, oriented north–south, and topped with several volcanic peaks. The main peaks, from north to south, are: El Ruiz (5325m), El Cisne (4750m), Santa Isabel (4950m), El Quindío (4750m) and El Tolima (5215m).

The Nevado del Ruiz is the largest and the highest volcano of the chain. Its eruption on 13 November 1985 killed over 20,000 people. Hot gases melted a part of the snow cap and swollen rivers of mud cascaded down the eastern slopes, sweeping away everything in their path. Armero, a town of about 25,000 inhabitants on the Río Lagunillas, disappeared entirely under the mud.

El Ruiz had previously erupted in 1845, but the results were far less catastrophic. Today, it seems that the volcano has returned to its slumber, and its activity is limited to the occasional puff of smoke hovering over the crater. It can wake up, however, at any time and several alerts have been raised over the past decade when the volcano's smoke was bigger than usual.

The Nevado del Tolima, the second highest volcano in the chain, is the most handsome of all with its classic symmetrical cone. On a clear day it can be seen from as far away as Bogotá. Its last eruption took place in 1943, but today it is considered almost extinct.

The park covers various climatic zones and its environments range from humid Andean cloud forest, through the *páramos* (open highlands) to perpetual snows. There are several mountain lakes in the park, mostly in the páramos between 3800m and 4200m. The Laguna del Otún is the largest.

## Orientation

The only road access into the park is from the north. This road branches off from the Manizales–Bogotá road in La Esperanza, 31km from Manizales, and winds up to the snowline at about 4800m at the foot of Nevado del Ruiz.

The entrance to the park is at Las Brisas (4050m) where individual visitors pay a US$3 admission fee (if you come with a tour group it's normally included in the tour price). About 4km uphill from Las Brisas is the Chalet Arenales (see Places to Stay & Eat later) and 10km further up the road is a shelter known as Refugio (4800m).

The volcano actually has three craters: Arenas, Olleta and Piraña. The main one, Arenas (5325m), responsible for the 1985 disaster, has a diameter of 800m and is about 200m deep. It's a three-hour hike from the Refugio up to the top. You walk on snow, but the ascent is relatively easy and no special mountaineering equipment is necessary.

The extinct Olleta crater (4850m), on the opposite side of the road, is covered with multicoloured layers of sandy soil and normally has no snow. The walk to the top will take about 1¼ hours from the road, and it's possible to descend into the crater.

The road continues for another 38km along El Cisne and Santa Isabel down to the Laguna del Otún, a large, beautiful lake at 3950m.

The southern part of the park is accessible only by foot. From Refugio La Pastora in the Parque Ucumarí (see that entry later in this chapter) a 15km trail goes uphill to the Laguna del Otún. Another access route begins from Cocora, from where a path heads uphill to the páramo and on to the extinct Nevado del Quindío. Neither of these routes is popular with hikers and there have been occasional instances of guerrilla activity on both trails.

### When to Go

The best months to trek in Los Nevados are January and February. December, March, July and August can be relatively good but are less sure of good weather. The rest of the year is quite rainy and the volcanoes are usually hidden in the clouds, showing themselves only on occasional mornings.

### Organised Tours

The northern access road is by far the park's most popular gateway, through which most tourists come on a day tour from Manizales. It's a 10-hour tour, which gives a glimpse of high-mountain scenery up to 5100m. It's by car or minibus, depending on the number of participants. See Organised Tours under Manizales earlier in this chapter.

From the Refugio, tour participants take a walk uphill (up to two hours return), but don't go as far as the crater. On the way back the tours call at the Hotel Termales del Ruiz for a bath in the hot springs.

Individual visitors can only enter the park with a registered park guide. The Bioturismo Arte y Café (see Organised Tours in the earlier Manizales section) has all the details and prices.

### Places to Stay & Eat

The park has some basic accommodation and food facilities, which allow for longer stays in the area. Information and booking

are available through the **national park office** (☎ 877 6794, 877 7518) and **Fundación para la Conservación de la Vida Silvestre en Colombia** (FCV; ☎ 884 4728; Carrera 21 No 23-21, Oficina 501, Manizales).

**Cabaña Las Brisas**, at the entrance to the park (4050m), provides basic accommodation for US$2.50, but you need a good sleeping bag. No food is available here.

**Chalet Arenales** (4150m) offers accommodation for 25 persons, rated at US$4/6 with your/their sleeping bag. You can also camp here. Food is available, but you need to order in advance.

**Refugio** (4800m) has no accommodation but sells snacks and hot drinks. Check whether it's open at the park's entrance.

Park facilities apart, there's the comfortable **Hotel Termales del Ruiz** (☎ 851 7069, 870 0944; singles/doubles/triples US$30/36/48), just outside the northern boundary of the park. Set at 3500m, this is the highest hotel in the country. It has a restaurant and thermal pools, and is on the route of the tours. There's no public transport on the access road to the hotel.

### Getting There & Away

There's no public transport to the park. Bioturismo Arte y Café in Manizales can provide transport in a car, jeep, minibus or buseta, but it can be costly if you are on your own or in a small party.

### SALAMINA
☎ 6 • pop 18,000 • elevation 1775m
• temp 19°C

Founded in 1825, Salamina is one of the oldest towns in the region and possibly the best architectural example left from the Antioquian colonisation of Caldas. Many old houses with nicely decorated doors and windows can still be seen around the main plaza and in the adjacent streets.

The unusual cathedral was designed by an English architect and built between 1865 and 1875. Its rectangular interior, without a single column, has a flat, very wide wooden ceiling. The fine wooden altar was made at the beginning of the 20th century. The cemetery chapel is also an interesting architectural design.

Salamina is usually visited as a half- or full-day trip from Manizales, although if you prefer to stay longer there are some budget hotels in the market area on Carrera 6 and around the main plaza. Regular minibuses (US$4, 2½ hours) and colectivos (US$4.50, 2¼ hours) operate between Manizales and Salamina, and all pass through Neira, another fine historic town, worth seeing if you like this kind of architecture.

## PEREIRA
☎ 6 • pop 475,000 • elevation 1410m
• temp 21°C
The capital of Risaralda, Pereira is Zona Cafetera's largest city and an important centre for the surrounding coffee-growing region. The town was founded in 1863 and within little more than a century it had developed into a lively modern city. It doesn't have many tourist marvels, but it's an agreeable place and is worth a stop if you are travelling this route.

Whereas the city itself may be a bit thin on tourist sights, there are quite a number of attractions in its environs, including Marsella, Termales de Santa Rosa and Ecotermales San Vicente. Pereira is also a launching pad for the Parque Ucumarí and Santuario Otún Quimbaya.

In 1995, a powerful earthquake shook the region of Pereira, and ruined a number of buildings in the city. At least 30 people were killed and about 200 others were injured. In 1999, another devastating earthquake hit Armenia and also seriously affected Pereira.

## Information
**Tourist Offices** The **Dirección de Fomento al Turismo** (☎ 335 7132, 335 7172; Carrera 7 No 18-55, Piso 2; open 8am-11.30am & 2pm-4pm Mon-Fri) is in the Palacio Municipal.

**Money** Reliable banks changing travellers cheques include **Bancolombia** (Carrera 8 No 17-56) and **Banco Unión Colombiano** (Carrera 8 No 20-61). Other banks may also cash your travellers cheques, and give cash advances on Visa and/or MasterCard.

The Centro Comercial Alcides Arévalo, Calle 19 No 6-48, shelters half a dozen casas de cambio, including **Titán Intercontinental** and **Cambios Country**. Another half a dozen casas de cambio are situated in the Centro Comercial El Paso, Carrera 8 No 18-37. The **Giros & Finanzas**, the agent of Western Union, is in the Centro del Comercio, Carrera 7 No 16-50.

**Email & Internet Access** There are plenty of Internet cafés in the city centre, including **Cybernet** (☎ 335 0554; Calle 19 No 7-49, Plaza de Bolívar), **C@fecopias** (☎ 333 6556; Carrera 7 No 15-75), **Mundo Digital** (☎ 334 2365; Carrera 7 No 16-50, Centro del Comercio) and **Matrix** (☎ 335 5708; Carrera 8 No 20-58). Internet access costs about US$1 per hour in most places.

## Bolívar Desnudo
The 8.5m-high, 11-tonne bronze sculpture of the naked Bolívar on horseback, in the Plaza de Bolívar, is probably the most unusual monument to El Libertador. The sculpture is the work of Arenas Betancur, Colombia's most outstanding creator of public monuments, who donated it to the city in 1963 to commemorate Pereira's centenary.

Pereira has three other Betancur works: **Monumento a Los Fundadores** (Monument to the Founders) is on the corner of Carrera 13 and Calle 13; **El Prometeo**, dedicated to the local university professor Juan Manuel Mejía Marulanda, is in Universidad Tecnológica de Pereira, south of the centre; and the **Cristo sin Cruz** (Christ without the Cross) is in the Capilla de la Fátima, on Av 30 de Agosto between Calles 49 and 50, on the way to the airport, west of the centre.

## Zoológico de Matecaña
The zoo (☎ 336 0044; admission US$2.50; open 8am-5pm daily) is opposite the airport. It is particularly known for its ligres (Pantera leotigris), a cross between an African lion and a Bengal tiger, bred here in Pereira. You can see lots of birds, including Andean condors, flamingos and toucans. You can even have a chat with the papagayos (macaws). Frequent urban buses marked 'Matecaña' run between the city centre and the zoo, and the trip takes 20 minutes.

## Organised Tours
The office of San Vicente thermal baths, **Ecotermales San Vicente** (☎ 333 6157; Calle 16 No 14-08) sells day packages to the springs (US$12), which include return transport, admission to the baths, lunch and two short walks. The office also provides information, books accommodation and runs transport to the springs (US$4 return). See Ecotermales San Vicente later in this chapter for more information.

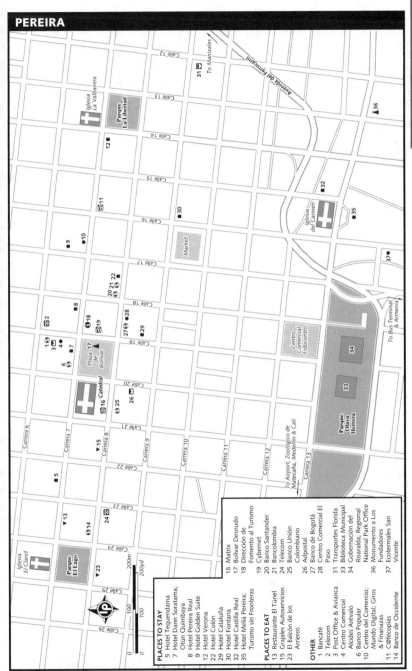

**PEREIRA**

**Otún Quimbaya** (☎ 324 2487; e *otun _quimbaya_excursiones@hotmail.com; Hotel Dann Soratama, Carrera 7 No 19-20, Piso 2)* organises ecotourist and adventure tours in the region and can provide guides.

**Turismo Sin Fronteras** (☎ 324 3136; e *turisinfronteras@hotmail.com; Hotel Meliá Pereira, Carrera 13 No 15-73)* operates some general-interest tours to cultural and natural attractions across Zona Cafetera.

## Places to Stay

The cheapest accommodation is found around and south of the former market square, but the area is not attractive and may not be perfectly safe at night. Most of the hotels here are basic and some are used for prostitution. One of the few acceptable places is the **Hotel Fontana** (☎ 334 2061; *Carrera 9 No 15-71; singles/doubles/triples US$3/5/8, with bath US$5/7/9)*. It's relatively clean and one of the cheapest in town, but it only has cold water.

It's more pleasant and probably safer to stay in the Plaza de Bolívar area, but the hotel prices are higher. One of the cheapest here is the **Hotel Colón** (☎ 335 6400; *Carrera 8 No 17-30; singles/doubles US$6/8, with bath US$8/12)*. It's an unremarkable place, but has hot water and acceptable rooms.

**Hotel Verona** (☎ 333 5525; *Carrera 7 No 14-19; singles/doubles/triples with bath US$8/14/17)*, just off Parque La Libertad, is a bit tucked away from the city heart, but is otherwise OK with 16 well-kept rooms. Some rooms are dim so have a look before checking in.

**Hotel Cataluña** (☎ 335 4527; *Calle 19 No 8-61; singles/doubles/triples with bath US$12/17/22)* is a reasonably cheap option just off the Plaza de Bolívar. It has 43 fairly spacious rooms; the ones facing the street are brighter.

**Hotel Tequendama** (☎ 335 7986; *Carrera 7 No 22-34; singles/doubles/triples with bath US$18/25/30)* is a small nine-room hotel with a family-like atmosphere and quiet rooms.

**Hotel Pereira Real** (☎ 335 9614; *Carrera 7 No 18-12; singles/doubles/triples US$25/35/40)* has just 10 rooms, recently fully refurbished. It's a good affordable option and may fill up at times. If this is the case, check the **Hotel Golden Suite** (☎ 334 7589; *Calle 17 No 6-57)*, managed by the same people, which offers and costs much the same.

**Hotel Dann Soratama** (☎ 335 8650; *Carrera 7 No 19-20; singles/doubles/triples US$30/45/60)*, overlooking Plaza de Bolívar, is possibly the best hotel in the heart of the city. It has spacious, air-conditioned rooms and prices include breakfast.

**Hotel Meliá Pereira** (☎ 335 0770; e *melia pereira@solmelia.com; Carrera 13 No 15-73; singles/doubles US$70/85)* is Pereira's poshest hotel with 200 air-conditioned rooms and most facilities you would wish for, including a swimming pool. Breakfast is included in the room price.

**Hotel Castilla Real** (☎ 333 2192; e *castilla real@pereira.multi.net.co; Calle 15 No 12B-15; singles/doubles US$65/75)* is a smaller alternative to the Meliá, just a few paces away. It has 25 comfortable, air-conditioned rooms, good service and discount rates on weekends; room prices include breakfast.

## Places to Eat

Like in all Colombian cities, eating is never a problem. The centre is packed with restaurants and snack bars, providing something for every pocket.

**Grajales Autoservicios** (*Carrera 8 No 21-60)* is a large, self-service 24-hour restaurant-cum-bakery, where you can put together your own lunch or dinner for US$3 to US$6. It's also good for breakfast.

**El Balcón de los Arrieros** (*Carrera 8 No 24-65; mains US$4-6)* is a pleasant paisa-style affair serving inexpensive dishes typical of the region and beyond.

**Restaurante El Túnel** (*Carrera 7 No 23-41; set meals US$2, mains US$3-7)* offers a variety of plates from different regions (including *lechona* and *sobrebarriga)* and serves a *menú del día*.

## Getting There & Away

**Air** The Matecaña airport is 5km west of the city centre, 20 minutes by urban bus, or US$2 by taxi. Avianca and Aces operate flights.

There are eight direct flights a day to Bogotá (US$50 to US$90), three to Medellín (US$40 to US$65), and one to Cartagena (US$80 to US$130). Flights to other destinations require a connection in either of the above-mentioned cities.

**Bus** The bus terminal is about 1.5km south of the city centre, at Calle 17 No 23-157.

Many urban buses will take you there in less than 10 minutes.

There are regular departures to Bogotá (US$15, nine hours); all buses go via Armenia, not Manizales. There are also a number of buses to Medellín (US$10, five hours) and Cali (US$8, four hours). Minibuses run every 15 minutes to Armenia (US$2, one hour), Manizales (US$2.50, 1¼ hours) and Marsella (US$1, one hour). Minibuses to Manizales pass via Santa Rosa de Cabal (US$0.50).

For Parque Ucumarí (see that entry later in this chapter), you need to go to El Cedral. **Transportes Florida** (Calle 12 No 9-40) has chivas departing to El Cedral (US$1.25, 1½ hours) from its office (not from the bus terminal) at 9am and 3pm on weekdays, and at 7am, 9am, noon and 3pm on Saturday and Sunday.

## MARSELLA
☎ 6 • pop 9000 • elevation 1600m
• temp 20°C

Set amid verdant, coffee-growing hills some 29km northwest of Pereira, Marsella is a pleasant, typical paisa town founded in 1860 by Antioquian colonists. It still has some old houses, including the Casa de la Cultura, a large three-storey *casona* (large house) laid out around a patio. The two-towered church, Iglesia de la Inmaculada Concepción, in the Parque La Pola (the main plaza), boasts a huge statue of Christ between its towers. However, Marsella's two main attractions are the botanical garden and the cemetery.

### Jardín Botánico Alejandro Humboldt

The botanical garden (☎ 368 5233; admission US$1.25; open 8am-6pm daily) is on a hill overlooking the town, two blocks from the main plaza. Created in 1979, the garden is still developing, but it's well-run and maintained. An array of cobbled footpaths has been laid, passing over small bridges built of guadua wood.

The Parque de la Ciencia y la Tecnología has been established in the garden, which consists of several simple mechanical devices to explain physical phenomena. Some of them are useful, eg, the windmill pumps water to the local toilet.

Another curiosity is Museo de la Cauchera (Museum of the Slingshot), probably the only one of its kind in the world. The museum is the by-product of a campaign to protect birds. It was launched among local kids who were killing birds with slingshots. The kids deposited their *caucheras* in exchange for free entrance to the park and other allurements. The museum is in the administrative building in the gardens, along with a café.

### Cementerio Jesús María Estrada

The cemetery (admission free; open 8am-6pm daily) is on the outskirts of town, a 10-minute walk from the plaza. Designed by Julio César Vélez and constructed in 1927, it is a masterpiece of funerary architecture. It has been built on a slope, and employs a system of terraces. Bodies are buried for a period of four years in the *gradas* (the terraced area of the cemetery), the *bóvedas* (concrete box-like constructions at the back) or *en tierra* (in the earth at the far right corner of the cemetery). After that time, the remains are permanently put to rest in the *osarios* (ossuaries), the openings in the cemetery's walls, which are then cemented over.

The osario is purchased to keep the bones of the entire family. The remains of those who can't afford an osario are deposited (after four years) in the *templetes*, two towers on each side of the front wall of the cemetery. In the centre of the cemetery is a statue of Christ, under which are the remains of Jesús María Estrada (Marsella's priest who founded the cemetery).

### Getting There & Away

Minibuses to and from Pereira run every 15 minutes approximately until about 7pm (US$1, one hour). The trip takes you through the spectacular coffee plantations.

## TERMALES DE SANTA ROSA
☎ 6 • elevation 1950m • temp 18°C

Also known as Termales Arbeláez, these popular hot springs are some 9km east of Santa Rosa de Cabal, a town on the Pereira–Manizales road. A tourist complex including thermal pools, a hotel, restaurant and bar, has been built near the springs amid splendid scenery at the foot of a 170m-high waterfall. The hot (70°C) water of the springs is cooled down to about 40°C in the main pool.

You can make a day trip to the thermal baths (admission US$6; open 8am-midnight daily) or stay there for longer. The springs are fairly quiet on weekdays, but tend to fill up with city dwellers during weekends and holidays.

## Places to Stay & Eat

The **Hotel Termales** (☎ *364 5500, 364 1322*) at the springs comprises two sections. The old part, Casa Vieja, has rooms to accommodate two to seven guests and costs about US$40 per person. The new part, La Montaña, offers cabañas with five to seven beds and costs US$35 per person. Both prices include full board and the use of the pools. The restaurant and bar are open for non-guests, but the food is expensive.

## Getting There & Away

Santa Rosa de Cabal is easily accessible from both Pereira (15km) and Manizales (36km) because it's on the road; minibuses between the two cities run every 10 to 15 minutes.

Transport from Santa Rosa de Cabal to the springs is operated by chivas from Calle 14 No 12-42 in the market area, with three departures daily, at 7am, noon and 3pm (US$0.80, 45 minutes). The chivas turn around and go back to Santa Rosa soon after their arrival at the springs. There may be some additional departures on weekends.

You can also go by jeep (they park in the same area), but they charge more. You can also contract them to pick you up in the evening (US$8).

## ECOTERMALES SAN VICENTE
☎ 6 • elevation 2250m • temp 16°C

These are other, newer thermal baths, quite close to the Termales de Santa Rosa. They are 18km east of the town of Santa Rosa de Cabal, linked by an unsurfaced road. A spacious purpose-built bath complex includes a hotel, cabañas, a camp site, restaurant, car park and, of course, the thermal pools themselves. Paths have been traced into the scenic environs, allowing for pleasant walks and access to a few charming waterfalls. Trout tanks have been built for fishing. Tourists can also have a massage and a bath in a mud pool.

The baths are operated from the office of Ecotermales San Vicente in Pereira (see Organised Tours under Pereira earlier), where inquiries and bookings can be made. The operator offers various packages (day plan, week plan), or you can come independently for a day and just pay a US$4 entrance fee.

## Places to Stay & Eat

The complex can accommodate 60 guests and another 100 at the camping ground. The different options are not cheap – stay in a double room without/with bath (US$23/25 per person), in a six-bed cabaña (US$22 per person) or camp in their/your tent (US$14/12 per person). All prices include breakfast and the use of the pools.

## Getting There & Away

There's no public transport to the baths. The operator provides its own transport from Pereira. Chivas, minibuses or busetas are supposed to depart daily from the Pereira office at about 8.30am and return from the baths around 5pm. The trip takes 1¼ hours each way and costs US$4 return. The admission fee to the complex is not included; it's an extra US$4.

## PARQUE UCUMARÍ

Parque Regional Natural Ucumarí is a nature reserve about 30km southeast of Pereira. Established in 1984 just outside the western boundaries of the Parque Nacional Los Nevados, the reserve covers about 42 sq km of rugged, forested land around the middle course of the Río Otún.

The reserve offers accommodation and food. It has ecological paths traced through verdant hills and you can see the lush vegetation and spot some of the park's rich wildlife. Birds are the reserve's most conspicuous inhabitants, with about 185 different species having been recorded here.

You can also make some longer excursions. The hike up the Río Otún, leading through a gorge to Parque Nacional Los Nevados, is the most popular. You can even get to Laguna del Otún (3950m) but it's a steady, six- to eight-hour walk uphill. It's possible to do the return trip within a day, though it's a strenuous hike. If you have camping gear, it's better to split the trek into a few days and do some side excursions up in the páramo.

The reserve offers a guide for US$20 per day, and also rents out mules and horses. Check the safety conditions with the rangers before setting off. Guerrillas have been reported in the Los Nevados park.

## Places to Stay & Eat

The **Refugio La Pastora** (at 2400m) provides accommodation for 28 visitors in four- to eight-bed dorms for US$6 per person. You can also camp for US$2.50 per person. The Refugio serves breakfast (US$1.50), lunch and dinner (US$2.50 each) for guests.

Accommodation has to be booked and paid for at **Grupos Ecológicos de Risaralda** *(GER;* ☎ *325 4781;* e *refugio_lapastora@hotmail .com; Centro Comercial Fiducentro, Local A-119)* in Pereira. If you plan on making a day trip to the park, you still have to visit the GER office to get the free permit.

### Getting There & Away
The reserve is accessible from Pereira over a rough road. Chivas will take you up to El Cedral, 24km from Pereira (see the Pereira section). From El Cedral (at 1950m), it's a pleasant two-hour (6km) walk uphill along the path following the Río Otún to La Pastora (1½ hours in the opposite direction).

## SANTUARIO OTÚN QUIMBAYA
The Santuario de Flora y Fauna Otún Quimbaya is a nature reserve 15km southeast of Pereira. It was created in 1996 to protect a 5-sq-km area of Andean forest between altitudes of 1800m and 2400m, characterised by high biodiversity. The reserve has a visitor centre, La Suiza, offering accommodation and meals, and a few ecological paths. The Santuario is close to Parque Ucumarí, so you can visit both reserves during one trip.

### Places to Stay & Eat
**La Suiza** *(beds US$8-15)* provides accommodation for 90 persons, in doubles and quads, plus meals (US$2 to US$3 each). The **regional national park office** *(*☎ *320 0200)* in Pereira, in the building of the Gobernación del Risaralda, Piso 4, provides information and takes bookings.

### Getting There & Away
Chivas from Pereira to El Cedral (see the earlier Pereira section for details) pass by La Suiza and can drop you off at the entrance. Should you then want to visit Parque Ucumarí, it's a four-hour walk to La Pastora.

## ARMENIA
☎ 6 • pop 250,000 • elevation 1550m • temp 22°C
Armenia was founded by Antioquian colonists as late as 1889. The town developed quickly around coffee production, and in

1966 it became the capital of the newly created department of Quindío. A catastrophic earthquake during January 1999 wrecked a number of buildings and the city's two important tourist attractions – the Museo Quimbaya and the market. According to the official estimates, about 30% of the buildings in the centre were destroyed. Armenia continues to recover from the disaster while the damage in the centre is still very much in evidence.

Whereas the city itself is not a great attraction, the surrounding region is well worth exploring. Quindío, Colombia's smallest department (except for the San Andrés archipelago), covers a mere 0.16% of the country's area, but it has a lot to offer. It shares a part of the mighty Parque Nacional Los Nevados and has several smaller nature reserves. Quindío also has a number of old charming towns founded by Antioquian settlers, as well as the Parque Nacional del Café, the department's most recent great attraction.

### Information
**Tourist Offices** The **Secretaría de Turismo** *(*☎ *741 4209; Plaza de Bolívar; open 8am-noon & 2pm-6pm Mon-Fri)* is situated on the ground floor of the Gobernación del Quindío building.

**Money** The **Bancolombia** *(Calle 20 No 15-26)* is the most likely bank to change travellers cheques, and can also change cash. Other banks marked on the map are only useful for cash advances on Visa and/or MasterCard.

The Centro Comercial IBG, Carrera 14 No 18-56, shelters half a dozen casas de cambio, including **Giros & Finanzas**, which represents Western Union.

**Email & Internet Access** Central facilities include **Internet Telecom** *(*☎ *744 1146; Carrera 14 No 20A-02),* **Zona Web** *(Carrera 14 No 16-31)* and **Mafenet** *(*☎ *741 3730; Centro Comercial IBG, Carrera 14 No 18-56, Local 34).*

### Plaza de Bolívar & Catedral
The Plaza de Bolívar is adorned with two monuments. One of them, predictably, is a monument to Bolívar, but unlike those in Pereira and Manizales, this statue is traditional. It was cast in Paris by Colombian

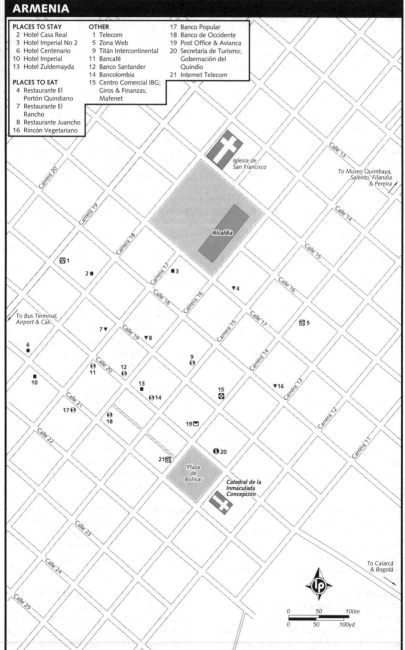

# ARMENIA

**PLACES TO STAY**
2  Hotel Casa Real
3  Hotel Imperial No 2
6  Hotel Centenario
10  Hotel Imperial
13  Hotel Zuldemayda

**PLACES TO EAT**
4  Restaurante El
   Portón Quindiano
7  Restaurante El
   Rancho
8  Restaurante Juancho
16  Rincón Vegetariano

**OTHER**
1  Telecom
5  Zona Web
9  Titán Intercontinental
11  Bancafé
12  Banco Santander
14  Bancolombia
15  Centro Comercial IBG;
   Giros & Finanzas;
   Mafenet

17  Banco Popular
18  Banco de Occidente
19  Post Office & Avianca
20  Secretaría de Turismo;
   Gobernación del
   Quindío
21  Internet Telecom

Iglesia de
San Francisco

To Museo Quimbaya,
Salento, Filandia
& Pereira

Calle 13

Calle 14

Carrera 20

Carrera 19

Carrera 18

Alcaldía

Calle 15

Carrera 17

Calle 16

2  ▮

☎1

▮3

▼4

Calle 18

Carrera 16

Calle 17

To Bus Terminal,
Airport & Cali

Carrera 15

Calle 19

7 ▼

▼8

6
▮

Calle 20

12

11

9

Carrera 14

☎5

▮
10

13
▮

◈14

15
✚

▼16

Carrera 13

17 ◈

9
18

19 ✉

Carrera 12

Calle 21

Calle 22

21 ⌨

ℹ 20

Carrera 11

Plaza
de
Bolívar

Catedral de la
Inmaculada
Concepción

Calle 23

Calle 24

To Calarcá
& Bogotá

Calle 25

| 0 | 50 | 100m |
|---|---|---|
| 0 | 50 | 100yd |

artist Roberto Henao Buriticá and unveiled on 17 December 1930, the centenary of Bolívar's death. The other monument on the square is the Monumento al Esfuerzo, yet another of Arenas Betancur's many extravaganzas.

The modern, tent-like concrete Catedral de la Inmaculada Concepción houses a series of abstract stained-glass windows.

## Museo Quimbaya

Also referred to as the Museo del Oro *(☎ 749 4426, 749 3820; Av Bolívar at Calle 40N)*, the museum was seriously damaged by the 1999 earthquake and was closed at the time of writing. It may reopen by the time you come, so check. Before the disaster, it was one of Colombia's best gold museums, featuring an excellent collection of ceramics and gold artefacts of Quimbaya culture. The museum is in the modern Centro Cultural, 5km northeast of the centre, on the road to Pereira.

## Places to Stay

Many of the budget hotels were clustered around Armenia's unusually large and vibrant market, but they were devastated by the 1999 earthquake. The market area has been turned into a park and the Alcaldía building was erected in place of a new market hall.

There are still some basic hotels found between Carreras 17 and 18, and Calles 17 and 19, but not many to be recommended. **Hotel Imperial No 2** *(☎ 741 2819; Carrera 17 No 17-31; singles/doubles US$5/6, with bath US$7/10)* is one of the cheapest of the acceptable ones.

**Hotel Casa Real** *(☎ 741 4550; Carrera 18 No 18-36; singles/doubles/triples with bath US$10/18/24)* is appreciably better than the Imperial No 2, although it's also in an unattractive area, which may not be that safe at night.

**Hotel Imperial** *(☎ 744 9151; Calle 21 No 17-43; singles/doubles/triples with bath US$10/12/17)* is better located and provides good value. Its rooms are neat, quiet, and perfectly acceptable.

**Hotel Zuldemayda** *(☎ 741 0580; Calle 20 No 15-38; singles/doubles/triples US$30/40/ 50)* has somehow survived the earthquake, unlike some of its neighbours. It has been solidly restored and offers satisfactory conditions, even though its rooms are rather small. Breakfast is included in the room price.

**Hotel Centenario** *(☎ 744 3143; Calle 21 No 18-20; singles/doubles/triples US$32/45/ 55)* is the best central option. It was the first hotel to be built in the city centre after the earthquake, so it feels new and neat. Breakfast is included in the price.

## Places to Eat

There's a number of budget restaurants serving set meals (US$1.50 to US$2) in the centre, including **El Portón Quindiano** *(Calle 17 No 15-40)*, **Restaurante Juancho** *(Calle 19 No 16-16)* and **Restaurante El Rancho** *(Carrera 17 No 19-10)*. Vegetarians can get budget meals at **Rincón Vegetariano** *(Calle 18 No 13-24)*.

There are several middle-range restaurants on Carrera 14, but most of the classier restaurants are outside the central area in the northeastern residential district.

## Getting There & Away

**Air** El Edén airport is 18km southwest of the city, near the town of La Tebaida on the road to Cali. Aces has four flights a day to Bogotá (US$50 to US$85) and one to Medellín (US$50 to US$110). Flights to other destinations have to connect in one of these cities.

**Bus** All buses arrive at and leave from the bus terminal on the corner of Carrera 19 and Calle 35. It is 1.5km southwest of the centre and can be reached by frequent city buses that run along Carrera 19.

There are plenty of buses to Bogotá (US$13, eight hours) and to Cali (US$7, four hours). Minibuses depart every 15 minutes or so to Pereira (US$2, one hour), Manizales (US$4.50, 2¼ hours), Filandia (US$1.25, one hour), Salento (US$0.80, 50 minutes) and Parque Nacional del Café (US$0.60, 25 minutes).

## PARQUE NACIONAL DEL CAFÉ
**☎ 6 • temp 21°C**

Established on the site of an old coffee hacienda and opened in 1995, the Parque Nacional del Café *(☎ 753 6095; admission US$4; open 9am-4pm Wed-Sun)* is a 52-hectare coffee theme park. It provides an easy and attractive insight into Colombia's coffee world, featuring its diverse aspects. The park is near the small town of Pueblo Tapao, about 15km west of Armenia, and is easily accessible by frequent minibuses from the city. It's Quindío's biggest tourist attraction, drawing in far more visitors than any other sight in the state.

The park is quite clearly divided into two parts. The first is the theme park proper, dedicated to the coffee, and there's a lot to see here. The other part, at the far back, is a large amusement park, with a collection of the usual distractions such as a roller-coaster, water slide, go-kart racetrack and a carousel.

In the high season (mid-December to mid-January, Easter, mid-June to mid-July) the park may be open daily. Put aside half a day to leisurely enjoy the park, and don't come if it's raining, as most attractions are outdoors.

## Things to See & Do

At the entrance of the park is the **Torre Mirador**, an 18m timber tower that provides views over the park and beyond. Next to the tower is the **Monumento a la Cosecha**, or the Harvest Monument, featuring a group of bronzed coffee workers with their mules loaded with sacks of coffee. Here is also the **Museo del Café**, housed in a rambling, old-style mansion, with numerous exhibits illustrating the history of coffee production in Colombia.

Behind the museum, you take the **Sendero Ecológico**, an ecological path that zigzags downhill to the river then climbs back to the museum. It's a 4km loop that winds through a number of attractions, including a traditional coffee plantation, a Quimbaya Indian cemetery and the stunning **Bambusario**, possibly the most impressive guadua forest you've ever seen.

Just behind the river is the **Pueblito Quindiano**, a re-created typical regional township, with its Plaza de Bolívar (actually, a replica of Armenia's main plaza from 1926) lined by houses built in traditional style. Some of these houses feature restaurants and snack bars offering local food. Beyond the Pueblito stretches the amusement park.

The Pueblito is linked with the museum by the **Teleférico**, or a cable car which provides some bird's-eye views, whereas the **Tren del Café**, pulled by a 1927 locomotive, can take you on a 6km ride around the amusement park.

## FILANDIA

☎ 6 • pop 4500 • elevation 1930m • temp 18°C

Filandia, a small town 30km north of Armenia, is one of the best examples of a typical pueblo left behind by Antioquian settlers in Quindío. The town has preserved its character remarkably well, with only the occasional intrusion of modern buildings. Uninterrupted lines of brightly painted houses dating from the beginning of the 20th century still stand on many streets.

There are two budget *residencias* on the main square, but most visitors just pop in for a few hours. Minibuses to and from Armenia run approximately every 15 minutes.

## SALENTO

☎ 6 • pop 3500 • elevation 1900m • temp 18°C

Founded in 1850, Salento is perhaps the oldest town in Quindío, and it's just about the smallest. One local saying charmingly summarises it thus: *el pueblo de calles cortas y recuerdos largos* ('the town of short streets and long memories').

Salento is a lovely place which gives the impression that the 20th century got lost somewhere down the road. Its plaza and main street, Calle Real (Carrera 6), boast many fine old houses, and its proximity to Los Nevados gives the town a noticeable mountain atmosphere and appearance.

You'll find more attractions outside the town, further to the east. Climb the Alto de la Cruz, a hill topped with a cross at the end of Calle Real, and you'll see the verdant Valle de Cocora with the mountains in the background. If the sky is cloudless (usually only early in the morning), you can spot the snow-capped tops of the volcanoes on the horizon.

## Places to Stay & Eat

Salento has half a dozen places to stay and many more places to eat. Additionally, the locals rent out rooms in their homes, which can be cheaper.

**Grocery of Miguel Gaviria** (*Calle 6 at Carrera 9; doubles/triples US$6/10*) is one of the cheapest places to stay. The owner rents out four rooms behind his shop. They are basic and without baths, but acceptable.

**Hostería Calle Real** (☎ 759 3272; *Carrera 6 No 2-20; rooms per person US$7*) is one

## Palma de Cera, World's Tallest Palm

There are more than 2500 known varieties of palm tree, of which the *palma de cera (Ceroxylon quindiunense)*, or wax palm, is a very particular kind. With its life span of 200 years, it's the world's tallest palm variety, growing up to 60m. At the same time, it has an unusually slim trunk, which makes it look striking, almost surreal.

The wax palm's favourite habitat is the cloud forest climatic zone, roughly between altitudes of 1500m and 3000m. It's actually the only palm species that can grow above 2500m and some specimens have been seen as high as 3300m. Yet it also grows at low altitudes.

The palm was first identified and classified by Alexander von Humboldt and Aime Bonpland during their expedition in Colombia in the early years of the 19th century. By then, the wax palm was commonly found all across the Andean region, but it was gradually depleted by forest clearing and the palm's commercial exploitation. Today, it's no longer a common species, and the areas where it grows are limited.

The region of Los Nevados in the Central Cordillera remains one of the palm's largest habitats. The Valle de Cocora is the best place in Colombia (and in the world for that matter) to see the 'forests' of this amazing palm. In 1985, the palma de cera was declared Colombia's national tree and placed under protection.

of the most pleasant places, and it's on the town's 'best' street. It has five rooms with bath and hot water. Optional breakfast costs US$1.50.

**La Posada del Café** (☎ 759 3012; *Carrera 6 No 3-08; rooms per person US$15)* is another charming place on the main street, but it's perhaps a bit overrated.

There are several restaurants on Calle Real and more on the main plaza, so there's little chance to starve.

You can also stay and eat in **Finca Mis Bohíos** (☎ 759 3202), 2km east of Salento on the road to Cocora.

### Getting There & Away

Minibuses to and from Armenia (US$0.80, 50 minutes) run roughly every 15 minutes. Two jeeps a day, normally around 7.30am and 4pm, depart from Salento's plaza and go up the rough 11km road to Cocora (US$1, 35 minutes). There may be more departures if there's a demand, but you either have to wait until six passengers have been collected or pay for the empty seats (US$1 each). On weekends, when tourists come, there are usu-

ally at least four departures daily. Otherwise, it's a pleasant two-hour walk to Cocora.

### VALLE DE COCORA

This long valley stretches from Salento eastwards to the tiny hamlet of Cocora and beyond. Cocora is just a collection of several houses, three restaurants serving delicious trout, and the **trout breeding station** (*admission US$1; open Sat afternoon, all day Sun)*.

The most spectacular part of the valley is east of Cocora. Take the rough road heading downhill to the bridge over the Río Quindío (just a five-minute walk from the restaurants) and you will see hills covered with the *palma de cera*, a very special kind of palm (see the boxed text 'Palma de Cera, World's Tallest Palm'). It's an astonishing sight. Walk further uphill and enjoy the scenery – you won't find that kind of landscape anywhere else.

The palms have made Cocora a tourist destination, with visitors mainly arriving on the weekends. On these days locals gather around the three restaurants to rent out horses (US$2.50 per hour).

# Southwest Colombia

Like almost every region in Colombia, the southwest is widely diverse, both culturally and geographically. Here you'll find jungles, deserts, beaches, snow-capped peaks, hot springs, icy streams, fertile valleys, arid wastelands, volcanoes, *páramos* (open highlands), lakes, caves and waterfalls – every kind of landscape imaginable. Some of these natural features are protected in the region's eight national parks.

On the cultural front, the southwest boasts a collection of colonial towns (of which Popayán undoubtedly heads the league), several important religious sanctuaries (don't miss Las Lajas), a number of old haciendas (among which El Paraíso and Piedechinche are the best known) and two of the most significant archaeological sites in all of the Americas (San Agustín and Tierradentro), which are possibly the region's most significant attractions, though not often visited these days due to security problems.

The Indian population of the region comprises several groups from different ethnic backgrounds. The dominant group is the Páez community living in the Tierradentro area, which belongs to the Chibcha linguistic family and numbers some 40,000 people. More traditional are the Guambianos (numbering about 12,000), from the mountainous region around Silvia, northeast of Popayán.

This chapter covers the departments of Valle del Cauca, Cauca, Huila and Nariño. With a population of nearly two million, Cali is the region's dominant urban centre, six times larger than the second biggest city, Pasto.

## Valle del Cauca

The department of Valle del Cauca bears the name of the Cauca Valley, the agricultural heart of the region. The valley accounts for most of Colombia's sugar production and it is possible to harvest the crop all year round. The valley produces many other crops, including cotton, tobacco, maize, grapes and coffee. Amid this rich agriculture sits Cali, the departmental capital.

The valley is flanked on its east and west sides by the mountain ranges of the Cor-

### Highlights

- Enjoy Cali's tropical pulse with its hot salsa and easy-going locals
- Explore Popayán, the region's most beautiful and best-preserved colonial town
- Discover the mysterious stone statues of San Agustín
- Visit the unique underground burial chambers of Tierradentro
- Experience Colombia's Catholic devotion at the striking Santuario de las Lajas

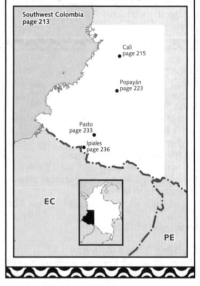

Southwest Colombia
page 213

Cali
page 215

Popayán
page 223

Pasto
page 233

Ipiales
page 236

EC

PE

dillera Central and Cordillera Occidental respectively. Beyond the latter stretches the wide lowland of thick rainforest which slopes down to the mangrove swamps on the Pacific Coast. Here is the port of Buenaventura, the second largest city of the department and Colombia's most important port on the Pacific.

### CALI
☎ 2 • pop 1,850,000 • elevation 1005m
• temp 24°C

Set in the verdant Cauca Valley, Cali is a lively city with a fairly hot climate. Apart from a few fine churches and museums, Cali has no great sights, but is appealing thanks to

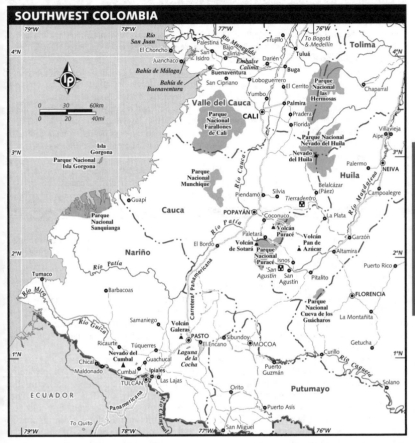

SOUTHWEST COLOMBIA

its vibrant atmosphere and amiable inhabitants. This ambience is best appreciated in the evening when a refreshing breeze dissipates the heat of day and city dwellers take to the streets, open-air cafés and salsa spots.

## History

Cali was founded in 1536 by Sebastián de Belalcázar, one of Francisco Pizarro's lieutenants, who had taken part in the conquest of the Incas.

Intrigues between these two conquerors, however, prompted Belalcázar to desert from Pizarro's army. When the Inca Empire was effectively at an end, after the execution of Atahualpa in 1533, Belalcázar made his way northward and founded Quito in 1534 on the ruins of a former Inca city.

It took him another year to get to the Cauca Valley.

At the time of the arrival of the Spaniards, the valley was inhabited by various indigenous groups, of which the Calima community was the most advanced. Despite Indian attacks, a new settlement was founded and called Santiago de Cali. Belalcázar briefly explored the region (founding Popayán in the process) and then moved further northward. He was only a little too late to found yet another important city, Bogotá, arriving there shortly after it had been founded by Jiménez de Quesada.

Cali's development was based principally on the fertile soil of the valley. The Spaniards shipped in thousands of African slaves to work on plantations of sugarcane and other

## What Is Cali Famous For?

Cali is renowned as a centre for sports. The Pan-American sports complex was built here in 1971 for the international games, with a stadium, Olympic-size gymnasium, swimming pools and the like. The city is also proud of its bullring: La Plaza de Toros de Cañaveralejo is the biggest in the country (19,000 seats) and one of the most modern in the Americas.

Cali is also noted for the beauty of its women, *las caleñas*, who are said to be the most graceful in the nation. Well, that's the popular local belief, but where in Colombia are they not beautiful? Colombian women won a number of titles in the Miss Universe and Miss World pageants.

Another source of Cali's pride is its salsa music. These hot rhythms originated in Cuba in the 1940s, matured in New York and spread throughout the Caribbean, reaching Colombia in the 1960s. Today, salsa is heard all over the country, but Cali and Barranquilla remain Colombia's major centres of this music. The African ancestry of a sizable part of the population in these cities has largely contributed to this.

Finally, Cali came to be known as home to the notorious Cali drug cartel and the major centre of cocaine trafficking. However, this is no longer true; since many of the cartel's top leaders were jailed in 1995, the cartel has been largely dismantled and the cocaine industry moved elsewhere.

crops. The African legacy is still very much in evidence today; a significant proportion of the population is black and mulatto.

Cali's political and religious importance was minor and eclipsed by the nearby Popayán, which was the province's capital and the principal centre of regional power during the whole colonial period and for a long time after. Cali's growth was slow and progress really came only at the beginning of the 20th century, primarily with the establishment of a large-scale sugar industry, followed by dynamic development in other sectors. A remarkable economic boom, especially since the 1940s, has helped the city to grow fivefold in the last 50 years. In the last two decades alone the city's population increased by half a million.

Today, Cali is Colombia's third-largest city, after Bogotá and Medellín, and the dominant industrial, agricultural and commercial centre of the southwest. It's the capital of the Valle del Cauca, housing more than half of the department's population.

## Orientation

The city centre is split in two by the Río Cali. To the south is the historic heart, laid out on a grid plan and centred on the Plaza de Caycedo. This is the area of most tourist sights, including historic churches and museums.

To the north of the river is the new centre, whose main axis is Av Sexta (Av 6N). This sector is modern, with trendy shops and restaurants, and it comes alive in the evening when a refreshing breeze tempers the day-time heat. This is the area in which to dine, drink and dance after a day of sightseeing on the opposite side of the river.

## Information

**Tourist Offices** The Secretaría de Cultura y Turismo (☎ 620 0000 ext 2410; open 8am-12.30pm & 2.30pm-6pm Mon-Fri) is on the 1st floor of the Gobernación del Valle del Cauca building.

The **national park office** (☎ 654 3719, 654 3720; Av 3GN No 37N-70) provides information on the national parks in the region, including the Isla Gorgona. The office no longer issues permits or books accommodation on the island, claiming that it has to be done in the Bogotá office. See Isla Gorgona later in this chapter.

The **Red de Reservas Naturales de la Sociedad Civil** (☎ 653 4538, 653 4539; W www.resnatur.org.co; Av 9N No 22N-07) provides information about nature reserves operated by individuals and nongovernmental organisations. See National Parks in the earlier Facts about Colombia chapter for further details.

**Money** For changing foreign cash and travellers cheques, you can try **Bancolombia** (Calle 15N at Av 8N) or **Banco Unión Colombiano** (Carrera 3 No 11-03 • Calle 22N No 6N-22). Central casas de cambio include the **Titán Intercontinental** (Calle 11 No 4-48, Plaza de Caycedo), **Univisa** (Carrera 4 No 8-67) and **Giros & Finanzas** (Carrera 4 No 10-12). All of the banks that are marked

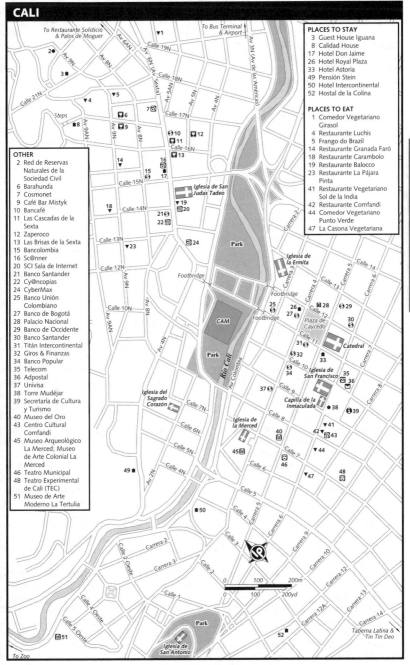

# CALI

SOUTHWEST COLOMBIA

on the Cali map provide peso advances on credit cards.

**Email & Internet Access** The SCI Sala de Internet (☎ 661 5886; Av 6N No 13N-66) is the largest and possibly the fastest central facility. Other Internet cafés in the new centre include the **Cy@ncopias** (☎ 668 8395; Av 6N No 13N-23), **Cosmonet** (☎ 668 6522; Av 6N No 17N-65), **Sc@nner** (☎ 664 4119; Av 6N No 15N-37) and the **CyberMax** (☎ 661 5945; Calle 12N No 4N-68).

In the historic centre, there's a convenient facility at the **Centro Cultural Comfandi** (☎ 334 0000 ext 1313; Calle 8 No 6-23, Piso 5). Any of the listed facilities will cost US$1 to US$1.50 per hour.

**Dangers & Annoyances** Even though Cali may look quieter and more relaxed than Bogotá or Medellín, don't be deceived by its easy-going air, summery heat and beautiful women. Muggers and thieves aren't inactive here, nor are they less clever or violent than elsewhere. Be careful while wandering around the streets at night. Avoid the park along Río Cali in the evening, and don't walk east of Calle 13 after dark.

## Museums

The **Museo Arqueológico La Merced** (☎ 889 3434; Carrera 4 No 6-59; admission US$1; open 9am-1pm & 2pm-6pm Mon-Sat) is housed in the former La Merced convent, Cali's oldest building, dating back to the city's early days. In its five rooms, you'll find a collection of pre-Columbian pottery left behind by the major cultures from central and southern Colombia, including Quimbaya, Tolima, Calima, Tierradentro, San Agustín, Nariño and Tumaco. There are some excellent pieces, worth closer inspection.

In the same building is the **Museo de Arte Colonial La Merced** (☎ 880 4737; Carrera 4 No 6-117) with a collection of colonial religious artefacts, but it was closed for refurbishing at the time of writing.

The **Museo del Oro** (☎ 684 7757; Calle 7 No 4-69; admission free; open 8am-11.30am & 2pm-6pm Mon-Fri), one block away from La Merced, has a small but well-selected and arranged collection of gold and pottery of the Calima culture.

The **Museo de Arte Moderno La Tertulia** (☎ 893 2942; Av Colombia No 5 Oeste-105; admission US$1; open 9am-1pm & 3pm-7pm Tues-Sat, 3pm-7pm Sun & Mon) presents temporary exhibitions of contemporary painting, sculpture and photography. It's a 15-minute walk from the city centre along Av Colombia.

## Churches

The **Iglesia de la Merced** (Carrera 4 at Calle 7) is the city's oldest church. It was begun around 1545 on the site where the first Mass was held in 1536 to commemorate the town's foundation. It's a lovely whitewashed building in the Spanish colonial style. Once inside, your attention will be captured by a heavily gilded baroque high altar topped by the Virgen de las Mercedes, the patron saint of the city. The church is likely to be open approximately 6.30am to 10am and 4pm to 7pm.

Overlooking the parks on the Río Cali, the Gothic-style **Iglesia de la Ermita** (Av Colombia at Calle 13), constructed between 1930 and 1948, has become one of the best-known landmarks in the city. The marble altar was brought from Italy. The 18th-century painting of El Señor de la Caña (Lord of the Sugarcane), to whom many miracles are attributed, is in the side altar. The church is open most of the day.

**Iglesia de San Francisco** (Carrera 6 at Calle 10) is a neoclassical construction dating from the 18th century. The large marble-and-wood altar was made in Spain at the beginning of the 20th century and shipped to Colombia. It landed at Buenaventura and was then carried to Cali by mule along the ancient camino de herradura (bridle path).

Next to the church are the Convento de San Francisco and the Capilla de la Inmaculada with the adjacent **Torre Mudéjar** (Carrera 6 at Calle 9), an unusual brick bell tower, which is one of the best examples of Mudéjar art in Colombia. The tower was built in the 18th century and its pealing bells served as the town's timepiece for many years.

The small 1757 **Iglesia de San Antonio** is set atop a hill, the Colina de San Antonio, west of the old centre. It shelters valuable tallas quiteñas, 17th-century carved-wood statues of the saints, representing the style known as the Quito School. The church's 19th-century bells are cast in a gold, copper and bronze alloy, and are said to have the merriest sound in Cali; they ring for Mass at 9am and 6pm (on Sunday at 5.30pm only). Even if you miss the opening hours of the church it's still worth walking there for a good view of the city; it's just a 10-minute walk west of the Torre Mudéjar.

## Zoológico de Cali
Founded in 1970, the zoo (☎ 892 7474; *Carrera 2A Oeste at Calle 14 Oeste; admission US$2.50; open 9am-5pm daily)* is in the suburb of Santa Teresita, 2km west of the centre. Its 10 hectares are home to about 1200 animals (belonging to about 180 species), both native and imported from other continents. It's Colombia's best zoo and it's well worth visiting.

## Organised Tours
There are plenty of travel agencies in Cali. They offer tours both within and outside the department (El Paraíso–Piedechinche, Popayán–Silvia), as well as city tours.

**Ecolombia Tours** (☎ 557 1957, 514 0829; e *ecolombiatours@yahoo.com; Carrera 37A No 6-18)* is arguably Cali's best specialist for tours to Isla Gorgona (US$250 to US$300). See Isla Gorgona later in this chapter for further details.

**Viajes Oganesoff** (☎ 892 2840, 892 0656; w *www.viajesoganesoff.com; Hotel Intercontinental, Av Colombia No 2-72)* organises night tours in *chiva* (US$15). Tours go on weekends if there are enough people to fill up a chiva (see Entertainment later).

## Special Events
The main city event is the **Feria de Cali**, which breaks out annually on 25 December and goes till the end of the year (some events continue into the first days of the new year), with parades, masquerades, music, theatre, bullfights and lots of fun. One of the highlights is a marathon concert of salsa bands, usually well attended by renowned international groups. Given the legendary beauty of the *caleñas* (Cali women), it's no surprise that the beauty pageant also draws in hordes of spectators.

## Places to Stay
Cali has two budget backpacker hostels conveniently located in the new city centre. They are close to the nightclubs and good restaurants and are popular with travellers:

**Guest House Iguana** (☎ 661 3522; *Calle 21N No 9N-22; singles/doubles US$7/10)*, run by a friendly Swiss woman, has ample clean rooms with shared facilities and offers laundry service and information.

**Calidad House** (☎ 661 2338; *Calle 17N No 9AN-39; dorm beds US$5)* is a bit more basic, with small four-bed dorms without baths, but it provides a range of facilities, including a laundry service, free use of the kitchen and luggage storage.

There are few budget hotels south of Río Cali, except for the maze of seedy *hospedajes* east of Calle 15, but don't walk there as it's unsafe. Farther west, in a quiet residential area near Iglesia de San Antonio, is **Hostal de la Colina** (☎ 893 7991; *Carrera 12 No 2-54; singles/doubles US$15/20)*, a large, pleasant family house with six good rooms all with bath.

There's a choice of mid-price accommodation around Plaza de Caycedo, including two places lining the plaza: the cheaper **Hotel Astoria** (☎ 883 0140; *Calle 11 No 5-16; singles/doubles/triples US$14/18/22)* and the better **Hotel Royal Plaza** (☎ 883 9243; *Carrera 4 No 11-69; singles/doubles/triples US$25/30/35)*. Both have rooms with private baths and fans. Some of the rooms overlook the plaza. In both hotels, ask for a room on one of the upper floors, for less noise and better views. Royal Plaza has a restaurant on the top floor.

**Pensión Stein** (☎ 661 4999; *Av 4N No 3N-33; singles/doubles with fan US$24/40, with air-con US$34/48)*, in a castle-like mansion, is a place with character and good value. Run by a Swiss couple, the hotel offers spotlessly clean rooms with bath and has a restaurant. All prices include breakfast.

**Hotel Don Jaime** (☎ 667 2828; *Av 6N No 15N-25; singles/doubles/triples with air-con US$35/45/55)* may be an option if you need somewhere affordable with air-con close to the city's pulse on Av Sexta. The hotel has 30 spacious rooms and you have half a dozen discos within a 100m radius.

Anyone with adequately lined pockets might take the plunge into the five-star **Hotel Intercontinental** (☎ 882 3225; w *www .interconti.com; Av Colombia No 2-72; doubles US$100)*, which is the best in Cali. It has most of what you'd wish for, including a swimming pool, gym, tennis court and Internet access.

## Places to Eat

There are loads of cafés and restaurants on and around Av Sexta, offering everything from simple snacks, burgers and pizzas to regional Colombian specialities and ethnic cuisines. Several budget restaurants serve set meals for around US$2. One of these is the long-established **Restaurante Balocco** (Av 6N No 14N-04; set meals US$1.75). Better is the small, family-run **Restaurante Luchis** (Calle 18N No 9N-111; set meals US$2, mains US$3), which also has some vegetarian dishes. If you prefer somewhere purely vegetarian, try **Comedor Vegetariano Girasol** (Av 5BN No 20N-30; set meals US$1.75).

There are also plenty of budget restaurants and snack bars in the historic centre on the other side of the river. One of the good places for a tasty lunch is the self-service **Restaurante Comfandi** (Carrera 6 No 8-22; set lunches US$2), which is hugely popular among locals. Vegetarians can get budget lunches at **La Casona Vegetariana** (Carrera 6 No 6-56; set meals US$2), **Restaurante Vegetariano Sol de la India** (Carrera 6 No 8-48; set meals US$2) and **Comedor Vegetariano Punto Verde** (Carrera 6 No 7-40; set meals US$2).

For finer dining, you can try some of the well-appointed restaurants on or just off Av 9N in the new centre.

**Restaurante Carambolo** (☎ 667 5656; Calle 14N No 9N-18; mains US$6-10) is a charmingly informal, two-level, cosy place full of flowers. It offers fine Mediterranean cuisine.

**Restaurante Granada Faró** (☎ 667 4625; Av 9N No 15AN-02; mains US$7-10) is a trendy local with an artistic touch, decorated with paintings. It serves international (mostly Mediterranean) cuisine and great salads.

**Restaurante La Pájara Pinta** (☎ 667 6786; Av 9N No 12N-76; mains US$7-10) occupies a spacious rambling mansion, which once was a family home, and the ladies' toilet still has its baths. It provides different ambiences and a great outdoor eating area. The service is first class, as is the food (international cuisine), even though the portions are rather small.

**Frango do Brazil** (☎ 660 1389; Av 9N No 17AN-36; mains US$7-12) is another attractive place with outdoor seating. It brings Brazilian cuisine to town, and it also has some international fare.

**Restaurante Solsticio** (☎ 668 2090; Av 6AN No 21N-77; mains US$6-10) offers a fine international menu which includes delicious meats and salads in colourful modern surroundings.

## Entertainment

Check the entertainment columns of local newspaper *El País*.

**Cinema** Cali has a number of commercial cinemas including **Multiplex Chipichape** (☎ 659 2199; Centro Comercial Chipichape, Calle 38N No 6N-35) and **Multiplex Unicali** (☎ 339 6626; Centro Comercial Unicentro, Carrera 100 No 5-169).

For more thought-provoking fare, check the programme of the **Cinemateca La Tertulia** (☎ 893 2942; Museo de Arte Moderno La Tertulia, Av Colombia No 5 Oeste-105), which has two shows daily from Tuesday to Sunday.

You can also try **Palos de Moguer** (☎ 660 2840; Av 6AN No 22N-26), which has a cine bar, where you can enjoy films and beer (see Nightlife later).

**Theatre** Colombia's national theatre came into being with the foundation of the **Teatro Experimental de Cali** (TEC; ☎ 884 3820; Calle 7 No 8-61). It continues to be one of the city's most innovative theatre companies. If you understand Spanish well enough, go to the TEC theatre and see one of its current productions.

**Teatro Municipal** (☎ 883 9106; Carrera 5 No 6-64) is the city's oldest existing theatre, completed in 1918. Today it's used for various artistic forms, including musical concerts, theatre and ballet, performed mostly by visiting groups.

**Nightlife** There are lots of bars, taverns, discos and nightclubs in the new centre. You'll find half a dozen discos around the corner of Av 6N and Calle 16N, of which **Las Brisas de la Sexta** (Av 6N No 15N-94) is one of the largest and most popular haunts. Just across the street is another vast disco, **Las Cascadas de la Sexta** (Av 6N No 16N-18), which has seven large screens and four dance floors. Tucked away a bit is the cosier **Zaperoco** (Av 5N No 16N-52), a likable *salsoteca*, with its magnetic salsa rhythms and hot atmosphere. Most places don't have a cover charge, so it's easy to move from one to the next, as you wish.

Several attractive bars have recently mushroomed on Calle 17N between Av 8N and Av 9N. The **Barahunda** *(Calle 17N No 8N-60)* was the most 'in' place at the time of writing, but check the others, including **Café Bar Mistyk**, directly across the street.

There are more bars further north, including the unusual **Palos de Moguer** *(Av 6AN No 22N-26)*, the only one that serves beer straight from its own in-house brewery. And the name? It's actually the name of the Spanish port from which Columbus departed on 3 August 1492 for his maiden journey across the Atlantic.

Another centre of night-time entertainment is on and around Calle 5 in southern Cali where you'll find two trendy discos, **Taberna Latina** *(Calle 5 No 38-75)* and **Tin Tin Deo** *(Carrera 22 No 4A-27)*. Both are frequented by university students and professors, adding intellectuality to the action.

Cali's best known salsa nightlife is in the legendary Juanchito, a popular outer suburb on the Río Cauca, largely populated by blacks. Far away from the centre, Juanchito was traditionally an archetypal salsa haunt dotted with dubious cafés and bars. Today, sterile and expensive salsotecas have replaced the old shady but charming venues. Juanchito's most famous salsa place is **Changó**, which is also probably the priciest. **Agapito**, next door, is cheaper and not necessarily poorer. **Parador** is frequented by some of the most acrobatic dancers in town. There are quite a few more venues to explore, including **Baracoa**. Come on the weekend and use a taxi. Note that the action starts late; places open at around 10pm and get crowded by midnight, peaking at about 2am.

A night tour in a chiva is a convenient and easy way of visiting some of the nightspots, if you are wary of setting off on a nocturnal adventure on your own. Chiva tours are organised on weekend nights by several operators, including the Viajes Oganesoff travel agency in the lobby of the Hotel Intercontinental. Its chiva, with a typical music band aboard, departs from the hotel on Friday and Saturday at 8pm. The five-hour tour calls at several music spots (usually one in Juanchito and one on Av Sexta), includes half a bottle of *aguardiente* per head and a snack, and costs US$15 per person.

Chivas also leave from other places, including the CAM (Centro Administrativo Municipal) and the Plazoleta de Avianca. These tours are usually cheaper but shorter. You don't need to book. Just watch out for parked chivas, ask for routes and prices, then decide for yourself.

## Getting There & Away

**Air** The Palmaseca airport is 16km northeast of the city, off the road to Palmira. Minibuses between the airport and the bus terminal run every 10 minutes until about 8pm (US$1, 30 minutes), or take a taxi (US$12).

There are plenty of flights to most major Colombian cities, including Bogotá (US$50 to US$110), Cartagena (US$80 to US$130), Medellín (US$80 to US$120), Pasto (US$50 to US$100) and San Andrés (US$100 to US$150). Aires and Satena fly to Ipiales (US$65 to US$100). Satena has daily flights to Guapí (US$50).

Avianca flies to Panama City (US$268 a 60-day return), while Tame has three flights per week to Tulcán in Ecuador (US$84 one way) and to Quito (US$118).

**Bus** The bus terminal is a 25-minute walk northeast of the centre, or 10 minutes by a frequent city bus. Buses run regularly to Bogotá (US$20, 12 hours), Medellín (US$16, nine hours) and Pasto (US$12, nine hours). Pasto buses will drop you off in Popayán (US$4, three hours) and there are also hourly minibuses to Popayán (US$5, 2½ hours). There are regular departures to Armenia (US$7, four hours), Pereira (US$8, four hours) and Manizales (US$10, five hours).

## HACIENDAS EL PARAÍSO & PIEDECHINCHE

There are a number of old haciendas in the Cauca Valley around Cali, most dating from the 18th and 19th centuries. They were engaged in the cultivation and processing of sugarcane, the region's major crop. El Paraíso and Piedechinche, close to each other about 40km northeast of Cali, are the best-known haciendas, both open as museums.

### El Paraíso

Also called the Casa de la Sierra, El Paraíso *(☎ 256 2378; admission US$1.50; open 9am-4pm Tues-Sun)* is a country mansion built in colonial style in 1815. It owes its fame to having been the setting for a tragic love story depicted by Jorge Isaacs in his tear-jerking romantic novel, *María*. The book was published in 1867 and has remained unwaveringly popular to this day.

The house has been restored and decked out with period furnishings, and looks much the same as it is described in the novel. The place will mean more to you if you have read the book, but if not, it is still a nice house surrounded by a pleasant garden.

### Piedechinche

Dating back to the second half of the 18th century, Piedechinche (☎ 438 4950, 550 6076; *admission US$1.50; open 9am-4pm Tues-Sun*) is a bigger hacienda and once had its own sugar refinery. The original *trapiche* (traditional sugarcane mill) is still in place, next to the colonial mansion.

The **Museo de la Caña de Azúcar** (Sugarcane Museum) was founded here in 1981 and is well organised. There is an exhibition hall where various aspects of sugarcane production are displayed, and a large park where a collection of old trapiches from all over the country have been put on view. The mansion itself, with its collection of period objects, can also be visited.

All the visitors are guided in groups. The tour takes about 1½ hours and includes visits to both the original mansion and the museum.

### Getting There & Away

The haciendas are near one another, so it's convenient to visit both of them in one trip. However, there's no regular public transport all the way to the haciendas; unless you come on a tour or by taxi, the trip will involve quite a bit of walking.

Many buses run along the Cali–Palmira–Buga road; get off on the outskirts of the town of Amaime (the drivers know where to drop you) and walk to Piedechinche (5.5km) or negotiate a taxi. El Paraíso is still further off the road.

Tours from Cali are run mostly on weekends; see Organised Tours in the earlier Cali section.

### SAN CIPRIANO

This is a village lost deep in the tropical forest near the Pacific Coast, off the Cali–Buenaventura road. There's no road leading

to the village, just a railway with occasional trains, but the locals have set up their own rail network with small man-propelled trolleys. This ingenious means of transport is a great attraction and justifies a San Cipriano trip if only for the ride.

San Cipriano boasts a crystal-clear river (ideal for swimming), informal budget accommodation and some simple places to eat. The village is a popular weekend destination with *caleños* (residents of Cali), but it's quiet on weekdays.

### Getting There & Away

To get to San Cipriano from Cali, take a bus or *colectivo* to Buenaventura, get off at the village of Córdoba (US$3, two hours) and walk down the hill into the village to the railway track. From here, the locals will take you to San Cipriano in their rail cars, a really great journey through the rainforest for US$1.

Check the safety conditions before setting off from Cali. The Cali–Buenaventura road has been known for the occasional presence of guerrillas.

### ISLA GORGONA

With an area of 24 sq km, Gorgona is Colombia's largest island in the Pacific Ocean. It's 9km long and 2.5km wide and lies 56km off the mainland. It's a mountainous island of volcanic origin, with its highest peak reaching 330m. It's covered with lush tropical rainforest and shelters diverse wildlife. The eastern coast, facing the continent, is calmer than the west, with several beaches (some of them white, which is uncommon on the Pacific Coast) and coral reefs along the shore. The Isla Gorgonilla, a smaller island off the southwestern tip of Gorgona, and a few rocky islets, the Rocas del Horno, on the northern end, complete the picture.

Gorgona is considered to be one of the peaks of the former fourth Cordillera, which once stretched from the Panama Isthmus to the Ecuadorian coast, but sank into the ocean over millions of years of geological activity. Today the island is separated from the continent by a 270m-deep underwater depression.

Gorgona is noted for a large number of endemic species resulting from the island's long separation from the continent. There are no big mammals, but there's a variety of smaller

## A Short History of Isla Gorgona

In the remote past Gorgona was reputedly inhabited by Indians, but which Indian group it was is a matter of speculation. Suggested groups range from the Cunas of Panama to the Sindaguas from the southern part of the Colombian coast. It's not clear either whether they were living there when Francisco Pizarro landed on the island in 1527.

Pizarro, the notorious Spanish conqueror responsible for the death of the Inca civilisation, stayed on Gorgona for several months before heading further south to discover the Inca Empire. He would perhaps have stayed longer had it not been for the poisonous snakes that caused the deaths of some of his soldiers. It was apparently due to the snakes that he named the island after the Gorgon, a three-winged monstrous deity in Greek mythology, who had live snakes for hair.

Later on, during the colonial period, the island wasn't permanently inhabited, but it served as a shelter for buccaneers and pirates marauding the sea in search of an easy prey. After Colombia's independence, the government wasn't really interested in the island until the bloody days of La Violencia of the 1950s, when a prison was established here (in 1959).

Tucked away off the mainland and permanently patrolled by a guard of sharks, Gorgona was a perfect place for a jail. Some witnesses say that it was extremely brutal and cruel. In 1975, the national park authorities included Gorgona on their list of proposed nature reserves. It took almost 10 years of effort and negotiations with the government before the prison was shut down and the island eventually became a national park in 1984. The park covers 617 sq km, comprising Gorgona, Gorgonilla and a wide belt of the surrounding ocean.

SOUTHWEST COLOMBIA

animals such as monkeys, lizards, bats, birds and snakes. About 15 species of snake have been identified here, including the boa. Two species of freshwater turtles and a colony of *babillas* (spectacled caimans) live at the Laguna Ayatuna. The waters surrounding the island are seasonally visited by dolphins, humpback whales and sperm whales, and sea turtles come for their breeding period and lay eggs on the beaches.

The climate of the area is hot and wet throughout the year. The mean temperature is about 27°C and relative humidity is close to 90%. The sky is frequently overcast. Average annual rainfall exceeds 4000mm. There's no dry season, but there are significant monthly differences in the amount of precipitation: September and October are the wettest months, whereas the rainfall is lowest in February and March.

The island is part of a national park and can be visited. The park management can provide accommodation in four- and eight-bed dorms and also has eating facilities.

### Visiting the Island

All visits to Gorgona are fixed four-day/three-night stays, which must be paid for in advance in the national park office in Bogotá. Previously the Cali office took bookings and payments, but now directs all prospective vis-

itors to the Bogotá office. This may change so check when you arrive in Colombia.

You need to pay the park's admission fee (US$5) and accommodation in the park's visitor centre (US$12 a night per person). Booking well in advance is advisable, especially for Colombian holiday periods. There may be a waiting time of up to two months in the tourist peaks. While you book, the office should give you information about the island and how exactly to get there.

Once on the island you'll be in the hands of park rangers and guides who will organise your stay and take you on excursions to the most interesting parts of the island. All the walks are accompanied by guides. The programme allows you time for recreational activities such as swimming, sunbathing and snorkelling. The local cafeteria serves meals (US$12 for three set meals), fast food, snacks, fruit juices and nonalcoholic drinks.

Bring boots, a long-sleeved shirt, some long trousers, rain gear, a swimsuit, hat and sunscreen. If you plan on snorkelling, bring along your gear. A torch is recommended; the use of candles is not permitted.

### Getting There & Away

The usual departure point for Gorgona has been the port of Buenaventura (a three-hour bus trip from Cali), where you catch a (usually overcrowded) cargo boat for a 10- to 12-hour night trip to the island (about US$30). It can be a hellish experience if the sea is rough. The boats depart daily from Muelle El Piñal, in the late afternoon or early evening. Information and reservation is available from the **Bodega Liscano** (☎ 2-244 6089, 244 6106), near the wharf.

Since the access road to Buenaventura was targeted by the guerrillas on various occasions in the past and may be not 100% safe, some independent tourists and most tours began to use Guapí as a launching pad for Gorgona. Guapí is a seaside village in Cauca, just opposite Gorgona, 56km away. Guapí is not connected by road with the rest of the country but can be reached by air on daily flights from Cali with Satena (US$50). From Guapí, boats take tourists to Gorgona in less than two hours (about US$200 per boat; up to 10 passengers). For information and reservation, call ☎ 2-825 7137, 825 7136.

If you desire more comfort, tours to Gorgona are available from Cali for US$250 to US$300 (see Organised Tours under Cali earlier). Tour operators offer all-inclusive tours in their own boats, providing a more comfortable and attractive way to visit the island than doing it on your own. It's usually the standard four-day/three-night programme, including excursions on the island, while you sleep and eat aboard the boat. Additional activities such as fishing and diving can be included in the tour's programme.

# Cauca & Huila

These two departments boast Colombia's most important archaeological sites, San Agustín (situated in Huila) and Tierradentro (in Cauca). Here also is the white pearl of colonial architecture, enchanting Popayán. The Popayán–San Agustín–Tierradentro triangle was one of Colombia's most popular loops among foreign travellers.

Unfortunately, both these departments suffer from the presence of guerrillas. Whereas Popayán remains a safe point on the map, the rural areas of San Agustín and Tierradentro may not be so safe. The number of foreign visitors to both these archaeological sites has slumped dramatically over recent years. Check safety conditions before setting off for either site.

## POPAYÁN

☎ 2 • pop 240,000 • elevation 1740m • temp 19°C

Popayán is one of Colombia's most beautiful colonial cities. Founded in 1537 by Sebastián de Belalcázar, the town soon became an important political, cultural and religious centre, and was an obligatory stopover on the route between Cartagena and Quito. Its mild climate attracted wealthy Spanish families from the sugar haciendas of the hot Cali region. They came to live here, building mansions and founding schools. Several imposing churches and monasteries were built in the 17th and 18th centuries, and the city flourished.

During the 20th century, while many Colombian cities were caught up in the race to modernise and industrialise, Popayán managed to retain its colonial character. Ironically, much of this historic fabric, including most of the churches, was seriously damaged by a violent earthquake in March 1983, moments before the much-celebrated Maundy Thursday religious procession was about to depart. The difficult and costly restoration was carried out for nearly two decades, and the results are truly admirable – little damage can be seen today and the city looks even better than it did before the disaster.

Apart from its beauty, Popayán is an inviting, tranquil and clean city. It has competent tourist offices and a range of places to stay and eat, and is not expensive by Colombian standards. Additionally it's pretty safe, unlike parts of the countryside.

The weather is pleasant most of the year, although the best time to visit is from November to February, when the rainfall is lowest. From June to September, the rains are more frequent and it is often cloudy.

### Information

**Tourist Offices** The **Oficina de Turismo de Popayán** (☎ 824 2251; Carrera 5 No 4-68; open 8am-noon & 2pm-6pm Mon-Fri, 9am-1pm Sat & Sun) is helpful and knowledgeable.

Another useful source of information is the **Policía de Turismo** (☎ 822 0916; Parque Caldas; open 8am-noon & 2pm-6pm Mon-Fri) in the Gobernación building on the main plaza.

The **national park office** (☎ 822 0996, 822 1097; Carrera 2 No 4-83) provides information on the two parks in the region,

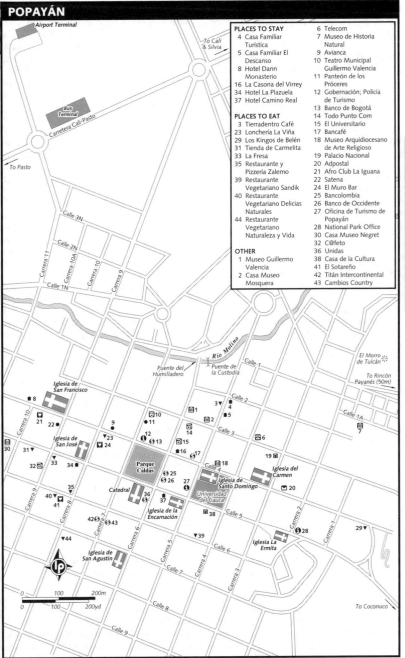

# POPAYÁN

**PLACES TO STAY**
4 Casa Familiar Turística
5 Casa Familiar El Descanso
8 Hotel Dann Monasterio
16 La Casona del Virrey
34 Hotel La Plazuela
37 Hotel Camino Real

**PLACES TO EAT**
3 Tierradentro Café
23 Lonchería La Viña
29 Los Kingos de Belén
31 Tienda de Carmelita
33 La Fresa
35 Restaurante y Pizzería Zalerno
39 Restaurante Vegetariano Sandik
40 Restaurante Vegetariano Delicias Naturales
44 Restaurante Vegetariano Naturaleza y Vida

**OTHER**
1 Museo Guillermo Valencia
2 Casa Museo Mosquera
6 Telecom
7 Museo de Historia Natural
9 Avianca
10 Teatro Municipal Guillermo Valencia
11 Panteón de los Próceres
12 Gobernación; Policía de Turismo
13 Banco de Bogotá
14 Todo Punto Com
15 El Universitario
17 Bancafé
18 Museo Arquidiocesano de Arte Religioso
19 Palacio Nacional
20 Adpostal
21 Afro Club La Iguana
22 Satena
24 El Muro Bar
25 Bancolombia
26 Banco de Occidente
27 Oficina de Turismo de Popayán
28 National Park Office
30 Casa Museo Negret
32 C@feto
36 Unidas
38 Casa de la Cultura
41 El Sotareño
42 Titán Intercontinental
43 Cambios Country

SOUTHWEST COLOMBIA

Puracé and Munchique. Both parks were closed due to safety concerns as we went to press.

**Money** Few of Popayán's banks change cash and/or travellers cheques, but fortunately, there are several casas de cambio, including **Titán Intercontinental** *(Centro Comercial Luis Martínez, Carrera 7 No 6-40, Interior 106)*, **Cambios Country** *(Carrera 7 No 6-41)* and **Unidas** *(Carrera 6 No 5-44)*. Banks marked on the map are useful for cash advances on credit cards.

**Email & Internet Access** Services are cheap in Popayán; you won't pay more than US$1 per hour in any of the listed places. Central facilities include **El Universitario** *(Carrera 6 No 3-47)*, **C@feto** *(Carrera 9 No 5-42)* and **Todo Punto Com** *(Calle 3 No 5-81)*.

## Museums

Popayán has quite a collection of museums, and most of them are set in splendid historic buildings.

**Casa Museo Mosquera** *(☎ 824 0683; Calle 3 No 5-38; admission US$1; open 8.30am-noon & 2pm-5.30pm Tues-Sun)* is a great colonial mansion built in the 1780s. It was home to General Tomás Cipriano de Mosquera, a politician and historian who was Colombia's president on four occasions between 1845 and 1867. The museum contains personal memorabilia of the general and his family, and a collection of colonial art, including some religious objects. Note the urn in the wall containing Mosquera's heart.

**Museo Arquidiocesano de Arte Religioso** *(☎ 824 2759; Calle 4 No 4-56; admission US$1; open 8.30am-12.30pm & 2.30pm-5.30pm Mon-Fri, 10am-3pm Sat)* has an extensive collection of religious art, including paintings, statues, altarpieces, silverware and liturgical vessels, most of which date from the 17th to 19th century.

**Museo Guillermo Valencia** *(☎ 824 2081; Carrera 6 No 2-65; admission US$1; open 10am-noon & 2pm-5pm Tues-Sun)* is dedicated to the Popayán-born poet who once lived here. The spacious late-18th-century building is full of period furniture, paintings, old photos and documents related to the poet and his son, Guillermo León Valencia, who was Colombia's president in 1962–66.

**Museo de Historia Natural** *(☎ 820 1952; Carrera 2 No 1A-25; admission US$1.50; open 8.30am-noon & 2pm-5pm Tues-Sun)* is possibly the best of its kind in the country, noted for its extensive collection of insects, butterflies and, in particular, stuffed birds. Part of the top floor is taken up by an archaeological display of pre-Columbian pottery from southern Colombia.

**Casa Museo Negret** *(☎ 824 4546; Calle 5 No 10-23)* features abstract sculpture by a noted Colombian artist, Edgar Negret, and works of art by some Latin American contemporary artists. It was closed as we went to press and it's not clear when, if ever, it will reopen.

## Churches

All the colonial churches have been meticulously restored after the 1983 earthquake. Most of them are only open for Mass, usually early in the morning and late in the afternoon, so plan your sightseeing accordingly.

The **Iglesia de San Francisco** *(Carrera 9 at Calle 4)* is the city's largest colonial church and arguably the best. Its spacious interior harbours a fine high altar and a collection of seven amazing side altarpieces, each different, in the aisles.

Other colonial churches noted for their rich colonial furnishings include the **Iglesia de Santo Domingo** *(Carrera 5 at Calle 4)*, **Iglesia de San José** *(Calle 5 at Carrera 8)* and the **Iglesia de San Agustín** *(Calle 7 at Carrera 6)*.

**Iglesia La Ermita** *(Calle 5 at Carrera 2)* is Popayán's oldest church (1546), worth seeing for its fine main retable and for the fragments of old frescoes, which were only discovered after the earthquake.

The neoclassical **Catedral** *(Parque Caldas)* is the youngest church in the centre, built between 1859 and 1906 on the site of a previous cathedral, which had been completely destroyed by an earthquake. The present one was seriously damaged by the 1983 quake, but rebuilt in its original shape over the following decade.

## Other Attractions

Museums and churches are only a part of what Popayán has to offer. The best approach is to take a leisurely walk along the central streets lined with whitewashed colonial mansions, savouring the architectural details and dropping inside to see the marvellous patios (many are open to the public).

While strolling about, have a look at the Italianate **Palacio Nacional** *(Calle 3 at Carrera 3)*, built in the 1930s, as well as the early 20th-century eclectic **Teatro Municipal Guillermo Valencia** *(Calle 3 at Carrera 7)*. Next door to the theatre is the neoclassical **Panteón de los Próceres**, which shelters the remains of Popayán's most illustrious sons, including General Tomás Cipriano de Mosquera and botanist Francisco José de Caldas (1770–1816). Enter the Universidad del Cauca, established in the old Dominican monastery, to see the ornate **Paraninfo Caldas** meeting hall, inaugurated in 1916 and named after the botanist.

Walk to the river to see two unusual old bridges. The small one, the **Puente de la Custodia**, was constructed in 1713 to allow the priests to cross the river to bring the holy orders to the sick of this poor northern suburb. About 160 years later, the solid 178m-long 12-arch **Puente del Humilladero** was built alongside the old bridge, and is still in use. Remarkably, the bridges haven't suffered damage from several serious floods, nor from the catastrophic quake of 1983.

The **Capilla de Belén**, a chapel set on a hill just east of the city centre, offers good views over the town. There were some armed attacks on travellers on the serpentine access alley to the chapel, so check with the Policía de Turismo for the current safety conditions before walking there. They now seem to patrol the area regularly and may even accompany you to the top.

**El Morro de Tulcán**, a hill topped with an equestrian statue of the town's founder, provides even better views, but here too, it's good to watch out for the tourist police, unless it's Sunday when crowds of locals go.

At the foot of the hill is the **Rincón Payanés**, a collection of replicas of Popayán's famous buildings. You will find here the Capilla de la Ermita, the Torre del Reloj and two historic bridges, plus a few craft shops and stands serving regional food.

## Special Events

If you are in the area during **Semana Santa** (Holy Week), you will have the opprtunity to see the famous night-time processions on Maundy Thursday and Good Friday. Popayán's Easter celebrations, held here since 1556, are the most elaborate in the country. Thousands of believers and tourists from all over Colombia come to take part in this religious ceremony. The festival of religious music is held at the same time. Note that hotels are full around this period, so get there earlier or book in advance.

## Places to Stay

Popayán has a good array of accommodation to suit every pocket. Many hotels are set in old colonial houses and have a style and atmosphere rarely found in Colombian hotels.

**Casa Familiar Turística** *(☎ 824 4853; Carrera 5 No 2-07; rooms per person US$3)* has recently moved from the 1st floor downstairs to the ground floor and now has just four rooms (all with shared facilities). It's no longer an attractive place but acceptable, clean and among the cheapest in town. **Casa Familiar El Descanso** *(☎ 824 0019; Carrera 5 No 2-41; rooms per person US$5)*, just half a block away, is a bit better but pricier, and its rooms don't have private baths either. Neither casa has its name on the door – you have to ring the bell.

**La Casona del Virrey** *(☎ 824 0836; Calle 4 No 5-78; singles/doubles/triples/quads with bath US$11/17/24/27)* has style and character and is good value. Choose one of the ample rooms facing the street. There are also some cheaper rooms without bath (US$6 per person).

Popayán has some splendid historic mansions that have been refashioned as stylish hotels, including **Hotel La Plazuela** *(☎ 824 1084; Calle 5 No 8-13; singles/doubles/triples US$30/40/50)* and **Hotel Camino Real** *(☎ 824 3595; Calle 5 No 5-59; singles/doubles/triples US$35/45/55)*. All rooms at both hotels have private baths and the prices include breakfast. In both, ask for a room facing the street.

**Hotel Dann Monasterio** *(☎ 824 2191; Calle 4 No 10-14; singles/doubles US$50/ 60)* is in a great colonial building with a vast courtyard that once was a Franciscan monastery. It's Popayán's top-notch offering, with 48 refurbished spacious rooms, a restaurant and a swimming pool (the only hotel with a pool in town).

## Places to Eat

Popayán has plenty of places to eat and the food is relatively cheap. Numerous budget restaurants serve set meals and there are also some interesting upscale options.

**Lonchería La Viña** (*Calle 4 No 7-79; set meals US$1.75, mains US$4-5*) is one of the best and most popular budget eateries. It has tasty food, generous portions and is open until midnight or even longer. Apart from set breakfasts, lunches and dinners, it has a good choice of à la carte dishes.

**Restaurante y Pizzeria Zalermo** (*Carrera 8 No 5-100; set meals US$1.75, mains US$4-8*) is a new place but has already become popular with locals. It's open till late and has a wide range including pizzas and chicken.

Vegetarians can find budget food in **Restaurante Vegetariano Sandik** (*Calle 6 No 4-52*), **Restaurante Vegetariano Delicias Naturales** (*Calle 6 No 8-21*) and **Restaurante Vegetariano Naturaleza y Vida** (*Carrera 8 No 7-19*).

Popayán has a number of places offering typical local food. **La Fresa** (*Calle 5 No 8-89*), a small cubbyhole with no sign on the door, serves delicious, cheap *empanadas de pipián*, a local variation of empanadas stuffed with potato and peanut. Half a block away, the unsigned place known locally as **Tienda de Carmelita** (*Calle 5 No 9-45*) serves good *tamales de pipián*. The more expensive **Los Kingos de Belén** (*Calle 4 No 0-55*) also has good regional specialities; try its *bandeja típica* (a local speciality) and wash it down with *champús* (a cold drink made from rice and *lulo* fruit).

With mouthwatering steaks and French specialities, the restaurant in **Hotel Camino Real** is one of the best in town. An excellent six-course meal will cost about US$12. The restaurant in the **Hotel Dann Monasterio** is not bad either, and is not that expensive. It serves international food, plus a few typical local dishes.

**Tierradentro Café** (*Carrera 5 No 2-12*) has the best choice of espressos and cappuccinos in town – 90 different flavours – an important stop for coffee addicts.

## Entertainment

With its 40-year history, the legendary **El Sotareño** (*Calle 6 No 8-05*) is a charming rustic bar playing nostalgic old rhythms such as tango, bolero, *ranchera* and *milonga* from scratched vinyls probably as old as the place itself, and serving some of the cheapest beer in town.

**Afro Club La Iguana** (*Calle 4 No 9-67*) has excellent salsa and Cuban *son* music at high volume, which is so hot and exciting that people dance all over the place, especially on weekends. For a quieter ambience, try **El Muro Bar** (*Carrera 8 No 4-11*), which plays soft rock and Latin-American ballads. There are several other places in the same area, which is regarded as Popayán's Zona Rosa.

## Getting There & Away

**Air** The airport is situated just behind the bus terminal, a 15-minute walk north of the city centre. Avianca and Satena have daily flights to Bogotá (US$70 to US$100).

**Bus** The bus terminal is a short walk north of the city centre. Note that travelling on some roads out of Popayán may be risky. Read below and check for recent news with the tourist offices.

Plenty of buses run to Cali (US$4, three hours), and there are also minibuses and colectivos every hour or so. Buses to Bogotá run every hour or two (US$24, 15 hours).

You shouldn't wait more than an hour for a bus to Pasto (US$8, six hours), but this spectacular road may be unsafe to travel, particularly at night. Buses have regularly been ambushed (mostly at night) and passengers robbed over the past decade. More recently, guerrillas have been stopping the traffic and burning buses or trucks, thus blocking the road for hours, but passengers were not harassed or robbed. If you plan to travel overland on this road, do it during daytime only.

For Tierradentro, take the Sotracauca bus at 8am or 10.30am, which will take you directly to San Andrés de Pisimbalá (US$6, five to six hours), passing the museum en route. Other buses (three daily) will drop you off in El Cruce de San Andrés, from where you have to walk 20 minutes to the museum plus another 25 minutes to San Andrés. The region between Popayán and Tierradentro is known for a guerrilla presence.

Three buses daily (two with Cootranshuila and one with Sotracauca) run to San Agustín via Coconuco and Isnos (US$8, seven to eight hours). The Línea Estelar minibus is a faster alternative (US$11, five to six hours). The road is very rough, but the trip through the lush cordillera cloud forest is spectacular. Part of this road is controlled by guerrillas and they have even put up a permanent checkpoint on the road. They stop passing traffic, control tourists' passports and let them go. So far, there haven't been any life-threatening incidents involving travellers, nor any hostage taking here.

## SILVIA
☎ 2 • pop 5000 • elevation 2620m
• temp 15°C

Silvia, a picturesque small town 60km northeast of Popayán, is the centre of the Guambiano Indian region. The Indians don't live in Silvia itself, but in the small mountain villages such as Pueblito, La Campana, Guambia and Caciques, scattered throughout the area. The whole community numbers about 12,000 Indians.

The Guambianos are considered one of the most traditional Indian groups in Colombia. They have preserved their culture remarkably well given their proximity to, and contact with, the 'civilised world'. They speak their own language, dress traditionally and still use rudimentary techniques in agriculture. They are excellent weavers.

On Tuesday, market day, they come to Silvia to sell their fruit, vegetables and handicrafts. This is the best time to visit the town – an attractive day trip from Popayán. Silvia market is possibly the most colourful Indian gathering in the country.

There are plenty of Indians in town on that day, almost all in traditional dress, the women in hand-woven garments and beaded necklaces, busily spinning wool. They come in chivas and tend to congregate around the main plaza. And they don't like cameras, so try to respect this.

The market begins at dawn and goes until the early afternoon. You can purchase *ruanas* (ponchos), shawls, blankets, scarves and sweaters, as well as an amazing variety of fruit and vegetables. Don't forget to bring a sweater (or buy one at the market) – it can be pretty cold if the weather is cloudy.

Virtually all travellers visit Silvia as a one-day trip from Popayán, but if you feel like staying longer, there are at least half a dozen cheap *residencias*.

To get to Silvia from Popayán, take the Coomotoristas or Tax Belalcázar minibus (US$1.50, 1½ hours). On Tuesday, there are also direct colectivos between Popayán and Silvia.

Consult Popayán's tourist offices before you set off – there has been a guerrilla presence in the Silvia region.

## SAN AGUSTÍN
☎ 8 • elevation 1695m • temp 18°C

San Agustín is one of South America's most important archaeological sites. The area was inhabited by a mysterious pre-Columbian civilisation, which left behind hundreds of freestanding monumental statues carved in stone. The site was a ceremonial centre where locals buried their dead and placed the statues next to the tombs. Pottery and gold objects were left in the tombs of the tribal elders.

So far, some 500 statues have been found and excavated. Many of them are anthropomorphic figures – some are realistic, others very stylised resembling masked monsters. Others are zoomorphic, depicting sacred animals such as the eagle, the jaguar and frog. The statues vary in size, from about 20cm up to 7m, and in their degree of detail.

SOUTHWEST COLOMBIA

### Mysteries of San Agustín Culture

There is still little known about the San Agustín culture and its enigmatic stone statues. Some archaeologists have drawn parallels between these monuments and the statues on Easter Island in the Pacific Ocean, but most experts relate San Agustín to the pre-Columbian Mesoamerican (Mexico, Guatemala) and Andean (Peru, Bolivia) cultures.

It is most likely that the culture began to evolve about the 6th century AD and reached its apogee around the 14th century. The best statuary was made only in the last phase of the development, and the civilisation had presumably vanished before the Spaniards came. Perhaps, like many other cultures of the Andean region, it fell victim to the Incas – this area of Colombia was the northernmost point of the Inca Empire. All this is still open to discussion. What is certain is that the statues were not discovered until the middle of the 18th century when a Spanish monk, Fray Juan de Santa Gertrudis, passed through San Agustín and gave a written account of the sculptures.

The area of San Agustín has witnessed intensive guerrilla activity over recent years. There have been ambushes on buses, as well as armed robberies of hikers. Also, there have been problems with theft in buses to and from San Agustín. Few travellers come these days to visit the statues and a number of hotels and restaurants have closed. In 2001, only about 1100 foreign tourists visited San Agustín, or just three per day. Check the current safety conditions before you go.

## Orientation

The statues and tombs are scattered in groups over a wide area on both sides of the gorge formed by the upper Río Magdalena. The most important sight is the Parque Arqueológico, which boasts the largest number of statues and a museum. The second most important place is the Alto de los Ídolos, another archaeological park. You buy one admission ticket (adult/student US$3/1.50), which is valid for two consecutive days for entry to both parks. There's no admission fee to other archaeological sites.

The region is centred on the town of San Agustín, which harbours most of the accommodation and restaurants. From there, you can explore the region on foot, horseback or by jeep. Give yourself three days for leisurely visits to the most interesting places. The weather is varied, with the driest period from December to February and the wettest from April to June.

## Information

There's no genuine tourist office in San Agustín, just a couple of travel agencies.

It's difficult to change travellers cheques in San Agustín. Cash US dollars can be exchanged at some travel businesses but at poor rates. It's a good idea to come with a cache of pesos.

The **Banco Agrario** (Carrera 13 at Calle 4) gives peso advances on Visa, but not on MasterCard; the closest places that accept MasterCard are in Pitalito. San Agustín had no ATMs as we went to press.

## Parque Arqueológico

The 78-hectare archaeological park (open 8am-6pm daily) is 2.5km west of the town of San Agustín, a pleasant half-hour's walk along a paved road. The park covers an area in which several important archaeological sites have been found close to each other. There are in total about 130 statues in the park, either found in situ or collected from other areas, and including some of the best examples of San Agustín statuary. Plan on spending at least three hours in the park.

At the entrance to the park is the **Museo Arqueológico** (open 8am-5pm Tues-Sun), which features smaller statues, pottery, utensils, jewellery and other objects, along with background information about the culture. It's a useful first stop to learn something about the people who created this strange cult of statuary.

In front of the museum is **Mesita D**, one of four burial sites identified by consecutive letters of the alphabet. The statues here date from the earlier phase of the culture's development and are noted for their cruder designs and less polished appearance.

Just south of the museum is the so-called **Bosque de las Estatuas** (Forest of Statues), where 35 statues of different origins have been placed along a footpath that snakes through the woods.

About 500m southeast of the museum is the **Mesita A**. It has two mounds, each with a central figure accompanied by a statue of a warrior on each side. There are also a few statues standing around, remaining at the sites where they were found.

The nearby **Mesita B** is the most important of all. It has three mounds and several freestanding figures, of which the most outstanding are a 4m-high statue known as the Bishop, unusual for the human faces carved on both top and bottom, and a statue depicting an eagle with a serpent in its talons.

The path continues south for about 500m to **Mesita C**, which features yet another cluster of statues.

A short walk downhill brings you to **Fuente de Lavapatas**, an important ceremonial site, presumably used for ritual ablutions and the worship of aquatic deities. In the rocky bed of the stream, a complex labyrinth of ducts and small, terraced pools, with representations of serpents, lizards and human figures, has been chiselled out.

From here, the path winds uphill to the **Alto de Lavapatas**, the oldest archaeological site found in San Agustín. Here you'll find a few tombs guarded by statues, and you'll get a panoramic view over the surrounding countryside.

## Alto de los Ídolos

This is another archaeological park *(open 8am-4pm daily)*, established on the site where a number of large stone sarcophagi and statues have been excavated. The largest statue in the San Agustín area, about 7m high, is here. The park is 4km southwest of San José de Isnos, on the other side of Río Magdalena from San Agustín town. You can get there on foot from San Agustín by crossing the deep Magdalena Gorge, a spectacular three-hour walk. Some travellers have been attacked and robbed on this route in the past, so check current safety conditions. You can also walk from Isnos, which is reached from San Agustín by road.

## Alto de las Piedras

This site is 7km north of Isnos and contains tombs lined with stone slabs painted red, black and yellow. One of the most famous statues, known as Doble Yo, is here; look carefully as there are actually four figures carved in this statue. You'll also find here an intriguing statue representing a female figure in an advanced state of pregnancy.

## El Tablón, La Chaquira, La Pelota & El Purutal

These four sites are relatively close to each other, so they can be seen in one trip. It is a pleasant five-hour walk from San Agustín town, or you can do it on horseback. La Chaquira is noted for its divinities carved into the mountain face, overlooking the gorge of the Magdalena River. In El Purutal you can see the only surviving painted statues in the region.

## Other Attractions

There are several more archaeological sites to see if you are not in a hurry, including La Parada, Quinchana, El Jabón, Naranjos and Quebradillas.

Apart from its archaeological wealth, the region is also noted for its natural beauty, and features two spectacular waterfalls, **Salto de Bordones** and **Salto de Mortiño**. It's also worth a walk or ride to **El Estrecho**, where the Río Magdalena passes through 2m narrows. All these sights are accessible by road.

## Places to Stay

There are a dozen budget residencias in and around town, most of which are clean and friendly and have hot water. Unless stated otherwise, hotels listed here charge US$2 to US$3 per person in rooms without bath, US$3 to US$4 with private bath.

If you don't feel like walking when you arrive there are a few budget hotels near the bus offices, including the basic but neat **Hospedaje El Jardín** *(☎ 837 3455; Carrera 11 No 4-10)*, the noisy **Hotel Colonial** *(☎ 837 3159; Calle 3 No 11-54)* and the run-down **Hotel Central** *(☎ 837 3027; Calle 3 No 10-54)*. All three have rooms with or without private baths.

A few blocks west, **Hotel Ullumbe** *(☎ 837 3799; Carrera 13 No 3-36; rooms per person US$5)* has good rooms with private baths and laundry service. Two blocks west is another good place, **Residencias Menezú** *(☎ 837 3693; Carrera 15 No 4-74; rooms per person US$5)*, which offers clean rooms with private baths and hot water. In the same area, **Residencias Mi Terruño** *(Calle 4 No 15-85)* has rooms with and without private bath and a pleasant balcony overlooking the garden.

There are more budget options outside the town, including the **Posada Campesina** *(☎ 837 3956)*, an agreeable family house 1km toward El Tablón. In the same area, **Casa de Francois** *(☎ 837 3847)* is also cheap and very popular with travellers, and you can use the kitchen. Another good choice is the French-run **Casa de Nelly** *(☎ 837 3221)*, a tranquil place 1km west of the town off the dirt road to La Estrella.

## Places to Eat

The **Restaurante Brahama** *(Calle 5 No 15-11)* serves cheap set meals, vegetarian food and fruit salads. **Restaurante Surabi** *(Calle 5 No 14-09)* also has inexpensive meals. You'll find several other budget eateries in the same area. There are more eating outlets on the road to the Parque Arqueológico, including **Restaurante La Brasa**, serving tasty grilled beef.

## Getting There & Away

The bus offices are clustered on Calle 3 near the corner of Carrera 11. Three buses a day go to Popayán via a rough but spectacular road through Isnos (US$8, seven to eight hours), and there are also minibuses (US$11, five to six hours). Guerrillas stop the traffic on this route, but so far have let tourists pass by without any problems.

Coomotor has two buses daily to Bogotá (US$15, 12 hours). There's also a faster and more comfortable Taxis Verdes service in vans (US$18, 10 hours).

There are no direct buses to Tierradentro; go to La Plata (US$7, five hours) and change for the bus to El Cruce de San Andrés (US$3, 2½ hours), from where it's a 20-minute walk to the Tierradentro museum. La Plata has several cheap residencias.

Frequent colectivos (both jeeps and cars) shuttle between San Agustín and Pitalito (US$1, 45 minutes).

## Getting Around

The usual form of visiting San Agustín's sights is by jeep tours and horseback excursions. The standard jeep tour includes El Estrecho, Alto de los Ídolos, Alto de las Piedras, Salto de Bordones and Salto de Mortiño. The trip takes seven to eight hours and costs US$10 per person if there are six people to fill the jeep (US$13 if there are four). There are few tourists in town these days, so there are few jeep tours.

Horse rental can be arranged through hotel managers or directly with the horse owners who frequently approach tourists. Horses are hired out for a specific route, or by the hour (US$2), half-day (US$6) or full day (US$10). One of the most popular horse riding trips includes El Tablón, La Chaquira, La Pelota and El Purutal; it costs US$6 per horse, and takes five hours. If you need a guide, add US$6 on to your budget for him and another US$6 for his horse.

## TIERRADENTRO

☎ 2 • elevation 1750m • temp 18°C

Tierradentro is an archaeological site noted for its underground burial chambers. They are elaborate circular tombs ranging from 2m to 7m in diameter, scooped out of soft rock in the slopes and tops of hills over a wide area. About a hundred of these unusual funeral temples have been discovered. They are the only example of their kind in the Americas.

The underground chambers have been hewn out to house the cremated remains of tribal elders. They vary widely in depth; some of them are just below ground level, while others are as deep as 9m, with spiral staircases of volcanic rock leading down into them. The dome-like ceilings of the larger vaults are supported by massive pillars.

The walls, the ceilings and pillars were decorated with geometric motifs painted in red and black (representing life and death, respectively) on a white background. Anthropomorphic figures were carved on the columns and walls of many chambers. In some of the chambers the decoration has been preserved in remarkably good shape.

Apart from the tombs, a number of stone statues similar to those of San Agustín have been found in the region, probably the product of a broad cultural influence. Human figures predominate, but animal representations are not unusual.

Little is known about the people who built the tombs and the statues. Most likely they were of different cultures and the people who scooped out the tombs preceded those who carved the statues. Some researchers have placed the 'tomb' civilisation somewhere between the 7th and 9th centuries AD, while the 'statue' culture shows links with the later phase of San Agustín development, which is estimated to have taken place some 500 years later. Today the region is inhabited by the Páez Indians, who have lived here since before the Spanish Conquest, but it is doubtful whether they are the descendants of the statue sculptors.

Much like San Agustín, the Tierradentro region has been notorious for a strong guerrilla presence over recent years. Guerrillas have been held responsible for the various cases of killing and kidnapping of locals. Very few foreigners visit Tierradentro these days. Check safety conditions before you decide to go.

## Orientation & Information

Tierradentro is far away from any significant urban centres, and is only accessible by dirt roads. You can get there from Popayán and San Agustín, but in each case it's a rough half-day bus ride.

Once in Tierradentro, you have four sites with tombs and one with statues, as well as two museums and the village of San Andrés de Pisimbalá. Except for the burial site of El Aguacate, all the sights are relatively close to each other, so they can be visited on foot. You can also visit them on horseback; horses are rented out near the museums and in San Andrés (US$8 per day). A torch is necessary for almost all the tombs – make sure to bring one with you.

There are no tourist offices or money-changing facilities in Tierradentro. General information is available from the museum staff and hotel managers. The owner of Los Lagos de Tierradentro (see Places to Stay & Eat later) is a good source of information.

## Museums

You begin your visit from the two museums, right across the road from one another, where you buy one combined ticket (adult/student US$3/1.50), valid for two consecutive days to all archaeological sites and the museums themselves. The museums are open 8am to 5pm daily.

The **Museo Arqueológico** contains pottery urns which have been found in the tombs. They were used to keep the ashes of the tribal elders. Some of the urns are decorated with dotted patterns and, in some cases, with representations of animals. The **Museo Etnográfico** has utensils and artefacts of the Páez Indians. Several small stone statues collected from the region have been placed in front of the museum buildings.

## Burial Sites & Statues

A 20-minute walk up the hill north of the museums will take you to **Segovia**, the most important burial site. There are 28 tombs here, some with well-preserved decorations. Seven of the tombs are lit; for the others, you need a flashlight. It is forbidden to take photos with a flash as it affects the paintings. The tombs are open 8am to 5pm daily.

A 15-minute walk uphill from Segovia will bring you to **El Duende**, where there are four tombs, but their decoration hasn't been preserved. More interesting is **Alto de San Andrés**, where you'll find five tombs, two of which boast their original paintings in remarkably good condition. In the same area is **El Tablón**, where there are 10 stone statues, similar to those of San Agustín, excavated in the area and now thrown together under a roof in a fenced-in field.

**El Aguacate** is the only remote burial site, located high on a mountain ridge, a two-hour walk from the museum (plus a two-hour walk back). There are a few dozen tombs there, but most have been destroyed by the *guaqueros* (tomb raiders). Only a few vaults still bear the remains of the original decoration. It's worth taking this walk anyway, for the sweeping views it provides over the whole region.

## San Andrés de Pisimbalá

This tiny village, a 25-minute walk west of the museums, is the major urban centre of Tierradentro, and has a few budget hotels and restaurants. It's particularly noted for its amazing thatched **church**. You can see its very simple interior through the gap in the entrance doors.

## Places to Stay & Eat

Accommodation and food in Tierradentro are simple but cheap – expect to pay US$2 to US$3 per person in rooms without bath. There's nothing upmarket in the area. You can stay either close to the museums or in San Andrés de Pisimbalá.

**Residencias Lucerna**, in a house just up the road from the museums, is clean, pleasant and friendly. About 150m farther on is **Hospedaje Pisimbalá**, one of the cheapest places to stay as well as eat – it serves set meals for about US$1.50. Another 150m farther up the road is the **Residencias Ricabet**. Next to it is the more expensive **Hotel El Refugio** *(singles/doubles US$10/15)*, but prices fall considerably in the low season. The hotel has a swimming pool and a restaurant.

In San Andrés de Pisimbalá, there are three budget residencias, of which **Los Lagos de Tierradentro** is the cheapest and perhaps the friendliest. The family running it serves meals and rents horses.

## Getting There & Away

Only two buses a day call at San Andrés de Pisimbalá. Most buses just pass El Cruce de San Andrés, from where you need to walk to the museums (20 minutes).

Three or four buses daily pass via El Cruce on their way to Popayán (US$6, five to six hours), and the same number to La Plata (US$2.50, 2½ hours). Two direct buses go from La Plata to Bogotá and two to San Agustín, or take a colectivo to Pitalito and change.

# Nariño

Nariño is Colombia's most southwesterly department, bordering Ecuador. In remote pre-Columbian times, this land was home to two remarkable centres of culture: Tumaco on the Pacific Coast and Nariño in the Andean highlands. In the mid-15th century, less than a century before the arrival of the Spanish, Nariño was conquered and incorporated into the Inca Empire. Once the Incas had been defeated by Pizarro, the Spaniards pushed northward into what is now Colombia. In effect, Nariño was conquered by the Spanish earlier than any other part of Colombia except for the Caribbean Coast, which was invaded independently from the north.

In geographical terms, Nariño comprises a vast lowland covered with thick rainforest on the Pacific Coast to the west, and the mountainous region topped with several volcanic peaks to the east. This area is a zone of serious seismic activity.

Nariño's inhabitants, known as the *pastusos*, are skilful artisans, and the local crafts are known for their originality and quality. Its history and people give Nariño a special atmosphere which reflects the cross of Colombian and Ecuadorian cultures.

Unfortunately, Nariño's picturesque countryside is now a bit difficult to explore, due to the massive invasion of guerrillas over recent years. Any longer side detours off the Panamerican Highway may be risky, not to mention that the highway itself is not perfectly safe.

## PASTO
☎ 2 • pop 320,000 • elevation 2530m
• temp 13°C

The capital of Nariño, San Juan de Pasto is set in the fertile Atriz Valley at the foot of the Volcán Galeras.

The town was founded by Lorenzo de Aldana in 1537 and played an active role in Colombia's history. It was an important cultural and religious centre during the colonial and republican times, and is a large commercial city today. Pasto has lost much of its historic character because of earthquakes that hit the city on various occasions, yet its churches were rebuilt in the original style and reflect some of the town's past splendour.

The city is noted nationwide for its *barniz de Pasto*, a processed vegetable resin used to decorate wooden bowls, plates, boxes and pieces of furniture with colourful patterns. The technique is not new; in the past, the Indians used the resin (known to them as *mopa mopa*) to coat their pottery and wooden articles.

## Information
**Tourist Offices** The **Oficina Departamental de Turismo de Nariño** *(☎ 723 4962; Calle 18 No 25-25; open 8am-noon & 2pm-6pm Mon-Fri)* is just off Plaza de Nariño (the main square).

**Money** Most of the major banks are around Plaza de Nariño. They pay advances on Visa and/or MasterCard, and some, including the **Banco Santander** and **Bancolombia**, also change cash and travellers cheques. There are also several casas de cambio, including **Titán Intercontinental** *(Carrera 26 No 18-71, Centro Comercial Galerías)* and **Giros & Finanzas** *(Carrera 26 No 17-12, Centro Comercial El Liceo)*.

**Email & Internet Access** Central facilities include **Global System** *(Calle 18A No 25-51)*, **Ciber C@fe PC Rent** *(Calle 18A No 25-36)*, **Cafelink** *(Centro Comercial Sebastián de Belalcázar)*, **Infonet** *(Calle 18 No 29-15)*, **Net Conección** *(Carrera 30 No 16B-82)* and **Cyber Café Net** *(Carrera 30 No 16B-60)*.

Internet access is relatively slow in Pasto. Expect to pay US$1 to US$2 per hour in any listed cafés.

## Museums
Pasto has half-a-dozen museums. They are small and relatively modest, yet may be worth a visit.

**Museo del Oro** *(☎ 721 9108; Calle 19 No 21-27; admission free; open 9am-6pm Mon-Fri, 9am-1pm Sat)* in the building of the Banco de la República features gold and pottery of the pre-Columbian cultures of Nariño.

**Museo Taminango de Artes y Tradiciones** *(☎ 723 5539; Calle 13 No 27-67; admission US$0.50; open 8am-noon & 2pm-6pm Mon-Fri, 9am-1pm Sat)*, in a meticulously restored *casona* (large house) from 1623 (reputedly the oldest surviving house in town), displays artefacts and antique objects from the region.

**Museo Juan Lorenzo Lucero** *(☎ 731 4414; Calle 18 No 28-87; admission US$1; open 8am-noon & 2pm-4pm Mon-Fri)* occupies the Casa Mariana, a fine historic building from the late 19th century. Named after a local priest and missionary, this is actually the museum of the city's history, featuring antiques, old weapons, photos, documents,

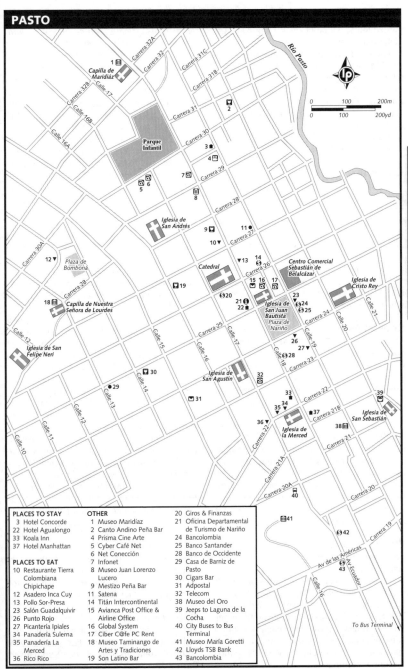

# PASTO

**PLACES TO STAY**
3 Hotel Concorde
22 Hotel Agualongo
33 Koala Inn
37 Hotel Manhattan

**PLACES TO EAT**
10 Restaurante Tierra
   Colombiana
   Chipichape
12 Asadero Inca Cuy
13 Pollo Sor-Presa
23 Salón Guadalquivir
26 Punto Rojo
27 Picantería Ipiales
34 Panadería Sulerna
35 Panadería La
   Merced
36 Rico Rico

**OTHER**
1 Museo Maridíaz
2 Canto Andino Peña Bar
4 Prisma Cine Arte
5 Cyber Café Net
6 Net Conección
7 Infonet
8 Museo Juan Lorenzo
   Lucero
9 Mestizo Peña Bar
11 Satena
14 Titán Intercontinental
15 Avianca Post Office &
   Airline Office
16 Global System
17 Ciber C@fe PC Rent
18 Museo Taminango de
   Artes y Tradiciones
19 Son Latino Bar

20 Giros & Finanzas
21 Oficina Departamental
   de Turismo de Nariño
24 Bancolombia
25 Banco Santander
28 Banco de Occidente
29 Casa de Barniz de
   Pasto
30 Cigars Bar
31 Adpostal
32 Telecom
38 Museo del Oro
39 Jeeps to Laguna de la
   Cocha
40 City Buses to Bus
   Terminal
41 Museo María Goretti
42 Lloyds TSB Bank
43 Bancolombia

furniture and paintings. All visits are by guided tours, which normally begin at 8am, 10am and 2pm.

There are two missionary museums: **Museo Maridíaz** (☎ 731 2094; *Calle 18 No 32A-01*) and **Museo María Goretti** (☎ 721 4915; *Av de las Américas No 15A-53*). Both have missionary collections and resemble antique shops crammed with anything from images of the saints to cannonballs. However, you may want to visit them for their archaeological and fauna collections.

## Churches

There are a dozen colonial churches in town, most of which are large constructions with richly decorated interiors.

The **Iglesia de San Juan Bautista**, with its ornate interior, is the city's oldest church, dating from Pasto's early days, but it was rebuilt in the mid-17th century after damage caused by earthquakes.

The **Iglesia de Cristo Rey**, with its beautiful stained-glass windows, is another church worth entering.

## Special Events

The city's major event is **Carnaval de Blancos y Negros** held on 5 and 6 January. Its origins go back to the times of Spanish rule, when slaves were allowed to celebrate on 5 January and their masters showed approval by painting their faces black. On the following day, the slaves painted their faces white.

The tradition is faithfully maintained. On these two days the city goes wild, with everybody painting or dusting one another with grease, chalk, talc, flour and any other available substance even vaguely black or white in tone. It's a serious affair – wear the worst clothes you have and buy an *antifaz*, a sort of mask to protect the face, widely sold for this occasion.

## Places to Stay

There are plenty of hotels throughout the central area.

**Koala Inn** (☎ 722 1101; *Calle 18 No 22-37; rooms without/with bath per person US$4/5*) is by far the most popular place with travellers. Set in a fine historic building, the hotel offers spotlessly clean and spacious rooms, laundry facilities, book exchange, a budget restaurant and a satellite TV in the patio. Warmly recommended.

**Hotel Manhattan** (☎ 721 5675; *Calle 18 No 21B-14; singles/doubles US$4/6, with bath US$5/7*) is also a stylish old building with fair-sized rooms and a spacious covered patio, but it rarely sees foreign travellers.

**Hotel Concorde** (☎ 731 0658; *Calle 19 No 29A-09; singles/doubles US$10/15*) is a small hotel close to the area of night entertainment. It has cosy tranquil rooms with bath.

**Hotel Agualongo** (☎ 723 5216; *Carrera 25 No 17-83; singles/doubles/suites US$40/50/70*) is the best central option. This 12-storey hotel has comfortable refurbished rooms, and the prices include breakfast. Choose a room facing east on one of the upper floors, and you'll enjoy great views of the main plaza.

## Places to Eat

There are loads of cheap restaurants and cafés in the city centre, where you can grab a set meal for no more than US$2. Also, many *panaderías* (bakeries) have tables and serve budget meals; try, for example, **Panadería La Merced** (*Carrera 22 No 17-31*) or **Panadería Sulerna** (*Carrera 22 No 17-69*).

The tiny restaurant in **Koala Inn** is good value. If you happen to get hungry at night, you can put together a reasonably priced meal at the 24-hour self-service **Punto Rojo** (*Plaza de Nariño*). **Pollo Sor-Presa** (*Calle 18 No 26-60*) and **Rico Rico** (*Calle 17 No 22-03*) are two of the better chicken outlets.

**Restaurante Tierra Colombiana Chipichape** (*Calle 18 No 27-19; mains US$3-4*) serves solid *comida criolla*, such as *sobrebarriga* (stewed, baked or fried brisket), *chuleta* (rib steak) and *arroz con pollo* (rice with chicken or vegetables). **Salón Guadalquivir** (*Plaza de Nariño*) is widely known for its hearty tamales and *empanadas*. **Picantería Ipiales** (*Calle 19 No 23-37*) has delicious *lapingachos* (fried pancake made from mashed potato and cheese).

**Asadero Inca Cuy** (☎ 723 8050; *Carrera 29 No 13-65*) offers the region's ultimate speciality, the *cuy*, or grilled guinea pig. The dish (the whole animal plus accompaniments) costs US$9 and is big enough for two people; order it one hour in advance.

## Entertainment

There are several pleasant bars in the city centre, including cosy **Cigars Bar** (☎ 729 3571; *Carrera 25 No 14-06*). **Son Latino Bar** (☎ 722 7032; *Calle 16 No 26-78*) plays salsa, *merengue* and *vallenato* and has a dance floor. For some Andean rhythms, try **Mestizo Peña Bar** (☎ 729 3395; Calle 18 No 27-67) or **Canto Andino Peña Bar** (☎ 730 5770; Calle 20 No 30-41); both have live music on weekends.

The local Zona Rosa, roughly between Calles 19 and 20 and Carreras 31C and 32, features some fast food, bars and discos, and comes alive on weekend nights.

Another concentration of bars and discos in the centre is on Calle 19 between Carreras 26 and 28 where you'll find about a dozen watering holes.

For more cultural fare, check the **Prisma Cine Arte** (☎ 731 0394; Calle 19 No 29-23), a bar which presents quality films on a large screen. Pick up the programme there.

## Shopping

Barniz de Pasto artefacts can be bought in **Casa del Barniz de Pasto** (Carrera 25 at Calle 13). **Plaza de Bomboná** (Calle 14 between Carreras 28 and 30) is a covered market, which has several craft shops. There are a few other handicraft shops around. Pasto is also a good place to buy leather goods (at Bomboná and nearby shops).

## Getting There & Away

**Air** The airport is 33km north of the city on the road to Cali. Colectivos go there from Calle 18 at Carrera 25 (US$2.50, 45 minutes). Pay the day before your flight at the airline office or at a travel agency, and the colectivo will pick you up from your hotel.

Avianca, Intercontinental and Satena all service Pasto, with daily flights to Bogotá (US$70 to US$125) and Cali (US$50 to US$100), and connections to other cities.

**Bus** The bus terminal is 2km south of the city centre. Urban buses go there from different points in the central area, including Carrera 20A at Calle 17, or take a taxi (US$1.25).

Frequent buses, minibuses and colectivos go to Ipiales (US$2 to US$3, 1½ to two hours); sit on the left for better views. Plenty of buses ply the spectacular road to Cali (US$12, nine hours). These buses will drop you off in Popayán in six hours. Avoid travelling this route at night – buses have been ambushed and passengers robbed. More than a dozen direct buses depart daily to Bogotá (US$32, 21 hours).

## AROUND PASTO
### Volcán Galeras

Galeras volcano (4267m) is 8km west of Pasto as the crow flies, or 22km by rough road (no public transport). The volcano's activity rose dangerously in 1989 putting the city and the surrounding region in a state of emergency. Since then, the volcano has erupted several times, but has recently calmed down. Tourists are again allowed to hike or ride to the top. The hike from Pasto to the top takes four to five hours. Pasto's tourist office can organise guides (US$20) and vehicles (US$40).

### Laguna de la Cocha

This is one of the biggest and most beautiful lakes in Colombia, about 25km east of Pasto. The small island of La Corota is a nature reserve, covered by dense forest and home to highly diverse flora. It is accessible by boat from the lakeshore.

Scattered around the lake are two dozen small private nature reserves, collectively known as the Reservas Naturales de la Cocha, established by locals on their farms. They will show you around, and some provide accommodation and food. However, many have been closed due to the guerrilla presence in the region. For the current situation, inquire at the **Asociación de la Red de las Reservas** (☎ 723 1022; Calle 10 No 36-28, Pasto).

Jeeps for the lake (US$1.50, 45 minutes) depart on weekdays from the Iglesia de San Sebastián in central Pasto (on weekends from the back of the Hospital Departamental, Calle 22 at Carrera 7).

## IPIALES
☎ 2 • pop 70,000 • elevation 2900m • temp 11°C

Ipiales, close the Ecuadorian border at Rumichaca, is an uninspiring commercial town driven by trade across the frontier. There is little to see or do here, except for the colourful Saturday market, where the *campesinos* from surrounding villages come to buy and sell goods. A short side trip to the Santuario de las Lajas is a must.

## Information
**Immigration** All passport formalities are processed in Rumichaca, not in Ipiales or Tulcán. The DAS office, on the Colombian

# IPIALES

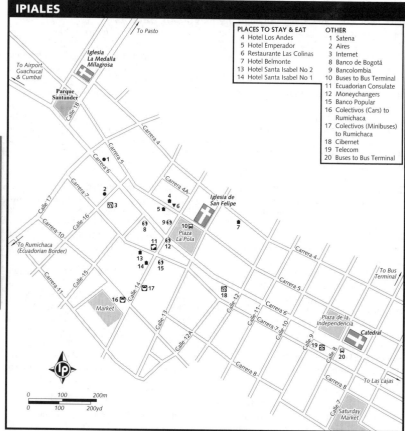

| PLACES TO STAY & EAT | OTHER |
|---|---|
| 4 Hotel Los Andes | 1 Satena |
| 5 Hotel Emperador | 2 Aires |
| 6 Restaurante Las Colinas | 3 Internet |
| 7 Hotel Belmonte | 8 Banco de Bogotá |
| 13 Hotel Santa Isabel No 2 | 9 Bancolombia |
| 14 Hotel Santa Isabel No 1 | 10 Buses to Bus Terminal |
| | 11 Ecuadorian Consulate |
| | 12 Moneychangers |
| | 15 Banco Popular |
| | 16 Colectivos (Cars) to Rumichaca |
| | 17 Colectivos (Minibuses) to Rumichaca |
| | 18 Cibernet |
| | 19 Telecom |
| | 20 Buses to Bus Terminal |

side of the border, is open 8am to 8pm daily, but the Ecuadorian post, just across the Río Rumichaca, may close for lunch from noon to 2pm.

**Ecuadorian Consulate** Few nationals need a visa for Ecuador, but if you need one, the consulate (☎ 773 2292; Carrera 7 No 14-10) is in the centre of Ipiales.

**Money** No bank in Ipiales changes cash or travellers cheques, but they are likely to give peso cash advances on credit cards. Bancolombia and Banco de Bogotá have ATMs.

Plenty of moneychangers on the Plaza La Pola (the main square) and a number of casas de cambio in the town's centre will change US dollars, Colombian pesos and Ecuadorian sucres. There are also money-changers at the border in Rumichaca.

**Email & Internet Access** There are several Internet cafés in town, but access can be slow. Try the **Internet** (Calle 16 No 6-51) or the **Cibernet** (Carrera 6 No 12-43, Centro Comercial Polo).

## Places to Stay

Ipiales has plenty of hotels and most are cheap. The nights are quite chilly here, so check the number of blankets before you book a room in a rock-bottom hospedaje.

**Hotel Belmonte** (☎ 773 2771; Carrera 4 No 12-111; rooms without/with bath per person US$3/4) is one of the cheapest and acceptable hotels. It is a small, friendly, family-run place, possibly the most popular with backpackers. It has some rooms with private baths, others not, but does have hot water.

**Hotel Emperador** (☎ 773 2311; Carrera 5 No 14-43; singles/doubles US$6/10) is nothing particularly memorable, but its rooms are OK and have private baths.

**Hotel Santa Isabel No 1** (☎ 773 3851; Calle 14 No 7-30; singles/doubles/triples US$7/12/15) is another budget option with private baths. The same owners have built the more respectable six-storey **Hotel Santa Isabel No 2** (☎ 773 4172; Carrera 7 No 14-27; singles/doubles/triples US$12/17/20), which provides more comfort and space.

**Hotel Los Andes** (☎ 773 4338; Carrera 5 No 14-44; singles/doubles/triples US$20/27/37) is one of the best in town, offering neat, quiet rooms, and a gym and sauna.

### Places to Eat

Many budget restaurants around the main plaza and the central streets serve budget meals and snacks. **Restaurante Las Colinas** (Carrera 5 No 14-42; mains US$4-7), next door to Hotel Los Andes, is one of the best in town. Several rustic asaderos, which serve roasted or grilled meats) are in the suburb of El Charco on the road to Las Lajas.

### Getting There & Away

**Air** The airport is 7km northwest of Ipiales, on the road to Cumbal, accessible by taxi (US$3). Satena and Aires have flights to Cali (US$65 to US$100) and to Bogotá (US$80 to US$130).

There are no direct flights from Ipiales to Ecuador, but you can easily get to Tulcán, from where Tame has daily flights to Quito. If you're heading to Tulcán from the border, you'll pass the airport 2km before reaching town.

**Bus** Ipiales has a new, large bus terminal, about 1km northeast of the centre. It's linked to the centre by urban buses (US$0.20) and taxis (US$1).

Expreso Bolivariano has a dozen buses daily to Bogotá (US$33, 23 hours). Several companies run regular buses to Cali (US$13, 11 hours). All these buses will drop you in Popayán in eight hours. Don't travel at night on this route – see the earlier Getting There & Away sections of Pasto and Popayán for more information.

There are plenty of buses, minibuses and colectivos to Pasto (US$2 to US$3, 1½ to two hours). They all depart from the bus terminal. Sit on the right for better views.

Frequent colectivos (cars and minibuses) travel the 2.5km to the border at Rumichaca (US$0.50), leaving from the bus terminal and the market area near the corner of Calle 14 and Carrera 10. After crossing the border on foot, take another colectivo to Tulcán (6km). On both routes, Colombian and Ecuadorian currency is accepted.

## SANTUARIO DE LAS LAJAS
**elevation 2600m • temp 14°C**

The Santuario de Nuestra Señora de Las Lajas, 7km southeast of Ipiales, is a neo-Gothic church built on a bridge spanning a spectacular deep gorge of the Río Guaitara. The church was erected to commemorate the appearance of the Virgin, whose image, according to a legend, emerged in the mid-18th century on an enormous vertical rock 45m above the river.

The first chapel was constructed in 1803, then replaced by another. Today's church, designed by Nariño architect Lucindo Espinoza, was built between 1926 and 1944, and is an unusual construction. It is set up against the gorge cliff so that the rock with the image is its main altar. The Virgin is accompanied by Santo Domingo and San Francisco.

Pilgrims from all over Colombia and from abroad come here year-round. Many leave thanksgiving plaques along the alley leading to the church. Note the number of miracles that are said to have occurred.

### Places to Stay

The Santuario is normally visited on a short trip out of Ipiales, but should you like to stay longer in Las Lajas, there are a dozen simple, small, budget hotels along the access alley to the church, plus a number of basic restaurants.

### Getting There & Away

Colectivos run regularly from Ipiales to Las Lajas (US$0.50, 15 minutes), leaving from Carrera 6 at Calle 4. A taxi from Ipiales to Las Lajas costs US$2.50. A return taxi (for up to four people), including an hour waiting in Las Lajas, shouldn't cost more than US$6. There's a spectacular view of the gorge and church just before you reach Las Lajas.

# Amazon Basin

Colombia's Amazon basin covers around 400,000 sq km, roughly equal in size to California or larger than Germany. Amazonia – as it's known to Colombians – takes up the entire southeast portion of the country, comprising more than a third of the national territory. Administratively, the region falls into six departments: Amazonas, Caquetá, Guainía, Guaviare, Putumayo and Vaupés.

Almost all the region is thick tropical rainforest crisscrossed by rivers and sparsely inhabited by several dozen different Indian communities and some colonists. The region is an ethnic and linguistic mosaic using more than 50 indigenous languages (not counting dialects) belonging to some 10 linguistic families. There are no roads, so transport is either by air or by river. Large parts of the region still remain largely untamed.

The longest rivers of Colombian Amazonia are the Río Caquetá (2200km) and Río Putumayo (1800km), both tributaries of the Amazon River. As for the Amazon itself, Colombia borders about 130km of its more than 6400km course. This is a result of a treaty signed in 1922 between Colombia, Brazil and Peru. The agreement granted Colombia a somewhat curious, narrow strip of land penetrating south between the two neighbouring countries down to the banks of the Amazon, with the town of Leticia sitting at its southeastern tip. Leticia has developed into by far the most popular tourist destination in the Colombian Amazon.

## LETICIA

☎ 8 • pop 35,000 • elevation 95m
• temp 27°C

Leticia is a small, hot town on the Amazon River where the borders of Colombia, Peru and Brazil converge. When it was founded in 1867, under the name of San Antonio, it was part of Peru, but it was transferred to Colombia under the treaty of 1922 and its name changed to Leticia.

The town is the only significant tourist centre in Colombian Amazonia, serving as a base for jungle trips around the region. Leticia is also a gateway to further Amazonian adventures, as it is linked via the Amazon with Iquitos (Peru) upriver and Manaus (Brazil) downriver.

## Highlights

- Go on a jungle tour to experience the lush rainforest and its rich wildlife
- Take a boat trip down the Amazon to Manaus

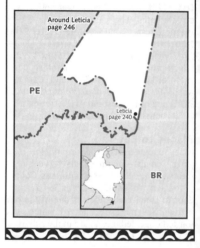

The town has reasonable tourist facilities and flight connections with Bogotá. Importantly, Leticia is a secure and easy-going place – guerrillas are not active in the area. Tourists arriving at Leticia's airport are charged a compulsory US$5 tax.

July and August are the only relatively dry months. The wettest period is from February to April. The Amazon River's highest level is reached between May and June, while the lowest is from August to October. The difference between low and high water can be as great as 15m.

### Orientation

Leticia lies right on the Colombia–Brazil border. Just south across the frontier sits Tabatinga, a Brazilian town much the same size as Leticia, with its own port and airport. Leticia and Tabatinga are virtually merging; there are no border checkpoints between them. Frequent *colectivos* link the towns, or you can just walk.

Both locals and foreigners are allowed to come and go between the two towns without

## Colombian Amazon's Poignant History

Very early on, the dream of El Dorado enticed the Spaniards into the Amazon region. Soon after the discovery of the Amazon River by Francisco de Orellana (in 1542), the region became the object of various expeditions. They didn't find the gold they were after, but opened up the region for missionaries. First the Jesuits, then the Franciscans and Capuchins followed the explorers, founding settlements, building churches and bringing Christianity to the Indians.

At the end of the 19th century, the rubber boom marked the beginning of the economic exploitation of the jungle on a large scale. It brought with it probably the cruellest period for the indigenous people. Slavery was introduced and decimated the Indian population. The Huitotos, the largest indigenous group of the Colombian Amazon, were almost totally wiped out. Between 1890 and 1935, their number slumped from about 60,000 to less than 10,000.

By the 1930s, when rubber fever came to an end, a new danger emerged. In 1932, the construction of the Altamira–Florencia and Pasto–Mocoa roads opened up the region. A stream of settlers rushed in, turning into a flood from the 1950s onwards. Uncontrolled colonisation resulted in a couple of hundred thousand newcomers settling along the fringes of the Amazon within a few decades. Fortunately, most settlers opted to establish their new homes in a belt at the foot of the Andes, with few migrants heading deeper into the jungle.

Yet, the heart of the Amazon didn't escape from intruders either. In the early 1980s, it became a playground for drug lords. Such a remote land with virtually no government control couldn't make for a more perfect shelter for coca plantations and cocaine laboratories, which mushroomed throughout the region. One of these, Tranquilandia, produced 3500kg of pure cocaine per month. Police couldn't believe their eyes when they seized it in 1984 and found 14 fully equipped modern laboratories, complete with water and electricity supply, roads, dormitories and an airstrip, plus 14 tonnes of cocaine ready to be sent overseas. This was the largest laboratory found, but are there others in this jungle?

During the 1990s, guerrillas largely replaced the drug lords, taking over their plantations and laboratories and establishing new ones. The Amazon, particularly the Caquetá and Putumayo departments, has become the FARC guerrillas' major stronghold and shelter. From here they began peace talks with the government in 1999, after authorities had agreed on withdrawing troops from part of the region and establishing a demilitarised zone. In effect, the FARC controlled an area the size of Switzerland without any government interference. A country within a country had been established.

Talks broke down in February 2002 and the government set about trying to reclaim the territory, yet guerrillas had strengthened their grip upon the region. They currently control large chunks of Caquetá and Putumayo and many other areas in the Amazon.

visas, but if you plan on heading further into either country, you must get your passport stamped at DAS in Leticia and at Polícia Federal in Tabatinga (not on the actual border).

On the island in the Amazon opposite Leticia/Tabatinga is Santa Rosa, a small Peruvian village. Boats go there from Leticia's Muelle Fluvial and the market, and Tabatinga's Porto da Feira.

On the opposite side of the Amazon from Leticia, about 25km downstream, is the Brazilian town of Benjamin Constant, the main port for boats downstream to Manaus. Boats shuttle regularly between Tabatinga and Benjamin Constant.

Of the four border towns, Leticia is the most pleasant and has the widest choice of tourist facilities – it's the best place to hang your hat no matter which way you're headed. Nonetheless, in the following sections we've included information on various Tabatinga services (money exchange, Internet access, hotels, restaurants) to allow you to easily move around the place and flexibly plan your itinerary.

### Information

**Tourist Offices** The **Secretaría de Turismo y Fronteras** (☎ 592 7505; Carrera 11 No 11-35; open 7am-noon & 2pm-5.30pm Mon-Fri) is just off Parque Santander.

The **national park office** (☎ 592 7124; Carrera 11 No 12-45) provides information about Parque Nacional Amacayacu

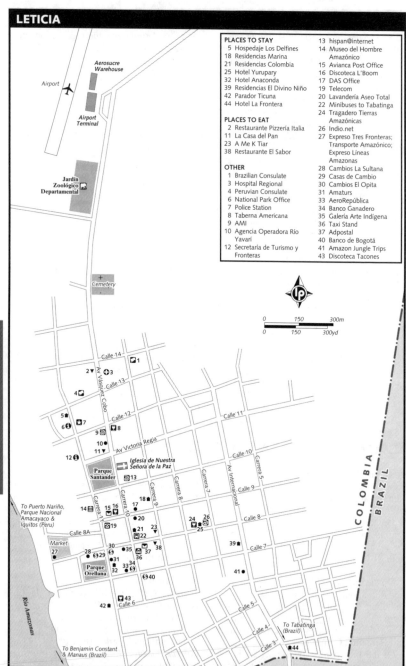

# LETICIA

**PLACES TO STAY**
5 Hospedaje Los Delfines
18 Residencias Marina
21 Residencias Colombia
25 Hotel Yurupary
32 Hotel Anaconda
39 Residencias El Divino Niño
42 Parador Ticuna
44 Hotel La Frontera

**PLACES TO EAT**
2 Restaurante Pizzería Italia
11 La Casa del Pan
23 A Me K Tiar
38 Restaurante El Sabor

**OTHER**
1 Brazilian Consulate
3 Hospital Regional
4 Peruvian Consulate
6 National Park Office
7 Police Station
8 Taberna Americana
9 AMI
10 Agencia Operadora Río Yavarí
12 Secretaría de Turismo y Fronteras
13 hispan@internet
14 Museo del Hombre Amazónico
15 Avianca Post Office
16 Discoteca L'Boom
17 DAS Office
19 Telecom
20 Lavandería Aseo Total
22 Minibuses to Tabatinga
24 Tragadero Tierras Amazónicas
26 Indio.net
27 Expreso Tres Fronteras; Transporte Amazónico; Expreso Líneas Amazonas
28 Cambios La Sultana
29 Casas de Cambio
30 Cambios El Opita
31 Amaturs
33 AeroRepública
34 Banco Ganadero
35 Galería Arte Indígena
36 Taxi Stand
37 Adpostal
40 Banco de Bogotá
41 Amazon Jungle Trips
43 Discoteca Tacones

and takes bookings for accommodation in the park (see Parque Nacional Amacayacu later in this chapter).

**Immigration** The **DAS office** *(Calle 9)* no longer stamps passports. You now need to get an entry or exit stamp in your passport from the DAS officials at Leticia's airport (open daily).

Entry and exit stamps for Brazil must be obtained at the **Polícia Federal** *(Av da Amizade 650)* in Tabatinga near the hospital.

A yellow-fever vaccination certificate is likely to be required by officials when you enter Brazil.

If heading for or coming from Iquitos, you get your entry or exit stamp in Santa Rosa.

**Consulates** The **Brazilian consulate** *(☎ 592 7530; Carrera 9 No 13-84; open 8am-noon & 1pm-4pm Mon-Fri)* is in the northern end of Leticia. Citizens of some countries, including the USA, Canada, Australia and New Zealand, need a visa and it may be costly (particularly for US nationals). Bring your photo and yellow-fever vaccination certificate.

The **Peruvian consulate** *(☎ 592 7204; Calle 13 No 10-70; open 9am-2pm Mon-Fri)* is also in Leticia's northern part.

Travellers coming from Brazil may need the **Colombian consulate** *(☎ 412 2104; Rua General Sanpaio 623; open 8am-2pm Mon-Fri)* in Tabatinga.

**Money** Leticia has two banks, both on the corner of Carrera 10 and Calle 7. **Banco Ganadero** changes AmEx travellers cheques (but not cash) and provides peso advances on Visa (but not on MasterCard), either by teller or the bank's ATM. The **Banco de Bogotá** won't touch your travellers cheques or cash dollars, but has an ATM that accepts Visa cards (but not MasterCard). **Cambios El Opita** *(☎ 592 5134; Carrera 11 No 7-96)* changes travellers cheques.

There are many *casas de cambio* on Calle 8 between Carrera 11 and the market. They change US dollars, Colombian pesos, Brazilian reais and Peruvian soles. They open around 8am or 9am until 5pm or 6pm weekdays and until around 2pm Saturday. Shop around, as rates vary.

There are also money-changing facilities in Tabatinga. The **Banco do Brasil** *(Av da Amizade)* gives cash advances in reais on

Visa. The **CNM Câmbio e Turismo** *(☎ 412 3281; Av da Amizade 2017)*, about 500m from the actual border, exchanges cash and travellers cheques, and pays in reais or pesos, but the rate may be a bit lower than in Leticia.

Check exchange rates on both sides of the border if these small differences are important to your budget or if you have a lot of money to change. Don't carry pesos any further into Brazil or Peru as it will be difficult to change them. By the same token, don't bring reais to Bogotá. Change all the money of the country you're leaving in Leticia/Tabatinga.

**Email & Internet Access** There are several Internet cafés in Leticia, including **hispan@internet** *(Calle 10 No 9-82)*, **Indio.net** *(Centro Comercial Acuarios, Carrera 7 at Calle 8)* and **AMI** *(Carrera 10 No 11-119)*. There are also Internet facilities in Tabatinga, including **Digital Net Internet Café** *(Rua Pedro Texeira)* and **D'Joy Internet Café** *(Rua da Pátria 568)*. Any of these will cost US$1 to US$1.50 an hour. Connections are rather slow.

**Laundry** The **Lavandería Aseo Total** *(Calle 9 No 9-85; open 7.30am-6.30pm daily)* will wash and dry your dirty linen for US$1.25 per kilogram.

## Things to See & Do
The **Jardín Zoológico Departamental** *(Av Vásquez Cobo; admission US$1; open 8am-noon & 2pm-5pm Mon-Fri, 8am-5.30pm Sat & Sun)*, near the airport, has animals typical of the region including anacondas, tapirs, monkeys, caimans, ocelots, eagles, macaws and a friendly manatee named Polo. The small lake at the far northern end of the zoo features the famous *Victoria amazonica*, a kind of water lily noted for its gigantic round leaves.

The small **Museo del Hombre Amazónico** *(☎ 592 7729; Carrera 11 No 9-43; admission free; open 9am-noon & 2.30pm-5pm Mon-Fri, 9am-1pm Sat)* features artefacts and household implements of Indian groups living in the region.

The **Galería Arte Indigena** *(☎ 592 7056; Calle 8 No 10-35)* is Leticia's largest craft shop selling artefacts of indigenous Indian groups. At the back of the shop is **Museo Uirapuru** featuring an exhibition of historic crafts (not for sale).

## Ticunas & Yaguas – Indigenous Groups of Leticia Region

The region around Leticia is inhabited by various indigenous groups, of which Ticunas and Yaguas are the main ones. Ticunas, the second most numerous community of the Colombian Amazon (after the Huitotos), occupy a vast area of Peru, Colombia and Brazil to the south of the Putumayo River. In the Leticia area, they live in Bellavista (on the Peruvian side), Atacuari, Puerto Nariño, Santa Sofía, Nazareth and on Mocagua Island.

The Ticuna men traditionally paint themselves with a black-blue dye extracted from the *huito* or *genipa*, an orange-like fruit, and dress in vegetable-fibre skirts. Only a few still do so. Their typical crafts include textiles, *cerbatanas* (blowpipes), necklaces and *yanchanas* (bark paintings).

The Yaguas are a seminomadic group, more traditional than the Ticunas, ethnically distinct and belonging to a different linguistic family. Most of them live in Peru; in Colombia they inhabit the Tucuchira and Atacuari Rivers but not the village of Atacuari itself. Some Yaguas live in the region of Santa Sofía and on Mocagua Island.

Yagua means 'red' in Quechua. The name comes from the red paint of the *achiote* plant, used on the face to prevent the approach of evil spirits. This paint also protects from insect bites and is employed as an ornament. The Yaguas are essentially hunters and fishers, but handicrafts have become an important source of revenue. They make fine seed necklaces, *mochilas* (bucket-shaped shoulder bags), ritual masks, bark paintings, blowpipes and totems, the most distinctive being the sticks with carved human figures on top.

---

Have a look around the market and take a stroll along the waterfront. Visit the Parque Santander before sunset for an impressive spectacle when thousands of small screeching parrots (locally called *pericos*) arrive for their nightly rest in the park's trees.

Leticia has become a base for touring the surrounding region, which is populated by several indigenous groups, among which the Ticuna and Yagua are the dominant communities. This is also a springboard for exploring the jungle and its exuberant flora and fauna.

### Organised Tours

There are a dozen tour operators in Leticia focusing on jungle trips. Most agencies offer standard one-day tours, which go up the Amazon to Puerto Nariño and include lunch and visits to the Isla de los Micos and to an indigenous village. These excursions are usually well organised, comfortable and trouble-free, but will hardly give you a real picture of the rainforest or its inhabitants.

The real wilderness begins well off the Amazon proper, along its small tributaries. The farther you go, the more chance you have to observe wildlife in relatively undamaged habitats and to visit indigenous settlements. This involves more time and money, but the experience can be much more rewarding. A three- to four-day tour is

perhaps the best way to balance the cost of the trip with the insight it will give you into the workings of the jungle.

Multiday tours are run by several companies, three of which have established small nature reserves and built jungle lodges. All three reserves – Zacambú, Río Yavarí and Palmarí – are along the lower reaches of the Río Yavarí, on the Brazil–Peru border. See the Río Yavarí section later in this chapter for information about the reserves, their lodges and tours.

Official tour agencies apart, you are likely to be approached by independent guides whose tours can be cheaper and are open to negotiation. They will find you in Leticia, in your hotel or in a restaurant, and will offer their services, usually starting the show by presenting thick albums of photos from previous tours. If you decide to go with them, always clearly fix the conditions, places to be visited, time and price. Insist on paying only a part of the cost of the trip before departure and the rest at the end.

If you are not up to a tour, there are some cheaper ways of getting a taste of the jungle, and they can be as good (or even better) than regular tours. Consider the following options: a budget backpacker offer of the Reserva Natural Palmarí; guided excursions in the Parque Nacional Amacayacu; and trips with the locals from Puerto Nariño.

See the relevant sections later in this chapter for details.

Bring enough mosquito repellent from Bogotá because you can't get good stuff in Leticia. Take high-speed film – the jungle is always dark.

## Special Events

July's week-long **Festival de la Confraternidad Amazónica** brings together popular and cultural events from the three countries.

## Places to Stay

**Leticia** There are a dozen places to stay in Leticia – more than sufficient to cope with relatively light tourist traffic.

**Residencias Colombia** (*Carrera 10 No 8-52; singles/couples US$4/7*) is one of the cheapest, but most basic, places. Rooms have hard double beds and fans, but baths are shared.

**Residencias Marina** (☎ 592 6014; *Carrera 9 No 9-29; singles/doubles/triples US$7/10/15*) is nothing particularly special, but all rooms have bath, fan and fridge.

**Residencias El Divino Niño** (☎ 592 5598; *Av Internacional No 7-23; singles/doubles US$6/10*) is another cheap, but undistinguished, option with private baths, but it's tucked a bit away from the centre.

**Hospedaje Los Delfines** (☎ 592 7388; *Carrera 11 No 12-81; singles/doubles US$10/15*) is a small family-run place offering nine spacious neat rooms with bath, fan and fridge. Rooms are arranged around a leafy patio.

**Hotel La Frontera** (☎ 592 5600; *Av Internacional No 1-04; singles/doubles/triples US$16/25/36*) is appropriately named as it's just 4m from the actual border. This new hotel offers 16 rooms with bath, fan, air-conditioning and cable TV.

**Hotel Yurupary** (☎ 592 7983; *Calle 8 No 7-26; singles/doubles/triples US$18/28/36*) is one of the best reasonably priced options in town. It has ample air-conditioned rooms with fridge and cable TV, and the price includes breakfast.

**Hotel Anaconda** (☎ 592 7119; *Carrera 11 No 7-34; singles/doubles/triples US$40/60/75*) is overrated, but you're likely to be able to negotiate the price. It may be worth the money if you are lucky enough to get a room on the top floor facing the Amazon. Here you'll have good views over the river, particularly attractive at sunset.

**Parador Ticuna** (☎ 592 7273; *Carrera 11 No 6-11; doubles/triples with fan US$25/30, with air-con US$36/45*) was once an amazing place, with large *cabañas*, palm-filled garden and big pool – a small tropical paradise. However, it has deteriorated sharply over the years. Some restoration work began when we were there. Check the situation when you arrive and decide for yourself.

**Tabatinga** This town also has a good range of accommodation, and it's a bit cheaper than Leticia. Both pesos and reais are accepted in most establishments.

**Traveler Jungle Home** (☎ 412 5060; **e** *mowglydiscovery@hotmail.com; Rua Marechal Rondon 86; US$5 per person*) belongs to an experienced jungle guide, Tony 'Mowgly' Vargas, and his French wife, Sophie Coyaud. They offer two simple rooms and the use of the kitchen, and organise tours.

**Hotel Pajé** (☎ 412 2774; *Rua Pedro Teixeira 367; rooms with fan/air-con US$4/6*) near the church is basic, but one of the cheapest places in town. All rooms have one double bed, suitable for a single or couple. Rooms are small, but have private baths.

**Hotel Cristina** (☎ 412 2558; *Rua Marechal Mallet 248; singles/doubles with fan US$6/8, with air-con US$8/12*) is OK and convenient if you plan on taking the early-morning boat to Iquitos (see Getting There & Away later). Alternatively, check the **Hospedaría Brasil**, 50m to the east, which offers and costs much the same.

**Hotel Rio Mar** (☎ 412 3061; *Rua Marechal Rondon 1714; doubles with fan & bath US$10*) is a small and friendly place just next to the market and Porto da Feira, convenient for enjoying the bustling port.

**Hotel Tarumã** (☎ 412 2083; *Rua da Pátria 70; singles/doubles/triples US$14/20/24*) faces the church and offers neat and quiet air-conditioned rooms with bath and breakfast.

**Pousada do Sol** (☎ 412 3987; *Rua General Sampaio; singles/doubles/triples US$20/24/36*) is one of the most pleasant places around. This large family-run mansion has seven air-conditioned rooms with bath and fridge and the prices include breakfast.

**Pousada Takana's** (☎ 412 3557; *Rua Oswaldo Cruz 970; singles/doubles US$16/24*) is another comfortable and enjoyable place with air-conditioned rooms and breakfast included, plus a restaurant and pool.

## Places to Eat

**Leticia** Food in Leticia is generally good and not that expensive. The local speciality is fish, including the delicious *gamitana* and *pirarucú*.

**Restaurante El Sabor** *(Calle 8 No 9-25)* is arguably Leticia's best budget eatery, with excellent-value set meals (US$2), vegetarian burgers, banana pancakes, fruit salads, plus unlimited free fruit juices with your meal. It's open 24 hours but closed on Monday.

**A Me K Tiar** *(Carrera 9 No 8-15; mains US$3-5)* offers some of the best *parrillas* (mixed grill) and barbecued meat in town, at very reasonable prices.

**Restaurante Pizzería Italia** *(Av Vásquez Cobo No 13-77; mains US$3-6)* serves delicious spaghetti, lasagne and pizza, cooked by a friendly Italian.

**La Casa del Pan** *(Calle 11 No 10-20)*, facing Parque Santander, is a great spot for breakfast (eggs, French bread, coffee and fruit juice for US$2).

**Tabatinga** The culinary picture here has improved recently.

**Restaurante Tres Fronteiras do Amazonas** *(Rua Rui Barbosa; mains US$4-7)* is one of the best eateries in town. This attractive palm-thatched open-air place offers a wide choice of fish and meat dishes, plus a selection of drinks, including *caipirinha* (Brazilian cocktail based on sugarcane rum).

**Restaurante Fazenda** *(Av da Amizade 1961; mains US$3-7)* is new, but already has become popular for its good-value Brazilian food and pleasant interior.

## Entertainment

There are several bars in Leticia's centre, including the popular **Tragadero Tierras Amazónicas** *(Calle 8 No 7-50)* next to Hotel Yurupary. **Discoteca Tacones** *(Carrera 11 No 6-14)* is probably the trendiest disco in town, closely followed by the **Discoteca L'Boom** *(Calle 9 No 10-40)*. Both play a mixed bag of music. **Taberna Americana** *(Carrera 10 No 11-108)* is a cheap, rustic bar playing salsa music till late.

## Getting There & Away

**Air** The only passenger airline servicing Leticia is **AeroRepública** *(☎ 592 7666; Calle 7 No 10-36)*. It flies between Leticia and Bogotá several days a week (US$100

to US$120). Avianca/Sam plans to restart services on this route. It may be difficult to get on flights out of Leticia in the holiday season – book as early as you can.

Before you book a commercial flight, you may want to check for cargo flights with Aerosucre, which shuttles between Leticia and Bogotá almost daily and sometimes takes passengers, though the pilots now charge almost as much as the commercial flights. Inquire at the Aerosucre *bodega* (warehouse) at the airport, just behind the passenger terminal. Go there early in the morning.

There are no flights into Brazil from Leticia, but from Tabatinga, Varig operates flights to Manaus on Monday, Wednesday and Friday (US$170 one way), while Rico flies on Tuesday, Thursday, Saturday and Sunday (US$165). Tickets can be bought from Tabatinga's travel agency, **Turamazon** *(☎ 412 2244; Av da Amizade 2271)*, or **CNM Câmbio e Turismo** *(☎ 412 3281; Av da Amizade 2017)*, both near the border. The airport is 2km south of Tabatinga; colectivos marked 'Comara' from Leticia will drop you off nearby. Remember to get your exit/entry stamps before departure.

A small Peruvian airline, TANS, flies its 15-seat hydroplane from Santa Rosa to Iquitos on Wednesday and Saturday (US$65). Information and tickets are available from **Cambios La Sultana** *(☎ 592 7071; Calle 8 No 11-57)* in Leticia. You need to go by boat from Leticia or Tabatinga to Santa Rosa to catch this plane.

**Boat** Leticia/Tabatinga is an important point for travellers looking for backwater Amazonian adventures, downstream to Manaus (Brazil) or upriver to Iquitos (Peru).

Boats down the Amazon to Manaus leave from Porto Fluvial de Tabatinga, beyond the hospital, and call at Benjamin Constant. There are two boats per week, departing from Tabatinga on Wednesday and Saturday around 2pm, and Benjamin Constant later those evenings. There may be more boats going on other days so check. Sometimes the boats are very crowded.

The trip to Manaus takes three days and four nights and costs US$40 in your own hammock, or US$180 for a double cabin. Food is included, but you're best advised to bring snacks and bottled water. The cheapest places to buy an ordinary cloth hammock

(US$5 to US$10) are **Esplanada Magazine** *(Av de Amizade)* near Banco do Brazil, and **Magazine Modas** *(Rua Marechal Mallet 378)*, both in Tabatinga; and the market area in Leticia.

Boats come to Tabatinga one or two days before their scheduled departure back down the river. You can string up your hammock or occupy the cabin as soon as you've paid the fare, saving on hotels. Food, however, is only served after departure. Beware of theft on board.

Upstream from Manaus to Tabatinga, the trip usually takes six days, and costs about US$70 in your hammock or US$220 for a double cabin.

Three small boat companies, **Transtur** *(☎ 412 3186; Rua Marechal Mallet 306)*, and **Mayco** and **Mi Reyna** *(both ☎ 412 2945; Rua Marechal Mallet 248)* in Tabatinga run *rápidos* (high-powered passenger boats) between Tabatinga and Iquitos. Each company has a few departures a week, so there is at least one boat almost every day. The boats leave from Tabatinga's Porto da Feira at 5am and arrive in Iquitos about 10 hours later. The boats call at Santa Rosa's immigration post. The journey costs US$50 in either direction, including breakfast and lunch. Don't forget to get an exit stamp in your passport from DAS at Leticia's airport the day before departure.

There are also irregular cargo boats from Santa Rosa to Iquitos, once or twice a week. The journey takes about three days and costs US$25 to US$30, including food. Downstream from Iquitos to Santa Rosa normally takes no longer than two days.

Note that there are no roads out of Iquitos into Peru. You have to fly or continue by river to Pucallpa (five to seven days), from where you can go overland to Lima and elsewhere.

For boats to the Parque Nacional Amacayacu and Puerto Nariño, see these following sections.

## PARQUE NACIONAL AMACAYACU

Amacayacu park takes in 2935 sq km of rainforest on the northern side of the Amazon, about 75km upstream from Leticia. The terrain is generally flat with some gently undulating areas in the park's northern fringes. Like the whole region, the park has a rich and diverse wildlife, featuring caimans, snakes (including the boa and anaconda) and various species of monkeys, not to mention a profusion of fish and birds. The park is a good place to get a glimpse of the Amazon wilderness for a reasonable price.

A spacious visitor centre built on the banks of the Amazon, at the confluence of the Quebrada Matamata, provides a base for excursions into the park. You can explore the park either by marked paths or by water. Local guides accompany visitors on all excursions and charge roughly US$10 to US$20 per group, depending on the route. In the high-water period (May to June), much of the land turns into swamps and lagoons, significantly reducing walking options, but then trips in canoes are organised. Bring plenty of mosquito repellent, a flashlight, a long-sleeved shirt and waterproof gear. Plan on staying at least three days.

### Places to Stay & Eat

The visitor centre offers large, mosquito-proofed dorms with beds and hammocks, and is well set up with showers and toilets. Blankets are provided so you don't need a sleeping bag. Accommodation in a bed/hammock costs US$9/7 per person, and three meals will run to about US$8. The park entry fee is US$3. Camping in the park is not permitted. You are allowed to bring in your own food provided you take the rubbish with you when you leave. However, you cannot use the cooking facilities at the centre.

You can book and pay accommodation at the national park office in Bogotá or in Leticia (see Tourist Offices under Leticia earlier in this chapter).

### Getting There & Away

Passenger boats that run daily from Leticia to Puerto Nariño (see the following section for details) will drop you off at the visitor centre (US$10, 1½ hours from Leticia). Buy your ticket early in the morning.

Returning from the park to Leticia may occasionally involve a day (or even two) of unexpected waiting. Boats pass through from Puerto Nariño (normally passing by the visitor centre around 8am), but can be full. If this is the case, they will simply pass by without stopping. Sometimes it's possible to wave down other boats, but they are mostly slow cargo vessels.

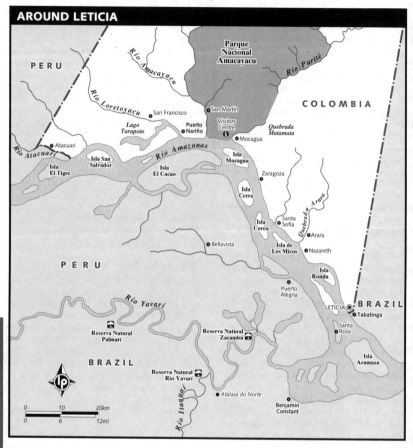

**AROUND LETICIA**

## PUERTO NARIÑO

☎ 8 • pop 2000 • elevation 110m
• temp 27°C

About 90km up the Amazon from Leticia
(15km upstream from the Amacayacu park),
Puerto Nariño is a tiny town on the banks of
the great river, but in the middle of nowhere.
It is built on a square plan and is inhabited
mainly by incomers, though there are some
Ticuna Indians living here as well. All incoming phone calls need to be connected
through the town's Telecom office (☎ 592
8190/91), and electricity is provided by the
local plant only between 3pm and 10pm.

### Things to See & Do

**Fundación Omacha** on the riverfront is a
conservation centre working to save the dol-

phins and manatees of the Amazon and has
a small exhibition. This apart, the town has
no great attractions, but is a good base for
budget jungle trips into the surrounding area,
which is interesting and worth exploring.

About 10km west of Puerto Nariño is the
**Lago Tarapoto**, a beautiful lake accessible
only by river, with varied flora including
the famous *Victoria amazonica* lily. If you
are in luck, you may see pink dolphins.
There are some Indian settlements scattered
around the lake. A half-day trip to the lake
in a small motorised boat (locally called
*peque-peque*) can be organised from Puerto
Nariño (around US$20 per boat for up to
four people). Locals can take you on boat
excursions to many other places, including
the Parque Nacional Amacayacu, or you

can just rent a canoe (US$7 per day) and do your own tour.

If you prefer walking, a popular destination is **San Martín**, a hamlet of Ticuna Indians northeast of Puerto Nariño, on the border of the national park. It's a two- to three-hour walk there and the same back. If you are not sure of going on your own, a local guide can accompany your party for US$10 to US$15.

### Places to Stay & Eat

Puerto Nariño has a choice of accommodation and eating options. Some of the cheapest accommodation is at **Cabañas Manguaré** *(US$5 per person)*, which is basic but acceptable. The **Brisas del Amazonas** *(singles/doubles/triples US$8/12/15)*, a fine mansion built in 1983, is past its best but remains a charming, if basic, place to stay.

**Casa Selva** *(US$12/10 per person in doubles/triples)* is at the top of local luxuries. It has impeccably clean rooms with private baths, plus a six-hammock dorm (US$5 per hammock). The hotel also serves meals (US$2 breakfast, US$3.50 lunch or dinner). For cheaper meals, try one of two basic local restaurants near the waterfront, **Doña María** or **Las Margaritas**.

### Getting There & Away

Puerto Nariño and Lago Tarapoto feature on the itineraries of Leticia tour operators. If you want to get there on your own, there's daily boat transport from Leticia. Three small boat companies, Expreso Tres Fronteras, Transporte Amazónico and Expreso Líneas Amazonas (all with offices near the waterfront in Leticia), operate scheduled fast passenger boats to Puerto Nariño, at 2pm on weekdays and at 1pm on weekends (US$11, two hours). There's one boat each day by one of the three carriers. At times the boats are full, so buy your ticket in the morning or a day before, just in case.

## RÍO YAVARÍ

This river forms the Brazil–Peru border for about 500km upstream from its confluence with the Amazon at Benjamin Constant. The Yavarí basin is very sparsely populated by small Indian communities and is little explored; large parts remain virtually virgin. It's therefore a good place to see a pristine habitat complete with wildlife.

Three Colombian tour operators have established small private nature reserves along the Yavarí's lower course: Zacambú, Río Yavarí and Palmarí. Each has built a jungle lodge in its reserve and runs tours from Leticia. The lodges provide accommodation and food, and serve as bases for trips by boat or foot into the surrounding area. All offer typical jungle lodge activities such as forest walks, fishing, night-time alligator spotting, bird-watching, dolphin-watching and visits to indigenous settlements.

All three operators offer three- to six-day all-inclusive packages, based at their lodges. Each package includes accommodation (in beds), meals, excursions with guides and return transport from Leticia. The cost largely depends on the number of people in the party, length of the stay, season etc; count on US$40 to US$80 a person per day. Tours don't usually have a fixed timetable; agents normally wait until they have enough people, but if you don't want to wait then be prepared to pay more.

Contact the agencies in advance to compare their programmes, conditions and prices. Legally, you should have a Brazilian or Peruvian visa to stay in the reserves, so check this issue with the agencies in advance. Following is a rundown of the three reserves.

### Reserva Natural Zacambú

Zacambú is the nearest to Leticia, about 70km by boat. Its lodge is on Lake Zacambú, just off Río Yavarí, on the Peruvian side of the river. It's reputedly a good area for wildlife spotting. The lodge is simple, with small rooms without baths, and a total capacity of about 30 guests. Most excursions from here go by boat, since walking possibilities around the lodge are limited, and in the period of high water almost nonexistent. Both the lodge and tours are run from Leticia by **Amazon Jungle Trips** (☎ 592 7377; e *amazonjungletrips@yahoo .com; Av Internacional No 6-25)*.

### Reserva Natural Río Yavarí

This reserve is about 20km upriver from Zacambú, on the opposite, Brazilian side of the Río Yavarí. The lodge is lovely, as is its location overlooking a small lake off the Río Itaquai, a southern tributary of the Yavarí. Rooms have private baths and there's a *maloca* (large, communal house) with hammocks. The lodge is run from Leticia by **Agencia Operadora Río Yavarí** (*☎ 592 7457; Carrera 10 No 11-27*). If you find the office closed, inquire at Hospedaje Los Delfines (see Places to Stay under Leticia earlier in this chapter).

## Reserva Natural Palmarí

Palmarí is another 20km further upstream on the Río Yavarí, about 110km by river from Leticia. Its rambling lodge sits on the high, south (Brazilian) bank of the river, overlooking a wide bend where pink and grey dolphins are often seen. The lodge itself features several cabañas with rooms with bath, a large round maloca with hammocks and a viewing tower providing sweeping vistas. The lodge has good food and helpful guides, and offers a wide choice of walking trips and boat excursions. The reserve is managed from Bogotá by its owner, **Axel Antoine-Feill** (*☎ 1-236 3813, 1-623 4265; Ⓦ www.palmari.org; Carrera 10 No 93-72*), who can speak several languages including English. His representative in Leticia is **Marcela Torres** (*☎ 592 7344*).

Tours apart, Palmarí has a budget offer for independent travellers who'd like to stay in the reserve but don't want to pay for an all-inclusive tour. The lodge simply charges for accommodation (US$10 per bed or US$7 per hammock) and food (US$3 breakfast, US$4 lunch, US$5 dinner), and you can plan your stay and excursions as you wish, using the reserve's canoes and guides sometimes for free or for a small charge if they are not too busy with tours or other tasks. Incidentally, Palmarí offers the best walking possibilities of the three reserves.

Getting cheaply from Leticia to Palmarí is a bit of an adventure. Go by colectivo boat from Tabatinga's Porto da Feira to Benjamin Constant (US$4, 30 minutes). Be there before 9am to catch the *recreo* boat that leaves then for Atalaia do Norte (US$4, three hours), where you need to hire a local boat to Palmarí (about US$10, 30 minutes to two hours depending on the boat). Contact Axel or check the website for further details.

# Language

Colombia's official language is Spanish, and apart from some remote Indian groups, all inhabitants speak it. On San Andrés and, particularly, Providencia, English is still widely used. Many Indian groups use their native languages. There are about 65 indigenous languages and nearly 300 dialects spoken in the country.

English-speakers can be found in large urban centres, but it's certainly not a commonly understood or spoken language, even though it's taught as a mandatory second language in the public school system. As soon as you leave urban areas, though, Spanish will virtually be the only medium of communication. You'll probably manage to travel without knowing a world of Spanish, but you'll miss out on a good part of the pleasure of meeting people. Your experience of the country will be limited.

Spanish is quite an easy language to learn, and is useful in most other Latin American countries as well. It's well worth making some effort to learn at least the essentials before setting off. Colombians will encourage you, so there's no need to feel self-conscious about vocabulary, grammar or pronunciation. For a more detailed guide to the Spanish of the region, pick up a copy of Lonely Planet's *Latin American Spanish phrasebook*. Another useful resource is the compact and comprehensive *University of Chicago Spanish-English, English-Spanish Dictionary*.

## Colombian Spanish

The Spanish spoken in Colombia is generally clear and easy to understand. There are regional variations, but these won't be noticeable to visitors, apart from perhaps the *costeños* from the Caribbean Coast who speak fast and may be difficult to understand.

The use of the forms *tu* ('you' informal) and *usted* ('you' polite) is flexible in Colombia, unlike Spain, where *tu* is generally only used among friends. Strangers can often use *tu*, while a husband and a wife may use *usted* when speaking to each other and to their children. While either form is OK, the best advice is to answer in the same form that you are addressed in – and always use *usted* when talking to the police.

Note that Colombians, like all Latin Americans, do not use *vosotros* (the plural of *tu)*; *ustedes* is commonly used.

### Vocabulary

Latin American Spanish vocabulary has lots of regional variations and differs noticeably from European Spanish. Colombian Spanish has altered the meaning of some words or taken their secondary meaning as the main one. Colombians have also created plenty of *colombianismos*, words or phrases used either nationally or regionally, but almost unknown outside Colombia. You'll find some colombianismos in the Glossary at the end of the book.

Colombians and other South Americans normally refer to the Spanish language as *castellano* rather than *español*.

Note that ll is a separate letter and comes after l in the alphabet; ch and ñ are also separate letters, appearing in the alphabet after c and n respectively.

### Pronunciation

Spanish pronunciation is, in general, phonetically consistent. For example, the Spanish a has one pronunciation rather than the numerous pronunciations we find in English, such as in 'cat', 'cake', 'cart', 'care', 'call'. The most significant pronunciation differences between the Spanish of Colombia and that of Spain are: ll – as 'y' in Colombia, as 'ly' in Spain; z and c before e and i – as 's' in Colombia, not the lisped 'th' of Spain.

### Vowels

| | |
|---|---|
| a | as in 'father' |
| e | as in 'met' |
| i | as in 'police' |
| o | as in 'for' |
| u | as in 'chute' |

The letter y is a consonant (pronounced as in 'yet'), except when it stands alone or appears at the end of a word (in which case it's pronounced as i).

## Consonants

| | |
|---|---|
| b | resembles its English equivalent, and is undistinguished from **v**; for clarification, refer to the former as 'b larga', and the latter as 'b corta' (the word for the letter itself is pronounced like English 'bay') |
| c | as the 's' in 'see' before **e** and **i**, elsewhere it's as English 'k' |
| ch | as in 'chair' |
| d | as in 'dog' in initial position and after **l** and **n**; elsewhere as 'th' in 'they' |
| g | similar to the 'h' in 'hell' before **e** and **i**; elsewhere as in 'go' |
| h | never pronounced |
| j | similar to the 'h' in 'hell' |
| ll | similar to the 'y' in 'yell' |
| ñ | similar to the 'ni' in 'onion' |
| q | as English 'k' (always followed by a silent **u** and in combination with **e** and **i** eg, *que/qui*) |
| r | strongly rolled at the beginning of a word, or after **n**, **l** and **s**; elsewhere it's pronounced with one trill |
| rr | always strongly rolled |
| v | see **b**, above |
| x | as the 'x' in 'taxi' |
| z | as the 's' in 'sun' |

## Word Stress

Words ending in a vowel or the letters **n** and **s**, are stressed on the second-to-last syllable, eg, *amigo* (friend) is stressed on 'mi'. For words ending in a consonant other than **n** or **s**, the stress is on the last syllable, eg, *amor* (love) is stressed on 'mor'. Any deviation from these rules is indicated by an acute accent, eg, *adiós* (pronounced 'ah-dee-OS').

## Basic Grammar

Nouns in Spanish are either masculine or feminine. The definite article ('the' in English) agrees with the noun in gender and number; for example, the Spanish word for 'train' is masculine, so 'the train' is *el tren*, and the plural is *los trenes*. The word for 'house' is feminine, so 'the house' is *la casa*, and the plural is *las casas*.

The indefinite articles (a, an, some) work in the same way: *un libro* (a book) is masculine singular, while *una carta* (a letter) is feminine singular. Their plurals are respectively: *unos libros* (some books), *unas cartas* (some letters).

Most nouns ending in **o** are masculine and those ending in **a** are generally feminine. Normally, nouns ending in a vowel add **s** to form the plural, while those ending in a consonant add **es**.

Adjectives usually come after the noun they describe, and agree with its gender and number. Possessive adjectives *mi* (my), *tu* (your), *su* (his/her) etc come before the noun and agree in number with the thing (or things) possessed, not with the possessor. For example, 'his suitcase' is *su maleta*, while 'his suitcases' is *sus maletas*. A simple way to indicate possession is to use the preposition *de* (of), eg *la habitación de Juan* (Juan's room – literally, 'the room of Juan').

A characteristic feature of Latin American Spanish is an extremely common use of diminutives. They either describe the smallness of something or, more often, express affection. They are formed by adding suffixes *-ito/a*, *-cito/a*, *-illo/a* and *-cillo/a* to nouns and adjectives. For example, *cafecito* is the diminutive form of *café* (coffee), and means 'small coffee'; *amorcito* is a tender version of *amor* (love) used as a form of address.

## Greetings & Civilities

Greetings in Colombia have become an elaborate ritual; the short Spanish *hola* has given way to an incalculable number of expressions, all of them meaning something between 'hello' and 'how do you do'. Here are some examples:

*¿Cómo está?*
*¿Cómo ha estado?*
*¿Qué ha hecho?*
*¿Cómo le va?*
*¿Cómo me lo han tratado?*
*¿Qué tal?*
*¿Q'hubo?* or *¿Quiubo?*
*¿Qué me cuenta?*
*¿Cómo le acabó de ir?*
*¿Qué más (de nuevo, de su vida)?*
*¿Qué hay (de cosas, de bueno)?*

This list could be continued for several more pages. When people meet or phone each other, they always begin the conversation with a long exchange of these and similar expressions.

You may find it funny, surprising, irritating, ridiculous, tiring, fascinating – but whatever you say about it, it is typically

Colombian and you should learn some of these expressions to keep to the local style.

| | |
|---|---|
| Good morning. | *Buenos días.* |
| Good afternoon. | *Buenas tardes.* |
| Good evening. | *Buenas noches.* |
| Good night. | *Buenas noches.* |
| Goodbye. | *Adiós/Chao.* |
| Please. | *Por favor.* |
| Thank you. | *Gracias.* |
| Excuse me. | *Disculpe/Excuse/ Perdone.* |
| I'm sorry. | *Disculpe/Lo siento.* |

## Useful Words & Phrases

| | |
|---|---|
| Yes. | *Sí.* |
| No. | *No.* |
| I'd like ... | *Me gustaría ...* |
| How much? | *¿Cuánto?* |
| How many? | *¿Cuántos?* |
| Where is ...? | *¿Dónde está/queda ...?* |
| Where? | *¿Dónde?* |
| When? | *¿Cuándo?* |
| How? | *¿Cómo?* |
| with | *con* |
| without | *sin* |
| here | *aquí* |
| there | *allí/allá* |

## People & Family

| | |
|---|---|
| Madam/Mrs | *Señora* |
| Sir/Mr | *Señor* |
| Miss | *Señorita* |
| man | *hombre* |
| woman | *mujer* |
| husband | *marido/esposo* |
| wife | *mujer/esposa* |
| boy | *chico/muchacho* |
| girl | *chica/muchacha* |
| child | *niño/a* |
| father | *padre/papá* |
| mother | *madre/mamá* |
| son | *hijo* |
| daughter | *hija* |
| brother | *hermano* |
| sister | *hermana* |
| grandfather | *abuelo* |
| grandmother | *abuela* |
| family | *familia* |
| friend | *amigo/a* |

| | |
|---|---|
| I | *yo* |
| you (singular) | *tú* (informal) |
| | *usted* (polite) |
| he/she | *él/ella* |
| we | *nosotros/as* (m/f) |
| you (plural) | *ustedes* |
| they | *ellos/ellas* (m/f) |

## Language Difficulties

Do you speak English?
   *¿Habla inglés?*
Does anyone here speak English?
   *¿Alguien habla inglés aquí?*
I don't speak Spanish.
   *No hablo castellano.*
I understand.
   *Entiendo.*
I don't understand.
   *No entiendo.*
Please speak more slowly.
   *Por favor hable más despacio.*
Could you repeat that, please?
   *¿Puede repetirlo, por favor?*
What does it mean?
   *¿Qué significa?/¿Qué quiere decir?*
Please write that down.
   *Por favor escríbalo.*

## Getting Around

Where is ...?
   *¿Dónde queda/está ...?*
How can I get to ...?
   *¿Cómo puedo llegar a ...?*
When does the next bus leave for ...?
   *¿Cuándo sale el próximo bus para ...?*
I'd like a ticket to ...
   *Quiero un boleto/pasaje a ...*
What's the fare to ...?
   *¿Cuánto cuesta a ...?*

| | |
|---|---|
| plane | *avión* |
| train | *tren* |
| bus | *bus* |
| small bus | *buseta* |
| ship | *barco/buque* |
| boat | *lancha/bote* |
| car | *carro* |
| taxi | *taxi* |
| truck | *camión* |
| pick-up truck | *camioneta* |
| bicycle | *bicicleta* |
| motorcycle | *motocicleta* |
| to hitchhike | *echar dedo* |

| | |
|---|---|
| airport | *aeropuerto* |
| train station | *estación del tren* |
| bus terminal | *terminal de buses* |
| bus stop | *paradero/parada* |
| port | *puerto* |
| wharf/pier | *muelle* |

| | |
|---|---|
| city | *ciudad* |
| town | *pueblo* |
| village | *pueblito, caserío* |
| road | *carretera* |
| freeway | *autopista* |
| tourist office | *oficina de turismo* |
| gas/petrol station | *bomba de gasolina* |
| police station | *estación de policía* |
| embassy | *embajada* |
| consulate | *consulado* |
| bank | *banco* |
| public toilet | *baño público* |
| | |
| entrance | *entrada* |
| exit | *salida* |
| open | *abierto/a* |
| closed | *cerrado/a* |
| | |
| ticket | *boleto, pasaje* |
| ticket office | *taquilla* |
| first/last/next | *primero/último/ próximo* |
| 1st/2nd class | *primera/segunda clase* |
| one way/return | *ida/ida y vuelta* |
| left luggage | *guardaequipaje* |

## Accommodation

Do you have rooms available?
  *¿Hay habitaciones?*
May I see the room?
  *¿Puedo ver la habitación?*
What does it cost?
  *¿Cuánto cuesta?*
Does it include breakfast?
  *¿Incluye el desayuno?*

| | |
|---|---|
| hotel | *hotel/residencias/ hospedaje* |
| room | *habitación* |
| single room | *habitación sencilla* |
| double room | *habitación doble* |
| bed | *cama* |
| double bed | *cama matrimonial* |
| toilet/bath | *baño* |
| shared bath | *baño compartido* |
| private bath | *baño privado* |
| shower | *ducha* |
| | |
| air conditioning | *aire acondicionado* |
| blanket | *manta, cobija* |
| fan | *ventilador* |
| key | *llave* |
| padlock | *candado* |
| pillow | *almohada* |
| sheets | *sábanas* |

| | |
|---|---|
| soap | *jabón* |
| toilet paper | *papel higiénico* |
| towel | *toalla* |
| | |
| cheap | *barato/a* |
| expensive | *caro/a* |
| clean | *limpio/a* |
| dirty | *sucio/a* |
| good | *bueno/a* |
| poor | *malo/a* |
| noisy | *ruidoso/a* |
| quiet | *tranquilo/a* |
| hot | *caliente* |
| cold | *frío/a* |

## Toilets

The most common word for 'toilet' is *baño*, but *servicios sanitarios*, or just *servicios* (services) is a frequent alternative. Men's toilets will usually be labelled by a descriptive term such as *hombres* or *caballeros*. Women's toilets will be labelled with *señoras* or *damas*.

## Post & Telecommunications

| | |
|---|---|
| post office | *oficina de correo* |
| letter | *carta* |
| parcel | *paquete* |
| postcard | *tarjeta postal* |
| airmail | *correo aéreo* |
| registered mail | *correo certificado* |
| stamps | *estampillas* |
| letter box | *buzón* |
| public telephone | *teléfono público* |
| telephone card | *tarjeta telefónica* |
| long-distance | *llamada de larga ca distancia* |
| international call | *llamada inter- nacional* |
| person to person | *persona a persona* |
| collect call | *llamada de pago revertido* |

## Shopping

How much is it?  *¿Cuánto cuesta/vale?*
I (don't) like it.  *(No) me gusta.*
Do you have ...?/  *¿Hay ...?*
  Are there ...?

| | |
|---|---|
| shop | *almacén/tienda* |
| shopping centre | *centro comercial* |
| price | *precio* |
| change | *vueltas* |
| money | *dinero/plata* |
| coin | *moneda* |
| banknote | *billete* |

| | |
|---|---|
| cash | *efectivo* |
| cheque | *cheque* |
| credit card | *tarjeta de crédito* |
| expensive | *caro* |
| cheap | *barato* |
| big | *grande* |
| small | *pequeño* |

## Geographical Terms

| | |
|---|---|
| bay | *bahía* |
| beach | *playa* |
| cave | *cueva* |
| channel | *caño* |
| hill | *cerro* |
| mount | *pico* |
| mountain | *montaña* |
| mountain range | *cordillera/sierra/ serranía* |
| pass | *paso* |
| rapids | *raudales* |
| ravine | *quebrada* |
| river | *río* |
| sea | *mar* |
| valley | *valle* |
| waterfall | *cascada/salto* |

## Times & Dates

Eight o'clock (8.00) is *las ocho*, while 8.30 is *las ocho y treinta* (literally, 'eight and thirty') or *las ocho y media* (eight and a half). Quarter to eight (7.45) can be *las ocho menos quince* (literally, 'eight minus fifteen'), *las ocho menos cuarto* (eight minus one quarter), *un cuarto para las ocho* (one quarter to eight) or *quince para las ocho* (fifteen to eight).

The 24-hour clock is often used for transport schedules. In everyday conversations, however, people commonly use the 12-hour system and, if necessary, add *de la mañana* (in the morning), *de la tarde* (in the afternoon) or *de la noche* (at night).

| | |
|---|---|
| What time is it? | *¿Qué horas son?/ ¿Qué hora es?* |
| It's 1pm. | *Es la una de la tarde.* |
| It's 7am. | *Son las siete de la mañana.* |
| It's 7.15. | *Son las siete y cuarto.* |
| It's late. | *Es tarde.* |
| It's early. | *Es temprano.* |

| | |
|---|---|
| today | *hoy* |
| now | *ahora* |
| tonight | *esta noche* |

### Emergencies

| | |
|---|---|
| Could you help me, please? | *¿Me podría ayudar, por favor?* |
| Where's the nearest hospital? | *¿Dónde queda el hospital más cercano?* |
| Could I use your telephone? | *¿Podría usar su teléfono?* |
| I want to call my embassy. | *Quiero llamar a mi embajada.* |
| I'm ill. | *Estoy enfermo/a.* |
| Please call ... | *Por favor llame a ...* |
| a doctor | *un doctor* |
| the police | *la policía* |
| accident | *accidente* |
| ambulance | *ambulancia* |
| help | *auxilio/ayuda* |
| hospital | *hospital* |
| police | *policía* |

| | |
|---|---|
| tomorrow | *mañana* |
| day after tomorrow | *pasado mañana* |
| yesterday | *ayer* |
| Monday | *lunes* |
| Tuesday | *martes* |
| Wednesday | *miércoles* |
| Thursday | *jueves* |
| Friday | *viernes* |
| Saturday | *sábado* |
| Sunday | *domingo* |
| January | *enero* |
| February | *febrero* |
| March | *marzo* |
| April | *abril* |
| May | *mayo* |
| June | *junio* |
| July | *julio* |
| August | *agosto* |
| September | *septiembre* |
| October | *octubre* |
| November | *noviembre* |
| December | *diciembre* |
| rainy season | *invierno* |
| dry season | *verano* |
| summer | *verano* |
| autumn/fall | *otoño* |
| winter | *invierno* |
| spring | *primavera* |

## Numbers

| | |
|---|---|
| 0 | *cero* |
| 1 | *uno* |
| 2 | *dos* |
| 3 | *tres* |
| 4 | *cuatro* |
| 5 | *cinco* |
| 6 | *seis* |
| 7 | *siete* |
| 8 | *ocho* |
| 9 | *nueve* |
| 10 | *diez* |
| 11 | *once* |
| 12 | *doce* |
| 13 | *trece* |
| 14 | *catorce* |
| 15 | *quince* |
| 16 | *dieciseis* |
| 17 | *diecisiete* |
| 18 | *dieciocho* |
| 19 | *diecinueve* |
| 20 | *veinte* |
| 21 | *veintiuno* |
| 30 | *treinta* |
| 40 | *cuarenta* |
| 50 | *cincuenta* |
| 60 | *sesenta* |
| 70 | *setenta* |
| 80 | *ochenta* |
| 90 | *noventa* |
| 100 | *cien* |
| 101 | *ciento uno* |
| 200 | *doscientos* |
| 500 | *quinientos* |
| 1,000 | *mil* |
| 100,000 | *cien mil* |
| 1,000,000 | *un millón* |
| 2,000,000 | *dos millones* |
| 1st | *primero/a* |
| 2nd | *segundo/a* |
| 3rd | *tercero/a* |
| 4th | *cuarto/a* |
| 5th | *quinto/a* |

## Health

| | |
|---|---|
| I'm ill. | *Me siento mal.* |
| I have a fever. | *Tengo fiebre/ temperatura.* |
| clinic | *clínica* |
| dentist | *dentista, odontólogo* |
| doctor | *doctor, médico* |
| medicine | *medicina, remedio* |
| pharmacy | *droguería* |

## FOOD & DRINKS
### Basics

| | |
|---|---|
| breakfast | *desayuno* |
| lunch | *almuerzo* |
| set lunch | *almuerzo corriente* |
| dinner | *comida* |
| set meal | *comida corriente* |
| soup | *sopa* |
| main course | *seco/bandeja* |
| dessert | *postre* |
| cake shop | *pastelería* |
| the bill/check | *la cuenta* |
| cup | *taza* |
| dish | *plato* |
| fork | *tenedor* |
| glass | *vaso* |
| knife | *cuchillo* |
| menu | *menú, carta* |
| plate | *plato* |
| spoon | *cuchara* |
| teaspoon | *cucharita* |
| bread | *pan* |
| butter | *mantequilla* |
| cheese | *queso* |
| chips | *papas fritas* |
| cream | *crema de leche* |
| hot dog | *perro caliente* |
| ice cream | *helado* |
| pastry | *pastel* |
| pepper | *pimienta* |
| popcorn | *maíz pira* |
| mashed potatoes | *naco* |
| rice | *arroz* |
| salad | *ensalada* |
| salt | *sal* |
| sugar | *azúcar* |
| toast | *calao* |
| tomato sauce/ ketchup | *salsa de tomate* |
| vegetables | *verduras* |
| vinegar | *vinagre* |
| salad dressing | *vinagreta* |

### Menu Decoder
#### Local Specialities

*agua de panela* – drink made of *panela* melted in hot water

*ajiaco* – soup with chicken, corn on the cob and three varieties of potato, served with cream and capers; speciality of Bogotá

*almojábana* – bread made from cornflour and cottage cheese

*arepa* – toasted or fried maize pancake; it's included as an accompaniment to some dishes

*arepa con queso* – fried maize pancake with cheese

*arepa de huevo* – maize dough fried with an egg inside, typical of the Caribbean Coast

*arequipe* – milk pudding made of milk and sugar (sometimes *panela*) boiled until thick; similar to fudge but a bit runnier

*arroz con chipichipi* – rice with small shell-fish; dish typical of the Caribbean Coast

*arroz con coco* – rice cooked in coconut milk; a speciality of the Pacific and Caribbean Coasts

*arroz con pollo* – rice with chicken and vegetables; one of the most common dishes, found on the menu of most restaurants

*avena* – cold drink made from oats and milk, with cinnamon and cloves

*bandeja paisa* – typical Antioquian dish made up of ground beef, rice, *chorizo*, *frijoles*, fried *plátano*, fried egg, *chicharrón* and avocado; also called *plato montañero*; today it's found almost everywhere

*bocachico* – river fish; very tasty but with plenty of bones

*bocadillo* – a sweet made of guava paste and wrapped in banana leaf; often eaten with a piece of cheese (*bocadillo con queso*)

*bofe* – beef lungs

*borojó* – grapefruit-sized round fruit with dirt-brown peel, endemic on the Pacific Coast; used for juices which are alleged to be aphrodisiacs

*brevas con arequipe* – figs stuffed with *arequipe*, served in syrup

*buñuelo* – small ball of deep-fried maize dough and cheese

*butifarras* – small, smoked meat balls, sprinkled with a few drops of lemon juice; typical snack of the Caribbean Coast

*cabro* or *cabrito* – grilled goat, usually served with yucca and *arepa*; dish typical of Santander

*cachama* – tasty river fish

*caldo de papa* – light soup with potatoes, pieces of beef and coriander; an energy-boosting Colombian breakfast

*canelazo* – hot drink made of *aguardiente*, *agua de panela* and cinnamon

*carne asada* – one of the most common dishes, appearing on almost every menu; roast or grilled beef, served with rice, chips, yucca etc, depending on the region

*casabe* – very large, dry, flat, round bread made from *yuca brava* (a kind of yucca), common in Los Llanos

*cazuela de mariscos* – stew of shellfish, fish, squid and vegetables; a speciality of the coast but also available in the interior

*ceviche* – raw fish or prawn marinated in lemon juice

*champús* – cold drink made from rice and *lulo* fruit; typical of Valle del Cauca

*changua* – light breakfast soup made of milk, containing an egg, a *calao* and coriander; in some regions potatoes are added

*chicha* – thick, alcoholic beverage made from corn

*chicharrón* – deep-fried piece of salted pork rind, added to the *bandeja paisa* and some other dishes

*chipichipi* – tiny shell fish

*chocolate santafereño* – cup of hot chocolate accompanied by a piece of cheese and bread (traditionally, you put the cheese into the chocolate); speciality of Bogotá

*chontaduro* – fruit of a palm, cooked and eaten with salt and lemon juice; very popular in Valle del Cauca

*chunchullo* – grilled or fried beef tripe

*churrasco* – large steak, typical of Argentina, now widespread in Colombia

*cocada* – a sweet made from coconut

*colaciones* – butter biscuits; a speciality of Cundinamarca

*cuajada* – unsalted, white, fresh cheese wrapped in banana leaf

*cuajada con melao* – typical desert, consisting of a piece of *cuajada* in *panela* syrup

*cuchuco* – heavy soup made of ground corn, wheat or maize with a piece of pork, potatoes and other vegetables; originally from Boyacá

*cuy* – guinea pig grilled on a spit; typical dish of Nariño

*curuba* – oval-shaped fruit, with soft, yellow peel and orange-coloured meat, growing only in Cundinamarca and Boyacá; the *sorbete de curuba* is second to none – don't miss it

*dedos de queso* – white cheese strips wrapped in pastry and deep-fried

*empanada* – fried pasty stuffed with rice, vegetables and meat; there are numerous regional variations which can include fish, seafood, chicken, and cheese

*empanada de pipián* – small, fried pasty stuffed with potato and peanut, accompanied by peanut sauce; typical snack of Popayán

*fraijoa* or *feijoa* – aromatic fruit with green peel and white meat similar in texture to the guava; the peel can be eaten

*fritanga* – popular dish, often sold in markets, street stalls, and in roadside restaurants; it may include any of these: *chicharrón, morcilla, chorizo, longaniza, bofe, papa criolla, papa salada, plátano* and *mazorca*

*fritanguería* – street stand serving *fritanga*

*fuente de soda* – budget cafeteria serving snacks, ice creams, fruit salads etc

*gamitana* – river fish typical of the Amazon; one of the most delicious fish

*granadilla* – round orange-sized fruit with a hard, yellow peel dotted with brown freckles; inside, it has grey, sweet flesh; comes from the same family as the passion fruit

*guama* – fruit with a hard, thick skin which looks like a huge string bean; the edible part is the inside cotton-like flesh covering the seeds

*guanábana* – soursop

*guarapo* – fermented drink made from fruit and sugarcane juice

*guasca* – herb typical of the Colombian highlands, used in soups; a must in the *ajiaco*

*haba* – large lima bean common in the Andes

*hormiga culona* – large fried ants; probably the most exotic Colombian speciality, unique to Santander and available only in season (March to May); it's not a dish you order in a restaurant, but a snack you buy by weight in shops

*jaiba* – species of crab

*lapingacho* – fried pancake made from mashed potato and cheese; Ecuadorian dish popular in Nariño

*lechona* – pig carcass, stuffed with its own meat, rice and dried peas and then baked in an oven; a speciality of Tolima, today popular in many regions

*lulo* – golf ball-sized, ideally round fruit with prickly yellow skin (don't handle it) and very soft flesh; makes a delicious juice

*mamey* – grapefruit-sized fruit with brown skin and bright yellow flesh

*mamoncillo* – grape-sized fruit, with green skin and reddish edible flesh which you suck until you get to the core

*manjarblanco* – kind of fudge made of milk, rice and sugar, sometimes with figs

*mantecada* – cake made of cornflour, butter, eggs and vanilla

*masato* – low-alcohol home-made beverage made of rice, wheat or corn, flavoured with cinnamon and cloves

*mazamorra* – boiled maize in milk; typical to Antioquia, but there are regional variations

*mazamorra chiquita* – hearty soup with meat, tripe, different types of potatoes and other vegetables; a speciality of Boyacá

*mistela* – home-made alcoholic drink made with *aguardiente* sweetened with herbs or fruits for several weeks

*mogolla chicharrona* – bread with small pieces of fried pork rind

*mondongo* – soup popular in many regions; seasoned tripe cooked in bouillon with maize, potatoes, carrots and other vegetables;

*morcilla* – tripe stuffed with rice, peas and herbs, boiled and then fried

*mute* – soup typical to Santander, prepared from pork, beef and tripe with potatoes, maize and other vegetables

*níspero* – perfectly round, billiard ball-sized, brown fruit with soft, fleshy meat; delicious in juices

*ñame* – type of yam, edible tuber

*oblea* – two thin, crisp pancakes with *arequipe* in the middle

*ostrería* – street stand serving seafood cocktails

*paella* – Spanish dish of rice, pork, chicken and seafood

*pan de bono* – small bun made of maize

flour, yucca starch and white cheese

*pan de yuca* – half-moon bread made of yucca starch and cheese

*panela* – unrefined and uncrystalised raw sugar obtained from sugarcane syrup and sold in brown-coloured blocks

*papa* – potato

*papa criolla* – literally 'creole potato', a species of small, yellow potato endemic to Colombian highlands, mainly Cundinamarca and Boyacá; essential in *ajiaco*

*papa salada* – skinned potato boiled and sprinkled with salt

*papayuela* – small and very aromatic papaya from the Andean region, with a different taste from the common lowland papaya

*patacón* – piece of plantain, squashed and then fried

*peto* – boiled maize in hot milk, sweetened with panela

*piqueteadero* – budget, short-order restaurant or roadside stand serving basic food

*pitaya* – tuna; prickly pear cacti fruit (don't handle it) that has yellow to red peel with a delicate soft, sweet meat and very small black seeds

*plato montañero* – another name for *bandeja paisa*

*pola* – popular name for beer

*postre de natas* – a dessert made from milk skin; speciality of Cundinamarca and Boyacá

*puchero* – broth with chicken, pork, beef, potato, yucca, cabbage, corn and plantain, accompanied by rice and avocado; a Bogotá speciality

*quesillo* – fresh, white cheese wrapped in banana leaf; a speciality of Tolima but also found elsewhere

*raspao* – ice ball made by scraping a block of ice and adding artificial flavours; sold only on the street

*refajo* – drink made of beer and soft drink (usually the 'Colombiana', the most popular Colombian fizzy drink)

*rellena* – tripe stuffed with rice, peas and herbs

*rondón* – the most typical dish of San Andrés, made with coconut milk, yucca, plantain, fish and sea snails

*roscón* – sweet bread with guava paste inside

*sabajón* – thick beverage made of *aguardiente*, egg and milk

*salpicón* – small pieces of various fruits in a fruit juice or fizzy drink

*sancocho* – kind of vegetable soup with fish, meat or chicken common throughout the country, with many regional varieties

*sancocho de gallina* – chicken soup with potatoes, plantain, yucca and corn on the cob

*sancocho de pescado* – fish soup typical of the Caribbean Coast

*sobrebarriga* – stewed, baked or fried brisket or flank of beef served with rice, potatoes and vegetables; dish popular in many regions

*tamal* – chopped pork with rice and vegetables folded in a maize dough, wrapped in banana leaves and steamed; originally from Tolima but today there are many regional varieties

*uchuva* – cherry tomato-sized, orange-coloured fruit; its flesh looks like that of a tomato, but it has a unique taste

*viudo de pescado* – river fish soup (mainly *bocachico*) cooked with potatoes, yucca and plantains; typical of Tolima and Huila

*zapote* – brown eggplant-shaped fruit with orange, fleshy-fibred meat around several seeds; there is another variety found on the coast, *zapote costeño*, which is like an ostrich egg and has softer meat around a single stone

## Eggs

*huevo* – egg

*huevos fritos* – fried eggs

*huevos fritos* – fried eggs

*huevos pericos/revueltos* – scrambled eggs

*tortilla* – omelette

## Fish & Seafood

*bagre* – catfish

*calamar* – squid

*camarón* – small shrimp

*cangrejo* – crab

*corvina* – blue fish

*langosta* – lobster

*langostino* – large shrimp, large prawn

*mariscos* – seafood

*mejillones* – mussels

*mero* – grouper or sea bass

*ostra* – oyster

*pargo* – red snapper

*pescado* – fish that has been caught and is considered to be food

*pez* – a live fish
*pulpo* – octopus
*róbalo* – snook, bass
*salmón* – salmon
*sierra* – king mackerel, sawfish
*trucha* – trout

## Meat, Poultry & Smallgoods

*caracol* – snail
*carne* – meat
*carne de cerdo* – pork
*carne de res* – beef
*carne guisada* – stewed beef
*carne molida* – mince meat
*chivo* – goat
*chorizo* – seasoned sausage
*chuleta* – chop, rib steak
*cordero* – lamb
*costilla* – rib
*gallina* – hen
*hígado* – liver
*jamón* – ham
*lomito* – sirloin
*lomo* – loin
*longaniza* – type of sausage
*menudencias* – chicken giblets
*milanesa* – thin steak
*muchacho* – roast beef
*pechuga* – breast (poultry)
*pernil* – leg of pork or poultry
*pollo* – chicken
*salchicha* – sausage
*ternera* – veal

## Fruit & Vegetables

*aguacate* – avocado
*ají* – red chilli pepper
*ajo* – garlic
*alcaparra* – caper
*breva* – fig
*chirimoya* – custard apple
*choclo* – sweet corn
*durazno* – peach
*fríjoles* – red beans
*fruta* – fruit

*guayaba* – guava
*habichuela* – string bean
*lechuga* – lettuce
*limón* – lemon
*maíz* – corn/maize
*maní* – peanuts
*maracuyá* – passion fruit
*mazorca* – sweet corn on the cob
*melao* – sugarcane syrup
*mora* – blackberry
*naranja* – orange
*patilla* – watermelon
*pimentón* – capsicum
*piña* – pineapple
*plátano* – plantain (green banana)
*tamarindo* – tamarind
*tomate de árbol* – tree tomato, tamarillo
*toronja* – grapefruit
*uva* – grape
*uva pasa* – raisin
*yuca* – yucca, cassava (edible root)
*zanahoria* – carrot

## Drinks

*agua* – water
*(agua) aromática* – herbal tea
*aguardiente* – sugarcane spirit flavoured with
    anise
*bebida* – drink/beverage
*carajillo* – black coffee with liquor
*cerveza* – beer
*coctel* – cocktail
*gaseosa* – bottled soft drink
*hielo* – ice
*jugo* – juice
*leche* – milk
*ron* – rum
*sorbete* – milk shake; fruit juice with milk
*té* – tea
*trago* – alcoholic drink
*vino* – wine
*vino blanco* – white wine
*vino espumoso* – sparkling wine
*vino rosado* – rosé
*vino tinto* – red wine

# Glossary

The solidus (/) in some words in bold separates masculine and feminine forms.

**arrecife** – coral reef

**asadero** – place serving roasted or grilled meats

**atarraya** – circular fishing net widely used on the coast and rivers

**AUC** – Autodefensas Unidas de Colombia; a loose alliance of paramilitary squads known as *autodefensas*

**autodefensas** – right-wing squads created to combat guerrillas, also called *paramilitares* or just *paras*

**ayudante** – driver's assistant on intercity buses

**azulejos** – ornamental handmade tiles which were brought to South America from Spain and Portugal during colonial times

**balneario** – seaside, lakeside or riverside bathing place with facilities

**bambuco** – musical genre of the Andean region

**bandola** – an instrument derived from the mandolin, used in the music of the Andean region; also an entirely different guitar-type instrument played in Los Llanos

**bandolero** – bandit, brigand; term used to refer to guerrillas to undermine their political aims, emphasising their criminal activities

**baquiano** – peasant who hires out horses or mules for horseback excursions, and usually accompanies the group as a guide

**basuco** or **bazuco** – base from which cocaine is refined; smoked in cigarettes

**boleteo** – the guerrilla practice of 'taxing' local landowners in exchange for leaving them in peace; 'a bourgeois contribution to the revolution'; people who refuse to pay are often hijacked or assassinated

**bomba** – petrol (gasoline) station

**brujo** – witch doctor, shaman

**burundanga** – drug extracted from a plant, used by thieves to render their victim unconscious

**buseta** – small bus; a popular means of city transport

**cabalgata** – horseback ride

**cabaña** – cabin, usually found on beaches or up in the mountains

**cachaco/a** – person from Bogotá, although for the *costeños* anyone not from the coast is a cachaco

**cacique** – Indian tribal head; today the term is applied to provincial leaders from the two traditional political parties, also called *gamonales*

**CAI** – Centro de Atención Inmediata; the network of police posts which were established in the cities in order to upgrade public security

**caipirinha** – Brazilian cocktail based on sugarcane rum

**caleño/a** – person from Cali

**caminata** – trek, hike

**camino de herradura** – bridle path, commonly paved with stone; these were the early tracks built under Spanish rule by Indian labour

**campero** – jeep

**campesino/a** – rural dweller, usually of modest economic means; peasant

**caneca** – wastepaper basket or bin

**carriel** – typical Antioquian leather bag used by men

**carro** – car

**casa de cambio** – money-exchange office

**caserío** – hamlet

**casona** – big, rambling old house

**caucheras** – slingshots

**cédula** – ID of Colombian citizens and residents

**ceiba** – common tree of the tropics; can reach a huge size

**celador** – security guard (usually armed) at a public building or private house; a very common job these days – there are at least 100,000 of them in Bogotá alone

**chalupa** – small passenger boat powered by an outboard motor

**chévere** – good, nice (informal)

**chichamaya** – traditional dance of the Guajiro Indians

**chigüiro** – capybara; the world's large rodent common to Los Llanos

**chimbo** – false; of bad quality; not as good as expected (informal)

**chinchorro** – hammock woven of cotton threads or palm fibre like a fishing net; typical of many Indian groups; the best known are the decorative cotton hammocks of the Guajiros

**chirimía** – street band popular on the Pacific Coast and in the Andean region

**chiva** – traditional bus with its body made of timber and painted with colourful patterns; still widely used in the countryside

**ciénaga** – shallow lake or lagoon

**cinemateca** – art-house cinema that screens quality films

**climatizado** – air-conditioned; term used for air-con buses

**colectivo** – shared taxi or minibus; a popular means of public transport

**corraleja** – dangerous kind of bullfight in which spectators can take their chances with the bull; popular mainly in the Sucre department, it originated in Pamplona, Spain

**corrida** – bullfight

**corriente** – ordinary bus

**costeño/a** – inhabitant of the Caribbean Coast

**criollo/a** – Creole, a person of European (especially Spanish) blood, but born in the Americas

**cuadrilla** – kind of popular theatre group or play, always using disguises, usually accompanied by music and sometimes by dance

**cuatro** – small, four-stringed guitar, used in the music of Los Llanos

**cumbia** – one of the most popular musical rhythms (and corresponding dance) of the Caribbean Coast; African in origin

**currulao** – popular dance of the Pacific Coast, of mixed African–Spanish origin, usually accompanied by a marimba

**danta** – tapir; large, hoofed mammal of tropical and subtropical forests

**dar papaya** – to give someone the opportunity to take advantage of you (informal)

**DAS** – Departamento Administrativo de Seguridad; the security police, responsible for immigration

**denuncia** – official report/statement to the police

**derrumbe** – landslide; the main cause of blocked roads, particularly during the rainy season

**(los) desechables** – literally 'the disposables'; term referring to the underclass including the homeless, beggars, street urchins, prostitutes, homosexuals and the like, who are treated as human refuse and are the objects of an abhorrent process of 'social cleansing' by death squads known as *los limpiadores*, or 'the cleaners'

**deslizador** – term used in some regions for a high-powered boat

**droguería** – pharmacy

**ELN** – Ejército de Liberación Nacional; the second-largest guerrilla group after the FARC

**esquina** – street corner

**estadero** – roadside restaurant which often offers accommodation

**FARC** – Fuerzas Armadas Revolucionarias de Colombia; the largest guerrilla group in the country

**finca** – anything from a country house with a small garden to a huge country estate

**fique** – sisal obtained from the agave, widely used in handicrafts

**flota** – general term for intercity buses

**frailejón** – espeletia, a species of plant typical of the *páramo*

**fresco** – take it easy (informal)

**fulano** – so-and-so; a person whose name has been forgotten or is unknown

**gallera** – cockfight ring

**gamín** – street urchin; originated from the French *gamin*; the word was adopted in Colombia when the French media began reporting on the appalling conditions of street children in Bogotá

**gamonales** – see *cacique*

**greca** – large, cylindrical coffee-maker; the old ones, often lavishly decorated with engraved patterns, are reminiscent of Russian samovars

**gringo/a** – any white male/female foreigner; sometimes, not always, used in a derogatory sense

**guacamaya** – macaw

**guacharaca** – percussion instrument consisting of a stick-like wooden body with a row of cuts and a metal fork; used in *vallenato* music

**guácharo** – oilbird; a species of nocturnal bird living in caves

**guadua** – the largest variety of the bamboo family, common in many regions of moderate climate

**guaquero** – robber of pre-Columbian tombs

**guardaequipaje** – the left-luggage office, checkroom

**guardaparque** – national-park ranger

**guayabera** – men's embroidered shirt, popular throughout the Caribbean region

**guayabo** – hangover (informal); warranted after an *aguardiente* session

**hacienda** – country estate
**hospedaje** – budget hotel

**indio** – literally 'Indian'; in Colombia it has acquired a pejorative connotation and is used to insult someone, regardless of race; to refer respectfully to Indians, use *indígena*
**invierno** – literally 'winter'; refers to the rainy season
**isleño/a** – literally 'islander'; inhabitant of San Andrés and Providencia
**IVA** – *impuesto de valor agregado*, a value-added tax (VAT)

**joropo** – typical music of Los Llanos, also referred to as *música llanera*

**lancha** – launch, motorboat
**ligre** – cross of Bengal tiger and African lion, first bred in Colombia (in Pereira's zoo)
**(los) limpiadores** – see *los desechables*
**liqui liqui** – men's traditional costume, typical of most of the Caribbean; a white or beige suit comprising trousers and a blouse with a collar, usually accompanied by white hat and shoes
**llanero/a** – inhabitant of Los Llanos
**(Los) Llanos** – literally 'plains'; vast plains between the Andes and the Río Orinoco

**mafioso** – member of the mafia; big fish of the drug business
**malecón** – waterfront promenade
**maloca** – large, communal house of certain Indian groups; usually a wooden structure thatched with palm leaves
**manta** – long, loose dress worn by Guajiro Indian women; also a bedspread
**maracas** – gourd rattles; an accompanying instrument of the *joropo* and other rhythms
**marimba** – percussion instrument
**matrimonio** – literally 'wedding'; hotel room with a double bed intended for married couples
**mecha** – small triangular envelope with gunpowder, used in *tejo*
**merengue** – musical rhythm originating in the Dominican Republic, today widespread throughout the Caribbean and beyond
**meseta** – plateau
**mestizo/a** – person of mixed European-Indian blood

**mirador** – lookout, viewpoint
**mochila** – bucket-shaped shoulder bag, traditionally made by Indians, today produced commercially
**mola** – colourful, hand-stitched applique textile of the Cuna Indians; a rectangular piece of cloth made of several differently coloured, superimposed layers sewn together
**mopa mopa** – also known as *barniz de Pasto*; vegetable resin used for decorating wooden crafts, typical of Pasto
**moriche** – palm common in Los Llanos, used for construction, household items, handicrafts etc
**motorista** – boat driver
**múcura** – kind of traditional pottery jar
**muelle** – pier, wharf
**mula** – literally 'mule'; a person hired by drug traffickers to smuggle drugs overseas
**mulato/a** – mulatto; a person of mixed Spanish-African blood

**narcotraficante** – drug dealer
**Navidad** – Christmas
**nevado** – snowcapped mountain peak

**ñapa** – a little bit extra for having bought something, eg, buy six oranges and get one free

**orquídea** – orchid
**oso hormiguero** – anteater

**paisa** – person from Antioquia; *pueblo paisa* – a typical Antioquian town
**palanca** – literally 'lever'; a connection or person with influence to help out when the regular avenues don't work (informal); it's very important to have them in Colombia
**papagayo** – popular term for macaw
**paradero** – bus stop; in some areas called *parada*
**paramilitares** – see *autodefensas*
**páramo** – open highlands between about 3500m and 4500m, typical of Colombia, Venezuela and Ecuador
**parapente** – paragliding
**parqueadero** – car park
**pasillo** – type of music/dance played in the Andean region
**pastuso/a** – person from Pasto, but also anyone a bit slow or dumb; the pastuso is the butt of many jokes
**perica** – cocaine (informal)
**pescadería** – fish (seafood) restaurant

**piso** – storey, floor

**pito** – car horn; used indiscriminately in and outside the city

**plaza de toros** – bullfight ring

**poporo** – a vessel made from a small gourd, used by the Arhuacos and other Indian groups to carry lime; while chewing coca leaves, Indians add lime to help release the alkaloid from the leaves

**porro** – musical rhythm of the Caribbean Coast

**propina** – tip (not a bribe)

**puente** – literally 'bridge'; also means a three-day-long weekend (including Monday)

**refugio** – rustic shelter in a remote area, mostly in the mountains

**requinto** – small 12-string guitar used as a melodic instrument

**requisa** – police document search, sometimes a body search

**residencias** – budget hotel

**retén** – police checkpoint on the road

**ruana** – Colombian poncho

**rumba** – fiesta; private or public party with music and drinking

**rumbeadero** – discotheque or other place to go to drink and dance

**rumbear** – to party; a Colombian speciality

**salinas** – seaside saltpans or shallow lagoons used for extraction of salt

**salsa** – type of Caribbean dance music of Cuban origin, very popular in Colombia

**salsoteca** – disco playing salsa music

**Semana Santa** – Holy Week, the week before Easter Sunday

**sicario** – a paid killer hired to eliminate adversaries

**SIDA** – AIDS

**soborno** – bribe

**son** – one of the main rhythms of Afro-Cuban music

**soroche** – altitude sickness

**sumercé** – originated from *Su Merced*, old-fashioned, respectful form of address; used mostly in rural areas of the Andean region

**taberna** – pub/bar/tavern

**tagua** – hard ivory-coloured nut of a species of palm; used in handicrafts

**tejo** – traditional game, popular mainly in the Andean region; played with a heavy metal disk, which is thrown aiming to make a *mecha* (a sort of petard) explode

**Telecom** – state telephone company

**teleférico** – cable car

**telenovela** – TV soap opera

**terminal de pasajeros** – bus terminal

**tiple** – small 12-stringed guitar used as an accompanying instrument

**tombos** – common informal term for police

**tonina** – freshwater dolphin

**torbellino** – music/dance typical of the Andean region

**totuma** – cup-like vessel made from the hollowed-out dried fruit of a tree cut in half; used in some areas for drinking, washing etc

**trapiche** – traditional sugarcane mill

**tugurios** – shantytowns built of waste materials by the poor on invaded public or private land around big cities, particularly extensive in Bogotá and Medellín; they are found throughout South America, though under a different name in each country: for example, *favelas* in Brazil, *villas miserias* in Argentina, *cantegriles* in Uruguay, *barriadas* in Peru, *callampas* in Chile and *ranchos* or *barrios* in Venezuela

**tunjo** – flat gold figurine, often depicting a warrior; typical artefact of the Muisca Indians

**vacuna** – literally 'vaccine'; term used to refer to the payments made to guerrillas by farmers to avoid being harassed

**vaina** – thing (informal); *qué vaina* – what a problem

**vallenato** – music typical of the Caribbean region, based on the accordion; it's now widespread in Colombia

**vaquero** – cowboy of Los Llanos

**verano** – literally 'summer'; refers to the dry season

**(La) Violencia** – bloody period of civil war (1948–57) between Colombia's two political parties

**vivero** – plant nursery

**voladora** – high-powered speedboat

**yagé** – plant with hallucinogenic properties used by traditional healers of some Indian groups

**yanchana** – bark paintings made by some Indian groups of the Amazon

**zambo/a** – person of mixed Indian-African ancestry

# Thanks

Many thanks to the travellers who used the last edition and wrote to us with helpful hints, useful advice and interesting anecdotes:

Carlos Enrique Jimenez Abad, Jadwiga Adamczuk, Scott Adams, Shane Adsett, Rose Ann V Albano, Jennifer Anders, Fredrik Andersen, Elizabeth Arango, Nicoletta Arena, Joel Aronson, Andrea Aster, Paolo Attanasio, Susie Badger, Terance Baker, Paul Bardwell, Ben Barker, Pina Belperio, Rachel Bentley, David Berguin, Catherine A Bernard, Gunter Bertram, Fabio Biserna, Allison Blaue, Harly Bonilla, Andres Botero, Angela Maria Botero, Phillip Boyd, Nicholas Branch, Richard J Bray, Mr & Mrs Roderick Brodie, Brad Brooks, Clinton W Broussard, Simon Brown, Jon A Buchli, Jayne Bull, Diane Bush, Ann Buttivant, Marcelo & Louise de Camago, Paul Campbell, Shannon Campbell, Tony & Lena Cansdale, L Mario Carmona, Aventis Maria Caro, Jose Carvalho, Carmel Castellan, Andrea Cel, Morag Chase, Catherine Clark, Aaron Clauson, Allison Cooper, Christophe Cornu, Brian Cox, Sophie & Mowgli Coyaud, Johanna Daranko, Nicholas Darton, Monica DaSilva, Carl Dirnbacher, Thomas Donegan, Carl Downing, Brigitte Dreyer, Leslie Dunton-Downer, Laurent Duport, Agnieszka Dziarmaga, Mike Esposito, H Insh, Clare Fairclough, Csaba Feher, Bjorn Fiedler, Albrecht Fischer, Rosel Flores, Diane E Floyd, Renee Simone Foster, Jonah Freedman, Max Friedman, Gabriel A Fuentes, Dave Fuller, Brian Furlong, Michael Gacquin, Davin Galbraith, Rosalie Gardner, Ricardo Garzon, Matthew Gauci, Peter Geerts, Georgie George, Timothy Gerson, Larry Gessler, Mirko Giulietti, Shay Gizbar, Jack Glass, W J Glass, Martin Gluckman, Tooker Gomberg, Diane B Goodpasture, Jeanne Goulding, Melissa Graboyes, Christopher Gratz, Rolf Grau, Dr Thilo Grotzinger, Ben Guezentsvey, Rui Guimaraes, Gillian Handyside, Deanne Harada, Donna & Dan Hardy, Megan Harker, Warren Harrington, Rocky Harris, Rob Hart, Martin Hartig, Louie Hechanova, Peggy Hendrickx, Lothar Herb, Peter Hertrampf, Cheryl Hicks, Lori Hill, Peter Hoell, Lawrence Holeman, Elaine Holloway, Niels Hollum, Wayne Hooper, Rose Hugh, Bianca Huls, Rene Huser, Patricia Inarrea, Christian Iyer, Ignacio Jaramillo, Ian Jenkins, Tahirah Johnson, Kryss Katsiavriades, Michael Keller, David Kendricks, Letitia Kennedy, Zia Asad Khan, Tuomas Kiiski, Bill Klynnk, Eric Knowlton, Hans Kolland, Martin Kopp, Anatolio Kronik, Mauricio Lanos, Joan Laparra, Justin Lawson, Shannon Lee-Rutherford, Noble Leland, Luciano Leon, Milton Lever, Steve Lidgey, Norbert Lies, Linda Locke, Saffron Lodge, Jose M Lomas, Monica Lopez, Helga Luise Hal, Daniel Lund, Ashley Lynch, Jonathan Lynn, Neil MacDonald, Ian Mace, Kenneth Mackie, Klemen Malovrh, Giovani Mancilla, Nick Manesis, Ilchtina Manga, Alain Maniciati, Debbie Mankovitz, John Manley, Eduardo Viteri Manticha, Nick Marbach, Jan Marco Muller, Lanny Marcus, Ann Marie, Michael Marquardt, L Marsden, James Mason, Carly Mattes, Edith Mayrhoffer, Michelangelo Mazzeo, Pablo McDermott, Adriana McMullen, H J Meerdinkveldboom, David Mesa Restrepo, Claudia Meyer, Lorenzo Millan, Chris Milliken, F Mirand, Ruedi Miller, Koen Moerman, Chris Moore, Andre Morissette, Rosemary Morle, Petra Mueller, Pamela Naessig, John T Nasci, Paige Newman, Greg Nielsen, David Nightingale, Ernest Nino-Murcia, Magnar Nordal, Kjetil Norvag, Claire O'Brien, Jane O'Callaghan, David Olson, Alexander Olufs, Johanna Oosterwyk, Guillermo Arbelaez Palacios, Sophie Parron, Gita Patel, Vera Pawlowski, Mike Pearce, Scott Pegg, Claire Pellet, Joseph Penny, Sabina Pensek, Luis Gabriel Perez, Giorgio Perversi, Sean Peterson, Alexander Pichler, Pablo Pinzon, Oliver Pogatsnik, Sandi Post, Katja Potzsch, Carolina Pulido, Patricia Ramfrez, William Redgrove, Trevor Reed, Vincent Reh, Bill Rhoades, Valerie Richards, Stefan Rickaert, Kirsty Ridyard, Francisco Rios, Branden Rippey, Julian Roberts, Simon Rochowski, Ramiro Rodriguez, Etienne Roger, Eduardo Rollox, Simon Rose, E Rowley, Maria Rutgerslaan, Rania Salameh, Matt Salmon, Valisa Saunders, Caroline Andrews & Paul Schmutz, Kurt Schumacher, Hans Schuurmans, Belinda Scotman, Brian Scowcroft, Henry M Segarra, Ms Antje Seidel, Prof Gour C Sen, Rachael Serrano, Phil Shah, Glen Shepard, James E Simpson, Randall Sinnott, Liv Sivertsen, Nick Smith, Ted Solis, Carlos Sanchez, Chris Stanley, Karin Steinkamp, Remco M Stomp, Monica Stripling, Simon Strong, Joanne Symington, Alexandra Taylor, Christine Escurriola Tettamanti, Sabine Thielicke, Celia Thompson, Alan Thornhill, Konstanze Thym, David Tickell, Gillie Tiffen, Rodrigo Torres, Jon Trost, Roland Ulrich, N Vaithilingam, Alex van Erp, Raf Vanvuchelen, Ruth Verhey, Jan Vermande, Daniel Vin, Michal Vit, Jens Vogt, Jadranka Vrsalovic, Robert Walton, Steve Watson, Doug Waugh, Harry Wetting, M White, Duncan Whiteman, Tanja Wielgorf, Tanja Wielgoss, Markus Wiget, Chris Wigginton, Vincent Wijnanga, Lori Willocks, Brian Winder, Robert Wingfield, Arno Witte, Carlos Wotzkow, Juan Zabala

# LONELY PLANET

You already know that Lonely Planet produces more than this one guidebook, but you might not be aware of the other products we have on this region. Here is a selection of titles that you may want to check out as well:

**South America on a Shoestring**
ISBN 1 86450 283 5
US$29.99 • UK£17.99

**Latin American Spanish Phrasebook**
ISBN 1 74059 170 4
US$7.99 • UK£4.99

**Healthy Travel Central & South America**
ISBN 1 86450 053 0
US$5.95 • UK£3.99

**Bolivia**
ISBN 0 86442 668 2
US$21.99 • UK£13.99

**Brazil**
ISBN 1 86450 146 4
US$24.99 • UK£14.99

**Venezuela**
ISBN 1 86450 219 3
US$19.99 • UK£12.99

**Ecuador & the Galapagos Islands**
ISBN 1 74059 464 9
US$21.99 • UK£13.99

**Peru**
ISBN 0 86442 710 7
US$17.95 • UK£11.99

**Panama**
ISBN 1 86450 307 6
US$16.99 • UK£10.99

**Available wherever books are sold**

# Index

## Text

**Bold** indicates maps.

**Bold** indicates maps.

## Boxed Text

# MAP LEGEND

## ROUTES

| City | Regional | |
|---|---|---|
| | ..........Freeway | ...........Pedestrian Mall |
| | ...........Toll Freeway | ...............Steps |
| | ......Primary Road | ...............Tunnel |
| | .......Secondary Road | ...............Trail |
| | ...........Tertiary Road | ........Walking Tour |
| | ............Dirt Road | ...............Path |

## TRANSPORTATION

........Train          ...........Tram
........Metro          ...........Ferry

## HYDROGRAPHY

......River; Creek     ...Spring; Rapids
............Canal      ......Waterfalls
............Lake       ....Dry; Salt Lake

## BOUNDARIES

— · — · — .... International          — ·· — ·· ...State; District          — — — — .......County

## AREAS

| | | | | |
|---|---|---|---|---|
| ..................Beach | ............Cemetery | ..........Golf Course | ...........Reservation |
| ..............Building | ................Forest | ...............Park | ...........Sports Field |
| ..............Campus | ..........Garden; Zoo | ...............Plaza | ...Swamp; Mangrove |

## POPULATION SYMBOLS

| | | | |
|---|---|---|---|
| ○ NATIONAL CAPITAL ...National Capital | ● Large City ..................Large City | ● Small City ........................Small City |
| ◉ State Capital .................State Capital | ● Medium City ............Medium City | ● Town; Village ...............Town; Village |

## MAP SYMBOLS

▪ ................................. Place to Stay          ▼ ...................................Place to Eat          ● .................................Point of Interest

| | | | | | |
|---|---|---|---|---|---|
| ....................Airfield | ........................Cinema | ......................Museum | ....................Snorkeling |
| ........................Airport | ....................Dive Site | ...............Observatory | ...............Stately Home |
| ...Archeological Site; Ruin | .......Embassy; Consulate | ........................Park | .......................Surfing |
| ..........................Bank | ....................Footbridge | ..............Parking Area | ................Synagogue |
| ........Baseball Diamond | ......................Fountain | .........................Pass | ...............Tao Temple |
| ......................Battlefield | ....................Gas Station | ..................Picnic Area | ..........................Taxi |
| ......................Bike Trail | ......................Hospital | .................Police Station | ...................Telephone |
| ................Border Crossing | ......................Information | .........................Pool | .......................Theater |
| .......Bus Station; Terminal | ...................Internet Café | .................Post Office | ..............Toilet - Public |
| ..........Cable Car; Chairlift | ....................Lighthouse | .........................Pub; Bar | ..........................Tomb |
| ...................Campground | .......................Lookout | .......................RV Park | ....................Trailhead |
| ..........................Castle | ..........................Mine | .......................Shelter | ...................Tram Stop |
| .......................Cathedral | .......................Mission | ...................Shipwreck | ...............Transportation |
| ..........................Cave | .......................Monument | .............Shopping Mall | .......................Volcano |
| ..........................Church | .......................Mountain | ...........Skiing - Downhill | ........................Winery |

*Note: Not all symbols displayed above appear in this book.*

---

# LONELY PLANET OFFICES

## Australia
Locked Bag 1, Footscray, Victoria 3011
☎ 03 8379 8000  fax 03 8379 8111
email: talk2us@lonelyplanet.com.au

## USA
150 Linden St, Oakland, CA 94607
☎ 510 893 8555  TOLL FREE: 800 275 8555
fax 510 893 8572
email: info@lonelyplanet.com

## UK
10a Spring Place, London NW5 3BH
☎ 020 7428 4800  fax 020 7428 4828
email: go@lonelyplanet.co.uk

## France
1 rue du Dahomey, 75011 Paris
☎ 01 55 25 33 00  fax 01 55 25 33 01
email: bip@lonelyplanet.fr
www.lonelyplanet.fr

**World Wide Web: www.lonelyplanet.com or AOL keyword: lp
Lonely Planet Images: lpi@lonelyplanetimages.com**